THE ILLUSTRATED GUIDE TO
JUDAISM

THE ILLUSTRATED GUIDE TO
JUDAISM

A COMPREHENSIVE HISTORY OF JEWISH RELIGION AND PHILOSOPHY,
ITS TRADITIONS AND PRACTICES, MAGNIFICENTLY ILLUSTRATED
WITH OVER 500 PHOTOGRAPHS AND PAINTINGS

DAN COHN-SHERBOK

LORENZ BOOKS

CONTENTS

Below Birthplace of the prophet Amos.

Below Jerusalem, mosaic, 6th century BCE.

Below Jewish teacher and pupil, 1395.

Above A rabbinical debate, 1888.   *Above Writing a Torah scroll by hand.*   *Above Girls celebrating bat mitzvah.*

INTRODUCTION

IS JUDAISM A UNIFIED RELIGIOUS TRADITION, OR HAVE A VARIETY OF JUDAISMS EXISTED THROUGH THE CENTURIES? DO ALL JEWS SUBSCRIBE TO THE SAME BELIEFS? DO THEY ALL OBSERVE THE SAME RITUALS?

These are the central questions that this volume seeks to explore. Divided into three major sections – Traditions, Belief and Practice – this work begins with an outline of the variety of forms of Jewish life that emerged in the history of the faith. Throughout it draws heavily on images of the Jew as portrayed in the Western artistic tradition.

JEWISH TRADITIONS
Beginning with ancient Judaism, the book examines a range of Judaisms that flourished from the time of Abraham to the Hellenistic period. Although all these ancient Judaisms embraced a belief in the God of the Hebrews, believers followed distinct spiritual paths in the quest to fulfill the divine will. Similarly, in the rabbinic and medieval periods, new forms of Judaism arose as Jews sought to make

Below A rabbinical disputation about Jewish law; a 17th-century Dutch painting by Jacob Toorenvliet.

sense of their world. Rabbinic Judaism, mystical Judaism, and philosophical Judaism were rooted in Scripture, yet these new forms of Judaism provided alternative interpretations of the tradition. The Karaites, Shabbateans and Frankists, however, were intensely critical of the rabbinic establishment and founded movements which were bitterly denounced by traditionalists. The modern world has witnessed the efflorescence of Jewish life and the establishment of a wide range of Judaisms each with its own religious ideology. From Orthodoxy to Humanism, from Zionism to Jewish feminism, modern Jews have strived to integrate Jewish values with contemporary concerns.

JEWISH BELIEF
This presentation of the multifarious nature of Judaism is followed by an extensive outline of Jewish belief, beginning with a discussion of the primary religious doctrines of the faith. Each section highlights biblical

Above A Jew wearing phylacteries and a prayer shawl, and holding a Torah. By Marc Chagall, c. 1930, a pioneer of modernism and leading Jewish artist.

teaching and traces its development from rabbinic times to the present. Commencing with a survey of Jewish belief about God's unity, the book goes on to examine traditional doctrines about God's nature, including such concepts as divine transcendence, eternal existence, omnipotence, omniscience and divine goodness. Turning to a consideration of God's action in the world, the subsequent sections focus on such subjects as providence, revelation, Torah and

Below A Sabbath Afternoon by Moritz Daniel Oppenheim, often regarded as the first Jewish artist of the modern era.

Above Jews praying at the Western Wall in Jerusalem. A 19th-century German painting by Gustav Bauernfeind.

mitzvot, and the promised land. There then follows an examination of ideas specifically connected with the Jewish spiritual path. Here such topics as the Bible, Talmud, midrash, sin, repentance, forgiveness, and reward and punishment are examined in detail. This discussion concludes with sections exploring the nature of Jewish eschatology.

JEWISH PRACTICE

The final part on Jewish practice, opens with a depiction of an outline of the Jewish calendar, and Jewish worship embracing such institutions as the sanctuary, Temple and synagogue. This is followed by an outline of the major festivals in the yearly cycle including Sabbath, Pilgrim Festivals, New Year, Day of Atonement, Days of Joy and Fast Days. The next sections discuss home ceremonies and personal piety as well as major life cycle events from birth through circumcision to marriage, divorce, death and mourning. Throughout this illustrated presentation of Jewish life, readers are encouraged to engage with the material and to reflect on the issues that emerge.

A LIVING FAITH

As this volume seeks to illustrate, in the past the Jewish community was united by belief and practice. Yet, all this has changed in the modern world. Prior to the Enlightenment in the 18th century, Jews did not have full citizenship rights of the countries in which they lived. Nevertheless, they were able to regulate their own affairs through an organized structure of self-government. Within such a context, Jewish law served as the basis of communal life, and rabbis were able to exert power and authority in the community.

However, as a result of political emancipation, Jews entered the mainstream of modern life, taking on all the responsibilities of citizenship. The rabbinical establishment thereby lost its status and control, and the Jewish legal system became voluntary. In addition, Jews took advantage of widening social advantages: they were free to choose where to live, whom to marry, and what career to follow. By gaining access to secular educational institutions, the influence of the surrounding culture also pervaded all aspects of Jewish life.

As a consequence of all this, Jewry in modern society has become fragmented and secularized. With the advent of the 21st century, the Jewish community faces new challenges as never before.

For nearly 4,000 years Judaism has been a living faith: if it is to continue, Jews will need to adapt to these changes in Jewish life and chart a new path into the future. What is at stake is no less than the survival of the Jewish heritage.

Below A boy reads the Torah during his bar mitzvah, a major life cycle event, with his rabbi and parents, at the Progressive Jewish community synagogue in Amsterdam.

TIMELINE

THIS IS A CHRONOLOGICAL TIMELINE OF THE JEWISH PEOPLE. IT LISTS SOME OF THE MAJOR EVENTS IN JUDAISM'S CULTURALLY AND POLITICALLY DIVERSE HISTORY OVER THOUSANDS OF YEARS.

Above 'We were slaves in Egypt', from a 14th-century Spanish illumination.

2000–700BCE

*c.*2000–1700BCE According to tradition, the age of the Patriarchs begins with Abraham. The Israelites leave Canaan for Egypt when famine strikes.

*c.*1700BCE Joseph is sold into slavery. He later welcomes his family to Egypt.

c. 1700–1300BCE Enslavement of the Israelites.

*c.*1300–1200BCE Moses leads the Israelites from Egypt.

*c.*1280BCE Torah, including the Ten Commandments, received by Moses at Mount Sinai.

*c.*1240BCE The Israelites conquer Canaan under Joshua.

*c.*1200–1000BCE Time of Judges.

1050BCE Philistines vanquish Shiloh and win the Ark of the Covenant. The time of Samuel, prophet and last judge.

1020BCE Saul is first King of the United Kingdom of Israel and Judah; rules until 1007BCE.

*c.*1004–965BCE King David crowned in Bethlehem. He makes Jerusalem his new capital and installs Ark of the Covenant.

*c.*965–928BCE Solomon is crowned. The Kingdom expands. First Temple is built.

*c.*928BCE Rehoboam is king. Kingdom splits into Judah and Israel (under Jeroboam).

918BCE Shishak of Egypt invades Israel.

*c.*900–800BCE Time of prophet Elijah.

727–698BCE King Hezekiah of Judah introduces major religious reforms.

722BCE Assyrians take over Israel. Ten Tribes disperse. Time of the prophet Isaiah.

700–100BCE

639–609BCE King Josiah makes religious reforms in Judah. Dies at Battle of Megiddo (Armageddon) fighting Assyrian and Egyptian forces.

586BCE Babylonians conquer Judah and destroy Jerusalem and the Temple. Most Jews are exiled to Babylon (the first Diaspora).

*c.*580BCE Jews establish colony on the Nile island of Elephantine, Egypt.

538–445BCE Under King Cyrus, the Persians defeat the Babylonians. Jews return to Israel, led by Zerubbabel and scribes Ezra and Nehemiah. Temple and city walls rebuilt in Jerusalem. Canonization of the Torah.

536–142BCE Persian and Hellenistic periods.

*c.*500–400BCE Canonization of Book of Prophets. Presumed period of Queen Esther and the Purim saga in Persia. Elephantine Temple destroyed in Egypt.

347BCE Time of the Great Assembly, end of kingship.

332BCE Land conquered by Alexander the Great; Hellenistic rule.

285–244BCE 72 Jewish sages translate Torah into Greek; called the Septuagint.

219–217BCE Rival Hellenistic dynasties fight for control of Israel. Seleucids finally displace Ptolemaids in 198BCE.

166–160BCE Maccabean (Hasmonean) revolt.

142–129BCE Jewish autonomy under Hasmoneans. In Jerusalem the zugot, or pairs of sages, acquire more power.

138BCE The rededication of the Second Temple. Foundation of Dead Sea Jewish sect at Qumran.

129–63BCE Jewish independence under Hasmonean monarchy.

100BCE–300CE

63BCE Romans invade Israel. Jerusalem captured by Pompey who names Judea a Roman vassal.

37BCE–4CE Herod the Great rules Israel. Temple in Jerusalem refurbished. Sanhedrin acts as Jewish legislature and judicial council.

*c.*30BCE–30CE Time of rabbis Hillel and Shammai.

6CE Judea becomes Roman province with capital at Caesarea.

*c.*20–36CE Ministry of Jesus of Nazareth.

30–100CE The birth of Christianity.

66–73CE The Great Revolt of Jews against Rome.

70CE Jerusalem conquered by Romans. Second Temple destroyed.

70–200CE Period of the tannaim, sages who organized the Jewish oral law.

115–117CE Jewish revolt against Rome.

131CE Hadrian renames Jerusalem Aelia Capitolina and forbids Jews to enter.

132–135CE Rebellion of Bar Kochba against Rome and Hadrian. Rome renames Judea 'Syria Palestina'.

*c.*210CE Mishnah (standardization of the Jewish oral law) compiled by Rabbi Yehuda Ha-Nasi. By now, Ketuvim (Writings) are canonized.

212CE Jews accepted as Roman citizens.

245CE Dura-Europos synagogue built in northern Syria.

300–600CE

220–500CE Period of the amoraim, the sages of the Talmud. The main redaction of Talmud Bavli (Babylonian Talmud) is completed by 475CE.

305CE Council of Elvira in Spain forbids Christians to socialize with Jews.

313–37CE Emperor Constantine converts Roman Empire to Christianity. The Empire is split into two, and the Eastern, or Byzantine Empire, becomes more powerful. Jews come under Byzantine rule in 330.

313–636CE Byzantine rule.

351CE A Jewish revolt in Galilee directed against Gallus Caesar is soon crushed.

361–3CE The last pagan Roman emperor, Julian, allows Jews to return to Jerusalem and rebuild the Temple. The project lapses when he dies and his successor Jovian re-establishes Christianity as the imperial religion.

c.390CE Mishnah commentary (written form of oral traditions) completed. Hillel II formulates Jewish calendar.

400–50CE Redaction of Talmud Yerushalmi (Talmud of Jerusalem).

425CE Jerusalem's Jewish patriarchate is abolished.

438CE The Empress Eudocia removes the ban on Jews praying at the Temple site.

489CE Theodoric, King of the Ostrogoths, conquers Italy and protects the Jews.

502CE Mar Zutra II establishes a Jewish state in Babylon.

525–29CE End of Himyar Jewish Kingdom in southern Arabia. Byzantine Emperor Justinian I issues anti-Jewish legislation.

550–700CE Period of the savoraim, sages in Persia who finalized the Talmud.

556CE Jews and Samaritans revolt against Byzantines. Midrashic literature and liturgical poetry developed.

600–750CE

7th century CE Foundation of the Khazar kingdom in Caucasus, southern Russia. Birth of Islam. The domination of Islam in the Arabian Peninsula results in the destruction of most Jewish communities there. Jews in the far southern realm of Yemen are mostly unaffected.

608–10CE Jews riot in Antioch, Syria, killing the Christians. This facilitates the entrance of Persian troops. Anti-Jewish pogroms break out from Syria to Asia Minor.

613CE, Jews gain autonomy in Jerusalem after a Persian-backed revolt.

613–14CE Persian invasion of Palestine brings the Byzantine period to an end.

629CE Byzantines retake Palestine and kill many Jews; survivors flee.

632CE Death of Islamic Prophet Mohammed.

636–1099CE Arab rule.

638CE Islamic and Arab conquest of Jerusalem. Arabs permit some Jews to return to Jerusalem, including immigrants from Babylon and refugees from Arabia.

640–2CE Arabs conquer Egypt.

691CE Dome of the Rock built by Caliph Abd el-Malik on site of the First and Second Temples in Jerusalem.

694–711CE The Visigoths outlaw Judaism.

700–1250CE Period of the Gaonim, presidents of the rabbinical colleges in Sura and Pumbedita, Babylon. New Jewish academies arise in Kairouan, Tunisia, and Fez, Morocco.

711CE Muslim armies invade and within a few years occupy most of Spain.

c.740CE Khazar Khanate royals and many Khazars convert to Judaism.

750–950CE Heyday of the Masoretes in Tiberias, Palestine, who codified Torah annotations, vocalizations and grammar.

750–1050CE

760CE The Karaites reject the authority of the oral law, and split off from rabbinic Judaism.

763–809CE Reign of Haran al Rashid (Persia), fifth Abbasid Caliph.

807CE Haran al Rashid forces Jews to wear a yellow badge and Christians to wear a blue badge.

808CE Fez (Morocco) becomes the capital of the Shiite dynasty under Idris II who allows Jews to live in their own quarter in return for an annual tax.

809–13CE Civil war in Persia.

900–1090CE The Golden age of Jewish culture in Spain.

912CE Abd-ar-Rahman III becomes Caliph of Spain.

940CE In Iraq, Saadia Gaon compiles his siddur (Jewish prayer book).

953CE Jewish historical narrative, Josippon, written in southern Italy.

960–1028CE Rabbenu Gershom of Germany, first great Ashkenazi sage, bans bigamy.

1013–73 Life of Rabbi Yitzhak Alfassi, who wrote the *Rif*, an important work of Jewish law.

1040–1105 Time of Rashi of France, Rabbi Shlomo Yitzhaki, who writes commentaries on almost the entire Tanakh (Hebrew Bible) and Talmud.

Below A 5th-century CE mosaic map from Madaba, showing Jerusalem.

1050–1250

1066 Jews enter England in the wake of the Norman invasion under William the Conqueror.

1090 Granada is conquered by the Muslim Berber Almoravides, ending the period of tolerance. Jews flee to Toledo.

1095–1291 Christian Crusades begin, sparking warfare with Islam in Palestine. Thousands of Jews are killed in Europe and in the Middle East.

1099 Crusaders temporarily capture Jerusalem.

1100–1275 Time of the tosafot, medieval talmudic commentators on the Torah carrying on Rashi's work.

1107 Moroccan Almoravid ruler Yoseph Ibn Tashfin expels Moroccan Jews who do not convert to Islam.

1135–1204 Rabbi Moses ben Maimon, aka Maimonides, is the leading rabbi of Sephardic Jewry. He writes the *Mishneh Torah* and the *Guide for the Perplexed*.

1141 Yehuda Halevi (1075–1141) issues a call for Jews to emigrate to Palestine.

1144 First Blood Libel, in Norwich, England. The trend spreads to Europe.

1179 Third Lateran Council in Vatican establishes Jewish-Christian relations.

1187 Arab leader Saladin (c.1138–1193) takes Jerusalem and most of Palestine; many Jews arrive.

1200–1300 Zenith of the German Jewish Hasidei Ashkenaz pietist movement.

1240 Paris Disputation. Monks publicly burn the Talmud.

1244–1500 Successive conquest of Palestine by Mongols and Egyptian Muslims. Many Jews die or leave.

1249 Pope Innocent IV in Italy forbids Christians to make false blood libels against Jews.

1250–1480

1250–1300 The time of Moses de Leon of Spain, reputed author of the Zohar. Modern form of Kabbalah (esoteric Jewish mysticism) begins.

1250–1516 Mamluk rule.

1250–1550 Period of the Rishonim, the rabbinic sages who wrote commentaries on the Torah and Talmud and law codes.

1263 The Great Disputation of Barcelona, where Nahmanides (Ramban) defends the Talmud against Christian accusations.

1267 Nahmanides settles in Jerusalem and builds the Ramban Synagogue.

1270–1343 Rabbi Jacob ben Asher of Spain writes the *Arba'ah Turim* (Four Rows of Jewish Law).

1290 Jews are expelled from England by Edward I by the Statute of Jewry.

1290–1301 Mamluk rulers allow attacks on churches and synagogues, and segregate Jews and Christians from Muslims.

1300 Time of Rabbi Levi ben Gershom (1288–1344), also known as Gersonides, a French philosopher.

1306–94 Jews are repeatedly expelled from France and readmitted. Last expulsion lasts 150 years.

1343 Persecuted in west Europe, Jews are invited to Poland by Casimir the Great.

1348–50 The Plague kills 30 to 60 per cent of Europe's people, and some blame Jews.

1391 Massacres in Spain; Jewish refugees find sanctuary in Algeria.

1415 Pope Benedict XII orders censorship of Talmud.

1458 Jews welcome Ottoman Turks who conquer Byzantine Constantinople.

1475 First Hebrew book printed, in Italy, Ben Asher's *Arba'ah Tumim*.

1478 The Spanish Inquisition begins.

1480–1550

1486 First Jewish prayer book published in Italy.

1487 Portugal's first printed book is a Pentateuch in Hebrew.

1488–1575 Life of Joseph Caro, born in Spain, who in later years wrote the *Shulkhan Arukh*, the codification of halakhic law and talmudic rulings.

1492 The Alhambra Decree – 200,000 Jews are expelled from Spain. Ottoman Sultan Bayezid II sends ships to bring Jews to safety in his empire. Many Jews survive as conversos (converts) or marranos, or flee. Columbus discovers America.

1493 Jews are expelled from Sicily.

1495 Jews expelled from Lithuania.

1497 Jews are forced to convert or leave Portugal.

1501 King Alexander of Poland readmits Jews to the Grand Duchy of Lithuania.

1516 Ghetto of Venice established.

1517 Martin Luther starts the Protestant Reformation.

1517–1917 Ottoman rule in Palestine.

1525–72 Rabbi Moses Isserles (The Rama) of Cracow writes an extensive gloss to the *Shulkhan Arukh* for Ashkenazi Jewry.

1525–1609 Life of Rabbi Judah Loew ben Betzalel, called Maharal of Prague.

1534 First Yiddish book published, in Poland.

1547 First Hebrew Jewish printing house in Lublin, Poland.

Below The 15th-century Rothschild Miscellany *details all of Jewish life.*

1550–1720

1534–70 Life of Isaac Luria, who founded the new school of Kabbalists.
1550 Moses ben Jacob Cordovero founds a Kabbalah academy in Safed.
1564 First printed version of Joseph Caro's Code of Jewish law published.
1567 First Jewish university yeshiva founded in Poland.
1577 Hebrew printing press established in Safed, the first of any kind in Asia.
1580–1764 First session of the Council of Four Lands (Va'ad Arba' Aratzot) in Lublin, Poland. Seventy delegates from local Jewish kehillot meet to discuss issues important to the Jewish community.
1626–76 Time of false Messiah Shabbetai Tzvi of Smyrna, Turkey.
1648–55 Ukrainian Cossack Bogdan Chmielnicki leads a massacre of Polish gentry and Jewry that leaves an estimated 130,000 dead. The total decrease in the number of Jews is estimated at 100,000.
1654 The first Jews go to North America.
1655 Jews are readmitted to England.
1675 The world's first Jewish newspaper is printed in Amsterdam.
1700 Rabbi Yehuda He-Hasid makes aliyah (immigrates) to Palestine with hundreds of followers. He dies suddenly.
1700–60 Life of Israel ben Eliezer, known as the Ba'al Shem Tov, who founded Hasidic Judaism in eastern Poland.
1701 Foundation of Bevis Marks Synagogue, London, the oldest synagogue in the United Kingdom still in use.
1720 Unpaid Arab creditors burn the unfinished synagogue built by immigrants of Rabbi Yehuda and expel all Ashkenazi Jews from Jerusalem.
1720–97 Time of Rabbi Elijah of Vilna, the Vilna Gaon.

1720–1800s

1729–86 Moses Mendelssohn and the Haskalah (Enlightenment) movement.
1740 Ottomans invite Rabbi Haim Abulafia (1660–1744) to rebuild Tiberias.
1740–50 Mass immigration to Palestine under messianic predictions.
1747 Rabbi Abraham Gershon of Kitov is the first immigrant of the Hasidic Aliyah.
1759 Time of Jacob Frank (who claimed to be the reincarnation of Shabbetai Tzvi and King David).
1772–95 Partitions of Poland between Russia, Kingdom of Prussia and Austria where most Jews live. Old Jewish privileges are renounced.
1775–81 American Revolution, which guaranteed the freedom of religion.
1789 The French Revolution leads France in 1791 to grant full citizen rights to Jews, under certain conditions.
1790 In the USA, George Washington writes to the Jews of Rhode Island that he wants a country 'which gives bigotry no sanction … persecution no assistance'.
1791 Emancipation of Jews begins in Europe. Russia creates the Pale of Settlement.
1799 Failed attempt by the French to seize Acre in Palestine.
1800–1900 The Golden Age of Yiddish literature, the revival of Hebrew as a spoken language, and the revival of Hebrew literature. First major Yiddish theatre founded in Romania in 1876.
1810 Reform Movement in Germany opens first synagogue in Seesen.
1820–60 The development of Orthodox Judaism, in response to Reform Judaism, the European emancipation and Enlightenment movements; it is characterized by strict adherence to halakha (Jewish religious law).

Above The Portuguese Sephardic Synagogue in Amsterdam, built 1671.

1800s–1870

Mid-1800s Rabbi Israel Salanter develops the Mussar Movement. Positive-Historical Judaism, later known as Conservative Judaism, is developed.
1841 David Levy Yulee of Florida is the first Jew elected to Congress. The *Jewish Chronicle* is first printed in the UK.
1851 Norway allows Jews to enter the country. They are emancipated in 1891.
1858 Jews emancipated in England.
1860 Alliance Israélite Universelle is founded in Paris with the goal to protect Jewish rights as citizens.
1860–1943 Time of Henrietta Szold, founder of Hadassah.
1861 The Zion Society is formed in Frankfurt am Main, Germany. The first Haskalah Russian journal, *Razsvet*, is founded.
1862 Jews are given equal rights in Russia's Congress Kingdom of Poland. Moses Hess writes his proto-Zionist tract, *Rome and Jerusalem*.
1867 Jews emancipated in Hungary.
1868 Converted Jew Benjamin Disraeli becomes Prime Minister of the United Kingdom.
1870–90 Russian Zionist group Hovevei Zion (Lovers of Zion) and Bilu (est. 1882) set up a series of Jewish settlements in Israel, financially aided by Baron Edmond James de Rothschild. Eliezer Ben-Yehuda revives Hebrew as a spoken modern language.

Above Memorial in Berlin for the murdered Jews of Europe.

1870–1914

1870-1 Jews are emancipated in Italy and then Germany.

1875 Reform Judaism's Hebrew Union College is founded in Cincinnati, USA.

1877 New Hampshire becomes the last US state to give Jews equal rights.

1881–4, 1903–6, 1918–20 Three waves of pogroms kill thousands of Jews in Russia and Ukraine.

1882–1903 First Aliyah (large-scale immigration) to Israel, mainly from Russia.

1887 Conservative Jewish movement founded in America.

1890 The term 'Zionism' is coined by Nathan Birnbaum.

1897 Theodor Herzl writes *Der Judenstaat* (The Jewish State). The Bund (General Jewish Labor Union) is formed in Russia. The first Zionist Congress meets in Switzerland; the Zionist Organization founded.

1902 The Jewish Theological Seminary becomes the flagship of Conservative Judaism. Theodor Herzl publishes utopian Zionist novel *Altneuland*.

1903 The Kishinev Pogrom is caused by accusations that Jews practise cannibalism.

1904–14 The Second Aliyah, mainly from Russia and Poland.

1905 Russian Revolution, accompanied by pogroms.

1909 The first kibbutz and Tel Aviv are founded.

1914–33

1914 American Jewish Joint Distribution Committee founded.

1915 Yeshiva College and Rabbinical Seminary is established in New York.

1917 British military governance over Palestine begins after Allenby's troops defeat Ottoman Turks. Balfour Declaration gives official British support for 'the establishment in Palestine of a national home for the Jewish people'. The Pale of Settlement in Russia is abolished, and Jews get equal rights. Russian civil war leads to more than 2,000 pogroms.

1918–48 British Rule of Palestine.

1919–23 Third Aliyah, mainly from Russia.

1920 Histadrut (Jewish labour federation) and Haganah (Jewish defence organization) are founded in Israel. Vaad Leumi (National Council) is set up by the Jewish community. Britain receives the League of Nations' British Mandate of Palestine.

1921 British military administration of the Mandate is replaced by civilian rule. Britain proclaims that all Palestine east of the Jordan River is closed to Jewish settlement, but not to Arab settlement. Polish-Soviet peace treaty in Riga. First moshav (cooperative village), Nahalal, founded in Israel.

1922 Transjordan set up on three-quarters of Palestine. Jewish Agency is established. Establishment of the Jewish Institute of Religion in New York. Reconstructionist movement is established.

1923 Britain awards Golan Heights to Syria. Arab immigration is allowed; Jewish immigration is not.

1924–32 Fourth Aliyah, mainly from Poland.

1929 Major Arab riots in Palestine.

1931 Etzel (Irgun) 'revisionist' Jewish underground organization, founded.

1933–67

1933 Hitler takes over Germany and begins imposing race laws against Jews.

1933–9 Fifth Aliyah, mainly from Germany.

1936 World Jewish Congress founded.

1938 9-10 November: Kristallnacht (Night of Glass) – Nazi violence against Jews.

1939 The British government announces a limit of 75,000 on future Jewish immigration to Palestine.

1939–45 World War II. Holocaust.

1945–8 Post-Holocaust refugee crisis.

1946–8 The struggle for the creation of a Jewish state in Palestine is resumed by Haganah, Irgun and Lehi militants.

1947 Discovery of Dead Sea Scrolls.

1947 29 November: The United Nations approves creation of a Jewish State and an Arab State in Palestine. Violence erupts between Jews and Arabs.

1948 14 May: The State of Israel declares independence.

1948 15 May: Arab–Israeli War.

1948–9 War of Independence. Almost 250,000 Holocaust survivors make their way to Israel. 'Operation Magic Carpet' brings Yemenite Jews to Israel.

1948–54 Mass immigration to Israel.

1952 Prague trials revive anti-Semitic fears in Communist eastern bloc.

1953 Establishment of Yad Vashem Holocaust Memorial in Israel.

1956 The Suez War.

1962–5 Jewish–Christian relations are revolutionized by Vatican II.

1964 Palestine Liberation Organization (PLO) founded.

1966 Shmuel Yosef Agnon (1888–1970) becomes the first Hebrew writer to win the Nobel Prize in literature; jointly with German Jewish author Nelly Sachs.

1967–80

1967 5–11 June: Six Day War fought between Jewish Israel and Arab Egypt, Syria and Jordan. Israel gains control of East Jerusalem, West Bank, Sinai Peninsula and Golan Heights.

1967 1 September: Arab Leaders meet in Khartoum: – the Three Nos of Khartoum: No recognition of Israel; No negotiations with Israel; No peace with Israel. UN 242 offers 'land for peace' formula and underpins most future peace plans.

1968–70 Egypt's War of Attrition against Israel, to recapture the Sinai held by Israel since the Six Day War. Jewish settlers occupy houses in Hebron, amid more than 100,000 Palestinians.

1972 After a brief window in 1971, Soviets clamp down on 'refusenik' Jews wishing to leave the USSR. Palestinian terrorists kill Israeli athletes at Munich Olympics.

1973 6–24 October: Yom Kippur War. Israel surprised by Egyptian–Syrian attack.

1974 Foundation of Gush Emunim (Bloc of the Faithful), religious settlers movement. Golda Meir, Middle East's first woman leader, resigns over post-Yom Kippur War anger.

1975 Amendment to the Trade Act of the USA ties trade benefits to the Soviet Union to freedom of emigration for Jews. United Nations adopts resolution equating Zionism with racism. Rescinded in 1991. Israel becomes an associate member of the European Common Market.

1977 Likud party takes power after Israeli elections, ousting Labour for the first time since independence.

1978 18 September: Israel and Egypt sign comprehensive peace accords at Camp David. Leftist Israelis found Peace Now.

1979 Israel–Egypt Peace Treaty signed. Prime Minister Menachem Begin and President Anwar Sadat are awarded Nobel Peace Prize.

1980–2000

1982 Israel's withdrawal from Sinai completed. Operation Peace for Galilee removes PLO fighters from southern Lebanon.

1982 June–December: The Lebanon War.

1983 American Reform Jews formally accept patrilineal descent. Menachem Begin resigns as prime minister, replaced by Yitzhak Shamir.

1984–5 Operations Moses and Joshua: Rescue of Ethiopian Jewry by Israel. Inconclusive elections result in Labour–Likud coalition; rotating prime-ministerial formula.

1987 Beginning of the First Intifada against Israel.

1989 Fall of the Berlin Wall. Four-point peace initiative proposed by Israel.

1990 The Soviet Union relaxes its emigration laws. Thousands leave for Israel.

1990–1 Iraq invades Kuwait, triggering a war between Iraq and Allied United Nations forces.

1991 Operation Solomon rescues most remaining Ethiopian Jews. The Madrid Peace Conference opens in Spain. First bilateral talks between Israeli and Jordanian, Syrian and Palestinian delegations since 1949.

1992 New government headed by Yitzhak Rabin of the Labour party.

1993 13 September: Israel and the PLO sign the Oslo Accords.

1994 26 October: Israel and Jordan sign an official peace treaty.

1994 10 December: Arafat, Rabin and Peres share the Nobel Peace Prize. Palestinian self-government in Gaza Strip and Jericho area.

1995 Broadened Palestinian self-government is implemented in West Bank and Gaza Strip.

1995 4 November: Israeli Prime Minister Yitzhak Rabin is assassinated.

1996 Palestinian Council elected.

1999 Ehud Barak elected Prime Minister of Israel.

2000–

2000 24 May: Israel withdraws its forces from southern Lebanon.

2000 Camp David II peace talks between Israel, PLO and USA fail.

2000 29 September: Start of second Palestinian uprising, al-Aqsa Intifada.

2001 Election of Ariel Sharon as Israel's Prime Minister.

2002 Spate of suicide attacks on Israeli towns. Israeli military reoccupation of Palestinian urban centres.

2003 US President George W Bush proposes Israeli–Palestinian roadmap to peace. Arab League re-airs Abdullah Plan for peace.

2005 31 March: Israeli government recognizes the Bnei Menashe people of north-east India as one of the Ten Lost Tribes of Israel.

2005 August: The Government of Israel withdraws military and Jewish settlers from the Gaza Strip.

2006 Prime Minister Ehud Olmert of Israel forms government. Islamist Hamas wins Palestinian elections.

2008 Israel celebrates 60 years of independence.

2009 Barack Obama becomes first US President to host Passover seder in the White House, Washington DC.

2013 Following attacks on Israel from Gaza, debate in the Jewish community about the feasibility of a two-state solution to the Middle East crisis.

Below Celebrating Israel Independence Day at the Western Wall, Jerusalem.

JEWS IN THE ANCIENT WORLD

JEWISH CIVILIZATION BEGAN IN A POLYTHEISITIC CONTEXT IN THE ANCIENT NEAR EAST. ACCORDING TO SCRIPTURE, GOD CALLED ABRAHAM TO GO FROM BABYLONIA TO THE LAND OF CANAAN.

The history of the Jewish people began in Mesopotamia where successive empires of the ancient world flourished and decayed before the Jews emerged as a separate people. The culture of these civilizations had a profound impact on the Jewish religion – ancient Near Eastern myths were refashioned to serve the needs of the Hebrew people. It appears that the Jews emerged in this milieu as a separate nation between the 19th and 16th centuries BCE. According to the Bible, Abraham was the father of the Jewish people. Initially known as Abram, he came from Ur of the Chaldeans. Together with his family he went to Harran and subsequently to Canaan, later settling in the plain near Hebron. Abraham was followed by Isaac and Jacob, whose son Joseph was sold

Below The Exodus from Egypt through the Red Sea, a 17th-century painting by Frans Francken the Younger.

into slavery in Egypt. There he prospered, becoming a vizier in the house of Pharaoh. Eventually the entire Hebrew clan moved to Egypt, where they remained and flourished for centuries before a new Pharaoh decreed that all male Hebrew babies should be put to death.

THE EXODUS

To persuade Pharaoh to let the Jewish people go, God sent a series of plagues upon the Egyptians. After this devastation, Moses, the leader of the Jewish people, led his kinsfolk out of Egypt. After wandering in the desert for 40 years, the Hebrews finally entered into the land that God had promised them. Under Joshua's leadership, the Hebrews conquered the existing inhabitants, the Canaanites. After Joshua's death the people began to form separate groups. At first there were 12 tribes named after the sons of Jacob. During this period the Hebrews

Above Moses receiving the Ten Commandments, during the 40-year sojourn in the desert. From the 14th-century Spanish Sarajevo Haggadah.

were ruled by 12 national heroes who served successively as judges.

Frequently the covenant between God and his chosen people was proclaimed at gatherings in national shrines such as Shechem. Such an emphasis on covenantal obligation reinforced the belief that the Jews were the recipients of God's loving kindness. Now in a more settled existence, the covenant expanded to include additional legislation, including the provisions needed for an agricultural community. During this period it became increasingly clear to the Jewish nation that the God of the covenant directed human history – the Exodus and the entry into the Promised Land – were viewed as the unfolding of a divine plan.

THE PERIOD OF THE JUDGES

Under the judges, God was conceived as the supreme monarch. When some tribes suggested to Gideon that he deserved a formal position of power, he declared that it was impossible for the nation to be ruled by both God and a human

king. None the less, Saul was subsequently elected as king despite the prophet Samuel's warnings against the dangers of usurping God's rule. Later, the Israelite nation divided into two kingdoms. The northern and southern tribes were united only by their allegiance to King David but when his successor, King Solomon, and his son Rehoboam violated many of the ancient traditions, the northern tribes revolted. The reason they gave for this rebellion was the injustice of the monarchy, but in fact they sought to recapture the simple ways of the generation that had escaped from Egypt. It is against this background that the pre-exilic prophets, including Elijah, Elisha, Amos, Hosea, Micah and Isaiah, endeavoured to bring the nation back to the true worship of God.

DECLINE AND DESTRUCTION

During the 1st millennium BCE the Jews watched their country emerge as a powerful state only to see it sink into spiritual and moral decay. As a punishment for the nation's iniquity,

Below Babylonian cuneiform tablet from 700–500BCE, with inscription and map of Mesopotamia. In the centre Babylon is surrounded by Assyria and Elam.

the northern kingdom was devastated by the Assyrians in 722BCE. Two centuries later the southern kingdom fell to the Babylonians. Following the Babylonian conquest in 586BCE the Temple lay in ruins and the people despaired of their fate. Yet, despite defeat and exile, the nation rose from the ashes of the old kingdoms. In the centuries that followed, the Jewish people continued their religious traditions and communal life. Though they had lost their independence, their devotion to God and his law sustained them through suffering and hardship.

RETURN TO JUDAH

In Babylonia the exiles flourished, keeping their religion alive in the synagogues. These institutions were founded so that Jews could meet together for worship and study; no sacrifices were offered since that was the prerogative of the Jerusalem Temple. In 538BCE King Cyrus of Persia permitted the Jews to return to their former home and the nation was transformed. The Temple was rebuilt and religious reforms were enacted. The period following the death of King Herod in 4BCE was a time of intense anti-Roman feeling among the Jewish population in Judea as well as in the Diaspora. Eventually such hostility led to war, only to be followed by defeat and the destruction of the Second

Above In 70CE, the Romans under Emperor Titus destroyed the Temple in Jerusalem. 15th-century Flemish picture.

Temple. In 70CE thousands of Jews were deported. Such devastation, however, did not quell the Jewish hope of ridding the Holy Land of its Roman oppressors. In the 2nd century CE, a messianic rebellion led by Simon Bar Kochba was crushed by Roman forces. Yet despite this defeat, the Pharisees carried on the Jewish tradition through teaching and study at Jabneh, near Jerusalem.

Below Abraham, father of the Jewish people, preparing to sacrifice his son Isaac, from a 1700s Arabian manuscript.

RABBINIC AND MEDIEVAL JUDAISM

THE EMERGENCE OF RABBINIC JUDAISM HAS FUNDAMENTALLY CHANGED THE NATURE OF JUDAISM. FROM THE HELLENISTIC PERIOD TO TODAY THE RABBIS HAVE DOMINATED ALL ASPECTS OF JEWISH LIFE.

From the 1st century BCE Palestinian rabbinic scholars engaged in the interpretation of Scripture. The most important scholar of the early rabbinic period was Yehuda Ha-Nasi (135–*c.*220CE), the head of the Sanhedrin (a group of distinguished Pharisaic scholars), whose main achievement was the redaction of the Mishnah, or 'compendium of Jewish law', in the 2nd century CE. This volume consisted of the discussions and rulings of sages whose teachings had been transmitted orally.

According to the rabbis, the law recorded in the Mishnah was given orally to Moses along with the written law. This implies that there was an infallible chain of

Below Medieval migration of Jews showing their expulsion from Spain and some Slavic countries and movement to Islamic and other lands.

transmission from Moses to the leaders of the nation and eventually to the Pharisees.

The Sanhedrin, which had been so fundamental in the compilation of the Mishnah, met in several cities in Galilee, but later settled in the Roman district of Tiberias. Other scholars simultaneously established their own schools in other parts of the country where they applied the Mishnah to everyday life, together with old rabbinic teachings, which had not been incorporated in the Mishnah.

During the 3rd century CE the Roman Empire encountered numerous difficulties including inflation, population decline and a lack of technological development to support the army. In addition, rival generals struggled against one another for power, and the government became increasingly inefficient. Throughout this time of upheaval,

Above Head of a colossal statue of Constantine the Great, who extended official religious toleration to Christians.

the Jewish community underwent a similar decline as a result of famine, epidemics and plunder.

THE RISE OF CHRISTIANITY

At the end of the 3rd century CE, the emperor Diocletian (ruled 284–305CE) inaugurated reforms that strengthened the Roman empire. In addition, Diocletian introduced measures to repress the spread of Christianity, which had become a serious challenge to the official religion of the empire. However Diocletian's successor, Constantine the Great (ruled 306–37CE), reversed his predecessor's hostile stance and also extended official toleration to Christians in the empire.

By this stage Christianity had succeeded in gaining a substantial number of adherents among the urban population; eventually Constantine became more involved in Church affairs and just before his death he himself was baptized. The Christianization of the empire continued throughout the century and by the early 400s CE Christianity was fully established as the state religion.

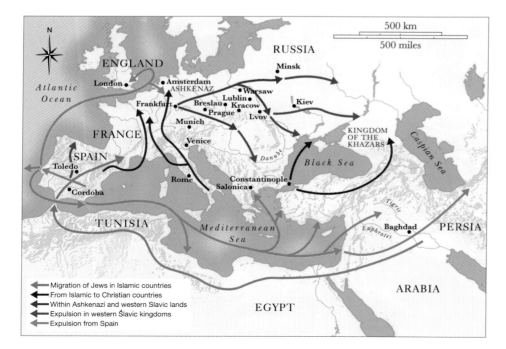

Migration of Jews in Islamic countries
From Islamic to Christian countries
Within Ashkenazi and western Slavic lands
Expulsion in western Slavic kingdoms
Expulsion from Spain

IN THE DIASPORA

By the 6th century CE the Jews had become largely a Diaspora people. Despite the loss of a homeland, they were unified by a common heritage: law, liturgy and shared traditions bound together the scattered communities stretching from Spain to Persia and from Poland to Africa. Living among Christians and Muslims, the Jewish community was reduced to a minority group and its marginal status resulted in repeated persecution. Though there were times of tolerance and creative activity, the threats of exile and death were always present in Jewish consciousness during this period.

UNDER ISLAM

Within the Islamic world, Jews along with Christians were recognized as 'Peoples of the Book' and were guaranteed religious toleration, judicial autonomy and exemption from the military. In turn they were required to accept the supremacy of the Islamic state. During the first two centuries of Islamic rule under the Umayyad and Abbasid caliphates, Muslim leaders confirmed the authority of traditional Babylonian institutions. When the Arabs con-

Right A Jewish scholar presents a translation of an Arabic treatise to Philippe d'Anjou, 13th century.

quered Babylonia, they officially recognized the position of the Jewish exilarch, who for centuries had been the ruler of Babylonian Jewry. By the Abbasid period, the exilarch shared his power with the heads of the rabbinical academies which had for centuries been the major centres of rabbinic learning.

During the 8th century CE messianic movements appeared in the Persian Jewish community, which led to armed uprisings against Muslim authority. Such revolts were quickly crushed, but an even more serious threat to traditional Jewish life was posed later in the century by the emergence of an anti-rabbinic sect, the Karaites. This group was founded in Babylonia in the 760s CE by Anan ben David. The growth of Karaism provoked the rabbis to attack it as a heretical movement since these various groups rejected rabbinic law and formulated their own legislation.

THE DECENTRALIZATION OF RABBINIC JUDAISM

By the 8th century CE the Muslim empire began to undergo a process of disintegration; this process was accompanied by a decentralization of rabbinic Judaism. The academies of Babylonia began to lose their hold on the Jewish scholarly world, and in many places rabbinic schools were established in which rabbinic sources were studied. In the Holy Land, Tiberias was the location of an important rabbinical academy as well as the centre of the masoretic scholars who produced the standard text of the Bible. But it was in Spain that the Jewish community was to

Left A 13th-century South German illumination showing Moses receiving the Ten Commandments, from the Regensburg Pentateuch.

attain the greatest level of achievement in literature, philosophy, theology and mysticism.

In their campaigns the Muslims did not manage to conquer all of Europe – many countries remained under Christian rule, as did much of the Byzantine empire. In Christian Europe, Jewish study took place in a number of important towns such as Mainz and Worms in the Rhineland and Troyes and Sens in northern France. In such an environment the study of the Talmud reached great heights; in Germany and northern France scholars known as 'the Tosafists' used new methods of talmudic interpretation. In addition Ashkenazic Jews of this period composed religious poetry modelled on the liturgical compositions of 5th- and 6th-centuries CE Israel.

Yet, despite such an efflorescence of Jewish life, the expulsion of the Jews from the countries in which they lived became a dominant policy of Christian Europe. They were driven out of Rome in 139BCE, from England in 1290, from Germany in 1348, from Spain in 1492 and from many other states. Repeatedly, Jewish communities throughout Europe suffered violent attack, and Jewish massacre became a frequent occurrence.

JEWS IN THE EARLY MODERN PERIOD

DURING THE EARLY MODERN PERIOD, JEWISH SCHOLARS CONTINUED
TO CONTRIBUTE TO JEWISH LIFE. HOWEVER THE LONGING FOR MESSIANIC
DELIVERANCE CONTINUED TO ANIMATE JEWISH CONSCIOUSNESS.

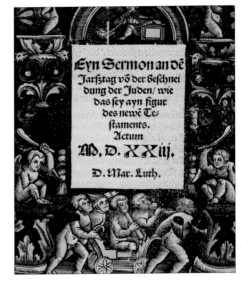

By the end of the 14th century political instability in Christian Europe led to the massacre of many Jewish communities in Castile and Aragon. Fearing for their lives, thousands of Jews converted to Christianity at the end of the century. Two decades later Spanish rulers introduced the Castilian laws that segregated Jews from their Christian neighbours. In the following year a public disputation was held in Tortosa about the doctrine of the Messiah; as a result increased pressure was applied to the Jewish population to convert. Those who became Maranos, or apostates, found life much easier, but by the 15th century anti-Jewish sentiment again became a serious problem. In 1480 King Ferdinand and Queen Isabella of Spain established the Inquisition to determine whether former Jews practised Judaism in

Below Many Jews fled Spain to escape the tortures of the Inquisition, shown here in a 19th-century engraving.

secret. To escape such persecution many Maranos sought refuge in various parts of the Ottoman empire.

RABBINIC SAGES

Prominent among the rabbinic scholars of this period was Joseph ben Ephraim Caro (1488–1575), who emigrated from Spain to the Balkans. In the 1520s he commenced a study of Jewish law, *The House of Joseph*, based on previous codes of Jewish law. In addition, he composed a shorter work, the *Shulkhan Arukh*, which has become the authoritative code of law in the Jewish world. While working on the *Shulkhan Arukh*, Caro emigrated to Safed in Israel, which had become a major centre of Jewish religious life. Talmudic academies were established and small groups engaged in the study of Kabbalistic (mystical) literature as they piously awaited the coming of the Messiah. In this centre of Kabbalistic activity one of the greatest mystics of Safed, Moses Cordovero (1522–70),

Above 16th-century Jews often found life insecure, as evidenced by this sermon of Martin Luther condemning the Jews. His anti-Semitism had a persistent influence on German attitudes towards Jews.

collected, organized and interpreted the teachings of earlier mystical authors. Later in the 16th century, Kabbalistic speculation was transformed by the greatest mystic of Safed, Isaac Luria (1534–72).

THE MYSTICAL MESSIAH

By the beginning of the 17th century Lurianic mysticism had made an important impact on Sephardic Jewry, and messianic expectations had also become a central feature of Jewish life. In this milieu the arrival of a self-proclaimed messianic king, Shabbetai Tzvi (1626–76), brought about a transformation of Jewish life and thought. After living in various cities, he travelled to Gaza where he encountered Nathan Benjamin Levi, who believed he was the Messiah. His messiahship was proclaimed in 1665, and Nathan sent letters to Jews in the Diaspora asking them to recognize Shabbetai Tzvi as their redeemer.

Eventually Shabbetai was brought to court and given the choice between conversion and death. In the face of this alternative, he converted to Islam. Such an act of

apostasy scandalized most of his followers, but others continued to revere him as the Messiah. In the following century the most important Shabbetean sect was led by Jacob Frank, who believed himself to be the incarnation of Shabbetai.

PERSECUTION

During this period Poland had become a great centre of scholarship. In Polish academies scholars collected together the legal interpretations of previous authorities and composed commentaries on the *Shulkhan Arukh*. However, in the midst of this general prosperity, the Polish Jewish community was subject to a series of massacres carried out by the Cossacks of the Ukraine, Crimean Tartars and Ukrainian peasants. In 1648 Bogdan Chmielnicki (1595–1657), head of the Cossacks, instigated an insurrection against the Polish gentry, and Jews were slaughtered in these revolts.

Elsewhere in Europe this period witnessed Jewish persecution and oppression. Despite the positive con-

Below A 17th-century engraving of Shabbetai Tzvi, a charismatic from Turkey and self-proclaimed Messiah.

THE ORIGINS OF HASIDISM
(ALSO SPELLED HASSIDISM OR CHASIDISM)

By the middle of the 18th century the Jewish community had suffered numerous waves of persecution and

was deeply dispirited by the conversion of Shabbetai Tzvi. In this environment the Hasidic movement sought to revitalize Jewish life. The founder of this new sect was Israel ben Eliezer, known as the Ba'al Shem Tov (1700–60), who was born in southern Poland. Legend relates that he performed various miracles and instructed his disciples in Kabbalistic lore. By the 1740s he had attracted many disciples who passed on his teaching. After his death, Dov Baer became the leader of his sect and Hasidism spread to southern Poland, the Ukraine and Lithuania.

Left The Ba'al Shem Tov (Israel ben Eliezer), founder of Hasidism.

---

tact between Italian humanists and Jews, Christian anti-Semitism frequently led to persecution and suffering. In the 16th century the Counter-Reformation Church attempted to isolate the Jewish community. The Talmud was burned in 1553, and two years later Pope Paul IV reinstated the segregationist edict of the Fourth Lateran Council, forcing Jews to live in ghettos and barring them from most areas of economic life. In Germany the growth of Protestantism frequently led to adverse conditions for the Jewish population. Though Martin Luther was initially well disposed to the Jews, he soon came to realize the Jewish community was intent on remaining true to its faith. As a consequence, he composed a virulent attack on the Jews.

By the mid-17th century, Dutch Jews had attained importance in trade and finance. Maranos and Ashkenazi Jews flourished in Amsterdam. In this milieu Jewish cultural activity grew: Jewish writers published works of drama, theology and mystical lore.

Though Jews in Holland were not granted full rights as citizens, they nevertheless enjoyed religious freedom, personal protection and liberty in economic affairs.

Below The Haari synagogue in Safed, home of rabbinic scholar Joseph Caro and mystic Isaac Luria.

JEWS IN THE MODERN WORLD

JEWISH EMANCIPATION IN THE 18TH CENTURY LED TO A REVOLUTION IN JEWISH LIFE. HOWEVER THE RISE OF ANTI-SEMITICISM IN THE 19TH CENTURY LED TO TERRIBLE CONSEQUENCES IN THE 1930S AND 40S.

During the late 18th century the treatment of Jews in central Europe improved owing to the influence of Christian polemicists.

JEWISH EMANCIPATION
Within this environment Jewish emancipation gathered force. The Jewish philosopher Moses Mendelssohn (1729–86) advocated the modernization of Jewish life. To further this advance he translated the Pentateuch into German so that Jews would be able to speak the language of the country in which they lived. Following his example, a number of followers known as the *maskilim* fostered the Haskalah, or Jewish Enlightenment, which encouraged Jews to abandon medieval forms of life and thought.

REFORM JUDAISM
Paralleling this development, reformers encouraged the modernization of the Jewish liturgy and reform of Jewish education. Although such changes were denounced by the

Below Proclamation of the Independence of the State of Israel by PM David Ben-Gurion, Tel Aviv, 14 May 1948.

Orthodox establishment, Reform Judaism spread throughout Europe. In 1844 the first Reform synod took place in Brunswick; followed by a conference in 1845 in Frankfurt. At this gathering one of the more conservative rabbis, Zacharias Frankel (1801–75), expressed dissatisfaction with progressive reforms to Jewish worship. He resigned and established a Jewish theological seminary in Breslau. Eventually this approach to the tradition led to the creation of Conservative Judaism. In 1846 a third synod took place at Breslau, but the revolution and its aftermath brought about the cessation of these activities until 1868, when another synod took place at Cassel.

In the United States, Reform Judaism became an important feature of Jewish life. The most prominent of the early reformers was Isaac Mayer Wise (1819–1900), who came to Albany, New York from Bavaria. Later he went to Cincinnati, Ohio where he published a new Reform prayer book as well as several Jewish newspapers. In 1869 the first Central Conference of American Rabbis was held in Philadelphia; followed in 1873 by the founding of the Union of American Hebrew Congregations. In 1875 the Hebrew Union College was established to train rabbinical students for Reform congregations.

ZIONISM
In eastern Europe conditions were less conducive to emancipation, and a series of pogroms took place in Russia in 1881–2. After these events, many Jews emigrated to the United States as well as Palestine. By the late

Above Theodor Herzl, founder of political Zionism, on a bridge in Basle during the 5th Zionist Congress.

1880s the idea of a Jewish homeland had spread throughout Europe. At the first Zionist Congress at Basle in 1897, Theodor Herzl (1860–1904) called for a national home based on international law.

By 1900 a sizeable number of Jews had emigrated to Palestine. After World War I, Jews in Palestine organized a National Assembly and an Executive Council. By 1929 the Jewish community numbered 160,000, and this increased in the next ten years to 500,000. At this time Palestine's population was composed of about one million Arabs consisting of peasants and a number of landowners, plus the Jewish population. In 1929 the Arab community rioted following a dispute about Jewish access to the Western Wall of the ancient Temple. This caused the British to curtail both Jewish immigration and purchase of Arab land.

By the 1920s Labour Zionism had become the dominant force in Palestinian Jewish life; in 1930 various socialist and Labour groups joined together in the Israel Labour Party. Within the Zionist movement a right-wing segment criticized Chaim Weizmann, President of the World Zionist Organization, who was committed to co-operation with the British. Vladimir Jabotinsky, leader

Above Scene at St Petersburg railway station in 1891 as many Jews fled from anti-Semitism in Russia.

of the Union of Zionist Revisionists, stressed that the central aim of the Zionist movement was the establishment of an independent state in the whole of Palestine. In 1937 a British Royal Commission proposed that Palestine be partitioned into a Jewish and Arab state with a British zone; this recommendation was accepted by Zionists but rejected by the Arabs.

In 1939, a British Government White Paper rejected the concept of partition, limited Jewish immigration, and decreed Palestine would become independent in ten years.

THE HOLOCAUST

As these events unfolded in the Middle East, Jews in Germany were confronted by increasing hostility. The Nazis gained control of the government and curtailed civil liberties. In November 1938 they organized an onslaught against the Jewish population known as *Kristallnacht*, a prelude to the Holocaust. Hitler invaded Poland in September 1939, and later that year incorporated much of the country into Germany; more than 600,000 Jews were gathered into a large area in Poland. This was

Right An Arab anti-Zionist demonstration in Palestine under the British mandate, 8 March 1920.

followed by the invasion of Russia in 1941, and the Nazis used mobile killing battalions, the *Einsatzgruppen*, to destroy Russian Jewry. In time fixed killing centres were created at six death camps where millions of Jews and others were murdered.

During the war and afterwards, the British prevented illegal immigrants entering the Holy Land, and Jews in Palestine campaigned against this policy. By 19 November 1947 the General Assembly of the United Nations endorsed a plan of partition, and the Arabs then attacked Jewish settlements. In May 1948, David Ben-Gurion (1886–1973) read out the Scroll of Independence of the Jewish state. Immediately a government was formed, and the Arabs stepped up their assault. Following the War of Independence, armistice talks were held and agreements signed with Egypt, Lebanon, Transjordan and Syria. Later President Gamal Abdel Nasser refused Israeli ships access to the Gulf of Aqaba in 1956, seized the Suez Canal and formed a pact with Saudi Arabia and various Arab states. In response, Israel launched a strike, conquering Sinai and opening the sea route to Aqaba. These events were followed by the Six Day War in 1967, the Yom

Above Existential philosopher Martin Buber deeply influenced Jewish religious thought with his I and Thou *(1923).*

Kippur War in 1973, and in 1982 an Israeli offensive against the PLO in Southern Lebanon.

In the ensuing years, hostility between Jews and Arabs has intensified. The *intifada* coupled with repeated suicide bombing led to the creation of a massive wall of defence in the Occupied Territories. Rocket attacks on Israel from Gaza in 2012 has hardened Israeli opinion and made a two-state solution more difficult. For Jews worldwide, the defence of Israel in the face of Arab opposition has become a major feature of contemporary Jewish life.

PART I

JEWISH TRADITIONS

For nearly 4,000 years the Jewish people have flourished, at times in the most adverse conditions. Throughout their long history, they remained faithful to the traditions of their ancestors. Yet, it would be an error to assume that the Jewish faith is monolithic in character. Rather, from ancient times to the present a wide variety of Judaisms have emerged, each with its own character.

In the ancient world, the simple faith of the patriarchs was replaced by an elaborate cultic system in the Jerusalem Temple. This was followed by the emergence of a number of religious groups including the Samaritans, Sadducees, Pharisees and Essenes. In the post-biblical period, the rabbis dominated Jewish life, creating mystical and philosophical systems. In later centuries, the Karaites were critical of the rabbinic establishment as were the Shabbateans and Frankists.

In modern times, traditional Judaism has been challenged by a range of non-Orthodox movements, each with its own ideology and religious orientation.

Opposite: The menorah, or seven-branched candlestick, is a classic symbol of Judaism that once stood in the Tabernacle and in the Temple in Jerusalem.

Above Lighting of the Hanukkah menorah by Barbara Aiello, who was the first female rabbi in Italy, at a synagogue in Milan, 2004.

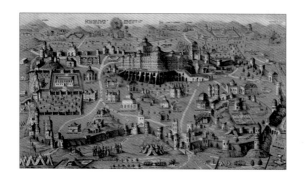

CHAPTER 1

ANCIENT JUDAISM

According to Scripture, Abraham was chosen by God to create a new nation. His descendants were to be as numerous as the stars in heaven. The Book of Genesis describes the faith of the patriarchs – Abraham, Isaac and Jacob – and the subsequent history of the ancient Hebrews.

Faith in one God sustained them in Canaan and their long sojourn in Egypt. They were enslaved by the Egyptian Pharaoh, but rescued by Moses who led them into the desert for 40 years. Under Joshua's leadership, the Jewish people conquered the Canaanites and established a monarchy. With the creation of a Temple in Jerusalem, a new form of Judaism emerged, rooted in cultic observance. The emergence of the prophets brought about a profound change in religious orientation with stress on moral action. Under the influence of Hellenism, the Jewish faith underwent further change. In the Northern Kingdom the Samaritans developed their own interpretation of the faith. As time passed, the Jewish nation divided into three major groups – the Sadducees, Pharisees and Essenes – with different religious orientations.

Opposite Moses and the Burning Bush. A 2nd-century painting from Dura-Europos, Syria, a synagogue with extraordinarily fine frescoes that was uncovered virtually intact in 1932.

Above A 19th-century print of the ancient city of Jerusalem showing the city walls and the magnificent Temple of King Solomon towering above it all.

ANCIENT HEBREWS

THE RELIGION OF THE ANCIENT HEBREWS WAS BASED ON TRADITIONS SURROUNDING THE PATRIARCHS, THE EXILE IN EGYPT AND GOD'S REDEMPTION OF HIS CHOSEN PEOPLE FROM BONDAGE.

The birth of the Jewish people occurred in ancient Mesopotamia. According to Scripture, God called Abraham to travel from Ur of the Chaldeans to Canaan where he promised to make his descendants as numerous as the stars in heaven.

THE ANCIENT NEAR EAST

The rise of ancient Mesopotamian civilization occurred at the end of the 4th millennium BCE in southern Mesopotamia, where the Sumerians created city states, each with its local god. During the 3rd millennium BCE waves of Semitic peoples settled amid the Sumerians. These Semites, known as Akkadians, identified some of their gods with the Sumerian deities. For these peoples, life was under these gods' control. To obtain happiness, it was essential to keep the gods in good humour through worship and sacrifice.

Below Jacob dreamt of a ladder to heaven during his flight from his brother Esau. 16th-century painting by Nicolas Dipre.

Right Abraham receives the divine promise that his descendants would be as numerous as the stars. A 2nd-century wall painting from Dura-Europos, Syria.

THE PATRIARCHS

It was in this polytheistic milieu that the Jews emerged as a separate people in the 19th–16th centuries BCE. According to the biblical narrative in Genesis, Abraham was the father of the Jewish nation. Originally known as Abram, he came from Ur of the Chaldeans – a Sumerian city of Mesopotamia. Together with his father Terah, his wife Sarai, and his nephew Lot, he travelled to Harran, a trading centre in northern Syria. There his father died, and God called upon him to go to Canaan: 'Go from your country and your kindred and your father's house to the land I will show you. And I will make of you a great nation.' (Genesis 12:1–2).

Abraham's belief in one God constituted a radical break from the past. Unlike the Sumerians and Akkadians, who believed in a pantheon of gods, Abraham was committed to the God who had revealed himself to him and ruled over heaven and earth. Scripture records that God made a covenant with Abraham symbolized by an act of circumcision: 'You shall be circumcised in the flesh of your foreskins and it shall be a sign of the covenant between me and you.' (Genesis 17:11). Later, God tested Abraham's dedication by ordering him to sacrifice Isaac, only telling him at the last moment to refrain. Repeatedly in the Book of Genesis God appeared to Abraham, reassuring him of his destiny. Similarly, God revealed himself to Abraham's son, Isaac, and to his grandson, Jacob.

Like Abraham, Jacob was told that his offspring would inherit the land of Canaan and fill the earth. When Jacob travelled to Harran, he had a vision of a ladder rising to heaven: 'And behold, the angels of God were ascending and descending on it! And behold, the

Below The Plagues of Egypt. An illumination from a Bohemian Haggadah of 1728.

THE JOSEPH NARRATIVES

The history of the three patriarchs is followed by a cycle of stories about Jacob's son Joseph. Like his ancestors, Joseph believed in a providential God who guided his destiny. When Joseph was in Shechem helping his brothers

tend his family's flocks he angered them by recounting dreams in which they bowed down before him. They reacted by plotting his death. Joseph was eventually taken to Egypt, where he became Pharaoh's chief minister. When his brothers came before him to buy grain because of a famine in Canaan, he revealed his true identity and God's providential care.

The Jewish people were later enslaved in Egypt, an event leading to the Exodus.

Left This remarkable 19th-century Russian painting has Jacob's eldest son Reuben showing him Joseph's coat.

Lord stood above it and said, "I am the Lord, the God of Abraham your father and the god of Isaac; the land on which you lie I will give to you and to your descendants, and your descendants shall be like the dust of the earth."' (Genesis 28:12–18).

THE EXODUS

The biblical narrative continues with an account of the deliverance of God's chosen people from Egyptian bondage. Here again, Scripture emphasizes that God is active in human history. The Book of Exodus relates that God revealed himself to Moses and commanded that he deliver the ancient Hebrews from bondage: 'I am the God of your father, the God of Abraham, the God of Isaac, and the God of Jacob ... I have seen the affliction of my people who are in Egypt, and have heard their cry because of their taskmasters. I know their sufferings ... Come, I will send you to Pharaoh that you may bring forth my people, the sons of Israel, out of Egypt.' (Exodus 3:6–7, 10)

In order to persuade Pharaoh that he should let the Jewish people go, God sent plagues on the Egyptians,

culminating in the slaying of every Egyptian first-born son. After the final plague, Pharaoh released the Israelites, and they fled without even waiting for their bread to rise. However, their perils did not end: Pharaoh changed his mind and sent his forces in pursuit. When the Israelites came to an expanse of water, it seemed that they were trapped. Yet miraculously it was converted to dry land so that they were able to escape. For the ancient Israelites, the belief in a providential

God who rescues his people from disaster became a central feature of the faith and is celebrated each year at the Passover festival.

REVELATION ON SINAI

This band of free people then entered the wilderness of Sinai, where God performed miracles to provide them with food and water. After travelling for about 90 days, they encamped before Mount Sinai. God called Moses up to the top of the mountain and told him that if his people would listen to him and keep his covenant they would become God's special people. Moses remained on the mountain for 40 days; at the end of this period, he returned with two tablets of stone on which were inscribed God's laws. These commandments served as the basis for Jewish life as they wandered through the desert for 40 years. Convinced that they were God's chosen people, the ancient Hebrews worshipped the Lord of creation who had chosen them from among all peoples and given them his sacred law so that they could become a priestly nation.

Below When the people of Israel danced before the Golden Calf, Moses condemned them for setting up an idol. 16th-century fresco by Raphael.

TEMPLE JUDAISM

THE LIFE OF THE JEWISH NATION WAS ANIMATED BY WORSHIP AND PRAYER. ONCE THEY HAD SETTLED IN THE PROMISED LAND, JEWS OFFERED SACRIFICES IN THE TEMPLE IN JERUSALEM.

Above Two rabbis celebrating Pesach (Passover), from the Agada Pascatis, *a 15th-century Haggadah manuscript.*

During the early history of the nation, the patriarchs prayed to God and offered sacrifices on high places. Later the Jewish people worshipped God in a portable sanctuary. There sacrifices were offered to the Lord of the universe who had delivered his people from slavery. Yet, in time this simple form of worship was replaced by an elaborate cultic system in the Jerusalem Temple. This magnificent structure and its surrounding buildings were constructed by King Solomon in the 10th century BCE.

THE SANCTUARY

For the ancient Hebrews, God was both transcendent and imminent. He had created the universe, yet was intimately involved in the life of his people. Throughout the Genesis narrative, the patriarchs turned to him in prayer. Worship took many forms: petition, confession, praise, thanksgiving, adoration and intercession. In addition, the patriarchs offered sacrifice to God on high places.

Later, Scripture records that Moses made a portable shrine (sanctuary), following God's instructions (Exodus 25–27). This structure travelled with the Israelites in the desert, and it was placed in the centre of the camp in an open courtyard 1,000 cubits (a cubit is the approximate length of a forearm) by 50 cubits (about 1500 X 75 ft/457 X 23m) in size. The fence surrounding it consisted of wooden pillars from which a cloth curtain was suspended. Located in the eastern half of the courtyard, the sanctuary measured 50 cubits by 10 cubits (about 75 X 15 ft/23 X 4.5m). At its end stood the Holy of Holies, which was separated by a veil hanging on five wooden pillars on which were woven images of the cherubim. Inside the Holy of Holies was the Ark of the Covenant, the table on which the shewbread, or 12 loaves representing the 12 tribes of Israel, was placed, the incense altar, and the menorah, or 'candelabrum'. In the courtyard there was also an outer altar on which sacrifices were offered, as well as a brass laver for priests.

THE JERUSALEM TEMPLE

Eventually this structure was superseded by the Temple, which was built by King Solomon on Mount

Below King Solomon overseeing the construction of the Temple in Jerusalem. From an illuminated 16th-century French Bible.

A NATIONAL CENTRE

Through the centuries the Temple was viewed as a national centre; moreover, since it was the abode of the Ark, it was considered to be the site of the revelation of the Divine Presence and the preferred place for prayer. For this reason individual worshippers directed their supplications towards the Temple even from afar. There the people also gathered in times of distress when the priests would weep between the vestibule and the altar. For the prophets, the Temple Mount (Mount Zion) was the mountain of the Lord, and the Temple was the house of the God of Jacob and the Lord's house. It was the place where God's name was called. In the words of the prophet Jeremiah, it was 'a glorious throne set on high from the beginning.' (Jeremiah 17:12).

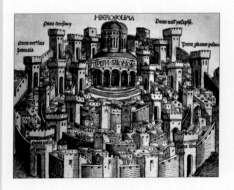

Left A woodcut of Jerusalem and the Temple of Solomon by Melchior Wolgemuth, from the Nuremberg Chronicle, *1493.*

Right *Preparations for the Passover, which in ancient times was observed in the Temple in Jerusalem. Bible illustration, 1470, by Leonardo Bellini.*

Moriah in Jerusalem in the 10th century BCE. Acting as the focus of prayer in ancient Israel, the Temple reoriented religious life and took the place of simpler forms of worship. The two principal sources for the plan of the Temple are 1 Kings 6–8 and 2 Chronicles 2–4. Standing within a royal compound, which also consisted of a palace, a Hall of Judgement, the Hall of Cedars, and a house for Solomon's wife, the Temple was 60 cubits long, 20 cubits wide, and 30 cubits high (about 88 ✗ 30 ✗ 46 ft/27 ✗ 9 ✗ 14m).

The main Temple was surrounded by a three-storeyed building divided into chambers with storeys connected by trap doors – these were probably storerooms for the Temple treasures. The main building consisted of an inner room – the Holy of Holies – on the west, and an outer room measuring 20 by 40 cubits (about 30 ✗ 60 ft/9 ✗ 18m) on the east. Around the Temple was a walled-in compound. At the entrance to the Temple stood two massive bronze pillars. Within the Holy of Holies stood the Ark, which contained the Two Tablets of the Covenant with the Ten Commandments.

In the outer room stood an incense altar, the table for the shewbread, and ten lampstands made of gold. In front of the Temple stood a bronze basin supported by 12 bronze cattle. A bronze altar also stood in the courtyard, which was used for various sacrifices.

THE LEVITES

In addition to sacrificial worship, it was customary for the Levites who served in the Temple to sing to the accompaniment of lyres with harps and cymbals. Many psalms in the Bible are ascribed to these Levite singers.

Primarily, the Temple was a place of assembly for the entire people for purposes of sacrifice, prayer and thanksgiving. They would come to Jerusalem to bring sin and guilt offerings as well as burnt offerings, peace offerings and meal offerings either in fulfilment of vows or as offerings of thanksgiving. These sacrifices had to be eaten within a day or two of their slaughter, and were apparently brought to the accompaniment of songs and in procession.

FESTIVAL WORSHIP

Special importance was attached to public processions in celebration of festivals. The people travelled to the Temple to worship before the Lord on Sabbaths and New Moons, at appointed seasons, and during the three pilgrim festivals (Pesach, Sukkot and Shavuot). Coming from Judah and beyond, the festal crowd would proceed in a throng with shouts and songs of thanksgiving; the procession was accompanied by the playing of musical instruments. The

right to serve in the Temple was assigned to the priests who were descended from Aaron, who were assisted by the Levites. The king enjoyed a status of holiness in the Temple, but in contrast to the priests, he was not permitted either to enter the sanctuary or to burn incense.

Below *Coin depicting the kind of lyre that may have been used in the Temple in Jerusalem, dated 134–5 CE, the third year of Bar Kochba's war against the Romans.*

PROPHETIC JUDAISM

THE PROPHETS OF ANCIENT ISRAEL WERE THE VOICE OF CONSCIENCE. REPEATEDLY THEY WARNED THE PEOPLE TO TURN FROM THEIR EVIL WAYS AND EMBRACE THE COVENANT IN ACCORDANCE WITH GOD'S WILL.

Above View of the River Tel and Tekoa, a village in the hills south of Jerusalem. The prophet Amos was born in Tekoa.

Once the ancient Hebrews settled in the Promised Land, they were ruled over by a series of judges. Eventually, a monarchy was established, at first over the entire country; and later, when there were two kingdoms (Israel in the north and Judah in the south), two royal houses reigned over their respective kingdoms. As time passed, a series of prophets emerged who pronounced against the evils of the nation. Prophetic Judaism championed the rule of justice and God's determination to punish his people for their iniquity unless they turned from their evil ways.

THE NORTHERN KINGDOM

In the 8th century BCE, Israel prospered for 40 years. Towards the end of Jeroboam II's reign, Amos, a shepherd from Tekoa who firmly differentiated himself from the official cultic prophets, proclaimed that

Israelite society had become morally corrupt. Many Israelites had become rich, but at the expense of the poor. Israel had sinned, he declared:

because they sell the righteous
  for silver
and the needy for a pair of shoes –
they that trample the head
  of the poor
into the dust of the earth,
and turn aside the way
  of the afflicted.
  (Amos 2: 6–7)

Amos's later contemporary, the prophet Hosea, echoed these dire predictions. Israel had gone astray and would be punished. Yet through personal tragedy – the infidelity of his wife, Gomer – Hosea was able to offer words of consolation and hope. Just as Hosea's love for his wife had been rejected, so God's love for Israel had been despised. But despite the coming devastation, God would not cease to love his chosen people.

Just as Hosea could not give up his wife, God could not abandon Israel: 'How can I hand you over, O Israel! My heart recoils within me, my compassion grows warm and tender.' (Hosea 11:8)

THE DESTRUCTION OF ISRAEL

As predicted by these pre-exilic Northern prophets, Amos and Hosea, the nation's fate was sealed. God had threatened destruction unless the people repented.

Left A stone stele showing two Assyrians driving a chariot, 8th century BCE.

At the beginning of the 8th century BCE the Assyrian King Shalmaneser V (727–722BCE) conquered Israel's capital Samaria after a siege of two years. The annals of Shalmaneser's successor, Sargon II (ruled 721–705BCE), record that 27,290 Israelites were deported as a result of this conquest. This marked the end of the northern kingdom. Following this assault, the kingdom of Judah was under threat.

Below According to Scripture, the tribes were descended from Jacob's sons, apart from Ephraim and Manasseh, who were sons of Jacob's son Joseph. Benjamin and Judah were in what became the southern kingdom of Judah, and the others in the northern kingdom of Samaria.

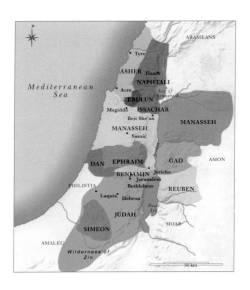

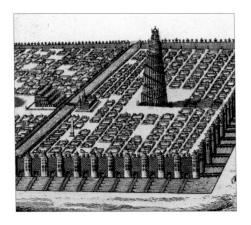

Above An 18th-century engraving of the Tower of Babel, the Hanging Gardens and the Royal Palace, Babylon.

THE SOUTHERN KINGDOM

To avoid a similar fate in the south, King Ahaz of Judah (*c.*735–720BCE) continued to pay tribute to Assyria and encouraged the nation to worship Assyrian gods. However, the prophet Isaiah was deeply concerned about such idolatrous practices. He believed the collapse of Israel was God's punishment for sinfulness, and he foresaw a similar fate for Judah. Isaiah warned his country that God was not satisfied with empty ritual in the Temple:

What to me is the multitude of
    your sacrifices? says the Lord.
I have had enough of burnt offerings
    of rams and the fat of fed beasts;
I do not delight in the blood of bulls,
    or of lambs, or of he-goats.
    (Isaiah 1:11)

A contemporary of Isaiah, the prophet Micah, also criticized the people for their iniquity and foretold destruction:

Hear this, you heads of the house
    of Jacob
and rulers of the house of Israel,
who abhor justice and pervert
    all equity ...
because of you Zion shall be
    ploughed as a field;
Jerusalem shall become a heap of
    ruins. (Micah 3:9,12)

Ahaz, however, refused to listen to these words; trusting in his own political alliances, he believed his kingdom was secure.

In the next century, the prophet Jeremiah similarly warned that the southern kingdom would eventually be devastated by foreign powers. The Lord, he declared, had this message for the southern kingdom:

Break up your fallow ground
and sow not among thorns.
Circumcise yourselves to the Lord,
remove the foreskins of your hearts,

O men of Judah and inhabitants
    of Jerusalem;
lest my wrath go forth like fire
and burn with none to quench it,
because of the evil of your doings.

Declare in Judah, and proclaim
    in Jerusalem, and say,
'Blow the trumpet through
    the land';
cry aloud and say,
'Assemble and let us go into the
    fortified cities!'
Raise a standard toward Zion,
flee for safety, stay not,
for I bring evil from the north,
and great destruction.
    (Jeremiah 4:3–6)

DESTRUCTION AND EXILE

In the following century Isaiah, Micah and Jeremiah's predictions were fulfilled: after a siege of 18 months, Jerusalem was conquered in 586BCE; all the main buildings were destroyed, King Zedekiah of Judah (597–86BCE) was blinded and exiled to Babylon.

The anguish of the people facing the tragedy of Babylonian conquest and captivity is reflected in the Book of Lamentations. Here the exiles

Right Hosea was a compassionate prophet who exhorted the people of Israel to reform. A panel from Sienna Cathedral, 1308.

bemoaned their fate as predicted by the prophets. The nation had betrayed the covenant and God poured out his wrath as he warned. Reflecting on their holy city, Jerusalem, they declared:

How lonely sits the city that was
    full of people!
How like a widow she has become,
She that was great among
    the nations! ...
The roads to Zion mourn,
for none come
    to the appointed feasts;
all her gates are desolate,
her priests groan;
her maidens have been
    dragged away
and she herself suffers bitterly.
    (Lamentations 1:1,4)

HELLENISTIC JUDAISM

GREEK CIVILIZATION HAD A PROFOUND IMPACT ON JEWRY, AFFECT-
ING ALL ASPECTS OF JEWISH LIFE. YET THESE CHANGES EVOKED A FIERCE
RESPONSE FROM PIOUS JEWS LOYAL TO THE TRADITION.

Although it is possible that there was some contact between Greeks and the ancient Hebrews, it was not until the 4th century BCE, during the reign of Alexander the Great (336–323BCE), that Greek civiliza-tion had a significant impact on Jewish life. The Hellenistic period was thus marked by the increasing influence of Greek ideas on the Jewish tradition.

THE HELLENISTIC PERIOD

During the centuries after Alexander the Great's reign, Palestine was part of Hellenistic kingdoms, first of Ptolemaic Egypt and then of Seleucid Syria. In the first third of the 2nd century BCE a group of Hellenizing Jews seized power in Jerusalem. Led by wealthy Jewish aristocrats who were attracted to Hellenism, their influence was primarily social rather than cultural and religious. Later, Jason the high priest (175–172BCE) established Jerusalem as a Greek city, Antioch-at-Jerusalem, with Greek educational institutions, such as the gymnasium.

Below A 2nd-century CE coin of Antiochus IV Epiphanes, the Seleucid king who caused the Maccabean revolt.

However, Jason was only a moder-ate Hellenizer compared with his successor as high priest, Menelaus, whose succession provoked a civil war. The Tobiads supported Menelaus, whereas the masses favoured Jason. It was these Hellenizers, including Menelaus and his followers, who influenced the Seleucid King Antiochus IV Epiphanes (175–164BCE) to under-take his persecutions of Jews in order to crush the rebellion of the Hasideans.

GREEK INFLUENCE

Yet, despite such rebellion the influ-ence of Hellenism was widespread in both Palestine and the Diaspora. Greek was substituted for Hebrew and Aramaic; Greek personal names were frequently adopted; Greek educational institutions were created; there was an efflorescence of Jewish Hellenistic literature and philoso-phy; and syncretism was widespread. The most obvious instance of Greek influence took place in the creation of Jewish literature during the Hellenistic period. The Jewish wisdom writer Ben Sira, for exam-ple, includes a number of aphorisms borrowed from Greek sources. The Testament of Joseph and the Book of Judith show Greek influ-ence. Similarly, the Book of Tobit shows Hellenistic influence in the form of its romance. In his para-phrase of the Bible, the Jewish historian made numerous changes. Abraham, for example, is presented as worthy of Greek political and philosophical ideals; Samson is an Aristotelian-like, great-souled man; Saul is a kind of Achilles; and Solomon is like Oedipus.

Above The battle of the Maccabees during the Hasmonean revolt by Jean Fouquet for Jewish historian Josephus's Antiquities of the Jews.

HELLENISM IN THE DIASPORA

It seems that there was no systematic pattern of Hellenizing in the Diaspora. Indeed, some Alexandrian Jewish writers argued that the Greeks had borrowed from the Jews. The Jewish Peripatetic philosopher Aristobulus asserted in the 2nd century BCE that Homer, Hesiod, Pythagoras, Socrates and Plato were all acquainted with a translation of the Torah into Greek. The first significant Graeco-Jewish historian, Eupolemus, reported that Moses taught the alphabet to the Jews, who then passed it on to the Phoenicians who transmitted it to the Greeks. The 1st-century BCE Jewish philosopher Philo was pro-foundly affected by Hellenism: the

Below Painting of the Temple of Solomon from the Hellenistic Dura-Europos synagogue in Syria, 3rd century CE.

Above Menelaus became high priest after bribing Antiochus IV with tribute money. 13th-century French illustration.

influence of Greek thought transcends mere language and affected his entire philosophical system.

ART AND LITERATURE

Beyond literary works, Greek influence is clearly illustrated in Hellenistic Jewish art and architecture. According to Josephus (37/38–100CE), the courts and colonnades of the Temple built by Herod in Jerusalem were in the Greek style. In synagogues in Palestine and the Diaspora, especially at Dura-Europos in Mesopotamia, the artwork was in direct violation of biblical and rabbinic prohibitions. The symbols used represent a kind of allegorization through art, similar to what Philo had attempted through philosophy. There is even evidence that some Jews adopted pagan elements in the charms and amulets they created. It is not surprising therefore that contact with Hellenism produced deviations from the Jewish tradition. Writers and artists who used extreme allegories in their work interpreted ceremonial laws as only a parable. Others relaxed their Jewish observance in order to become citizens of Alexandria. Indeed, the city of Alexandria, where Hellenism was most manifest, was

the only place where Christianity seems to have made real inroads in converting Jews.

JEWISH RESISTANCE

The spread of Hellenism gave rise to powerful resistance among the observant. Jewish struggle against Greek and Roman domination was provoked by a reaction to what was seen as spiritual corruption. Jewish monotheism and observance of the covenant were challenged by the influence of foreign ideas. This was most manifest in the Hasmonean revolt. When Antiochus IV conquered Jerusalem in 167BCE, he banned circumcision, Sabbath observance and the reading of the Torah; he also decreed that the Temple should be dedicated to the worship of the Greek god Zeus, that pigs should be sacrificed on the altar, and that all people, including non-Jews, should be allowed to worship there. In championing Hellenism, he underestimated Jewish resistance to such reforms. Many Jews were prepared to die rather than violate their traditions, and in the end the nation triumphed against its oppressors.

Below Seleucid general Nicanor attacked the Palestinian rebel leader Judah ha-Maccabee and the Jews on the Sabbath, during the Hasmonean revolt. Drawing by Gustave Doré, 1865.

SAMARITANS

IN THE NORTHERN KINGDOM THE SAMARITANS KEPT THEIR OWN
TRADITIONS BASED ON SCRIPTURE. AS TIME PASSED, HOSTILITY GREW
BETWEEN THE JEWISH AND THE SAMARITAN PEOPLES.

In ancient times the Samaritans constituted a separate people originating
from within the Jewish community.
This Jewish sect, which occupied
Samaria after the conquest of the
Northern Kingdom by the
Assyrians, developed its own interpretation of the faith. Intermingling
with the resident non-Jewish population, its mixed community
continued to follow the Jewish way
of life while simultaneously adopting pagan practices.

When Cyrus of Persia
(590/580–529BCE) conquered
Babylon in the 6th century CE, he
allowed the Jews to return from
Babylonia to their homeland. When
the Samaritans offered to help these
returning exiles rebuild the Temple,
the governor of Judea Zerubbabel,
who supervised the repair and
restoration of the Temple, refused
their offer since he regarded them as

*Below On Passover eve, Samaritans
today sacrifice a lamb, which is roasted
whole and eaten by the community.*

of uncertain racial origin and was
suspicious of their worship.
Recognizing that they would be
excluded from the state which these
exiles were intent on creating, the
Samaritans persuaded the Persian
officials responsible for the western
empire that the plans for restoration
were illegal, thereby delaying work
on the Temple for ten years or more.
This was the beginning of the
enmity between the Jewish and
Samaritan peoples, which continued
for hundreds of years.

BELIEF AND PRACTICE

Despite their rejection from the
Jewish community, the Samaritans
remained loyal to traditional belief
and practice. In its earliest form,
the Samaritan creed consisted of a
simple belief in God and the Torah
(Pentateuch). For the Samaritans,
God is the wholly other – he is
manifest in all things, all powerful
and beyond comprehension. His
purposes for Israel and all peoples
were communicated to Moses

*Above In the 1920s, arranged marriages
among Samaritan children of the West
Bank were still common.*

on Mount Sinai. According to
Samaritan tradition, Moses was
God's representative who wrote
the Torah and authorized Mount
Gerizim as the place that God
chose for sacrifice. In addition, the
Samaritans subscribed to a belief
in resurrection and anticipated
the arrival of one who would restore
all things prior to the final judgement of God.

Given that the Samaritans possessed only the Torah as the sole
authoritative source, the Pentateuch
served as the basis of their religious
practices. Frequently the Samaritans
were stricter about the interpretation of biblical law than the rabbis
because of their adherence to the
letter of the law. In other cases,
Samaritan law deviated from rabbinic traditions because of different
interpretations of the text.

Regarding the Sabbath, for
example, the Samaritans held four
prayer services. The first, on the
Sabbath eve, lasted for about an hour
before the setting of the sun. This
was followed on the Sabbath morning by a second service, which began
between 3 and 4 a.m. The afternoon
service was held only on regular
Sabbaths and those that fall during

the counting of the Omer; it began at noon and lasted for about two hours. The fourth prayer service took place at the end of the Sabbath and continued for about half an hour until the sun set.

BELIEF AND PRACTICE

In addition to Sabbath observance, the Samaritans also celebrated the other festivals recorded in Scripture. For the Samaritan community, the Passover was of central significance. On the eve of the festival, the Samaritans carried out the sacrifice of the paschal lamb on Mount Gerizim. At twilight on the 14th day of the first month, all members of the community gathered at the site of the altar in two groups; the first carried out the sacrifice and the second engaged in prayer. The High Priest then climbed on to a large stool and gave the signal to slaughter the sheep while reading the account of the Exodus from Egypt. Then a number of sheep corresponding to the families present were slaughtered.

Another major festival is Shavuot, when the Samaritans made a pilgrimage to Mount Gerizim. This

Below A magnificent Samaritan Torah case decorated in gold with images of objects used in the Temple.

Above At Shavuot, Samaritans parade at Mount Gerizim, Israel, celebrating the giving of the law on Mount Sinai.

holiday was celebrated on the 50th day of the counting of the Omer. The period is divided into seven weeks; in each week the Samaritans devoted the Sabbath to one of the places that the children of Israel passed on the Exodus from Egypt before arriving at Mount Sinai. On the first day after the sixth Sabbath, the Samaritans celebrated the day standing on Mount Sinai – there they prayed and read from the Torah (Pentateuch) from the middle of the night until the following evening. The seventh Sabbath is called the celebration of the Ten Commandments. The pilgrimage itself began early in the evening and all places holy to the Samaritans were visited.

Turning to the literature of the Samaritan community, the earliest work was the Pentateuch, which served as the centre of Samaritan life. The *Defter* constituted the oldest part of the liturgy and was probably written in the 4th century CE. There were also Samaritan chronicles, including the *Asatir*, a midrashic work, and *Al-Tolidah*, which contained various genealogical lists. The Samaritan Book of Joshua recounted the history of the Samaritan people from the initiation of Joshua to the days of Baba Rabbah. The *Annals* by Abu al-Fath were composed in the 14th century and were explained in the 19th to 20th centuries by Jacob

ben Harun. The *New Chronicle* was written in Samaritan Hebrew by Av-Sakhva ben Asad ha-Danfi and related events from Adam to 1900CE. The Samaritan corpus included a variety of halakhic works, Pentaetuch commentaries, and grammatical studies.

In all cases, Samaritan literature was centred around the Pentateuch and the religious life of the community. The purpose of these works was to guide the community in understanding the meaning of Scripture, ensuring that the biblical precepts were fulfilled in the lives of the adherents. This religious orientation illustrates the traditionalism of the Samaritan sect despite its deviation from mainstream Judaism. Holding fast to the religious tenets of the faith, the Samaritans strictly adhered to the Jewish way of life as they understood it. In this respect they regarded themselves as following an authentic form of Judaism despite their divergence from the rabbis.

Throughout its history the Samaritan community was committed to observing the law and fulfilling its covenant duties as it understood them.

Below A Samaritan priest with the ancient Pentateuch in the Samaritan synagogue in Nablus, West Bank.

SADDUCEES

MEMBERS OF A 2ND-CENTURY BCE JEWISH SECT, POSSIBLY FORMED AS A POLITICAL PARTY, THE SADDUCEES BELIEVED THE TORAH WAS DIVINELY REVEALED AND BIBLICAL LAW MUST BE STRICTLY FOLLOWED.

According to tradition, the Sadducees were followers of the teachings of the High Priest Zadok. Scholars, however, have pointed out that this explanation is unlikely since the Sadducees made their debut in history as supporters of the Hasmonean high priests. Thus, the term 'Sadducees' may be a Hebraization of the Greek word *sundikoi*, or 'members of the council'. This would mark them out as councillors of the Hasmoneans even though they themselves came to associate their name with the Hebrew *zedek*, or 'righteous'. According to rabbinic sources, the Sadducees were not named after the High Priest Zadok, but rather

Below A fanciful 19th-century lithograph showing the breastplate and supposed costume of the Jewish high priest.

Right Jewish historian Flavius Josephus, who described the Hasmonean revolt, is brought before Titus, Roman commander in Judea during the Jewish revolt 66CE.

another Zadok who rebelled against the teachings of Antigonus of Soko, a government official of Judea in the 3rd century BCE who was a predecessor of the rabbis.

Despite these different interpretations, it is clear that the Sadducees were a priestly group, associated with the leadership of the Jerusalem Temple. Possibly, the Sadducees belonged to the aristocratic clan of the Hasmonean high priests who replaced the previous high priestly lineage that permitted the Syrian Emperor Antiochus IV Epiphanes to desecrate the Temple of Jerusalem with idolatrous sacrifices. The festival of Hanukkah celebrates the overthrowing of the Syrian forces, the re-dedication of the Temple, and the instalment of a new Hasmonean priestly line.

In the following years the Hasmoneans ruled as priest-kings; like other aristocracies across the Hellenistic world, they were increasingly influenced by Hellenistic ideas. Like the Epicureans, the Sadducees rejected the existence of an afterlife, thereby denying the Pharisaic doctrine of the resurrection of the dead. The Dead Sea Scrolls community – identified with the Essenes – were led by a high priestly caste who were believed to be the descendants of the legitimate high priestly lineage which the Hasmoneans removed. According to the Dead Sea Scrolls, the current high priests were interlopers since the Hasmoneans constituted a different priestly line.

THE INTERPRETATION OF SCRIPTURE

Most of what is known about the Sadducees is derived from the writings of the Jewish historian Josephus; other information is contained in the Talmud. According to these sources, the Sadducees rejected the Pharisaic belief in an oral Torah. Instead, they interpreted the Torah literally. In their personal lives this led to an excessively stringent lifestyle.

The fact that the Sadducees had a high opinion of the Five Books of Moses does not mean that they denied that the other books of the Bible – the prophets and historical writings – were divinely inspired. Yet they refused to accept the other biblical books as sources of law. When a Sadducee had to judge a case he would look in the written Torah and ignore the oral traditions that the Pharisees accepted as normative. One of the consequences of such an approach was that the Sadducees stressed the importance of the priests in the Temple cult, while the Pharisees insisted on the participation of all Jews.

In developing their approach to Scripture, the Sadducees had interpretative traditions of their own which were written down in a

Above Ceremonies at the Temple in Jerusalem, from the Bible Mozarabe, a 10th-century Spanish manuscript.

book of jurisprudence known as the Book of Decrees. The existence of this code is known from a rabbinical source, the *Megilla Ta'anit*, a calendar-like text, which states that the Book of Decrees was revoked on the 4th of Tammuz, although no year is given. The code that is described is very harsh. An example of the

Below A section of the oldest surviving map of the Holy Land. This part of the 5th-century CE mosaic map from Madaba, Jordan, shows Jerusalem and the area around.

Sadducean approach concerns the interpretation of the biblical law concerning 'an eye for an eye.' The Pharisees believed that the value of an eye was to be sought by the perpetrator of its loss rather than actually removing his eye in accordance with the law. The Sadducees, however, insisted that the law should be taken literally.

SADDUCEAN THEOLOGY

Regarding Sadducean belief, many sources stress that the Sadducees believed that souls die with their bodies. The rabbinical text known as *Avot de Rabbi Nathan* states that a discussion about this subject was the cause of the schism between the Sadducees and the Pharisees.

According to the *Avot de Rabbi Nathan*, the Pharisee teacher Antigonus of Soko had two disciples who used to study his words. They taught them to their disciples, and their disciples to their disciples. These proceeded to examine the words closely and demanded, 'Why did our ancestors see fit to say this thing? Is it possible that a labourer should do his work all day and not take his reward in the evening? If our ancestors, forsooth, had known that there is no other world and that there will be a resurrection of the dead, they would not have spoken in this manner.'

So they arose and withdrew from the study of the oral Torah, and split into two sects.

TEMPLE PRACTICES

With regard to Temple ritual, the Sadducees insisted that the daily burnt sacrifices were to be offered by the high priest at his own expense, whereas the Pharisees maintained that they were to be furnished as a national sacrifice at the cost of the Temple treasury. The Sadducees also held that the meal offering belonged to the priest's portion, whereas the Pharisees claimed

Above A 15th-century miniature showing that ritual animal slaughter is a part of the Jewish way of life.

it was for the altar. The Sadducees insisted on a high degree of purity in those who officiated at the preparation of the ashes of the Red Heifer. By contrast, the Pharisees opposed such strictness.

With regard to the kindling of the incense in the vessel with which the high priest entered the Holy of Holies on the Day of Atonement, the Sadducees claimed it should take place outside so that he might be wrapped in smoke while meeting the Shekhinah (divine presence) within; the Pharisees insisted that the incense be kindled inside.

In addition, the Sadducees opposed the popular festivity of the water libation and the procession that preceded it on each night of Sukkot, marking the end of the agricultural year. They also opposed the Pharisaic assertion that the scrolls of the Torah have the power to render ritually unclean the hands that touch them; the Pharisaic idea of the *eruv* (the merging of several private precincts into one so that food and vessels can be carried from place to place); and the formula introduced by the Pharisees in divorce documents.

PHARISEES

ALONGSIDE THE SADDUCEES AND THE ESSENES, THE PHARISEES CON-
STITUTED A MAJOR JEWISH PARTY IN THE HELLENISTIC PERIOD. AFTER
THE FALL OF THE TEMPLE, THE PHARISEES DOMINATED JEWISH LIFE.

The Pharisees were a Jewish religious and political party who
emerged shortly after the
Hasmonean revolt in about
165–160BCE. In all likelihood they
were the successors of the Hasideans
who had promoted the observance
of Jewish ritual and the study of the
Torah. Regarding themselves as followers of Ezra, they maintained the
validity of the Oral Torah as well as
of the Written Torah.

THE EMERGENCE
OF THE PHARISEES

The origin of their name is uncertain, though it is generally believed
that the name Pharisees derives from
the word *parash*, or 'to be separated'
– thus Pharisees would mean the

*Below Jesus on trial before the
Sanhedrin, the Jewish supreme court,
which was dominated by the Sadducees.
A 6th-century CE mosaic from Ravenna.*

separated ones or the separatists.
Determined to adapt biblical law to
new conditions, they formulated a
complex system of scriptural interpretation. Initially the Pharisees were
small in number, but by the 1st century CE they had profoundly
influenced the religious beliefs, practices and social attitudes of the
majority of the nation.

The Pharisees' first bid for power
took place in a period two centuries
after the Babylonian exile, during the
struggle to remove the Temple and
religious control from the leadership
of the Sadducees. The inception of
synagogue worship was an attempt
by the Pharisees to undermine the
privileged authority of the Sadducees;
in addition, ceremonies that were
originally part of the Temple cult
were carried over to the home, and
scholars of non-priestly descent
came to play an important role in
national affairs. Unlike the Sadducees,

*Above The prophet Ezra reads the law,
which was expanded by the Pharisees.
A 2nd-century CE painting from
Dura-Europos synagogue, Syria.*

the Pharisees believed that the
Written Torah required expansion.
As a consequence, Phari-saic sages
developed an elaborate system of
biblical interpretation.

PHARISAIC SCHOLARSHIP

According to rabbinic writings,
Pharisaic sages first appeared as the
men of the Great Assembly.
Subsequently there were five gener-
ations of *zugot* (pairs) of outstanding
Pharisees who served as leaders of
the Pharisaic supreme court until the
beginning of the 1st century CE.
During the civil war of the reign of
Alexander Janneus, the Pharisees
were among the king's enemies.
Later they were restored by Salome
Alexandra. The Pharisees then
exacted retribution on the
Sadducees. The Jewish historian

Josephus records there were about 6,000 Pharisees during King Herod's reign. By the second or third decades of the 1st century CE, the Pharisees had become divided into two schools of thought: the school of Hillel and the school of Shammai.

While scholars disagree on whether the Pharisees were the dominant group in Erez Israel before 70CE, there is no doubt that once the Temple in Jerusalem was destroyed by the Romans they became the leading party. As such, the Pharisees exerted a profound influence on Jewish life. The hereditary priestly caste was superseded by a new form of leadership that was based on learning, knowledge and wisdom. The most important relationship among the Pharisees was between a teacher and student. A sage's reputation was based on learning transmitted orally from him to his students. Pharisaic maxims from this period deal with such ethical issues as honesty in judging, ethical responsibility and serving God.

THE DEVELOPMENT OF PHARISAIC JUDAISM

Towards the end of the 1st century CE under Rabban Gamaliel II, the Sanhedrin (rabbinical assembly) at Yavneh strengthened a post-Temple form of Judaism. The term rabbi came into general use for a sage recognized as such by his peers. The sages at Yavneh summarized the

Above Giacomo Giaquerio's shifty painting of a Pharisee from a 15th-century north Italian fresco about the life of Jesus, at the Castello della Manta.

teachings of the earlier schools of Hillel and Shammai. In addition, they canonized the Scriptures, gave a more precise form to daily prayer, and transferred to the synagogue and the Sanhedrin various observances associated with the Temple. An ordination procedure for rabbis was instituted and the Sanhedrin exerted control over all aspects of Jewish life.

As far as the belief system of the Pharisees was concerned, Pharisaic theology was based on the conviction that God is an omnipotent, spiritual being who is all-wise, all-knowing and all-merciful. God, they believed, loves all his creatures and expects human beings to act justly and compassionately. Although God is omniscient and omnipotent, he endowed human beings with the power to choose between good and evil. Every person, the Pharisees stressed, has two impulses: the *yetzer tov* (good inclination) and the *yetzer ha-ra* (evil

Left This floor mosaic from an ancient synagogue in Jericho shows a menorah above the inscription 'Shalom al Israel' (Peace upon Israel').

inclination). Yet despite the belief in free will, the Pharisees held that everything in the world was ordained by God. Unlike the Sadducees, Pharisees believed in the resurrection of the dead. This concept of a future life made possible the belief in the divine justice in the face of calamity and suffering.

Pharisaic theological reflection is found in various collections of midrashim (commentaries on Scripture). Unlike the Mishnah, which consists of legislation presented without explicit reference to Scriptural sources, rabbinic aggadah (commentary on the Bible) focuses on the contemporary relevance of specific texts. Though the sages were not speculative philosophers, they expressed their religious views in these works and attempted to apply this teaching to daily life. These midrashic sources, along with the aggadic sections of the Talmud, serve as the basis for reconstructing the theology of early rabbinic Judaism.

Below A 15th-century German Torah scroll. Unlike the Sadducees, the Pharisees believed the Written Torah needed expansion.

ESSENES

THE ESSENES WERE THE THIRD PRINCIPAL SECT IN THE HELLENISTIC PERIOD. CONGREGATED IN SEMI-MONASTIC COMMUNITIES, THEY SAW THE HELLENIZERS AND SADDUCEES AS VIOLATORS OF GOD'S LAW.

The dispute between the Pharisees and the Sadducees centred around the religious leadership of the Jewish people. However, there were other smaller groupings that withdrew from society into holy communities who rejected the priests who controlled the Temple. Pre-eminent among these groups were the Essenes, who, according to the Jewish historian Josephus (37/38–100CE), believed in fate and the immortality of the soul. They lived as a separatist association in the towns of Judea and also in rural communes, where members engaged in agricultural and artisan labour as well as the study of religious writings.

Admission to this order occurred only after several periods of probation and preparation. Those initiated into the faith had to swear obedience to the rules and leadership of the community and promise that they would keep secret its special doctrines. Discipline was enforced by the expulsion of lax members after a vote by the council. Among the inner circle, property was owned jointly. Food, clothing and other necessities were administered by overseers. Essene rituals included wearing white garments, taking frequent ritual baths and eating community meals accompanied by prayer and a reading from Scripture.

According to Josephus, the Essenes numbered about 4,000 in the 1st century CE. He asserted that Essene prophets were held in high regard by the masses and the kings for the accuracy of their predictions and medical knowledge.

THE DEAD SEA SECT

According to modern scholars, an Essene-like group lived between 150BCE and 68CE in the Judean desert near the Dead Sea. In 1947 Arab shepherds discovered a group of documents – the Dead Sea Scrolls – which were traced to 11 caves not far from Jerusalem where they were preserved by the desert climate. The Dead Sea Scrolls include communal rule books, hymns and biblical commentaries. Near this site was uncovered the remains of a community that flourished from about 130BCE to the time of the Roman–Jewish war. The ruins discovered on a cliff north of the Wadi Qumran include a tower, assembly chamber, kitchen, writing room and worship space. It appears that the members of this sect slept in tents, caves or upper rooms of this building.

Above El Greco's 16th-century painting of John the Baptist, cousin of Jesus, who may have had contact with the Essenes.

An elaborate system of cisterns ensured an adequate supply of water for the members of this group. The community's cemetery contained a thousand burials. For nearly two centuries, Qumran was the headquarters of a well-organized settlement,

Below This fragment of the Dead Sea Scrolls shows the Song of Degrees, one of the Psalms of King David.

Below A ritual bath or mikveh *of the Essene sect at Qumran, 2nd century* BCE. *Water in* mikvehs *should come from natural springs or rivers.*

which at its height numbered about 200. The Dead Sea Scrolls were most likely the remains of the Qumran library, which was hidden during the Roman–Jewish war when Qumran was destroyed by the Romans.

QUMRAN AND THE ESSENES

Assuming that Qumran was an Essene community and the Dead Sea Scrolls a collection of their writings, then the movement was both quietistic and philosophical. The scrolls depict a priest-dominated group who viewed the Temple as dominated by corrupt men who had usurped power.

From references in Qumran texts, the site seems to have been founded by a priestly 'Teacher of Righteousness', who was persecuted as a wicked priest. The community regarded the *Kittim* (possibly the Romans) with hostility and regarded itself as the true heir of the Mosaic covenant and of God's promises. Members of the order had been preserved from the domination of evil powers. The group had been saved from the domination of these forces in order to settle in the wilderness

INDIVIDUAL CHARISMATICS

In the Judean desert there were also individual charismatics who, though not formally affiliated with the Essenes, adopted similar attitudes and practices. John the Baptist, for example, was described in the New Testament as clothed with camel's hair, a leather girdle around his waist, and eating locusts and wild honey. According to Scripture, he preached a baptism of repentance for the forgiveness of sins. Another figure was John's mentor, Bannus. According to the Jewish historian Josephus, Bannus dwelt in the wilderness, wearing only such clothing as trees provided, feeding on such things as grew of themselves and using frequent ablutions of cold water, by day and night for purity's sake. In the 40s of the 1st century CE, Theudas declared himself a prophet and persuaded crowds to follow him to the River Jordan. A decade later an Egyptian prophet led his group to the Mount of Olives outside Jerusalem, proposing to force his way into the city, overpower the Roman garrison and set himself up as ruler of the people.

under the leadership of true priests, until they could return to a Temple that had been purified.

As members of the covenant, these individuals constituted the divine elect of God, who had predetermined whether they would join the holy community (Sons of Light) or remain outside with those hostile to God (Sons of Darkness). Eventually the Sons of Light would issue forth in ritual combat under the leadership of their divinely appointed leaders to re-establish the remnant of Israel in the Promised Land and to witness the victory of God over the entire earth.

CHAPTER 2

RABBINIC JUDAISM

From the 1st century BCE to the 2nd century CE, rabbinic scholars engaged in the interpretation of Scripture. In their view, the Five Books of Moses were given by God to Moses on Mount Sinai. This belief implies that God is the direct source of all laws recorded in the Torah, and is also indirectly responsible for the authoritative legal judgements of the rabbis. Alongside their exegesis of biblical law, scholars also produced interpretations of Scripture in rabbinic commentaries and the Talmud. Within these texts is a wealth of theological, philosophical and mystical speculation.

The Karaites, a radical sect, later challenged rabbinic Judaism. Their guiding interpretative principle was: 'Search thoroughly in Scripture and do not rely on my opinion.' Further challenges were posed by the Shabbateans and Frankists. In the 17th century, a self-proclaimed messianic king, Shabbetai Tzvi, electrified the Jewish world with his claims. After his conversion to Islam, the majority of his followers were despondent, yet a number continued to believe in his messiahship. These Shabbateans and a later Shabbatean sect, the Frankists, remained convinced that the messianic era had begun.

Opposite The title page of a Hebrew manuscript of the Guide for the Perplexed *by the 12th-century Jewish philosopher and rabbinic scholar Moses Maimonides.*

Above *In 1999, Menachem Joskowicz, Chief Rabbi of Poland, asked John-Paul II to remove a large Christian cross from land bordering the concentration camp of Auschwitz.*

RABBINIC JUDAISM

THE RABBIS CONSTITUTED A SCHOLARLY CLASS DRAWN FROM THE PHARISEES. THEY PRODUCED A MASSIVE CORPUS OF LEGAL TEXTS, BIBLICAL EXEGESIS, THEOLOGICAL WORKS AND ETHICAL REFLECTIONS.

With the destruction of the Second Temple in 70CE, the Pharisees emerged as the dominant religious group. These sages were determined to forge a new form of Judaism based on scriptural precedent. In their view, both the written and the oral Torah were expressions of God's will.

RABBINIC LAW

During the Tannaitic period (1st century BCE–2nd century CE) and the Amoraic period (2nd–6th century CE) rabbinic scholars – referred to as the Tannaim and the Amoraim respectively – actively engaged in the interpretation of Scripture. According to the Pharisaic tradition, both the written Torah and its interpretation (oral Torah) were given by God to Moses on Mount Sinai. This belief, which implies that God is the direct source of all laws recorded in the Pentateuch and indirectly responsible for the authoritative legal judgements of the rabbis, served as the justification for the rabbinic exposition of scriptural ordinances.

INTERPRETING SCRIPTURE

Alongside the halakha, or the 'exegesis of Jewish law', scholars also produced aggadah, or 'interpretations of Scripture in which new meanings of the text were expounded' in midrashim or 'rabbinic commentaries', and in the Talmud. Within the aggadic texts is found a wealth of theological speculation about such topics as the nature of God, divine justice, the coming of the Messiah and the hereafter. In addition, ethical considerations were of considerable importance in the discussions of these teachers of the faith.

Early rabbinic Judaism thus covered a wide variety of areas that were all embraced by the holy word revealed on Mount Sinai, and this literature served as the foundation of later Judaism as it developed through the centuries.

Above Sage and pupil learning Hillel's golden rule –'What is hateful to you, do not do to another'. From the Coburg Pentateuch by Samuel Halevi, 1395.

RABBINIC EXEGESIS

The exegesis found in rabbinic literature of the Tannaitic and Amoraic periods is largely of two types: direct and explicit exegesis where the biblical text is commented on or accompanied by a remark, and indirect exegesis where a scriptural text is cited to support an assertion. In the case of direct exegesis, the rabbis frequently reinforced their exhortations by a biblical sentence which expressed their sentiments. It was also a usual custom in rabbinic circles to cite a text and then draw out its meaning. Further, the rabbis frequently stressed that a word should be understood in its strictest sense. Occasionally they also employed typological exegesis to explain the meaning of Scripture.

Turning to the method of indirect exegesis, it was a common practice in rabbinic literature to draw deductions from scriptural texts by means of a number of formal hermeneutical rules. Hillel the elder, who flourished about a century before the destruction of the Second Temple, is reported to have been the first to lay down these principles. In the 2nd century CE Ishmael ben Elisha expanded Hillel's seven

Below Moses ben Yekuthiel Hakohen commissioned what is now known as The Rothschild Miscellany *in 1479 to show customs of religious and secular life as expounded by rabbinic sages in a Jewish Renaissance household.*

Above A rabbi reads to his people from a Sefer Torah, *the handwritten copy of the Pentateuch. From the 14th-century Barcelona Haggadah.*

rules into thirteen by sub-dividing them, omitting one, and adding a new one of his own.

These various methods of exegesis were based on the deeply held conviction that the Bible is sacred, that it is susceptible of interpretation and that, when properly understood, it will guide the life of the worthy. By means of this process of explanation of God's revelation, rabbinic

Below Rabbinic study group at Bircas Hatorah in Jerusalem, 1994, a yeshiva which is dedicated to Torah education.

authorities were able to infuse the tradition with new meaning and renewed relevance.

RABBINIC THEOLOGY

Unlike the Mishnah, which consists of legislation presented without explicit reference to a Scriptural source, rabbinic aggadah focuses on the contemporary relevance of specific biblical texts. The early halakhic midrashim consists of Tannaitic commentaries on the legal verses of the Bible. Narrative midrashim, on the other hand, derive from sermons given by the Amoraim in synagogues and academies. Within these texts the rabbis propounded their theological views by means of stories, legends, parables and maxims based on Scripture. Within aggadic sources, the rabbis expressed their profound reflections on human life and God's nature and activity in the world. Unlike the legal precepts of the Torah and the rabbinic expansion of these scriptural ordinances, these theological opinions were not binding on the Jewish community. They were formulated instead to educate, inspire and edify those to whom they were addressed. Study of the Torah was a labour of love that had no end, a task whose goal was to serve the will of God.

Above A contemporary North African rabbi wearing Arab-style headgear and clothing and studying a Hebrew book.

RABBINIC ETHICS

Supplementing these theological reflections, the rabbis in midrashic and talmudic sources also encouraged the Jewish people to put the teachings of the law into effect in their everyday lives. In their view the kingdom of God is inconsistent with injustice and social misery – the effort to bring about the perfection of the world so that God will reign in majesty is the responsibility of every Jew. Jewish ethics as enshrined in rabbinic literature were inextricably related to the coming of God's Kingdom. Throughout rabbinic sources, Jews were encouraged to strive for the highest conception of life, in which the rule of truth, righteousness and holiness will be established among humankind. Such a desire is the eternal hope of God's people – a longing for God's Kingdom. The coming of his rule requires a struggle for the reign of justice and righteousness on earth. This Kingdom is not an internalized, spiritualized, other-worldly concept, rather it involves human activity in a historical context.

EARLY MYSTICAL JUDAISM

ALONGSIDE OTHER MODES OF SCRIPTURAL INTERPRETATION, RAB-
BINIC SCHOLARS ENGAGED IN MYSTICAL EXEGESIS. THEY FORMULATED
COSMOLOGICAL THEORIES AS WELL AS METHODS OF HEAVENLY ASCENT.

Within aggadic sources, the rabbis also engaged in mystical speculation. These doctrines were often of a secret nature; in a midrash on Genesis it is reported that these mystical traditions were repeated in a whisper so that they would not be overheard by those for whom they were not intended. These secret doctrines served as the basis for the evolution of a mystical form of the Jewish tradition.

THE DIVINE CHARIOT

In the rabbis' mystical reflections, the first chapter of Ezekiel played an important role. In this biblical text the *merkavah*, or 'divine chariot', is described in detail, and this scriptural source served as the basis for rabbinic speculation about the nature of the deity. It was the aim of the mystic to be a 'merkavah rider' so

Below God creating the earth, planets and stars, from a 15th-century Armenian Sefer Yezirah or 'Book of Creation'.

Right The Vision of Ezekiel from a 15th-century Bible, showing the winged symbols of the four Christian evangelists – a man, a lion, an ox and an eagle.

that he would be able to penetrate the heavenly mysteries. Within this contemplative system, the rabbis believed that the pious could free themselves from the fetters of bodily existence and enter paradise. A further dimension of this theory is that certain pious individuals can temporarily ascend into the unseen realm and, having learnt the deepest secrets, may return to earth. These mystics were able to attain a state of ecstasy, to behold visions and hear voices. As students of the merkavah they were the ones to attain the highest degree of spiritual insight.

THE MYSTICS AND CREATION

Closely associated with this form of speculation were *Maaseh Bereshit*, or 'mystical theories about creation'. Within aggadic sources the rabbis discussed the hidden meanings of the Genesis narrative. The most important early treatise, possibly from the 2nd century CE, which describes the process of creation is *Sefer Yezirah*, or 'Book of Creation'. According to this cosmological text, God created the universe by 32 mysterious paths consisting of 22 letters of the Hebrew alphabet together with ten *sefirot*, or 'emanations'. Concerning these 22 letters, the *Sefer Yezirah* states: 'He hewed them, combined them, weighed them, interchanged them and through them produced the whole creation and everything that is destined to come into being.'

DIVINE EMANATION

These recondite doctrines were supplemented by a theory of divine emanation. The first of the sefirot is the spirit of the living God; the second is air and is derived from the first – on it are hewn the 22 letters. The third sefirah is the water that comes from the air; the fourth is the fire that comes from water through which God made the heavenly wheels, the seraphim and the ministering angels. The remaining six sefirot are the six dimensions of space – north, south, east, west, height and depth.

These ten sefirot are the moulds into which all created things were originally cast. They constitute form

---

HEAVENLY HALLS

A description of the experiences of these merkavah mystics is contained in *hekhalot*, or 'heavenly hall', literature from the later Gaonic period (from the 7th to the 11th century CE). In order to make their heavenly ascent, these mystics followed strict ascetic disciplines, including fasting, ablution and the invocation of God's name. After reaching a state of ecstasy, the mystic was able to enter the seven heavenly halls and attain a vision of the divine chariot.

rather than matter. The 22 letters are the prime cause of matter: everything that exists is due to the creative force of the Hebrew letters, but they receive their form from the sefirot. According to this, God transcends the universe; nothing exists outside him. The visible world is the result of the emanations of the divine. God is the cause of the form and matter of the cosmos. By combining emanation and creation, the *Sefer Yezirah* tries to harmonize the concept of divine imminence and transcendence. God is imminent in that the sefirot are an outpouring of his spirit. He is transcendent in that the matter, which was shaped into the forms, is the product of his creative action.

MEDIEVAL MYSTICISM

Drawing on these ideas, early medieval Jewish mystics elaborated a complex system of mystical thought. Referring to the traditions of early rabbinic mysticism, writers expanded and elaborated many of the doctrines found in midrashic and talmudic sources as well as in the *Sefer Yezirah*. In their writings these mystics saw themselves as the transmitters of a

Above This 19th-century Russian icon shows the prophet Elijah contemplating his ascent to heaven in a fiery chariot. Jewish mystics saw themselves as chariot riders on an ascent towards the Divine.

Below A medieval Jewish hamsa, sometimes known as the hand of Miriam. Amulets like this were used to protect people from evil spirits.

secret tradition which describes the supernal world to which all human beings are linked. One strand of this heritage focused on the nature of the spiritual world and its relationship with the terrestrial plane. The other more practical side attempted to use energies from the spiritual world to bring about miracle-working effects. According to these mystics, all of creation is in a struggle for redemption and liberation from evil, and their goal was to restore world harmony so that universal salvation would be attained through the coming of the Messiah and the establishment of the Kingdom of God.

Pre-eminent among these early medieval mystics were Jewish settlers in the Rhineland, the Hasidei Ashkenaz. Among the greatest figures of this period were the 12th-century Samuel ben Kalonymus of Speyer, his son Judah ben Samuel of Regensburg, and Eleazar ben Judah of Worms, who composed the treatise *The Secret of Secrets*. In their writings these mystics were preoccupied with the mystery of divine unity. God himself, they believed, cannot be known by human reason. The aim of the Hasidei Ashkenaz was to attain a vision of God's glory through the cultivation of the life of piety, which embraced devotion, saintliness and contemplation.

KABBALISTIC JUDAISM

MEDIEVAL MYSTICS, KNOWN AS KABBALISTS, CONTINUED THE TRADITIONS OF EARLIER THINKERS. THE AIM OF THE KABBALISTS WAS TO ATTAIN THE HIGHEST LEVELS OF SPIRITUAL ILLUMINATION.

Parallel with the emergence of the Hasidei Ashkenaz, Jewish Kabbalists in southern France engaged in speculation about the nature of God, the existence of evil and the religious life. In 12th-century Provence the earliest Kabbalistic text, the *Bahir*, reinterpreted the concept of the sefirot as depicted in the *Sefer Yezirah*. According to the *Bahir*, the sefirot are conceived as vessels, crowns or words that constitute the structure of the divine realm.

Basing themselves on this work, various Provence Jews engaged in similar mystical reflection. Isaac the Blind conceived of the sefirot as emanations of a hidden dimension of the Godhead. Using neo-Platonic

Below A Hebrew book in the garden of the Nahmamid Institute, housed in a former synagogue in Gerona, Spain, once a centre of Jewish Kabbalah.

ideas, he argued that out of the *En Sof*, or 'infinite', emanated the first supernal essence (divine thought) from which came the remaining sefirot.

KABBALISTS IN GERONA

In Gerona, the traditions from Isaac the Blind were broadly disseminated. One of the most important was Azriel ben Menahem who replaced divine thought with the divine will as the first emanation of the En Sof. The most famous figure of this circle was Nahmanides (1194–1270CE) who helped this mystical school gain general acceptance. In his commentary on the Torah he frequently referred to Kabbalistic notions to explain the true meaning of the text. During the time these Geronese writers were propounding their Kabbalistic theories, other mystical schools of thought developed in Spain. Influenced by the Hasidei Ashkenaz and the Sufi traditions of Islam, Abraham ben Samuel Abulafia wrote meditative texts concerning the technique of combining the letters of the alphabet as a means of realizing human aspirations toward prophecy. They developed a complex system of mystical speculation coupled with mystical practice.

SPANISH KABBALISTS

Other Spanish Kabbalists were more attracted to Gnostic ideas. Isaac ha-Kohen elaborated the theory of a demonic emanation. The mingling of such Gnostic teaching with the Kabbalah of Gerona resulted in the major mystical work of Spanish Jewry, the Zohar, composed by Moses ben Shem Tov de Leon in Guadalajara. The author places the work in a 2nd-century CE setting, focusing on

Above A Kabbalist at festivities in Meron, Israel, to celebrate Simeon ben Yohai, commemorated in the Zohar.

Simeon ben Yohai and his disciples, but the doctrines of the Zohar are of a much later origin. Written in Aramaic, the text is largely a midrash in which the Torah is given a mystical or ethical interpretation.

THE EN SOF

According to these various Kabbalistic systems, God in himself lies beyond any speculative comprehension. To express the unknowable aspect of the Divine, the early Kabbalists of both Provence and Spain referred to the Divine Infinite as En Sof – the absolute perfection in which there is no distinction or plurality. The En Sof does not reveal itself; it is beyond all thought and at times is identified with the Aristotelian First Cause. In Kabbalistic teaching, creation is bound up with the manifestation of the hidden God and his outward movement.

DIVINE EMANATION

These sefirot emanate successively from above to below, each one revealing a stage in the process. The common order of the sefirot and the names most generally used are: (1) supreme crown; (2) wisdom; (3)

intelligence; (4) greatness; (5) power (or judgement); (6) beauty (or compassion); (7) endurance; (8) majesty; (9) foundation (or righteous one); (10) kingdom.

These ten sefirot are formally arranged in threes. The first triad consists of the first three sefirot and constitutes the intellectual realm of the inner structure of the Divine. The second triad is composed of the next three sefirot from the psychic or moral level of the Godhead. Finally, sefirot 7, 8 and 9 represent the archetypes of certain forces in nature. The remaining sefirah, kingdom, constitutes the channel between the higher and the lower worlds. The ten sefirot together demonstrate how an infinite undivided and unknowable God is the cause of all the modes of existence in the finite plane.

SPIRITUAL REALITY

In explaining this picture of Divine creation, Kabbalists adopted a neo-Platonic conception of a ladder of spiritual reality composed of four worlds in descending order. First is the domain of Atzilut, or 'emana-tion', consisting of the ten sefirot which form Adam Kadmon, or 'primordial man'. The second world, based on hekhalot, or 'heavenly hall', literature, is the realm of Beriyah, or 'creation', which is made up of the throne of glory and the seven heavenly palaces. In the third world, Yezirah, or 'formation', most of the angels dwell, presided over by the angel Metatron. This is the scene of the seven heavenly halls guarded by angels to which merkavah, or 'chariot', mystics attempt to gain admission. In the fourth world of Asiyah, or 'making', are the lowest order of angels – the ophanim, who combat evil and receive prayers. This is the spiritual archetype of the material cosmos, heaven and the earthly world.

Asiyah is both the last link in the Divine chain of being and the domain where the Sitra Ahra, or 'the realm of demonic powers', is manifest; in this sphere the forces of good struggle with the demons.

COSMIC REPAIR

For the mystic, deeds of *tikkun*, or 'cosmic repair', sustain the world, activate nature to praise God, and bring about the coupling of the tenth and the six sefirot. Such repair is accomplished by keeping the commandments which were conceived as vessels for establishing contact with the Godhead and for ensuring divine mercy. Such a religious life provided the Kabbalist with a means of integrating into the divine hierarchy of creation – the Kabbalah was able to guide the soul back to its Infinite source. The supreme rank attainable by the soul at the end of its sojourn is *devekut*, or 'mystical cleaving to God'. Devekut does not completely elim-

Left A Kabbalistic roll of 1604 by Jacob Hebron, showing the names of God, the 10 sefirot, the 32 paths, the mystery of the letters and vowels, and the Temple.

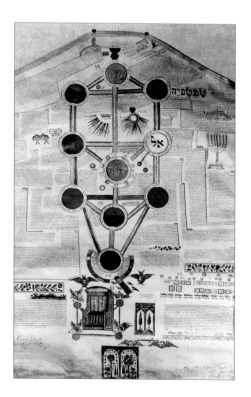

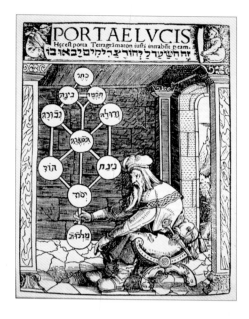

Above German woodcut from 1516 showing a Jewish Kabbalist holding the Sefirot Tree of Life.

inate the distance between God and human beings – it denotes instead a state of beatitude and intimate union between the soul and its source.

Below Tree of Life Showing the Ten Spheres or sefirot, by Mark Penney Maddocks, 1976, illustrating the ten sefirot or divine emanations.

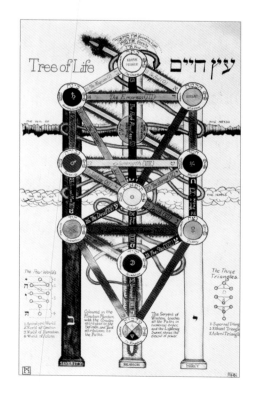

PHILOSOPHICAL JUDAISM

JEWISH THINKERS INTERPRETED THEIR TRADITION PHILOSOPHICALLY.
THE INTERPRETATION OF THE NATURE OF GOD AND HIS ACTION
CONSTITUTED AN ALTERNATIVE CONCEPTION OF THE JEWISH FAITH.

In the Hellenistic world the Jewish philosopher Philo tried to integrate Greek philosophy and Jewish teaching into a unified whole. By applying an allegorical method of interpretation to Scripture, he explained the God of Judaism in Greek philosophical categories and reshaped Jewish notions about God, human beings and the world. Philo was the precursor of medieval Jewish philosophy which also attempted to combine alternative philosophical systems with the received biblical tradition. The beginnings of this philosophical

Below Islamic theology had a profound impact on Jewish medieval thought. This 1237 illustration of medieval Muslim scholars is from Maqamat *by poet and Seljuk empire government official al-Hariri of Basra (1054–1122).*

development took place in 9th-century CE Babylonia during the height of the Abbasid caliphate, when rabbinic Judaism was challenged by Karaite scholars who criticized the anthropomorphic views of God in midrashic and talmudic sources.

Added to this internal threat was the Islamic contention that Mohammed's revelation in the Koran superseded the Jewish faith. In addition, Zoroastrians and Manicheans attacked monotheism as a viable religious system. Finally, some gentile philosophers argued that the Greek scientific and philosophical world view could account for the origin of the cosmos without reference to an external deity. In combating these challenges, Jewish writers were influenced by the teachings of *kalam*, or 'Muslim

Above This statue of Spanish poet and philosopher Solomon Ibn Gabirol stands in Malaga, where he was born in 1022.

schools' of the 8th to the 11th century CE; in particular the contributions of one school of Muslim thought – the Mutazilite kalam – had a profound effect on Jewish thought. These Islamic scholars maintained that rational argument was vital in matters of religious belief and that Greek philosophy could serve as the handmaiden of religious faith. In their attempt to defend Judaism from internal and external assault, rabbinic authorities frequently adapted the Mutazilite kalam as an important line of defence, and as time passed they also employed other aspects of Graeco-Arabic thought in their expositions of the Jewish faith.

SOLOMON IBN GABIROL

After the 11th century CE the Mutazilite kalam ceased to play a central role in Jewish philosophical thought. In Islam the Mutazilites were replaced by the more orthodox Asharyites, who attempted to provide a rational basis for unquestioning traditionalism. During this period the first Spanish Jewish

Above Hebrew manuscript of 1356 of Maimonides' classic Guide for the Perplexed. *From Huesca, Spain.*

negative ones – they lead to a knowledge of God because in negation no plurality is involved.

MAIMONIDEANS AND ANTI-MAIMONIDEANS

By the 13th century, most of the important philosophical texts of medieval thinkers had been translated into Hebrew by Jews living in southern France. This led to bitter antagonism between Maimonideans and anti-Maimonideans who believed that Maimonides had corrupted the tradition. Yet, in later centuries other philosophers emerged who continued to produce treatises grounded in Greek thought. The most prominent Jewish philosopher after Maimonides who was attracted to Aristotelianism was Gersonides (1288–1344). In his *The Wars of the*

Above Statue of Maimonides, the greatest medieval Jewish philosopher, in his birthplace, Cordoba in Spain.

philosopher to produce a work in the neo-Platonic tradition was Solomon Ibn Gabirol (1022–58). In his *Fountain of Life*, he argued that God and matter are not opposed as two ultimate principles – instead matter is identified with God. It emanates from the essence of the creator, forming the basis of all subsequent emanations.

MAIMONIDES

In the following century, Moses Maimonides (1135–1204), arguably the greatest philosopher of the Middle Ages, produced *The Guide for the Perplexed*, based on Aristotelianism. Like Saadia, he addressed the question of anthropomorphic terms in the Bible. In his view, a literal reading of these passages implies that God is a corporeal being. Yet, according to Maimonides, this is a mistake. No positive attributes should be predicated of God, he argued, since the Divine is an absolute unity. Thus when God is described positively in the Bible, such ascriptions must refer to his activity. The only true attributes are

SAADIA GAON

The earliest philosopher of the medieval period was the 10th-century CE thinker, Saadia ben Joseph al-Fayyumi. As *Gaon*, or 'head', of one of the Babylonian academies, he wrote treatises on a wide range of subjects and produced the first major Jewish theological treatise of the Middle Ages, *The Book of Beliefs and Opinions*. In this study Saadia attempted to refute the religious claims of Christians, Muslims and Zoroastrians. Adapting the teaching of the Mutazilites, he argued that religious faith and reason are fully compatible. On this basis he sought to demonstrate that God exists since the universe must have had a starting point. The divine creator, he believed, is a single, incorporeal being who created the universe out of nothing. Anthropomorphic descriptions of God in the Bible, he argued, should therefore be understood figuratively rather than literally.

Lord, he wrestled with the question of divine omniscience. In his opinion, God only knows human events if they are determined by heavenly bodies; he does not know them in so far as they are dependent on individual choice. This limitation to divine knowledge, Gersonides believed, is entirely consonant with Scripture and is coherent with the concept of the freedom of the will.

Gersonides was followed by other Jewish philosophers such as the 14th-century Spanish thinker Hasdai Crescas (1340–1410), whose work *The Light of the Lord* offered an alternative account of the basic principles of the Jewish faith in opposition to Maimonides' 13 principles.

However, after Crescas the philosophical approach to religion lost its appeal for most thinkers in Spain. By the end of the 15th century, the impulse to rationalize the Jewish tradition in the light of Greek philosophy had come to an end, and succeeding generations of Jews turned to the mystical tradition as a basis for speculation about God's nature and his creation.

LURIANIC KABBALAH

IN THE 1500s ISAAC LURIA MADE MAJOR CONTRIBUTIONS TO JEWISH MYSTICISM. HIS INFLUENCE ON A CIRCLE OF DISCIPLES HAD HUGE CONSEQUENCES FOR THE DEVELOPMENT OF KABBALISTIC JUDAISM.

By the early modern period the centre of Kabbalistic activity had shifted to Israel. In this milieu Isaac Luria (1534–72), the greatest mystic of the period, reinterpreted Kabbalistic doctrine – his teaching propounded theories about divine contraction, the shattering of the vessels and cosmic repair. These reflections profoundly influenced the subsequent development of Jewish mysticism.

MOSES CORDOVERO

One of the greatest mystics of the town of Safed, Moses Cordovero (1522–70), collected, organized and interpreted the teachings of earlier mystical scholars. His work is a systematic summary of the Kabbalah up to his time, and in his most important treatise, *Pardes*, he outlined

Below A view of Safed and Mount Meron, Israel. Simeon ben Yohai is buried on Mount Meron, and thousands camp out near the tomb on the anniversary of his death on Lag B'Omer, or the 'Scholars' Feast'.

the Zoharic concepts of the Godhead, the sefirot, the celestial powers and the earthly processes.

In this study he described the sefirot as vessels in which the light of the En Sof is contained and through which it is reflected in different forms. For Cordovero, the Godhead is in this way manifest in every part of the finite world. In another important work, *The Palm Tree of Deborah*, he expressed the notion that in order to achieve the highest degree of the religious life, one should not only observe the commandments but also imitate divine processes and patterns.

ISAAC LURIA AND CREATION

Originally brought up in Egypt where he studied the Talmud and engaged in business, Isaac Luria withdrew to an island on the Nile where he meditated on the Zohar for seven years. In 1569 he arrived in Safed and died some two years later after having passed on his teaching to a small group of disciples. Of primary

Above Torah shrine at Ha'ari synagogue in Safed, Israel, where Rabbi Isaac Luria lived and taught.

importance in the Lurianic system is the mystery of creation. In the literature of early Kabbalists creation was understood as a positive act. For Luria, however, creation was a negative event: the En Sof had to bring into being an empty space in which creation could occur since divine light was everywhere, leaving no room for creation to take place. This was accomplished by the process of *zimzum*, or 'the contraction of the Godhead into itself'.

After this act of withdrawal, a line of light flowed from the Godhead into *tehiru*, or 'empty space', and took on the shape of the sefirot in the form of Adam Kadmon. In this process divine lights created the vessels – the external shapes of the sefirot – which gave specific characteristics to each divine emanation. Yet these vessels were not strong enough to contain such pure light and they shattered. This *shevirat ha-kelim*, or 'breaking of the vessels', brought disaster and upheaval to the emerging emanations: the lower vessels broke down and fell; the three highest emanations were damaged; and the empty space was divided into two parts. The first

part consisted of the broken vessels with many divine sparks clinging to them; the second part was the upper realm where the pure light of God escaped to preserve its purity.

THE COSMOS

Following the shattering of the vessels the cosmos was divided into two parts: the kingdom of evil in the lower part and the realm of divine light in the upper part. For Luria evil was seen as opposed to existence; therefore it was not able to exist by its own power. Instead it had to derive spiritual force from the divine light. This was accomplished by keeping captive the sparks of the divine light that fell with them when the vessels were broken and subsequently gave sustenance to the satanic domain. Divine attempts to bring unity to all existence now had to focus on the struggle to overcome the evil forces. This was achieved by a continuing process of divine emanation, which at first created the sefirot, the sky, the earth, the Garden of Eden and human beings.

Below A Hasidic Jew studying in Safed, Israel. The blue colour on the door is thought to protect against the evil eye. Hasidic Judaism is deeply influenced by Kabbalistic thought.

Above Strictly Orthodox Jews pray for peace in the Lebanon at the grave of mystic Isaac Luria in Safed, Israel.

Humanity was intended to serve as the battleground for this conflict between good and evil. In this regard Adam reflected symbolically the dualism in the cosmos – he possessed a sacred soul while his body represented the evil forces. God's intention was that Adam defeat the evil within himself and bring about Satan's downfall. But when Adam failed, a catastrophe occurred parallel to the breaking of the vessels; instead of divine sparks being saved and uplifted, many new divine lights fell and evil became stronger.

THE JEWISH PEOPLE

Rather than relying on the action of one person, God then chose the people of Israel to vanquish evil and raise up the captive sparks. The Torah was given to symbolize the Jews' acceptance of this allotted task. When the ancient Israelites undertook to keep the law, redemption seemed imminent. Yet the people of Israel then created the golden calf, a sin parallel to Adam's disobedience. Again, divine sparks fell and the forces of evil were renewed. For Luria, history is a record of attempts by the powers of good to rescue these sparks and unite the divine and earthly spheres. Luria and his disciples believed that they were living

in the final stages of this last attempt to overcome evil, in which the coming of the Messiah would signify the end of the struggle.

TIKKUN

Related to the contraction of God, the breaking of the vessels and the exiled sparks, was Luria's conception of tikkun. This concept refers to the mending of what was broken during the breaking of the vessels. After the catastrophe in the divine realm, the process of restoration began and every disaster was seen as a setback in this process. In this battle, keeping God's commandments was understood as contributing to repair – the divine sparks which fell down can be redeemed by ethical and religious deeds. According to Luria, a spark is attached to all prayers and moral acts; if the Jew keeps the ethical and religious law these sparks are redeemed and lifted up.

By the beginning of the 17th century Lurianic mysticism had had a major impact on Sephardic Jewry, and in succeeding centuries Luria's mystical theology became a central feature of Jewish life.

KARAITES

THE EMERGENCE OF THE KARAITE MOVEMENT IN THE 8TH CENTURY CE POSED A MAJOR CHALLENGE TO THE RABBINIC ESTABLISHMENT. IT CONTINUED TO EXERT A PROFOUND INFLUENCE ON JEWISH LIFE.

In the early medieval period the emergence of Karaism as an anti-rabbinic movement constituted a major threat to the tradition. Deriving its name from the Hebrew word *mikrah*, or 'Scripture', the Karaites believed that God had revealed his word exclusively in the Written Torah. In their view, the oral Torah as passed down by rabbinic sages was a human reflection on the divine commandments.

ORIGIN OF THE KARAITES

During the 8th century CE messianic movements appeared in the Persian Jewish community, leading to armed

Right An 18th-century silver yad *or finger pointer used when reading from the Torah. For the Karaites the Torah was of pre-eminent importance.*

uprisings against Muslim authorities. Such revolts were quickly crushed, but an even more serious threat to traditional Jewish life was posed later in the century by the emergence of an anti-rabbinic sect, the Karaites. This movement was founded in Babylonia in the 760s by Anan ben David, who had earlier been passed over as exilarch (head of the Jewish community in Babylonia). The Karaites traced its origin to the time

of King Jeroboam in the 8th century BCE. According to some scholars, Anan's movement absorbed elements of an extra-talmudic tradition and took over doctrines from Islam.

The guiding interpretative principle formulated by Anan, 'Search thoroughly in Scripture and do not rely on my opinion', was intended to point to the Bible as the sole source of law. Jewish observances, the Karaites insisted, must conform to biblical legislation rather than rabbinic ordinances. Anan, however, was not lenient concerning legal matters. For example, he did not recognize the minimum quantities of forbidden foods fixed by the rabbis; in addition, he introduced more complicated regulations for circumcision, added to the number of fast days, interpreted the prohibition of work on the Sabbath in stricter terms than the rabbis, and extended the prohibited degrees of marriage. In short, he made the yoke of the law more burdensome.

THE DEVELOPMENT OF THE KARAITE MOVEMENT

After the death of the founder, new parties within the Karaite movement soon emerged. The adherents of

Left A prophet of God denounces the idolatry of Jeroboam. Painting by William Hole (1846–1917). For the Karaites God's world was revealed exclusively in Scripture.

Above The Karaite synagogue is the oldest active synagogue in Jerusalem, founded in the 8th century CE. The synagogue is currently below street level, which has risen over the years.

Anan were referred to as the 'Ananites' and remained few in number. In the first half of the 9th century CE, the Ukarite sect was established by Ishmael of Ukbara (near Baghdad). Some years later another sect was formed in the same town by Mishawayh Al-Ukbari. Another group was formed by a contemporary of Mishawayh, Abu Imram Al-Tiflisi. In Israel, yet another sect was established by Malik Al-Ramli. By the end of the 9th century CE, Karaism had become a conglomerate of groups advocating different anti-rabbinic positions, but these sects were short-lived and in time the Karaites consolidated into a uniform movement.

The central representative of mainstream Karaism was Benjamin ben Moses Nahavendi (of Nahavendi in Persia), who advocated a policy of free and independent study of Scripture, which became the dominant ideology of later Karaism. By the 10th century CE, a number

Right The Karaite synagogue in Yevpatoria, Ukraine. Yevpatoria became a residence of the Hakham, spiritual leader of the Karaites, when Russia annexed the Crimea in 1738.

of Karaite communities were established in Israel, Iraq and Persia. These groups rejected rabbinic law and devised their own legislation, which led eventually to the foundation of a Karaite rabbinical academy in Jerusalem. There the Karaite community produced some of the most distinguished scholars of the period, who composed legal handbooks, wrote biblical commentaries, expounded on Hebrew philology and engaged in philosophical and theological reflection.

ANTI-KARAITES AND THE DEVELOPMENT OF KARAISM

The growth of Karaism provoked the rabbis to attack it as a heretical movement. The first prominent authority to engage in anti-Karaite debate was Saadia Gaon, who in the first half of the 9th century CE wrote a book attacking Anan. This polemic was followed by other anti-Karaite tracts by eminent rabbinic authorities.

By the 10th century CE, the Karaites had successfully established a network of synagogues in the Middle East. In addition, the movement produced some of the most distinguished literary figures of eastern Jewry. Karaite scholars composed handbooks of law, wrote commentaries

on the Bible, contributed to theology and philosophy, and furthered the growth of Hebrew philology.

However, traditionalists continued to compose diatribes against what they perceived as a heretical sect. But as the social composition of the movement changed, Karaism became less severe, and members of the movement in Egypt and elsewhere became prosperous merchants. As a consequence, the ascetic features of Karaite ritual were modified, and the concept of a post-biblical tradition was gradually accepted.

After the Jerusalem community was destroyed during the First Crusade, the centre of Karaite literary activity shifted to the Byzantine empire. From there Karaites established communities in the Crimea and medieval Poland and Lithuania. In Egypt the Karaite community continued to maintain itself. Subsequently, relations between Karaites and Rabbanites (the rabbinical establishment) varied – at times ties were close whereas at other periods the differences between the Karaism and traditional Judaism were emphasized. Yet, after the 11th century Karaism lost its base of support, and it survived only as a small minority group.

SHABBATEANS

THE ARRIVAL OF SHABBETAI TZVI ELECTRIFIED THE JEWISH WORLD.
CONVINCED THAT THE LONG-AWAITED MESSIAH HAD COME, FOLLOWERS
ANTICIPATED THAT MESSIANIC REDEMPTION WAS IMMINENT.

*Above Shabbetai Tzvi, who declared
he was the Messiah or the Anointed of
the God of Jacob, engraved in 1666.*

Through the centuries, Jews antici-pated the coming of a messianic redeemer who would bring about the transformation of human history. In the middle of the 17th century, Jewry was electrified by the arrival of Shabbetai Tzvi who was pro-claimed the long-awaited Messiah by his disciple Nathan of Gaza. Despite his subsequent apostasy and death in 1676, a circle of followers – the Shabbateans – continued to proclaim his messiahship.

THE ARRIVAL OF
SHABBETAI TZVI

By the beginning of the 17th cen-tury, Lurianic mysticism had made a major impact on Sephardic Jewry, and messianic expectations had also become a central feature of Jewish life. In this milieu the arrival of a self-proclaimed messianic king, Shabbetai Tzvi, brought about a transformation of Jewish life and

*Below A view of 19th-century Smyrna,
Turkey, where the false Messiah
Shabbetai Tzvi was born in 1626.*

thought. Born in Smyrna into a wealthy family, Shabbetai had received a traditional Jewish educa-tion and later engaged in the study of the Zohar.

After leaving Smyrna in the 1650s Shabbetai spent ten years in various cities in Greece as well as in Constantinople (Istanbul) and Jerusalem. Eventually he became part of a Kabbalistic group in Cairo and travelled to Gaza where he encoun-tered Nathan of Gaza who believed that Shabbetai was the Messiah. In 1665 Shabbetai's messiahship was announced, and Nathan sent letters to Jews in numerous communities asking them to repent and recognize Shabbetai Tzvi as their redeemer. Shabbetai, he announced, would take the Sultan's crown, bring back the lost tribes and inaugurate the period of messianic redemption.

After a brief sojourn in Jerusalem, Shabbetai went to Smyrna, where he encountered strong opposition on the part of some local rabbis. In response he denounced the disbe-lievers and declared that he was the

Anointed of the God of Jacob. This action evoked a hysterical response – a number of Jews fell into trances and had visions of him on a royal throne crowned as king of Israel. He journeyed to Constantinople in 1666, but on the order of the grand vizier he was arrested and put into prison. Within a short time the prison quar-ters became a messianic court; pilgrims from all over the world made their way to Constantinople to join in messianic rituals and asce-tic activities. In addition, hymns were written in his honour and new fes-tivals were introduced. According to Nathan who remained in Gaza, the alteration in Shabbetai's moods from illumination to withdrawal symbol-ized his soul's struggle with demonic powers. At times he was imprisoned by the *kelippot*, or 'powers of evil', but at other moments he prevailed against them.

DEFENDING SHABBETAI'S
MESSIAHSHIP

Such an act of apostasy scandalized most of Shabbetai's followers, but he defended himself by asserting he had become a Muslim in obeisance to

God's commands. Many of his followers accepted this explanation and refused to give up their belief. Some thought it was not Shabbetai who had become a Muslim, but rather a phantom who had taken on his appearance; the Messiah himself had ascended to heaven.

Others cited biblical and rabbinic sources to justify Shabbetai's action. Nathan explained that the messianic task involved taking on the humiliation of being portrayed as a traitor to his people.

Furthermore, Nathan argued on the basis of Lurianic Kabbalah that there were two kinds of divine light – a creative light and another light opposed to the existence of anything other than the En Sof (Infinite). While creative light formed structures of creation in empty space, the other light became after *zimzum*, or 'divine contraction', the power of evil. According to Nathan, the soul of the Messiah had been struggling against the power of evil from the beginning; his purpose was to allow divine light to penetrate this domain and bring about *tikkun*, or 'cosmic repair'. In order to do this, the soul of the Messiah was

Below Interior of the house of Shabbetai Tzvi in Izmir, formerly Smyrna, in Turkey.

not obligated to keep the law, but was free to descend into the abyss to liberate sparks and thereby conquer evil. In this light, Shabbetai's conversion to Islam was explicable.

THE SHABBATEAN MOVEMENT

After Shabbetai's act of apostasy, Nathan visited him in the Balkans and then travelled to Rome where he performed secret rites to bring about the end of the Papacy. Shabbetai remained in Adrianople and Constantinople where he lived as both Muslim and Jew. In 1672 he was deported to Albania where he disclosed his own Kabbalistic teaching to his supporters. After he died in 1676, Nathan declared that Shabbetai had ascended to the supernal world.

Eventually a number of groups continued in their belief that Shabbetai Tzvi was the Messiah,

Above The anointing of Shabbetai Tzvi as King of the Jews by Nathan of Gaza, in a 17th-century engraving.

including a sect, the Doenmeh, or 'dissidents', which professed Islam publicly but nevertheless adhered to its own traditions. Marrying among themselves, they eventually evolved into antinomian sub-groups, which violated Jewish sexual laws and asserted the divinity of Shabbetai and their leader, Baruchiah Russo.

In Italy several Shabbatean groups also emerged and propagated their views. In the 18th century the most important Shabbatean sect was led by Jacob Frank, who was influenced by the Doenmeh in Turkey. Believing himself to be the incarnation of Shabbetai, Frank announced that he was the second person of the Trinity and gathered together a circle of disciples who indulged in licentious orgies.

FRANKISTS

IN THE 18TH CENTURY, JACOB FRANK ESTABLISHED A SHABBATEAN MOVEMENT. ALARMED BY THE RADICAL NATURE OF THIS GROUP, THE RABBINIC ESTABLISHMENT DENOUNCED THE FRANKISTS AS HERETICS.

The 18th-century Jacob Frank (1726–91) established a new Shabbatean group, the Frankists, whose theology constituted a radical departure from the tradition. Not surprisingly, Frank and his followers were anathematized by the rabbinic establishment for their heretical views and practices.

ORIGIN OF THE FRANKISTS

Jacob Frank was born Jacob ben Judah Leib in Korolowka, a small town in Podolia. Educated in Czernowitz and Sniatyn, he lived for a number of years in Bucharest. Although he went to heder, or 'Jewish primary school', he had no knowl-

Below Caricature of Archbishop Dembowski of Lemberg, who arranged a public burning of the Talmud and other Hebrew writings after the Shabbateans informed him they rejected the Talmud in the late 1750s.

edge of the Talmud. In Bucharest he began to earn his living as a dealer in cloth and precious stones.

Frank appears to have been associated with Shabbateans during his youth. He began to study the Zohar, making a name in Shabbatean circles as a person possessed of certain powers. In 1752 he married Hannah, the daughter of a respected merchant in Nikopol. Accompanied by Shabbateans, he visited Salonika in 1753 and became involved with the Doenmeh, a radical wing of this group. Eventually he became the leader of the Shabbateans in Poland where he was perceived by his followers as a reincarnation of the divine soul which had previously resided in Shabbetai.

Subsequently, Frank journeyed through the communities of Podolia, which contained Shabbatean groups. Although he was received enthusiastically by Shabbateans, Frank's

Above Jonathan Eybeschutz, rabbi of the 'Three Communities', was accused by Jacob Emden of being a secret Shabbatean. He was cleared in 1753.

appearance in Lanskroun caused considerable consternation when he was discovered conducting a Shabbatean ritual with his followers – his Jewish opponents claimed that a religious orgy was taking place. Although Frank's followers were imprisoned, he was released because the authorities thought he was a Turkish subject.

At the request of the local rabbis an enquiry was instituted that examined the practices of the Shabbateans.

FRANKIST THEOLOGY

In his teaching, Frank revealed himself as the embodiment of God's power who had come to complete Shabbetai's task. He was, he believed, the true Jacob, like Jacob in the Bible who had completed the work of his predecessors, Abraham and Isaac. In short statements and parables, Frank explained the nature of his mission. It was necessary, he argued, for those who belonged to his group to adopt Christianity outwardly in order to keep their true faith secret. In his view, all religions were only stages through which believers had to pass, like a person putting on different suits of clothes that could later be discarded.

Above Kamenietz: the capital of Podolia in Russian Poland, where the Frankist movement developed.

In place of the Shabbatean trinity in which all were united in divinity, Frank argued that the true and good God is hidden and divested of any connection with the created order. It is he who conceals himself behind 'the King of Kings'

THE NEW ROAD

According to Frank all great religious leaders from the patriarchs to Shabbetai Tzvi and Baruchiah, had endeavoured to find the way to God, but failed. In Frank's view, it is necessary to embark on a completely new road, untrodden by the people of Israel. This path is the road to consistent religious anarchy – in order to achieve this goal it is necessary to abolish and destroy Jewish laws, teachings and practices that constrict the power of life. Some believers had already passed through Judaism and Islam; now they had to complete their journey by taking on the Christian faith, using its beliefs and practices to conceal the real core of their belief in Frank as the true Messiah and the living God.

whom Frank also refers to as 'the Great Brother', or 'He who stands before God'. He is the God of the true faith whom one must attempt to approach; in doing so, it is possible to break the domination of the three 'leaders of the world' who rule earth, imposing on it an inappropriate system of law.

FRANKISTS AND THE CHURCH

Frank prepared his followers to accept baptism as the step that would open before them this new way. Paralleling the pattern in the Gospels, he appointed 12 emissaries who were destined to become his chief disciples. At the same time he appointed 12 'sisters' who were to act as his concubines. Continuing

the tradition of the Baruchiah sect, Frank also instituted licentious sexual practices.

As time passed, it became clear that Frank and his followers would need to be baptized, and they requested that Archbishop Lubienski in Lvov receive them into the Church. In making this application, they expressed the desire to be allowed to lead a separate existence. The Church, however, replied that no special privileges would be granted.

In July 1759 a disputation took place in Lvov, as a precondition of conversion, when the leading rabbis and members of the Frankist sect debated a variety of theological topics. In September 1759 Frank was baptized, and by the end of 1760 in Lvov alone more than 500 Frankists followed his example. Despite such widespread conversion, the Church became increasingly suspicious of the Frankists: it appeared that the real object of their devotion was Frank as the living incarnation of God.

In February 1760 Frank was arrested and an inquisition took place, resulting in Frank's imprisonment, though he was later released. In 1791 Frank died, mourned by hundreds of his followers.

Below Street in the Jewish area of Lvov, in the Ukraine, where a Frankist disputation took place in 1759.

CHAPTER 3

MODERN JUDAISM

On the far right of the religious spectrum, Orthodox Judaism and Hasidism hold tenaciously to the belief system of the past, believing the Torah in its entirety was given by God to Moses on Mount Sinai; in addition, the rabbinic interpretation of the law is sacrosanct. However, recent times have seen the emergence of new forms of Judaism with radically different ideologies some of which do not accept the Torah as the basis of Jewish life.

In the early 19th century, Reform Jews were anxious to modernize the tradition. They felt it was no longer necessary for Jews to adhere to the minutiae of the law and set aside certain central tenets of traditional Judaism. Conservative Jews adopted a less radical view, yet also sought to make Judaism relevant in the modern world. More recently, Reconstructionist and Humanistic Jews argued that Judaism must divest itself from supernaturalism. A growing number of Jews sought to revitalize the faith through Jewish renewal. And, at the margin of Jewish life, Messianic Jews believed that a new era had dawned with the coming of the messianic age.

Opposite A Hasidic Jew, arms outstretched with joy, celebrates the reunification of Jerusalem on the first Jerusalem Day in 1968. He is carried by a soldier at the Western Wall.

Above In 1954, US architect Frank Lloyd Wright designed his only synagogue, Beth Shalom at Elkins Park, Pennsylvania, a startling modernist version of an ancient temple.

ORTHODOX JUDAISM

BOUND BY THE JEWISH LEGAL SYSTEM, ORTHODOX JEWS KEEP ALIVE THE TRADITIONS OF THEIR ANCESTORS. THE RITUALS OF ORTHODOX JUDAISM BRING THE CHAIN OF TRADITION INTO THE PRESENT AGE.

The origins of Orthodox Judaism stretch back 4,000 years to the birth of the Jewish nation. From the time of the patriarchs to rabbinic Judaism, Jews were bound by the covenant with Moses. Orthodox Jews today adhere to the tenets of the faith in an uncompromising fashion.

ORIGINS OF ORTHODOXY

Orthodox Judaism is the branch of Judaism that adheres most strictly to halakha, or 'Jewish law'. By the 18th century local Jewish communities had lost much of their authority. This led to the disintegration of the traditional religious establishment as well as the prestige of communal leaders. Coupled with the aspirations of Jewish emancipationists, new interpretations of the faith and an altered conception of the relationship between Jews and non-Jews, Orthodox Judaism was a response to these changes in Jewish life.

Below Sephardic Mordechai Eliyahu and Ashkenazi Avraham Shapira were Orthodox chief rabbis of Israel, 1983–93.

In the first half of the 19th century, traditionalist Jews in Hungary and Germany were profoundly critical of the efforts of Reform Jews to adapt halakha to modern society as well as modify the traditional synagogue service. These reformers argued such alterations were a condition for Jewish emancipation as well as civil equality. Traditionalists viewed this attitude a violation of God's will.

At the end of the 19th century, Eastern European Orthodox leaders similarly championed Torah Judaism in the face of increased secularism.

ORTHODOX THEOLOGY

Until the growth of the Enlightenment in the 18th century, the Jewish people affirmed their belief in one God who created the universe. As a transcendent deity he brought all things into being, continues to sustain the cosmos, and guides humanity to its ultimate destiny. In the unfolding of this providential scheme, Israel has a central role – as God's chosen people, the nation is to serve as a light to all peoples.

Above A strictly Orthodox family in Jerusalem. Note the girls' sober clothing and the boy's side curls and fringes.

Scripture does not contain a dogmatic formulation of such beliefs, but the Orthodox prayer book contains the medieval philosopher Moses Maimonides' formulation of the '13 Principles of the Jewish Faith'.

As Maimonides explained, anyone who denies any of these tenets is to be regarded as a heretic: God's existence; God's unity; God's incorporeality; God's eternity; God alone is to be worshipped; prophecy; Moses is the greatest of the prophets; the divine origin of the Torah (Pentateuch); the Torah is immutable; God knows the thoughts and deeds of human beings; reward and punishment; the Messiah; resurrection of the dead. Maimonides' principles as well as parallel dogmatic formulations by other medieval thinkers served as the basis for theological speculation through the centuries.

MODERN TRADITIONALISTS

Today Orthodox Jews continue to subscribe to these fundamental doctrines, secure in the knowledge that they are fulfilling God's will. Such a commitment serves as the framework for the traditional Orthodox way of life. Wary of modernity, traditional Orthodox Jews are anxious to preserve the Jewish way of life through a process of intensive

Right Friday night in Jerusalem. Jewish tradition encourages everyone to dress finely for Shabbat.

education – for these Jews there can be no compromise with secularism. Such attitudes permeate all aspects of Jewish life from the earliest age. Among traditional Orthodox Jews, education for boys is rigorous, following the curriculum laid down in ancient times. Within strictly Orthodox circles, expectations for girls are of a different nature; Jewish young women are reared to become loyal and dedicated mothers and homemakers.

Strict adherence to Jewish law is demanded within the context of traditional orthodoxy. Committed to the doctrine of Torah Mi Sinai (the belief that God revealed the Torah to Moses on Mount Sinai), Orthodox Jews are obliged to keep all biblical and rabbinic ordinances. To accomplish this in a modern setting requires both determination and scrupulous care. Although the traditional Orthodox constitute only a minority of the Jewish community, there is a growing element anxious to draw other Jews to the traditional faith.

Below Pupils crowd round the desk of a teacher at an Orthodox elementary school in Jerusalem.

ORTHODOX JUDAISM TODAY

The dominant trend in Orthodoxy since World War II has been its increased emphasis of adherence to the traditional Jewish way of life. What is required is religious zealotry, observance of the mitzvot, or commandments, and a rejection of modern values and culture.

Throughout the Jewish world, Orthodox Jews have actively encouraged the establishment of schools, synagogues, political organizations, a press and summer camps. Both Orthodox rabbis and lay leaders have been anxious to counter the threats of secularism and modernity.

Today most Orthodox Jews reside in Israel or the United States. In Israel religiously observant Jews make up about 15–20 per cent of the Jewish population. These neo-traditionalists, who were once marginal to Israeli society, play an increasingly important role in communal and political life. Within their ranks the Edah Haredit (community of the pious) consist of thousands of families with numerous sympathizers. These are the most intransigent of the Orthodox. They relate to the state of Israel with various degrees of hostility. A more moderate neotraditionalism is found in Israeli Agudah circles.

Among Israeli Orthodox Jews, the heads of the yeshivot and a number of Hasidic rebbes are dominant. In the United States, neo-traditionalists have been supportive of their own institutions.

With the exception of pockets of neo-traditional extremists such as the Edah Haredit in Israel, American Orthodox Jews are generally familiar with modern culture, and most are willing to work with the non-Orthodox on behalf of general Jewish interests.

Below An Orthodox Jew wearing the traditional prayer shawl and tefillin, boxes worn on the forehead and arm.

HASIDISM

SINCE THE 18TH CENTURY HASIDISM HAS BEEN A POWERFUL FORCE IN JEWISH LIFE. TODAY THE HASIDIC COMMUNITY IS DIVIDED INTO A NUMBER OF SUB-GROUPS, EACH WITH ITS OWN REBBE.

In the 18th century, Hasidism emerged as a challenge to the rabbinic establishment. Founded by the Ba'al Shem Tov (1700–60), this pietistic movement stressed the importance of eliminating selfhood and the ascent of the soul to divine light. Unlike the arid scholasticism of traditional Judaism, Hasidism offered to the Jewish masses a new outlet for religious fervour.

THE ORIGINS OF HASIDISM

During the second half of the 18th century, this new popular movement attracted thousands of followers. Pietistic in orientation, Hasidism was based on Kabbalistic ideas and reinterpreted the role of the rabbi as a spiritual guide. It first appeared in the villages of the Polish Ukraine, especially Podolia, where Shabbatean Frankists had been active. According

Below A Hasidic Jew holds the lulav and etrog in a sukkah built for Sukkot in Williamsburg, New York.

to tradition, Israel ben Eliezer, known as the Ba'al Shem Tov or Besht, was born in Southern Poland and in his twenties journeyed with his wife to the Carpathian mountains. In the 1730s he travelled to Mezhbizh where he performed various miracles and instructed his disciples in Kabbalistic lore. By the 1740s he had attracted a considerable number of disciples who passed on his teaching. After his death in 1760, Dov Baer became the leader of this sect and Hasidism spread to southern Poland, the Ukraine and Lithuania.

CRITICISM

The growth of Hasidism engendered considerable hostility on the part of rabbinic authorities. In particular the rabbinic leadership of Vilna issued an edict of excommunication. The Hasidim were charged with permissiveness in their observance of the commandments, laxity in the study of the Torah, excess in prayer, and preference for

Above Hasidic women behind a mechitza screen that affords them a limited view of the service at Viznitz synagogue, Stamford Hill, London.

the Lurianic rather than the Ashkenazic prayer book. In subsequent years the Hasidim and their opponents (Mitnaggedim) bitterly denounced one another. Relations deteriorated further when Jacob Joseph of Polonnoye published a book critical of the rabbinate; his work was burned, and in 1791 the Mitnaggedim ordered that all relations with the Hasidim cease.

By the end of the century, the Jewish religious establishment of Vilna denounced the Hasidim to the Russian government, an act resulting in the imprisonment of several leaders. Despite such condemnation, the movement was eventually recognized by the Russian and Austrian governments. In the ensuing years the movement divided into a number of separate groups under different leaders who passed on positions of authority to their descendants.

HASIDIC THEOLOGY

Hasidism initiated a profound change in Jewish religious pietism. In the medieval period, the Hasidei Ashkenaz attempted to achieve perfection through various mystical activities. This tradition was carried on by Lurianic Kabbalists who engaged in various forms of self-

Above *Dancing at a Chabad-Lubavitch bar mitzvah in Paris in 2008. Chabad-Lubavitch is now one of the largest Hasidic organizations in the world.*

mortification. In opposition to such ascetic practices, the Ba'al Shem Tov and his followers emphasized the omnipresence of God rather than the shattering of the vessels and the imprisonment of divine sparks by the powers of evil. For Hasidic Judaism there is no place where God is absent; the doctrine of *zimzum*, or 'divine contraction', was interpreted by Hasidic sages as only an apparent withdrawal of the divine light. Divine light, they believed, is everywhere. As the Ba'al Shem Tov explained, in every one of a person's troubles, physical and spiritual, even in that trouble God himself is there.

For some Hasidim, devekut, or 'cleaving to God in prayer', was understood as the annihilation of selfhood and the ascent of the soul to divine light. In this context joy, humility, gratitude and spontaneity were seen as essential features of Hasidic worship. The central obstacles to concentration in prayer are distracting thoughts; according to Hasidism, such sinful intentions contain a divine spark which can be released. In this regard, the traditional

Right *The Rebbe and his Hasidim during Hanukkah at the Premishlan congregation in Bnei Brak, Israel.*

Kabbalistic stress on theological speculation was replaced by a preoccupation with mystical psychology in which inner bliss was conceived as the highest aim rather than *tikkun*, or 'repair of the cosmos'.

For the Hasidim, it was also possible to achieve devekut in daily activities including eating, drinking, business affairs and sex. Such ordinary acts became religious if in performing them one cleaves to God, and devekut is thus attainable by all Jews rather than just by a scholarly elite. Unlike the earlier mystical tradition, Hasidism provided a means by which ordinary Jews could reach a state of spiritual ecstasy. Hasidic worship embraced singing, dancing and joyful devotion in anticipation of the period of messianic redemption.

THE ZADDIK
Another central feature of this new movement was the institution of the zaddik, which gave expression to a widespread disillusionment with rabbinic leadership. According to Hasidism, the zaddikim are spiritually superior individuals who have attained the highest level of devekut. The goal of the zaddik was to elevate the souls of his flock to the divine light. His tasks included

Above *Rabbi Menachem Schneerson giving funds to a follower as a blessing. He led the Chabad-Lubavitch movement in the late 20th century.*

pleading to God for his people, immersing himself in their everyday affairs, and counselling and strengthening them. As an authoritarian figure, the zaddik was seen by his followers as possessing the miraculous power to ascend to the divine realm. In this context, devekut to God involved cleaving to the zaddik. Given this emphasis on the role of the zaddik, Hasidic literature included summaries of the spiritual and Kabbalistic teachings of various famous zaddikim as well as stories about their miraculous deeds.

CONSERVATIVE JUDAISM

CONSERVATIVE JUDAISM ADOPTS A MIDDLE POSITION BETWEEN ORTHODOX AND REFORM JUDAISM, ADVOCATING LOYALTY TO THE TRADITION COUPLED WITH AN ACCEPTANCE OF MODERN VALUES.

In the wake of the Enlightenment of the 18th century, reformers sought to modernize the Jewish tradition. Initially, Reform Judaism constituted a radically new approach to the tradition. Yet more conservative reformers were alarmed by the radicalism of their co-religionists. Eventually, Conservative Judaism emerged as a more moderate form of Jewish modernism.

ZACHARIAS FRANKEL

The founder of what came to be known as Conservative Judaism was Zacharias Frankel (1801–75). An advocate of moderate reform, Frankel was committed to a historically evolving dynamic Judaism. The aim of such an approach (positive historical Judaism), he believed, would be to uncover the origins of the Jewish people's national spirit and the collective will. Both the past as enshrined in tradition and the

present as embodied in the religious consciousness of the people, he argued, should determine the nature of Jewish life.

In 1845 Frankel left the Reform rabbinical conference in Frankfurt because a majority of the participants had voted that there was no need to use Hebrew in the Jewish worship service. Although he agreed with other reformers that Judaism needed to be revised, he disputed with them over the legitimate criteria for religious change. None the less, he broke with Orthodoxy in asserting that the Oral law was rabbinic in origin, that the halakha, or 'Jewish law', had evolved over time, and that the source of religious observance was not divine.

SOLOMON SCHECHTER

In the United States a similar approach to the tradition was adopted by a number of leading figures including

Above Seder plate showing traditional foods eaten at Passover – an egg, lamb, green vegetables, haroset and bitter herbs. Conservative Judaism stresses the importance of ritual in Jewish life.

the Jewish scholar Solomon Schechter (1847–1915) who argued that Conservative Judaism should combine elements of both traditional and non-traditional Judaism. Disdainfully Schechter rejected both Reform and Orthodoxy. Instead, he emphasized the importance of traditional rituals, customs, observances as well as belief, while simultaneously stressing the need for a historical perspective.

In February 1913 a union of 22 congregations was founded, committed to maintaining the Jewish tradition in its historical continuity. In the preamble to its constitution, the United Synagogue stated its intention to separate from Reform Judaism – it was committed to a heterogeneous, traditional mode of belief and practice through the observance of ritual in the home and synagogue. As Conservative Judaism expanded in the 1920s and 1930s a degree of uniformity developed in congregational worship. Services usually began late Friday evening and early Saturday morning; head coverings were required; prayer shawls were usually worn on

Left Prime Minister David Ben-Gurion of Israel and Louis Finkelstein, Chancellor of the Jewish Seminary for Conservative Judaism, New York, look at rare books at the seminary, 1960.

Sabbath morning; rabbis conducted the service and preached English sermons; prayer books other than the Union Prayer Book of the Reform movement were used; and many congregants participated in afternoon study with the rabbi. In addition, many synagogues had organs, mixed choirs, family pews, and *minyans*, or 'quorum for a religious service', that met three times a day for prayer.

CONSERVATIVE THEOLOGY

Conservative Jews viewed Judaism as an evolving organism that remained spiritually vibrant by adjusting to environmental and cultural conditions. In consequence, Conservative thinkers attempted to preserve those elements of the tradition that they believed to be spiritually meaningful while simultaneously setting aside those observances that actually hinder the continued growth of Judaism. Such obsolete practices were not abrogated, but simply ignored. In a similar spirit, Conservative Jews, in contrast with the Orthodoxy, felt no compulsion to accept theological doctrines which they believed were outmoded – thus Conservative Judaism broke with Orthodoxy regarding the belief that the Torah was revealed in its entirety to Moses on Mount Sinai.

In its quest to modernize the faith, Conservative scholars sought to establish an authoritative body to adapt Judaism to contemporary circumstances. As early as 1918 there was a considerable desire to establish a body of men learned in the law who would be able to advise the movement concerning pressing contemporary issues. Thus, even though the Conservative movement refused to formulate a detailed platform or series of credal statements, these features of Conservative Judaism provided a coherent and imaginative approach to the tradition.

CONSERVATIVE BELIEFS

Regarding belief in God, Conservative thinkers have generally subscribed to the traditional understanding of the Deity as omnipotent, omniscient, and all-good. Yet, in contrast with Orthodoxy, there remains considerable ambiguity about the nature of divine communication. Unlike Orthodox thinkers who view revelation as verbal in nature and Reform theologians who conceive of the Torah as a largely human product, the Conservative movement has generally attempted to bridge these two extremes. Within Conservative Judaism revelation is understood as a divinely initiated process involving human composition. As to what constitutes the nature of such a divine human encounter, Conservative writers vary: some argue that human beings correctly recorded the divine will as revealed at Sinai; others that those who wrote the Scriptures were simply divinely inspired.

Regarding halakha, Conservative thinkers emphasized the importance of conserving the laws of traditional Judaism, including dietary observances, Sabbath, festival and liturgical prescriptions, and ethical precepts. Nevertheless, Conservative scholars

Above In 1963, Martin Luther King received the Solomon Schechter Award. Schechter (1847–1915) was a leading figure of the Conservative movement.

advocated change and renewal. On the whole they stressed the historical importance of the Jewish heritage. Guided by such an approach to law, the Conservative movement resorted to what Schechter called 'the conscience of catholic Israel' in reaching decisions about the status of biblical and rabbinic law.

Concerning Jewish peoplehood, the Conservative movement has consistently affirmed the pre-eminence of K'lal Yisrael, or 'the body of Israel'. Yet despite this insistence there has not been the same unanimity about the nation of God's chosen people. Although the Sabbath and High Holy Day prayer books have retained the traditional formula ('You have chosen us from all the nations'), there has been a wide diversity of interpretation of the concept of chosenness among Conservative thinkers. Yet, as a consequence of its dedication to the peoplehood of Israel, the Conservative movement has from its inception been dedicated to the founding of the State of Israel.

REFORM JUDAISM

THE ENLIGHTENMENT HAD A DEEP IMPACT; NO LONGER WERE JEWS FORCED TO LIVE IN GHETTOS. REFORM JUDAISM EMERGED AS A REVOLUTIONARY MOVEMENT WHOSE AIM WAS TO MODERNIZE THE FAITH.

At the end of the 18th century, such advocates of Jewish enlightenment as Moses Mendelssohn encouraged fellow Jews to integrate into the mainstream of western European culture. Subsequently early reformers tried to reform Jewish education by widening the traditional curriculum of Jewish schools. Pre-eminent among these figures was Israel Jacobson, who founded a boarding school for boys in Westphalia and subsequently established other schools throughout the kingdom. In these new foundations, general subjects were taught by Christian teachers while a Jewish instructor gave lessons about Judaism.

Simultaneously a number of Reform temples were opened in Germany with innovations to the liturgy, including prayers and sermons in German as well as choral singing and organ music. The central

Below The West London Synagogue of British Jews, founded 1840. They chose this name to emphasize their patriotism.

aim of these early reformers was to adapt Jewish worship to contemporary aesthetic standards. For these innovators, the informality of the traditional service seemed foreign and undignified. They therefore insisted on greater decorum, more unison in prayer, a choir, hymns and music responses, as well as alterations in prayers and service length.

REFORMING JUDAISM

In response to such developments, Orthodoxy asserted that any change to the tradition was a violation of the Jewish heritage. For these traditionalists the Written and Oral Torah constitute an infallible chain of divinely revealed truth. Despite this reaction, some German rabbis began to re-evalute the Jewish tradition. In this undertaking the achievements of Jewish scholars who engaged in the scientific study of Judaism had a profound impact. In Frankfurt the Society of Friends of Reform was founded and published a proclamation stating that they recognized the

Above US Reform rabbi Isaac Mayer Wise became President of the Hebrew Union College, the rabbinical seminary of the Reform movement in 1875.

possibility of unlimited progress in the Jewish faith and rejected the authority of the legal code as well as the belief in messianic redemption.

A similar group was founded in Berlin in 1844 and called for major changes in the Jewish tradition. That year the first Reform synod took place at Brunswick in which the participants formulated a programme of reform. This was followed by a series of synods. In England similar developments took place with the establishment of the West London Synagogue in the 1840s. In the USA, Reform congregations were established first in Charleston, South Carolina and later in New York City. Isaac Mayer Wise founded the Union of American Hebrew Congregations with lay and rabbinical representatives in 1873, and the Hebrew Union College, the first Reform rabbinical seminary in America in 1875.

PHILOSOPHY

In 1885 a gathering of Reform rabbis met in Pittsburgh, Pennsylvania, and adopted a programme of reform: the Pittsburgh Platform. This document insisted on a number of central principles of this new movement. According to these reformers,

Above Reform rabbi Sally Priesand was ordained in 1972. She is reputedly the world's first woman rabbi.

Judaism presents the highest conception of the God-idea as taught in holy Scripture and developed and spiritualized by Jewish teachers. They believed the Bible is the record of the consecration of the Jewish people to its divine mission, yet it should be subjected to scientific research. The Mosaic legislation, they declared, is a system of training the Jewish people, but today only the moral laws are binding; rabbinic legislation is apt to obstruct rather than further modern spiritual elevation. Further, the reformers rejected the belief in the Messiah as well as the doctrine of heaven and hell. It is the duty of modern Jewry, they asserted, to strive for justice in modern society.

Fifty years after the Pittsburgh meeting of 1885, the Jewish world had undergone major changes: America had become the centre of the Diaspora; Zionism had become a vital force in Jewish life; and Hitler was in power.

The Columbus Platform of the Reform movement adopted in 1937 reflected a new approach to liberal Judaism. In later years the Reform movement underwent further change. In the 1960s new liturgies were used, and in the 1970s a new Reform prayer book was published

which changed the content as well as the format of worship. In 1972 the first woman rabbi was ordained, and by the early 1980s more than 75 women had entered the rabbinate. In 1976 the Reform movement produced the San Francisco Platform – the purpose of this statement was to provide a unifying document which would bring a sense of order to the movement.

More recently, another platform was issued by the Central Conference of American Rabbis in 1991. At the onset of the 21st century, this rabbinic body set out a new statement of principles that affirmed the central tenets of Judaism – God, Torah and Israel – while acknowledging the diversity of Reform Jewish belief and practice. In this platform the movement affirmed the reality and

oneness of God despite the differing theological interpretations. Further, it affirmed that the Jewish people are bound to God by an eternal covenant and that all human beings are created in the image of God. The Torah was conceived as the foundation of Jewish life; in this context the study of Hebrew, the language of Torah and the Jewish liturgy were extolled. The Jewish quest to bring Torah into the world was regarded as a central aspect of the faith. Finally, the movement stressed that the Reform movement is committed to strengthening the people of Israel and to furthering the interests of the Jewish State.

Below A Reform Yom Kippur service held at the Reform Temple De Hirsch Sinai, Seattle, Washington.

RECONSTRUCTIONIST JUDAISM

SEEKING TO MODERNIZE THE CENTRAL TENETS OF THE FAITH, RECONSTRUCTIONIST JUDAISM EMERGED IN THE EARLY 1900S AS A RADICAL ALTERNATIVE TO MAINSTREAM JEWISH MOVEMENTS.

The Reconstructionist movement emerged in the first half of the 20th century in the United States as a radical interpretation of the faith. Inspired by its founder, Mordecai Kaplan (1881–1983), the movement rejected the concept of a supernatural deity, and focused on the sociological dimensions of the tradition. Reconstructionists view Judaism as an evolving religious civilization in which spiritual symbols play a fundamental role.

ORIGINS

Unlike Reform and Conservative Judaism, Reconstructionist Judaism developed out of the thinking of an individual teacher. Born in Lithuania in 1881, Mordecai Kaplan served as

Below The Reconstructionist, 1959. Since 1935 the magazine has traced the growth of Reconstructionist Judaism in North America.

professor of homiletics at the Jewish Theological Seminary in New York. During the 1910s and 1920s he engaged in wide-ranging congregational work; later he officiated as a rabbi at a synagogue-centre in New York. In 1922 Kaplan initiated a policy of reconstructing Judaism to meet the demands of modern life. After publishing *Judaism as a Civilization* in 1934, he launched the *Reconstructionist* magazine.

In *Judaism as a Civilization* Kaplan evaluated the main religious groupings of American society. In his view, Reform had correctly recognized the evolving character of Judaism, yet it ignored the social basis of Jewish identity as well as the organic character of Jewish peoplehood. Neo-Orthodoxy, on the other hand, acknowledged Judaism as a way of life and provided an intensive programme of Jewish education. None the less, it mistakenly regarded the Jewish religion as unchanging. In contrast, Conservative Judaism was committed to the scientific study of the history of the Jewish faith while recognizing the unity of the Jewish people. However it was too closely bound to the halakha, or 'Jewish law' to respond to new circumstances. All of these movements failed to adjust adequately to the modern age; what was needed, Kaplan argued, was a definition of Judaism as an evolving religious civilization.

A RECONSTRUCTED JUDAISM

In the light of this vision of a reconstructed Judaism, Kaplan called for the re-establishment of a network of organic Jewish communities that

Above First page of the manuscript of Mordecai Kaplan's Judaism as a Civilization, dated New York, 1934, with handwritten notes by Kaplan.

would ensure the self-perpetuation of the Jewish heritage. Membership of this new movement would be voluntary; leadership should be elected democratically; and private religious opinions would be respected. Kaplan proposed a worldwide Jewish assembly, which would adopt a covenant defining the Jews as a trans-national people. In Kaplan's

Below Mordecai Kaplan, founder of Reconstructionist Judaism, at Camp Modin, Maine, 1958. Modin began in 1922 as 'The Camp with a Jewish Idea'.

Above Reconstructionist rabbi Sharon Kleinbaum dances the Hora, a popular Jewish circle dance, after officiating at a same-sex wedding in New York, 2010.

view, religion is the concretization of the collective self-consciousness of the group, which is manifest in spiritual symbols such as persons, places, events and writings. These symbols inspire feelings of reverence, commemorate what the group believes to be most valuable, provide historical continuity, and strengthen the collective consciousness of the people. In order for the Jewish community to survive, Kaplan believed it must eliminate its authoritarian dogmatic features.

SUPERNATURAL BELIEF

In particular, Judaism must divest itself of supernatural belief. The spiritual dimension of the faith must be reformed in humanistic and naturalistic terms. For Kaplan, God is not a supernatural being but the power that makes for salvation. God, he wrote, is the sum of all the animating organizing forces and relationships that are forever making a cosmos out of chaos. In Kaplan's view, the idea of God must be understood fundamentally in terms of its effect. In his view, God is a 'trans-national', 'super-factual' and 'super-experiential' transcendence, which does not infringe on the laws of nature. Such a notion was far-removed from

RECONSTRUCTIONIST LITURGY

Many of the ideas found in Kaplan's writings were reflected in the movement's religious literature. *The New Haggadah for Passover*, for example, applied Kaplan's theology to liturgical texts, subordinating miracles and plagues in the traditional Haggadah to the narrative of Israel's redemption from Egypt. *The Sabbath Prayer Book* was designed for those who were dissatisfied with synagogue worship – its aim was to arouse emotion by eliminating theologically untenable passages and adding inspirational material drawn from the tradition. This new prayer book deleted all references to the revelation of the Torah on Mount Sinai, the chosenness of Israel, and the doctrine of a personal Messiah.

the biblical and rabbinic concept of God as the creator and sustainer of the universe who chose the Jewish people and guides humanity to its final destiny.

THE MOVEMENT

In the 1940s and 1950s the leaders of Reconstructionist Judaism insisted they were not attempting to form a new branch of Judaism. Throughout this period, Reconstructionists hoped to be able to infuse the three major groups within North American Judaism (Orthodox, Conservative and Reform) with its ideas.

However, by the end of the 1960s the Reconstructionist movement had become a denomination – it had established a seminary to train Reconstructionist rabbis and had instituted a congregational structure. Regarding halakha or Jewish law,

the Reconstructionist Rabbinical Association issued a statement of its 1980 convention that placed authority in the Jewish people (as opposed to the rabbis) and created a process whereby each congregation would be free to evolve its own *minhag*, or 'customs'. Three years later, the Association produced guidelines on intermarriage, encouraging rabbis to welcome mixed couples (a Jew and a non-Jew), permit them to participate in Jewish synagogue life, and recognize their children as Jewish if raised as Jews. In addition, the Association decreed that rabbis could sanctify an intermarriage as long as it was accompanied by a civil, rather than a religious, ceremony.

Below Celebrating Sukkot at the Reconstructionist Rabbinical College in Wyncote, Pennsylvania, USA.

HUMANISTIC JUDAISM

THIS RADICAL MOVEMENT HAS BECOME AN ALTERNATIVE FOR SOME
JEWS. IT OFFERS JEWISH SECULAR HUMANISTS A NEW FORM OF JUDAISM
DEVOID OF A BELIEF IN A SUPERNATURAL DEITY.

Like Reconstructionist Judaism, Jewish humanism offers a non-theistic interpretation of the Jewish faith. Originating in the 1960s in Detroit, Michigan under the leadership of Rabbi Sherwin Wine, Humanistic Judaism now numbers about 40,000 members in the United States, Israel, Europe and elsewhere. The movement originated in 1965, when the Birmingham Temple in a suburb outside Detroit began to publicize its philosophy of Judaism. In 1966 a special committee for Humanistic Judaism was organized at the Temple to share service and educational material with rabbis and laity. The following year a meeting of several leaders of the movement met, issuing a statement, which affirmed that Judaism should be governed by

Below Blowing the Shofar for Yom Kippur at a humanistic service at Morris County, NJ, USA, 2005.
In a break with tradition, the service is about atonement – but not to God.

empirical reason and human needs. A new magazine, *Humanistic Judaism* was founded. Two years later, two new Humanistic congregations were established: Temple Beth Or in Deerfield, Illinois, and a Congregation for Humanistic Judaism in Fairfield County, Connecticut.

In 1969 the Society for Humanistic Judaism was established in Detroit to provide a basis for cooperation among Humanistic Jews, and in 1970 the first annual conference of the Society took place. During the next ten years new congregations were established in Boston, Toronto, Los Angeles, Washington, Miami, Long Beach and Huntington, New York. In subsequent years Secular Humanistic Judaism became an international movement with supporters on five continents. The National Federation currently comprises nine national organizations in the United States, Canada, Britain, France, Belgium, Israel, Australia, Argentina and Uruguay.

Above Rabbi Sherwin Wine founded the Society for Humanistic Judaism in North America, in 1969.

THE IDEOLOGY OF HUMANISTIC JUDAISM

In 1986 the Federation issued a proclamation stating its ideology and aims. According to this document, Humanistic Jews value human reason and the reality of the world which reason discloses. In their view, the natural universe stands on its own, requiring no supernatural intervention. In this light, Humanists believe in the value of human existence and in the power of human beings to solve their problems individually and collectively. Life, they maintain, should be directed to the satisfaction of human needs. In their view, Judaism, as the civilization of Jews, is a human creation: it embraces all manifestations of Jewish life, including Jewish languages, ethical traditions, historic memories, cultural heritage, and especially the emergence of the state of Israel in modern times.

The Jewish people, Humanists insist, is a world with a pluralistic culture and civilization all its own. Judaism, as the culture of the Jews, is thus more than theological content. It encompasses many languages, a vast body of literature, historical memories and ethical values. Yet, unlike other modern movements, Humanistic Judaism seeks to

welcome all people who seek to identify with Jewish culture and destiny. Hence, Humanists have redefined the notion of Jewishness. A Jew, they state, is a person of Jewish descent or any person who declares himself or herself to be a Jew and who identifies with the history, ethical values, culture, civilization, and community of the Jewish nation.

JEWISH FESTIVALS

Dedicated to Jewish survival, Humanistic Judaism emphasizes the importance of Jewish festivals in fostering Jewish identity. Yet, for Humanistic Jews, they must be detached from their supernatural origins and reinterpreted in the light of modern circumstances. Such a reorientation provides a basis for extolling human potential.

So, too, does Humanistic Judaism's understanding of life-cycle events: the ceremonies connected with these events emphasize the importance of group survival. Beginning with birth, Humanistic Jews stress the connection of the child with the future of the family, the Jewish people and humanity. Likewise, Humanistic Judaism fosters a Humanistic maturity ceremony, which reflects the ethical commitments of Humanistic

Jews. As an important transitional event, the marriage ceremony should also embody Humanistic values. For Humanistic Jews, the wedding should embrace the conception of the bride and groom publicly declaring their commitment and support and loyalty to one another.

Rituals connected with death should similarly be expressive of Humanistic principles. Humanistic Judaism asserts that mortality is an unavoidable and final event. Accepting this truth, it is possible to live courageously and generously in the face of tragedy. A Humanistic Jewish memorial service serves as

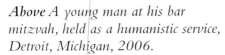

Above A young man at his bar mitzvah, held as a humanistic service, Detroit, Michigan, 2006.

an opportunity to teach a philosophy of life. Both the meditations and the eulogies are designed to remind people that the value of personal life lies in its quality, not in its quantity.

A NEW APPROACH

Humanistic Judaism, then, offers an option for those who wish to identify with the Jewish community despite their rejection of the traditional understanding of God's nature and activity. Unlike Reconstructionist Judaism, with its emphasis on the observances of the past, Humanistic Judaism fosters a radically new approach. The Jewish heritage is relevant only in so far as it advances Humanistic ideals.

In addition, traditional definitions and principles are set aside in the quest to create a Judaism consonant with a scientific and pluralistic age. Secular in orientation, Humanistic Jews seek to create a world in which the Jewish people are dedicated to the betterment of all humankind.

Left Altar at a humanistic wedding scattered with natural objects – flowers, stones, incense and a glass goblet.

JEWISH RENEWAL

FOSTERING A NON-TRADITIONAL COMMITMENT TO JEWISH HERITAGE, JEWISH RENEWAL IS A PRODUCT OF THE COUNTER-CULTURE MOVEMENTS, ORGANIZED AROUND EXPERIMENTAL FELLOWSHIPS.

The Jewish Renewal movement brings Kabbalistic and Hasidic theory and practice into a non-Orthodox, egalitarian framework. In this respect, Jewish Renewal is characterized by its Hasidic orientation. Renewal Jews often add ecstatic practices such as meditation, chant and dance to traditional worship. In addition, some Renewal Jews borrow from Buddhism, Sufism and other faiths to enhance their spiritual approach.

HISTORY

Jewish renewal has its origins in the North American counter-movements of the late 1960s and early 1970s. During this period, a number of young rabbis, academics and political activists founded experimental havurot, or 'fellowships', for prayer and study in a reaction to what they perceived as the overly organized institutional structures of mainstream Judaism. Initially the main inspiration was the pietistic fellowship of the Pharisees as well as other early

sects. In addition, some of these groups attempted to function as fully fledged communes after the model of their secular counterparts. Others formed communities within urban and suburban contexts.

Founders of the havurot movement included the liberal political activist Arthur Waskow, Conservative rabbi Michael Strassfeld and perhaps Jewish Renewal's most prominent leader, Zalman Schachter-Shalomi. Even though the original leadership consisted of men, US Jewish feminists were later actively engaged in Jewish Renewal, including Rabbis Shefa Gold, Lynn Gottlieb and Waskow's partner Phyllis Berman. Initially the movement attracted little attention in the US Jewish community despite various articles in Jewish magazines. However, in 1973 Michael and Sharon Strassfeld published *The Jewish Catalogue: A Do-It-Yourself Kit*. This was patterned after the counter-culture *Whole Earth Catalogue* and served as a basic reference book dealing with a wide

Above *Liberal political activist Rabbi Arthur Waskow (right), co-founder of the havurot movement and a leading figure in Jewish Renewal, with Muslim imam Mahdi Bray.*

range of Jewish subjects, including traditional observances as well as crafts, recipes and meditational practices. In time the havurah movement increased in numbers and included self-governing havurot within Reform, Conservative and Reconstructionist congregations. By 1980 a number of havurot moved away from traditional patterns of Jewish worship as members added English readings, chants, poetry and other elements from various spiritual traditions.

RENEWAL LEADERSHIP

Pre-eminent among leaders of this new movement was Zalman Schachter-Shalomi, a Hasidic-trained rabbi who was ordained in the Lubavitch movement. In the 1960s he broke with Orthodox Judaism and founded his own organization, the B'nai Or Religious Fellowship. The name 'B'nai Or' means 'sons' or 'children' of light, and was taken

Left *Rabbi Zalman Schachter-Shalomi, with the Dalai Lama in Dharamsala, India, 1990. The rabbi is holding a chart explaining the similarities between Jewish and Tibetan views.*

from the Dead Sea Scrolls where the sons of light battle with the sons of darkness.

Schachter-Shalomi viewed B'nai Or as a semi-monastic ashram community, based on various communal models of the 1960s and 70s. The community never materialized as he wished, yet it produced a number of important Renewal leaders. The *B'nai Or Newsletter* presented articles on Jewish mysticism, Hasidic stories and Schachter-Shalomi's philosophy, which was influenced by Buddhism and Sufism. Rabbi Zalman later held the Wisdom Chair at Naropa Institute, America's only Buddhist university.

After the first national Kallah conference in Radnor, Pennsylvania in 1985, the name B'nai Or was changed to P'nai Or (Faces of Light) to reflect the more egalitarian nature of Jewish Renewal. Together with Arthur Waskow, Schachter-Shalomi broadened the focus of the organization. In 1993 it merged with the Shalom Centre, founded by Rabbi Waskow to become ALEPH (Alliance for Jewish Renewal). This organization served as an overarching association for like-minded havurot.

However, some more Orthodox members of B'nai Or were not content with these changes and left the Renewal movement. This brought

Right Wearing a prayer shawl and skullcap, a Jew practises yoga on the beach at Ashdod, Israel – an example of how Judaism is revitalised in contemporary life.

about significant leadership changes, with Waskow taking an increasingly important role. During this period his magazine *Menorah* merged with the *B'nai Or Newsletter* to become *New Menorah*. This new publication addressed such issues as Jewish feminism, the nuclear arms race, new forms of prayer, social justice, and gay rights.

B'nai Or/ALEPH and its magazine led to the spread of Jewish Renewal throughout the United States and other countries. This has brought about the institutionalization of the movement in the form of the administrative ALEPH, the rabbinical association OHaLaH, and formalized rabbinic ordination programme.

THE MOVEMENT

Statistical information about the number of Jews who affiliate with Jewish Renewal is not available. None the less, the movement has had a profound impact on various non-Orthodox streams of Judaism within the United States. Arguably the greatest impact has been on

Reconstructionist Judaism. Initially Reconstructionism was based on the rationalistic philosophy of Mordecai Kaplan, but, under the influence of Jewish Renewal, it has come to embrace Jewish mystical beliefs and practices, particularly in the prayer books that were issued in the 1990s.

Jewish Renewal has also had an impact on other non-Orthodox movements in terms of the increased leadership roles of women, the acceptance of gays and lesbians, and liberal political activism.

In addition, it is not uncommon for synagogues not associated with Jewish Renewal to feature workshops on Jewish meditation and yoga. Various melodies and liturgical innovations have been introduced through the influence of Renewal.

Despite such an impact on Jewish life, critics of Jewish Renewal maintain that the movement puts too much emphasis on individual spiritual experience over communal norms. Dismissed as a 'New Age' phenomenon, they argue that the borrowing from non-Jewish traditions has had a deleterious effect on Jewish life.

Left Rabbi Zalman Schachter-Shalomi, perhaps Jewish Renewal's most prominent leader, in conversation with Tibetan Buddhist monks in Dharamsala, India, 1990.

MESSIANIC JUDAISM

AT THE CENTRE OF MESSIANIC JEWISH BELIEF AND PRACTICE IS THE CONVICTION THAT JESUS, WHO IS REFERRED TO AS YESHUA, IS THE LONG-AWAITED MESSIAH OR ANOINTED ONE.

Firmly rejected by the Jewish community as a whole, Messianic Judaism claims to be an authentic interpretation of the Jewish tradition. In the last few decades it has emerged as a controversial movement on the religious scene. Although followers see it as a legitimate interpretation of the tradition, this claim is firmly rejected by the Jewish community.

At the core of Messianic Jewish theology is the belief that Jesus (whom Messianic Jews refer to as Yeshua) is the long-awaited Messiah. Messianic believers contend that they are not Christians – rather they are determined to live Jewish lives in fulfilment of God's will. In this quest, Messianic Jews have reinterpreted the major Jewish festivals including Sabbath, Passover, Shavuot and Sukkot as well as festivals of joy and life-cycle events. At the centre of their practice and worship is the belief that the world has been redeemed and transformed.

Below Rembrandt's Head of Christ, *painted in 1748, shows the Christian Messiah as a Jewish man.*

BIRTH OF A MOVEMENT

In the early 1970s a considerable number of American Jewish converts to Christianity (known as Hebrew Christians) were committed to a church-based conception of Hebrew Christianity. At the same time emerged a growing segment of the Hebrew Christian community seeking a more Jewish lifestyle. Particularly among the youth, there was a strong urge to identify with their Jewish roots. In their view, the acceptance of Yeshua should be coupled with a commitment to the cultural and religious features of the faith.

Eventually a clear division emerged between those who wished to forge a new lifestyle and those who sought to pursue traditional Hebrew Christian goals. The advocates of change sought to persuade older members of the need to embrace Jewish values, yet they remained unconvinced. In time the name of the movement was changed to Messianic Judaism – this brought about a fundamental shift in orientation. Any return to Hebrew Christianity was ruled out, and a significant number of older members left the movement.

THEOLOGY

Messianic Judaism is grounded in the belief that Yeshua is the long-awaited Messiah. In this respect, Messianic Judaism and the earlier Hebrew Christian movement are based on the same belief system. None the less, Messianic Jews are anxious to point out there are important distinctions between their views and those of Hebrew Christians. Hebrew Christians see themselves as of Jewish origin and may desire to affirm their background, yet at the same time they

Above Messianic Jews do not celebrate Mass but they mark festivals, such as the blessing of bread and wine on the Sabbath.

view themselves as coming into the New Covenant. The Old Covenant has passed away. Hence, the direct practice of anything Jewish is contrary to their being part of the new people of God and the body of Christ. Messianic Jews, however, believe that the Jew is still called by God.

In the view of Messianic Jews, all of the prophecies in the *Tanakh* (Hebrew Bible) relating to messianic atonement were fulfilled in Yeshua. Repeatedly they affirm that the Messiah Yeshua came to the Jews, and his followers transmitted his message to the world. Although the Torah demands a blood sacrifice, the Messiah is able to offer himself as a means of atonement. Whereas traditional Judaism stresses that human effort is futile, what is required instead is belief in God's word and acceptance of the Messiah's atonement for sin. Only in this way can the faithful receive God's forgiveness and the promise of salvation.

Messianic Judaism asserts the world will be changed during the Second Coming. Drawing on the Suffering Servant passages in the Book of Isaiah, Messianic Jews argue that Yeshua fulfilled this role on earth but he will come again to deliver the world, defeat Israel's enemies, and establish God's Kingdom on earth.

Above Members of Sha'ar Adonai, a Messianic congregation, dancing in Central Park in New York.

Right A painting of Jesus, the Virgin and the Child *by Jewish master Marc Chagall. The artist stresses the Jewishness of Jesus as the suffering Messiah.*

OBSERVANCE

Messianic Jews see themselves as the true heirs of the early disciples of the risen Lord. Anxious to identify with the Jewish nation, Messianic Jews have sought to observe the central biblical festivals. In their view, the Sabbath and the various festivals prescribed in Scripture are as valid today as they were in ancient times.

Customs regulating the life-cycle and lifestyle of Jews in biblical times are binding on members of the Messianic community. Believers are united in their loyalty to the Jewish heritage as enshrined in Scripture.

None the less, Messianic Jews are not legalistic in their approach to Judaism. Traditional observance is tempered with the desire to allow the holy spirit to permeate the Messianic community and animate believers in their quest to serve the Lord. For this reason, there is considerable freedom among Messianic Jews in the ways they incorporate the Jewish tradition into their daily lives.

Right Minister Jacques Elbaz preaches to Messianic Jews in Tel Aviv, Israel.

The nature of contemporary Messianic practice, means that congregations do not rigidly follow the patterns recommended in the various Messianic prayer books produced by the movement; instead, they modify their observance in accordance with their own spiritual needs. Visitors to Messianic congregations will thus be struck by the considerable variation that exists within the movement.

נקיון העיר בידך !

CHAPTER 4

UNTRADITIONAL JUDAISM

Over the last two centuries, new interpretations of Jewish life have emerged. In the 1900s, Zionist thinkers argued a Jewish commonwealth must be established in the Holy Land. A few religious Zionists argued Jewry must actively bring about the creation of a Jewish presence in Palestine prior to the arrival of the Messiah. Secular Zionists maintained Jews would never be secure from anti-Semitism unless they had a nation state.

In recent years, other non-traditional movements have emerged in the Jewish community. Modern Kabbalists have tried to revitalize traditional Kabbalistic doctrines in the quest to live a more spiritual life. Jewish socialists have pressed for the restructuring of modern society. Jewish feminists have pressed for gender equality. Jewish Buddhists have reinterpeted Judaism. Jewish vegetarians espouse animal welfare. Other Jews advocate the acceptance of the pluralistic nature of modern Jewish life. Today Jews in Israel and the Diaspora follow a wide variety of different and conflicting paths in their quest to live an authentically Jewish existence.

Opposite The years following the establishment of the State of Israel in 1948 saw the creation of many Jewish posters, such as this one from 1955 stressing environmental urban issues.

Above Jewish women reach out to touch the Western Wall in Jerusalem, 2010. In modern times, Jewish feminists have re-evaluated the role of women in Jewish life.

RELIGIOUS ZIONISM

TRADITION IS THAT THE MESSIAH WILL LEAD THE JEWS BACK TO ZION. IN CONTRAST, RELIGIOUS ZIONISTS ADVOCATED THE RETURN OF JEWRY TO ISRAEL IN ANTICIPATION OF MESSIANIC DELIVERANCE.

For thousands of years Jews anticipated that the coming of the Messiah would bring about a final ingathering of the Jewish people to their ancient homeland. This was to be a divinely predetermined miraculous event, which will inaugurate the messianic age. However, in the early 19th century within religious Orthodox circles there emerged a new trend, the advocacy of an active approach to Jewish messianism.

THE STIRRINGS OF RELIGIOUS ZIONISM

At the beginning of the 19th century, a number of Jewish writers maintained that, rather than adopt a passive attitude towards the problem of redemption, the Jewish nation must engage in the creation of a homeland in anticipation of the advent of the Messiah. Pre-eminent

Below A Theological Debate *by Eduard Frankfort, 1888. By this date, the idea of a Jewish state was being fiercely debated among Orthodox Jews.*

among such religious Zionists was Yehuda hai Alkalai, born in 1798 in Sarajevo to Rabbi Sholomo Alkalai, the spiritual leader of the local Jewish community. During his youth, Yehuda lived in Palestine, where he was influenced by Kabbalistic thought. In 1825 he published a booklet entitled *Shema Yisrael* in which he advocated the establishment of Jewish colonies in Palestine, a view at variance with the traditional Jewish belief that the Messiah will come through an act of divine deliverance.

When in 1840 the Jews of Damascus were charged with the blood libel (killing a child and using its blood in an act of ritual), Alkalai became convinced that the Jewish people could be secure only in their own land. Henceforth he published a series of books and pamphlets explaining his plan of self-redemption. In *Minhat Yehuda* he argued on the basis of the Hebrew Scriptures that the Messiah will not miraculously materialize; rather, he will be preceded by various preparatory

Above Abraham Isaac Kook, philosopher, mystic and defender of religious Zionism, who became the first Ashkenazi chief rabbi of Palestine before independence.

events. In this light the Holy Land needs to be populated by Jewry in preparation for messianic deliverance. For Alkalai, redemption is not simply a divine affair – it is also a human concern requiring labour and persistence.

THE GROWTH OF RELIGIOUS ZIONISM

Another early pioneer of religious Zionism was Zvi Hirsch Kalischer, the rabbi of Toun in the province of Posen, in Poland. An early defender of Orthodoxy against the advances made by Reform Judaism, he championed the commandments in prescribing faith in the Messiah and devotion to the Holy Land. In 1836 he expressed his commitment to Jewish settlement in Palestine in a letter to the head of the Berlin branch of the Rothschild family. The beginning of redemption, he maintained, will come through natural causes by human effort to gather the scattered of Israel into the Holy Land. Later he published *Derishat Zion.* In this work he argued that the redemption of Israel will not take

place miraculously. Instead, it will occur slowly through awakening support from philanthropists and gaining the consent of other nations to the gathering of the Jewish people into the Holy Land.

Following in the footsteps of Alkalai and Kalischer, Abraham Isaac Kook formulated a vision of messianic redemption integrating the creation of a Jewish state. Born in Latvia in 1865, Kook received a traditional Jewish education and in 1895 became rabbi of Bausk. In 1904 he emigrated to Palestine, eventually becoming the first Ashkenazi chief rabbi after the British Mandate. Unlike secularists who advocated practical efforts to secure a Jewish state, Kook embarked on the task of reinterpreting the Jewish religious tradition to transform religious messianic anticipation into the basis for collaboration with the aspirations of modern Zionism.

ORTHODOXY AND RELIGIOUS ZIONISM

Although some Orthodox Jewish figures endorsed the Zionist movement, Orthodoxy in Germany, Hungary and Eastern European countries protested against this new development in Jewish life.

To promote this policy, an ultra-Orthodox movement, Agudat Yisrael, was created to unite rabbis and laity against Zionism. Determined to counter Zionist ideology, Agudat denounced the policies of modern Zionists and refused to collaborate with religious Zionist parties such as the Mizrachi. In Palestine itself the extreme Orthodox movement joined with Agudat Israel in its struggle against Zionism.

Eventually, however, these critics of Zionist aspirations modified their position and began to take a more active role in Jewish settlement. This was owing to the immigration of members of Agudat Yisrael to Palestine, as well as the massacre of Orthodox Jews in Hebron, Safed and Jerusalem during the riots of 1929. None the less, the ultra-right refused to join the National Council of Palestinian Jewry, which had been established in the 1920s. In the next decades the rise of the Nazis and the events of the Holocaust brought about a split in the movement.

In 1934 Isaac Breuer, a leading Orthodox spokesman, cautioned that it would be a mistake to leave Jewish

Left Hasidic Jew in Mea Shearim, home to ultra-Orthodox Jews in Jerusalem, 1985. Some Hasidic Jews oppose the idea of a Zionist state.

Above Entrance to a house in Mea Shearim, Jerusalem, a quarter outside the Old City walls, whose name means 'Hundred Gates'.

history to the Zionists. If Agudat wished to gain the upper hand against the Zionists, it was obligated to prepare the Holy Land for the rule of God. In the unfolding of God's providential plan, he declared, the extreme Orthodox had a crucial role to play. Between the end of the war and the founding of the Jewish state, a zealous extreme group, the Neturei Karta in Jerusalem, accused the Agudat of succumbing to the Zionists. Yet, despite such criticism, the leaders of Agudat continued to support the creation of a Jewish homeland, and a year before its establishment they reached an understanding with Palestinian Zionists concerning such matters as Sabbath observance, dietary laws and regulations regarding education and marriage. Such a conciliatory policy paved the way for the creation of Orthodox religious parties in Israel, which continue to play a central role in the government of the Jewish state. Today, religious Zionists in Israel and the Diaspora regard the modern State of Israel as the fulfilment of God's promise to Abraham, Isaac and Jacob.

SECULAR ZIONISM

IN THE 1880S AND 90S SECULAR ZIONISTS PROMOTED THE CREATION OF A JEWISH HOMELAND IN PALESTINE. IN THEIR VIEW, ONLY THE CREATION OF A JEWISH STATE WOULD PROTECT JEWS FROM THEIR ENEMIES.

The Russian pogroms of 1881–2 forced many Jews to emigrate to the United States, but a sizeable number were drawn to Palestine. These earlier pioneers were the vanguard of the Zionist movement, which agitated for the creation of a Jewish commonwealth in the Holy Land. In their view, anti-Semitism was inevitable; hence, they argued, Jewry could only be secure in a country of their own. This ideology was fuelled by an intense commitment to Jewish survival in a hostile world.

ORIGINS

In the Russian Pale of Settlement, nationalist zealots organized Zionist groups (Lovers of Zion) which collected money and organized courses in Hebrew and Jewish history. In 1882 several thousand Jews left for Palestine, where they worked as shopkeepers and artisans; other

Below Portrait of Theodor Herzl, founder of political Zionism, painted in 1914 on the eve of World War I.

Jewish immigrants known as Bilu (from the Hebrew 'House of Jacob, let us go') combined Marxist ideals with Jewish nationalist fervour and worked as farmers and labourers.

During this period, Leo Pinsker, an eminent Russian physician, published *Autoemancipation* in which he argued that the liberation of Jewry could only be secured by the establishment of a Jewish homeland. 'Nations', he wrote, 'live side by side in a state of relative peace, which is based chiefly on fundamental equality between them. But it is different with the people of Israel. This people is not counted among the nations, because when it was exiled from its land it lost the essential attributes of nationality.'

THE ZIONIST MOVEMENT

In the 1890s the idea of Jewish nationalism had spread to other countries in Europe. Foremost among its proponents was the Austrian journalist Theodor Herzl (1860–1904) who was profoundly influenced by the Dreyfus affair. In 1897, the first Zionist Congress took place in Basle, which called for a national home for Jews based on international law. At this congress Herzl stated that emancipation of the Jews had been an illusion. Jews were everywhere objects of contempt and hatred. The only solution to the Jewish problem, he argued, was the re-establishment of a Jewish homeland in Palestine.

In the same year the Zionist Organization was created with branches in Europe and America. After establishing these basic institutions of the Zionist movement, Herzl embarked on diplomatic

Above French editor Jean Jaurès, one of the most energetic defenders of Alfred Dreyfus. The Dreyfus affair persuaded Theodor Herzl of the necessity of a Jewish state to protect Jews.

negotiations. In 1898 he met with Kaiser Wilhelm II (ruled 1888–1918) who promised he would take up the matter with the Sultan. When nothing came of this, Herzl himself attempted to arrange an interview, and in 1901 a meeting with the Sultan took place. In return for a charter of Jewish settlement in Palestine, Herzl suggested that wealthy Jewish bankers might be willing to pay off the Turkish debt. In the following year the Sultan agreed to approve a plan of Jewish settlement throughout the Ottoman empire but not a corporate Jewish homeland in Palestine.

Unwilling to abandon a diplomatic approach, Herzl sought to cultivate contacts in England. In 1903 Joseph Chamberlain, the Secretary of State for Colonial Affairs, suggested the possibility of Uganda as a homeland for the Jews. At the next Zionist Congress in Basle this proposal was presented for ratification. When Chamberlain's scheme was explained, it was emphasized that Uganda was not meant to serve as a permanent solution but

Above During an 1880s pogrom in Kiev, Russian Jews were assaulted while police did nothing. Such attacks convinced Zionists of the need for a Jewish state.

rather as a temporary residence. When the resolution was passed by a small margin, delegates from eastern Europe walked out. Eventually the offer was withdrawn.

EVOLUTION
After Herzl's death in 1904, David Wolffsohn became President of the Zionist movement. Under his leadership Orthodox Jews joined the Zionist Organization as members of the Mizrahi Party; socialist Jews also became members through the Labour Zionist Party. In the 1907 congress a resolution was passed which pledged the movement to the quest for a charter, the physical settlement of Palestine and the revival of the Hebrew language. During the next decade the major developments in the Zionist movement took place in Israel and by the beginning of the 20th century a sizeable number of Jews had migrated to Palestine.

Most of these pioneers lived in cities, but a small minority worked on farm colonies under the control of the Palestine Jewish Colonization Association. By 1929 the Jewish community in Palestine (*yishuv*) numbered 160,000 with 110 agricultural settlements; in the next ten years the community increased to 500,000 with 233 agricultural communities. During this time, rival Jewish factions emerged within Palestine with different political

Above Arabs ready to attack Jewish buses from Jerusalem, 1948. As the Jewish population in Palestine increased, Zionists were constantly threatened by Arabs.

orientations. The President of the World Zionist Congress, Chaim Weizmann (1874–1952), for example, was committed to co-operating with the British. Vladimir Jabotinsky (1880–1940), leader of the Union of Zionist Revisionists, stressed that the central aim of Zionism was the establishment of an independent state in the whole of Palestine.

THE CREATION OF A JEWISH STATE

The Holocaust and the establishment of the State of Israel were organically related events: the death of millions of Jews in World War II profoundly affected Jewry throughout the world.

Left David Ben-Gurion, the first Prime Minister of modern Israel, appointed two days after independence.

During the war and afterwards, the British prevented illegal immigrants entering the Holy Land. In response, Jewish military forces joined together in resisting British policy. Eventually the British Government handed the problem of Palestine over to the United Nations. The UN discussed the Palestinian problem in May 1947. A special committee issued two reports; a minority recommended a federated bi-national state; the majority advocated a new plan of partition with a Jewish and Arab state as well as an international zone in Jerusalem.

This latter proposal was endorsed by the General Assembly of the United Nations on 29 November 1947. Once the UN plan of partition was endorsed, the Arabs began to attack Jewish settlements. By March 1948 more than thousand Jews had been killed, but in the next month David Ben-Gurion (1886–1973) ordered the Haganah to link up all the Jewish enclaves and consolidate the territory given to Israel under the UN partition plan.

On 14 May 1948 Ben-Gurion read out the Scroll of Independence in which he reiterated the goal of the Zionist movement: 'The Land of Israel was the birthplace of the Jewish people ... In the year 1897 the First Zionist Congress, inspired by Theodor Herzl's vision of the Jewish State, proclaimed the right of the Jewish people to national renewal in their own country.'

MODERN KABBALISM

DRAWING ON ANCIENT KABBALISTIC TEACHING, MODERN KABBALISTS STRESS THE IMPORTANCE OF JEWISH MYSTICAL BELIEF AND PRACTICE. IN RECENT YEARS, THE KABBALAH CENTRE HAS ATTRACTED MILLIONS.

In contemporary society the Kabbalistic tradition has served as a rich spiritual resource for many Jews. In their quest to attain enlightenment, these religious seekers have embraced the teachings of modern Kabbalists. Pre-eminent among contemporary mystics Rav Philip Berg has drawn millions of Jews to the Kabbalistic tradition through the creation of Kabbalah Centres throughout the Jewish world.

ORIGINS

The fundamentals of the medieval Kabbalistic system were expanded by such luminaries as Moses Cordovero, Isaac Luria, the Ba'al Shem Tov, Nachman of Bratslav, Levi Yitzhak of Berdichev, Kalonymus Kalman Epstein, Dov Baer of Mezhirich and Shneur Zalman. In

Below The Chamsah, an amulet used to ward off the evil eye, from Safed, Israel, where Kabbalah developed.

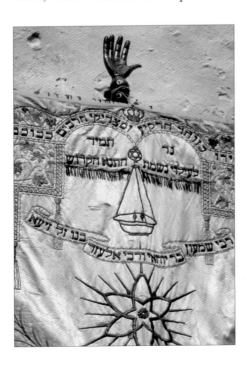

the modern period, interest in Kabbalistic thought outside the Hasidic circle generally diminished with the exception of such figures as Yehuda Ashlag, the author of *Sulam*, or 'Ladder', who influenced the development of popular Kabbalah. In recent years through his disciple Rav Berg, the international Kabbalah Centre has today become the most influential proponent of Kabbalistic thought worldwide.

Born in Warsaw in 1885, Ashlag was a descendent of scholars connected to the Hasidic courts of Prosov and Belz. In 1921 he moved to Palestine and worked as a labourer; later he was appointed rabbi of Givat Shaul, Jerusalem. In the 1930s he gathered around him a group of disciples who studied Kabbalah and promoted the study of Kabbalistic doctrine even for those who had not mastered rabbinic texts. In his view, knowledge of Kabbalah can provide all persons with a taste of Godliness that will enable them to conquer their evil inclinations and advance spiritually.

During this period Ashlag published *The Talmud of the Ten Sephirot*, which was a reworking of the thought of Isaac Luria; in addition he wrote an extensive commentary on the Zohar. In this work Ashlag stressed the transformation of human consciousness from a state of desiring to receive, to desiring to give. Through the study of Kabbalah, he believed, the mind opens to God's light, and the desire to give to others is developed. Ashlag believed that the coming of the Messiah meant that humans would give up their selfishness and devote themselves to loving each other.

Above American rabbi Philip Berg of the Kabbalah Centre, which has had a powerful effect on Jews seeking inspiration from the Kabbalistic tradition.

THE KABBALAH CENTRE

Ashlag's main disciples included his sons Baruch Shalom and Shlomo Benyamin as well as Rabbi Yehuda Brandwein. Rabbi Baruch and Rabbi Brandwein influenced students who spread Ashlag's interpretation of Kabbalah. Brandwein's son-in-law Rabbi Avraham Sheinberger founded a commune in Israel, Or Ganuz, or 'The Hidden Light', which combines Ashlag's communal ideas with a devotion to Kabbalistic teaching.

In 1962 Rabbi Brandwein met Rav Philip Berg who had visited Israel from America. Trained in traditional yeshivot, Rav Berg was no longer a practising rabbi, but was deeply influenced by Rabbi Brandwein's teaching. In his autobiography, *Education of a Kabbalist*, Berg explained that he received the honour and responsibility of bringing the ancient wisdom of Kabbalah to the world.

As Brandwein's devoted student, Berg established the Kabbalah Research Centre, which today has 50 branches worldwide and has become the leading educational institution teaching the wisdom of the Kabbalah. Together with his sons Michael Berg and Yehuda Berg, Rav Berg has spread Kabbalistic teaching to millions of

Above The return of Jewish mysticism is marked by a deepening interest in the way of Kabbalah.

adherents. In a wide range of publications the Bergs have spread Ashlagian Kabbalism to disciples seeking spiritual knowledge and insight.

KABBALISTIC THEOLOGY

Of central importance in the Kabbalistic system propounded by Rabbi Ashlag as explained by Rabbi Brandwein is the Desire to Share. This, he argued, should replace the Desire to Receive. According to Brandwein, human beings have been the gift of the desire to receive; this can be understood as an unusually large spiritual vessel containing the divine light. Yet it is a mixed blessing. Although it allows them to be persons to be filled with light, it can block them from true goodness. If individuals cannot transform their desire to receive into a Desire to Share, this will have the most negative results. The Desire to Receive will grow larger and larger until it swallows everything around it. Human history, Brandwein observed, is simply a record of self-serving desire run rampant, fuelled by hatred, envy and distrust.

Developing Brandwein's views, Rav Berg explains how spiritual growth is possible. Our souls, he asserted, are created for one reason only – the Creator in whom all things are invested, had a Desire to Share. But, when the Creator existed alone, sharing could not occur. There were no vessels to hold the endless bounty pouring out of him. So, with nothing more than desire, he created those vessels which are our souls. Initially these created souls received the divine light with no motive other than to receive for themselves alone. But as they were filled, a new yearning evolved – one that put them on a collision course with the Creator. Suddenly, in emulation of the Creator, our souls developed a Desire to Receive for the purpose of sharing. But they were faced with the same dilemma as that which faced the Creator himself before he created the vessels. With every soul filled, there was no one and nothing with whom to share.

Thus what Berg referred to as the 'Bread of Shame' came into being. This was shame at receiving so much and giving nothing in return. Shame at being in a position in which the soul had no opportunity to say yes or no to the Creator and, by that exercise of will, prove itself worthy to receive and thus dispel the shame. The shame led to rebellion – a mass rejection of the Creator's beneficence. When that happened, the light was withdrawn, darkness and the unclean worlds were created and all became finite – or limited – and thus in need of receiving. With those worlds came the clay bodies – vessels desiring only to receive for themselves alone – in which our souls reside. Here they forever struggle against body energy, to share. For the modern Kabbalist, this quest to eliminate the 'Bread of Shame' by sharing with others is the fundamental spiritual goal.

Below Kabbalistic Jews mark the end of the Sabbath with Havdalah, reciting blessings over wine, a candle and spices.

THE JEWISH LEFT

IN THE LATE 19TH CENTURY SOCIALIST IDEALS INSPIRED A GROWING SEGMENT OF THE JEWISH COMMUNITY. CONTINUING THIS TRADITION, THE JEWISH LEFT PROMOTES SOCIAL ACTION IN MANY CONTEXTS.

The term Jewish Left refers to Jews who identify with or support left-wing causes either as individuals or through organizations. The Jewish Left is not a movement, yet those who support this political stance have been identified with various groups, including the US labour movement, the women's rights movement and anti-fascist organizations.

In contemporary society many well-known figures on the left have been Jews; these individuals were born into Jewish families and have in various ways been connected with the Jewish community, Jewish culture and the Jewish faith.

ORIGINS
In the age of industrialization in the 19th century, a Jewish working class emerged in Eastern and Central Europe. Before long, a Jewish labour movement had emerged. The Jewish Labour Bund (or federation) was formed in Vilna in Lithuania in 1897. In addition, Jewish anarchist and socialist organizations were formed and spread across the Jewish Pale of Settlement in the Russian Empire. As Zionism grew in numbers, socialist Zionist parties were established. There were also non-Zionist left-wing forms of Jewish nationalism, such as territorialism (which advocated the creation of a Jewish national home but not necessarily in Palestine), autonomism (which supported non-territorial national rights for Jews in multinational empires), and folkism (which celebrated Jewish culture).

As Eastern European Jews emigrated in the 1880s, these ideological positions took root in various Jewish communities, particularly in England, New York and Buenos Aires. In the United States, the Jewish socialist movement embraced various organs including the Yiddish-language daily, the *Forward*, trade unions such as the International Ladies Garment Workers' Union, and the Amalgamated Clothing Workers.

Above Rose Pesotta, a Ukrainian Jew who came to the USA in 1917, became a feminist organizer and vice president of the International Ladies' Garment Workers' Union.

In the late 19th and early 20th centuries, Jews played a major role in the Social Democratic parties in Germany, Russia, Austria–Hungary and Poland.

STALINISM AND FASCISM
Many Jews worldwide welcomed the Russian Revolution of 1917, celebrating the eclipse of a regime which had fostered anti-Semitism. In their view, the new order in Russia would bring about the amelioration of Jewish life. A number of Jews joined the Communist party in Great Britain and the United States. As a result, there were Jewish sections of various Communist parties such as the Yevsektsiya in the Soviet Union. In the USSR the Communist regime adopted an ambivalent attitude

Left Many Jews welcomed the Russian Revolution. These members of the Jewish Society in St Petersburg are holding a banner in Yiddish that reads, 'Jewish Socialist Workers Party', 1918.

fascism. During World War II the Jewish left played a major role in the resistance to Nazism.

THE LEFT IN CENTRAL AND WESTERN EUROPE

Alongside Jewish working-class movements, assimilated middle-class Jews in Central and Western Europe began to search for sources of radicalism in the Jewish tradition. Martin Buber, for example, was influenced by Hasidic texts in formulating his philosophy; Walter Benjamin was inspired by Marxism and Jewish messianism; Jacob Israel de Haan combined socialism with Orthodox Judaism; in Germany, Walther Rathenau was an important figure of the Jewish Left.

SOCIALIST ZIONISM

In the 20th century, socialist Zionism became an increasingly important factor in Palestine. Poale Zion, or 'Workers of Zion', the Histadrut labour union and the Mapai party were important in Israel and included within their ranks such politicians as Israel's first and fourth prime ministers David Ben-Gurion and Golda Meir. At the same time, the kibbutz movement was grounded in socialist ideals.

In the 1940s many on the left advocated a bi-national state in Israel/Palestine rather than an exclusively Jewish state. This position was supported by such figures as Hannah Arendt and Martin Buber. Since Israeli independence in 1948, the left has been represented by the Labour Party, Meretz and the Palestine Communist Party, Maki. There are two worldwide left-wing Zionist organizations: namely the World Labour Zionist Movement and the World Zionist Organization.

Above Political theorist Hannah Arendt, a German Jew, who reported for the New Yorker *on the war crimes trial of the Nazi Adolf Eichmann.*

towards Jewry and Jewish civilization; at times it supported the development of a Jewish national culture, yet the party also carried out anti-Semitic purges. With the rise of fascism in Europe in the 1920s and 1930s, many Jews became involved in the left, particularly within Communist circles, which were fiercely opposed to

Left This anti-Semitic cartoon of 1900 alleges Jews were plotting to destablize Russia. Many Russian Zionists supported the creation of a Jewish homeland in Palestine.

Above Israel's first and fourth prime ministers Golda Meir and David Ben-Gurion at London Airport, 1961.

THE CONTEMPORARY LEFT

The Jewish working class died out following World War II, but there are still some survivals of the Jewish working class left, including the Jewish Labour Committee and *Forward* newspaper in New York, the Bund in Melbourne, Australia, and the Labour Friends of Israel in the UK.

Throughout the 1960s and 1970s there was a renewal of interest in the West in working-class culture and in various radical positions of the past. This interest led to the development of a new form of radical Jewish organizations that were interested in Yiddish culture, Jewish spirituality and social justice, such as the New Jewish Agenda, the Jewish Socialists' Group in Britain, and the magazine *Tikkun*.

In addition, there has been a strong Jewish presence in the anti-Zionist movement, including such figures as Norman Finkelstein and Noam Chomsky. In Israel, left-wing political parties and blocs continue to play a significant role in the Jewish state.

JEWISH FEMINISM

INSPIRED BY THE FEMINIST MOVEMENT, JEWISH FEMINISM PROMOTES THE RIGHTS OF JEWISH WOMEN. CRITICAL OF MALE DOMINANCE IN RELIGIOUS LIFE, THEY WORK FOR AN EQUAL ROLE IN ALL SPHERES.

The Jewish feminist movement seeks to improve the status of women within Judaism and to open up new opportunities for religious experience and leadership. An offshoot of the feminist movement, it originated in the early 1970s in the United States and has had a profound influence on contemporary Jewish life.

ORIGINS
Jewish feminism was spurred by a grassroots development that took place in the 1970s. In the previous decade, many Jewish women had participated in the second wave of American feminism. At this time most of these women did not link their feminism to their religious or their ethnic indentification. However, eventually some women whose Jewishness was central to their self-understanding applied feminist insights to their condition as American Jewish women. Faced with a male religious establishment,

Below Jewish feminists. Politician Bella Abzug with writer Gloria Steinem and the Revd Jesse Jackson.

these women envisaged a new form of Jewish life, one that would embrace women's concerns.

At this stage two important articles appeared which pioneered the evolution of American Jewish feminism. In the fall of 1970 Trude Weiss-Rosmarin criticized the liabilities of Jewish women in 'The Unfreedom of Jewish Women' which appeared in the *Jewish Spectator* which she edited. Several months later, Rachel Adler, an Orthodox Jew, published an indictment of the status of women in *Davka*, a counter-culture journal.

THE DEVELOPMENT OF JEWISH FEMINISM
Following these publications, Jewish feminism became a public phenomenon. A small group of feminists, calling themselves Ezrat Nashim (women's help), associated with the New York Havurah, a counter-cultural fellowship and took the issue of equality of women to the 1972 convention of the Conservative Rabbinical Assembly. In meetings with rabbis and their wives, members of Ezrat

Above Bertha Pappenheim, Austrian feminist and founder of the Jüdischer Frauenbund (League of Jewish Women) in 1904.

Nashim called for a change in the status of Jewish women. In their view, women should have equal access with men in occupying public roles of status and honour in the Jewish community. The group focused on eliminating the subordination of women by equalizing their rights in marriage and divorce laws, the study of sacred texts, including women in the *minyan*, or 'quorum necessary for communal prayer', and providing

Below French feminist writer Elisabeth Badinter is a Jew and author of Mother Love: Myth and Reality *(1980).*

opportunities for women to assume positions of leadership in the synagogue as rabbis and cantors. In the same year, the Reform movement took a fundamental step in this direction by ordaining Sally Priesand as the first female Reform rabbi.

In the following year, secular and religious Jewish feminists under the auspices of the North American Jewish Students' Network convened a conference in New York City. The next year a short-lived Jewish feminist organization was founded at a similar Jewish feminist conference. As time passed, Jewish feminists brought their message to a wider audience through various publications. Activists from Ezrat Nashim and the North American Jewish Students' Network published an issue of *Responsa* magazine dedicated to Jewish feminist concerns. In 1976, an expanded version entitled *The Jewish Woman: New Perspectives* appeared. The same year a Jewish feminist magazine *Lilith* was published.

RITUALS AND RABBIS

Through their efforts, Jewish feminists gained increasing support. Innovations, such as baby-naming ceremonies, feminist Passover seders and ritual celebrations of the New Moon were introduced into communal settings in the home or synagogue. These ceremonies were

aimed at the community rather than the individual; in this way, Jewish feminists aimed to enhance women's religious roles in Jewish life. The concept of egalitarianism evoked a positive response from many American Jews. In the Reform movement, the principle of equality between the sexes became a cardinal principle. Similarly, within the Reconstructionist movement women were granted equal status, and in 1974 Sandy Eisenberg Sasso was ordained as a rabbi. In time the Conservative movement also accepted

Above Women of the Wall wear prayer shawls and tallit, ritual garments traditionally associated with men, at the Western Wall, Jerusalem, 2010.

the principle of equality: Amy Eilberg became the first female Conservative rabbi in 1985, and women were welcomed into the Conservative cantorate in 1987.

BLU GREENBERG AND JOFA

In support of feminist principles, Blu Greenberg founded the Jewish Orthodox Feminist Alliance (JOFA) in 1997 to advocate women's increased participation in modern Orthodoxy and to create a community for women and men dedicated to principles of equality. In its mission statement, JOFA declares: 'The mission of the Jewish Orthodox Feminist Alliance is to expand the spiritual, ritual, intellectual and political opportunities for women within the framework of halakha. We advocate meaningful participation and equality for women in family life, synagogues, houses of learning and Jewish communal organizations to the full extent possible within halakha.'

ORTHODOX FEMINISM

Even though the Conservative movement led the way for Jewish feminism in the 1970s and 1980s, Jewish feminism was interpreted in different ways in the Orthodox community. In 1981 Blu Greenberg made a case for Orthodox feminism in *On Being a Jewish Feminist*. Alongside this work, a small number of Orthodox feminists established women's *tefilah*, or 'prayer', groups that respected halakhic restraints on the role of women in Jewish life.

Even though the Orthodox leadership deny feminist claims of the secondary status of women within traditional Judaism, Jewish feminism has had an important impact on American Orthodoxy. Girls are provided with a more comprehensive education in Orthodox schools, and Orthodoxy has embraced such rituals as celebrations of the birth of a daughter and bat mitzvah rites.

GENDER ISSUES

WITHIN THE JEWISH WORLD THERE ARE A SUBSTANTIAL NUMBER OF
GAY AND LESBIAN JEWS. YET THE VARIOUS MOVEMENTS WITHIN JUDAISM
DIFFER IN THEIR VIEW OF HOMOSEXUALITY.

In the Western world, many states now legalize civil partnerships between people of the same sex. Orthodox Jews may condemn such unions, but some non-Orthodox communities adopt a more liberal attitude.

TRADITIONAL JUDAISM AND HOMOSEXUALITY

In the Bible, homosexual conduct between men is more frequently mentioned and condemned than homosexual practices between women. There is no reference to a homosexual tendency, rather it is the act which is forbidden. Thus Leviticus 19:20 states: 'Thou shalt not lie with mankind, as with

Below A mother and her lesbian partner with their newborn son and female rabbi, California, 2004, the first year that same-sex marriages were permitted in the US state.

Right Chabad Lubavitch Hasidim protesting at the annual gay pride parade in Tel Aviv, Israel.

womankind, it is an abomination.' Again, Leviticus 20:13 declares: 'And if a man lie with mankind, as with womankind, both of them have committed abomination; they shall surely be put to death; their blood shall be upon them.'

In the 2nd century CE, a debate is recorded in the Mishnah in which Rabbi Judah forbids two unmarried men to sleep together in the same bed, while the sages permit it. According to the Talmud, the reason why the sages disagree with Rabbi Judah is that Jews are not suspected of engaging in homosexual practices. Although the code of Jewish law records the opinion of the sages, it states: 'But in these times, when there are many loose-livers about,

a man should avoid being alone with another male.' According to the rabbis, Gentiles too are commanded by the Torah to abstain from male homosexual acts.

The sources, however, are less clear about lesbianism. The *Sifra* (midrash on Scripture) comments on Leviticus 18:3 ('After the doings of the land of Egypt wherein ye dwelt shall ye not do; and after the doings of the land of Canaan,

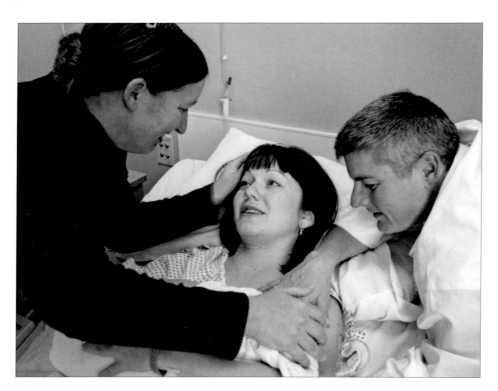

WORLD CONGRESS

Today the movement for the acceptance of gay and lesbian Jews is a worldwide phenomenon. The World Congress of Gay, Lesbian, Bisexual and Transgender Jews, Keshet Ga'avah, consists of more than 25 member organizations. The Hebrew subtitle Keshet Ga'avah – Rainbow of Pride – emphasizes the importance of Hebrew and of Israel to the World Congress. Since its establishment in 1975, conferences have been held all over the world. Their vision is 'an environment where Lesbian, Gay, Bisexual and Transgender Jews worldwide can enjoy free and fulfilling lives.'

whither I bring you, shall ye not do; neither walk in their statutes.'), stating that what is being referred to are the sexual practices of the Egyptians and the Canaanites. The sin being referred to is marrying off a man to a man and a woman to a woman. The Talmud rules that women who perform sexual acts with one another should not be viewed as harlots, but as indulging in lewd practices.

According to the 12th-century Jewish philosopher and legalist Moses Maimonides, while lesbian practices are forbidden, a woman guilty of them should not be treated as an adulteress.

CONSERVATIVE JUDAISM AND HOMOSEXUALITY

Despite such teaching, the more liberal branches of Judaism have in recent years embraced both gays and lesbians. Conservative Judaism did not allow for the ordination of openly gay men and women for over one hundred years. In addition, Conservative rabbis who performed same-sex commitment ceremonies did so without the Law Committee's sanction. Yet on 6 December 2006 the Committee on Jewish Law and Standards of the Rabbinical Assembly decreed that Conservative rabbis, synagogues and institutions can perform or host same-sex commitment ceremonies and are free to hire openly gay rabbis and cantors if they so wish. The decisions of the CJLS are only advisory, yet this body does represent the movement as a whole.

Above A same-sex couple participating in a Jewish wedding ceremony at Beverly Hills, California, in 2008.

REFORM JUDAISM

More liberal in its outlook, the Reform movement actively supports the rights of gays and lesbians. Over the last two decades the Union of American Hebrew Congregations has admitted to membership several synagogues with an outreach to gay and lesbian Jews. Hundreds of men and women who previously felt alienated from Judaism have joined these synagogues and added their strength to the Jewish community.

In 1977 the Union of American Hebrew Congregations called for an end to discrimination against homosexuals, and in 1987 they expanded upon this by calling for inclusion of gay and lesbian Jews in all aspects of synagogue life. Subsequently the movement has embarked on a programme of heightened awareness and education to achieve the fuller acceptance of gay and lesbian Jews.

Left Portrait of a gay Jewish couple marrying under the traditional huppah (a canopy with open sides) in Manhattan, New York.

JEWISH BUDDHISTS

JUBUS OR BUJUS SEEK TO BLEND THEIR JEWISH BACKGROUND WITH PRACTICES DRAWN FROM THE BUDDHIST TRADITION. THIS SPIRITUAL PATH OFFERS BELIEVERS A MEANS OF ENTRY INTO JUDAISM.

The members of the Jewish Buddhist movement (known as Jubus or Bujus) seek to combine their Jewish background with practices drawn from the Buddhist tradition. The term Jubu was first brought into circulation with the publication of *The Jew in the Lotus* by Rodger Kamenetz. The majority of Jewish Buddhists maintain their religious convictions and practices in Judaism coupled with Buddhist beliefs and observances.

The first instance of an American being converted to Buddhism in the USA occurred at the 1893 exposition on world religions. The convert, Charles Strauss, stated that he was a Buddhist at a public lecture that followed the World Conference on Religions in the same year. Strauss later became an author and an expositor of Buddhism in the West. After World War II there was an increasing interest in Buddhism among Jews associated with the Beat generation. At that time Zen Buddhism was the most widely known form of the Buddhist tradition.

In the 1960s more Jews became interested in Buddhist teachings; prominent teachers included Joseph Goldstein, Jack Kornfield and Sharon Salzberg who founded the Insight Meditation Society and learned vipassana meditation primarily through Thai teachers.

THE ATTRACTION OF JUDAISM
Jewish Buddhists report that the encounter between Jews and Buddhism leads to a journey into a deeper spirituality by blending

***Above** An iconic image of a stone Buddha embedded in tree roots at Wat Mahathat temple, Ayutthaya, Thailand.*

various elements of both traditions. For Jubus the Buddhist tradition provides a means of entry into the religious treasures of their own faith. As many individual followers are keen to point out, both Judaism and Buddhism contain a number of common practices: they both emphasize acting ethically. Each is based on a body of teachings passed on for thousands of years. Each teaches respect for spiritual teachers. Both stress that actions have consequences, but that errors can be atoned for and purified. Neither Jubus nor Bujus proselytize, though both accept newcomers. Jews and Buddhists alike treat their texts and holy objects with veneration. And significantly, some of their mystical teachings are similar.

BRIDGING TRADITIONS
On the surface it appears that the beliefs and rituals of Judaism and Buddhism could not be more different. Yet, Jubus argue that an immersion into Buddhism can serve to help Jews to discover their Jewish roots. The Jewish history of persecution and displacement, for example, is echoed by the treatment of Tibetan Buddhists at the hands of the Chinese; both Moses and the

THE JEW IN THE LOTUS

In October 1990, the Jewish poet Rodger Kamenetz journeyed to Dharamsala, India, with a small group of rabbis and other Jewish leaders. There they met the Dalai Lama, the leader of Tibetan Buddhism who had been exiled from Tibet by the Chinese regime.

The book that emerged from this expedition was *The Jew in the Lotus: A Poet's Rediscovery of Jewish Identity in Buddhist India* (1994). This volume explores Kamenetz's reflections on his own Jewishness and the attraction that Buddhism holds for a significant number of Jews whom he referred to as Jubus.

In this study, Kamenetz expounds an interpretation of Judaism that offers a new form of spirituality to Jews so they need not turn to Buddhism or anywhere else. Candidly he chronicles his own struggles with what it means to be Jewish. Without knowing why, he sensed it is not enough to be a secular Jew; rather, he insisted, life calls for a spirituality of some sort.

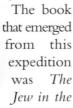

***Above** Rodger Kamenetz's* The Jew in the Lotus.

Above The Dalai Lama, the leader of Tibetan Buddhism, praying at the Western Wall in Jerusalem.

Buddha had life-changing experiences that caused them to flee the royal court: both wandered – Buddha as a yoga practitioner and Moses as a shepherd. There is also a similarity between the tree of knowledge in Genesis and the Bodhi tree under which the Buddha was first enlightened. Jubus further point out that both traditions encourage questioning and debate. Despite the icons and statues associated with Buddhism, both religions reject images and forms of the Ultimate, conceiving the Absolute to transcend all form and limitation. For some Jubus, the eight-fold path of Buddhism helps to focus their spiritual and moral life.

JUDAISM AND BUDDHISM
Critics of the Jewish–Buddhist movement are anxious to point out the differences between Judaism and Buddhism. The most conspicuous difference concerns belief in God. While Judaism is the foundation of monotheism, Buddhists do not espouse belief in a supernatural deity.

Right Singer Leonard Cohen was ordained as a Buddhist monk but says 'I'm not looking for a new religion. I'm quite happy with the old one, with Judaism.'

According to tradition, when the historical Buddha was asked whether or not God exists, he remained silent. This silence was interpreted in two ways: either he intended to demonstrate that God is beyond words, or that he considered theism as irrelevant to his doctrine. This latter approach has been widely accepted among Buddhists through the centuries.

The doctrine of no-self is also foreign to Jewish consciousness. According to Buddhist philosophy, the annihilation of the ego is conceived as seeing through the illusion of the historically conditioned self as a fixed entity. Even though Jewish

Above Rabbi David Saperstein, the Dalai Lama and Rodger Kamenetz at the Seder for Tibet, 1997, a concrete example of Jewish–Buddhist dialogue.

mysticism extols the transcendence of the ego, this path is not an end in itself. The Jewish mystic is obliged to continue to keep the mitzvot and to remain an individual member of a Jewish community. Selfhood is fundamental to the Jewish notion of obedience to the divine will. Yet, despite such observations, Jubus insist that they are living an authentic Jewish existence enlightened by insights from a rich tradition of spiritual resources.

JEWS AND THE ENVIRONMENT

ALONGSIDE CONCERNS ABOUT ANIMAL WELFARE, MANY JEWISH PEOPLE TODAY ALSO FOCUS ON THE SIGNIFICANCE OF NUMEROUS ENVIRONMENTAL THREATS.

Acid rain, the greenhouse effect, ozone layer depletion, erosion of topsoil, destruction of forests and other habitats, pollution of water and soil, and toxic waste pose fundamental problems in the modern world. Given that Judaism teaches that the earth is the Lord's and that we are to be partners and co-workers with God in protecting the environment, Jews have ecological responsibilities towards the planet. Across the religious spectrum, a growing number of Jews embrace ecological principles rooted in the tradition.

HUMAN RESPONSIBILITY FOR NATURE

In the 21st century, concern with the preservation of the planet has become of central importance. The proliferation of vast industries throughout the globe, the danger of

Above An Ultra-Orthodox Jewish man showers after bathing in the Dead Sea, where Orthodox Jews have dedicated areas. Such rituals are linked to respect for the natural world.

overpopulation, the risk of global warming – these and a range of other issues have contributed to anxiety about the ecological state of the world. In the past, these problems were not central to Judaism. On the contrary, Scripture asserts that human beings are to master the environment: 'And replenish the earth, and subdue it; and have dominion over the fish of the sea, and over the fowl of the air, and over every living thing that creepeth upon the earth' (Genesis 1:28). This does not mean, however, that in the older Jewish sources there was no concern with conservation. On the

contrary, human beings are to exercise care in dealing with nature. Human freedom to act should be in God's name and by his authority.

CREATION & STEWARDSHIP

Genesis 1.31 declares that God found all of creation 'very good'. This implies that creation is sufficient, structured and harmonious. Scripture teaches that God has absolute ownership over creation. The environmental implications are that human beings are not to misuse nature. Everything belongs to God – as a consequence the use of the natural world must always be related to the larger good, and human concerns should not be elevated above everything else. Having been created in the image of God, humans are to have a special place and role. Of all of God's creatures, only they have the power to disrupt the natural world. This power comes from special characteristics that no other creature possesses. Humanity was placed on earth to act as God's agents and to actualize his presence as his stewards.

Left Much of the Amazon rainforest has been destroyed in recent years. Jewish environmentalists seek to take responsibility for protecting the planet from such devastation.

LOVE AND AWE

As God's representatives on earth, humanity is connected to the rhythms of nature, the biogeochemical cycles, and the complex diversity of ecological systems. In Judaism, human responsibility growing out of such awareness is perceived as the fulfilment of the commandment to love and fear God. As the 12th-century Jewish philosopher Maimonides explained in the *Mishnah Torah*: 'When a person observes God's works and God's great and marvellous creatures, and they see from them God's wisdom that is without estimate or end, immediately they will love God, praise God and long with a great desire to know God's great name ... And when a person thinks about these things they draw back and are afraid and realizes that they are small lowly and obscure, endowed with slight and slender intelligence, standing in the presence of God who is perfect knowledge.'

THE BIBLE AND THE ENVIRONMENT

A central text in understanding the Jewish concern for the environment concerns the prohibition of cutting down trees in a time of war. Deuteronomy 20:19–20 teaches: 'When in your war against a city you have to besiege it a long time in order to capture it, you must not destroy the trees wielding the axe against them. You may eat of them, but you must not cut them down. Are trees of the field human to withdraw before you into the besieged city? Only trees that you know do not yield field food may be destroyed; you may cut them down for constructing siegeworks against the city that is waging war on you, until it has been reduced.'

In rabbinic sources this law was expanded to include the prohibition of the wanton destruction of household goods, clothes, buildings,

springs, food and the wasteful consumption of anything. The underlying idea is the recognition that everything we own belongs to God. When we consume in a wasteful manner, we damage creation and violate the commandment to use creation only for legitimate ends. Restraint in consumption is hence a cardinal value within the tradition.

THE SABBATH

Sabbath observance is one way to engender this sense of love and humility before creation. For one day out of seven, observant Jews limit their use of resources. Traditionally

Above Since Israel's founding in 1948, agriculture and ecology has played an important part there. Poster of an Israeli farmer harvesting grapes, 1949.

they do not do any work; the day is set aside for contemplation of the meaning of life.

Through Sabbath prayer the Jewish community is able to recognize that everything comes from God. Hence when Jews recite a blessing, they create a sacred pause in the flow of time to contemplate their place in the universe. At this moment they can see the world as an object of divine concern and place themselves beyond selfish desire.

95

JEWISH VEGETARIANISM

IN THE MODERN WORLD, A GROWING NUMBER OF JEWS FROM ACROSS THE RELIGIOUS SPECTRUM HAVE EMBRACED VEGETARIANISM AS AN AUTHENTIC MODE OF JEWISH LIVING.

Many people see Jewish vegetarianism as both a philosophy and a life style based on Jewish theology.

THE BIBLICAL BACKGROUND

According to Rabbi Abraham Isaac Kook (1865–1935), the first chief rabbi of Israel, vegetarianism is the ideal, symbolizing the ultimate peace between human beings and the animal kingdom. In his view, in the Messianic Age as prophesied in the Book of Isaiah, everyone will adopt a vegetarian diet. The only sacrifices that will be offered in the Temple will be the minhah sacrifice, which is of vegetable origin. Even though

Below Jewish rug depicting Adam and Eve, made in Turkey, late 19th century. According to tradition, humans were vegetarian until the time of the Flood.

there has been some debate regarding Kook's consistency in following a vegetarian diet, Rabbi She'ar Yashuv Cohen, the Chief Rabbi of Haifa, declared: 'I am a vegetarian, following in the footsteps of my late father, Rabbi David Cohen, and his teacher, the saintly first Chief Rabbi of Israel, Abraham Isaac Kook.'

According to Jewish vegetarians, in the ideal state of Gan Eden (the Garden of Eden) humans were described as vegetarian, and this state of affairs continued until after the Great Flood in the time of Noah. Other prominent figures who have followed a vegetarian lifestyle based on such biblical ideas include Rabbi David Rosen, former Chief Rabbi of Ireland, the late Rabbi Shlomo Goren, Chief Rabbi of Israel, and Avraham Burg, an elected Knesset Speaker.

Above Abraham Isaac Kook, 20th-century philosopher, who promoted vegetarianism as a Jewish ideal.

ETHICAL PRINCIPLES

Judaism forbids the infliction of unnecessary pain and suffering. The principle of *tsaar baalei hayyim*, or 'preventing the suffering of living creatures', is extolled in biblical and rabbinic sources. Although this principle is not explicitly formulated in Scripture, it is based on biblical teaching concerning the compassionate treatment of God's creatures. Such an attitude shows an early appreciation of the sentiency of other creatures, and according to the rabbis, Israel was unique among the nations in advocating this approach.

On this assumption, rabbinic codes of law enshrine the principle of tsaar baalei hayyim as an important feature of the faith. Specifically, the rabbis continued to legislate concerning Sabbaths and festivals. For example, rabbinic legislation stipulates that animals – like human beings – should be allowed to move about wearing bandages and splints for their wounds, and that cushions should be supplied if needed.

Further, one is allowed to put salve and oil on an animal's wound and seek assistance of a gentile if milking is required. Again, it is

allowed to put an animal in cold water so as to cool it off as a remedy for congestion, or raise it out of a body of water into which it has fallen. It is also permitted to relieve a burden from an animal if it is in pain. Given the centrality of this concept of tsaar baalei hayyim, Jewish vegetarians maintain that their life style is the ideal ethical option, one that more clearly approximates to the original will of the creator.

HEALTH CONCERNS

Recently a number of medical scientists have stressed that a plant-based diet is more healthy than a diet which includes meat. The Jewish tradition emphasizes the importance of maintaining health. Hence Jews are commanded in Deuteronomy 4:15: 'You shall guard yourselves most diligently.' This implies that everything possible must be done to protect health and avoid unnecessary risks. Further, Jews are obliged to 'choose life above all'. (Deuteronomy 30:19). The Talmud states that a danger to health takes precedence over ritual obligations. The Torah also declares that preven-

tion is the highest form of health. In this light, Jewish vegetarians maintain that they are following both biblical and rabbinic principles in adopting a vegetarian lifestyle.

In this regard, Jewish vegetarians point out that elevated blood cholesterol levels, high blood pressure and diabetes, all of which contribute to heart disease, can be alleviated by a high fibre, low-fat vegetarian diet coupled with a vigorous regime of exercise and stress reduction.

Similarly, the risk of lung cancer may be increased by animal-fat consumption. Meat consumption is a major risk factor for prostate cancer. Breast cancer may be linked with higher oestrogen levels and may reflect childhood dietary practices. Cancer of the colon is strongly linked to red and white meat consumption. Further, meat consumption is a risk factor for pancreatic cancer. Ovarian cancer has also been linked with dairy, egg and meat consumption.

Left Jewish writer and Nobel Prize winner Isaac Bashevis Singer eating a vegetarian lunch in his apartment in Miami Beach, Florida, 1981.

Above The deforestation of the Amazon in recent years is an issue important to Jews concerned with the conservation of our planet.

Further, lymphoma has been linked with beef and dairy consumption. Finally, the risk of bladder cancer in non-vegetarians is twice that of vegetarians.

ECOLOGICAL CONCERNS

As an extension of the concern with animal welfare, many Jewish vegetarians also focus on the significance of numerous environmental threats. Acid rain, the greenhouse effect, ozone layer depletion, erosion of topsoil, destruction of forests and other habitats, pollution of water and soil, and toxic waste pose fundamental problems in the modern world.

Given that Judaism teaches that the earth is the Lord's and that we are to be partners and co-workers with God in protecting the environment, Jews have ecological responsibilities towards the planet. Hence, it is vital that Jewish values be applied in the solution of these pressing problems.

PART II

JEWISH BELIEF

The Jewish religion is grounded in belief about the nature of God and his relation to the world. The God of the Jewish people has no beginning nor end; he is the eternal deity who lives forever. In this respect there is an unbridgeable gap between God and humanity: God outlasts all that he has created and continues eternally. He does not dwell in time — time itself is part of creation. Consequently God is in the Eternal Now.

According to tradition, the Bible traces God's providential care for his chosen people from their origins in the 2nd millennium BCE through the Second Temple period. For the Jews, Scripture serves as the foundation of the faith. Later rabbinic sources amplify biblical doctrines about creation, revelation, Torah and mitzvah, sin and repentance, the Promised Land, the Messiah and the afterlife.

Despite the diversity of a multitude of Jewish movements in the contemporary world, Jews today can continue to look back to their sources for an understanding of God's nature and the spiritual life.

Opposite: A 12th-century Spanish illustration of the Temple of Solomon showing the menorah, the Ark of the Covenant and other traditional symbols.

Above Jew praying at the Western Wall in Jerusalem, the only structure still standing from the Temple Mount destroyed by the Romans in 70CE.

CHAPTER 5

GOD

According to the Bible, the struggle against Canaanite belief and practice was a constant concern. Later in the rabbinic period, scholars cautioned against worshipping two gods in heaven. Worship of one God was of paramount importance. With the rise of Christianity, Jews were admonished to remain faithful to monotheism, and Jewish theologians insisted on God's unity. For the Jewish people, God is both imminent and transcendent. He created the universe, yet is in no sense remote from his creation. In the rabbinic period, Jewish sages formulated the concept of the *Shekhinah* to denote God's abiding presence. It is the Shekhinah that serves as an intermediary between God and human beings.

For God there is no past, present, nor future. In rabbinic literature, the word *emet*, or truth, one of the names of God, is interpreted as having the first, middle and final letters of the Hebrew alphabet. According to Jewish thinkers, God is both omnipotent and omniscient. His power is unlimited as is his knowledge. Past, present and future lie unrolled before his eyes, and nothing is hidden from him. It is he who has created all things in his infinite goodness. From him benevolence and compassion flow as a mighty stream.

Opposite Abraham smashing idols. From the Leipnik Haggadah (1740) by Joseph of Leipnik, the most influential scribe of the Hamburg-Altona school of Hebrew illuminated manuscripts.

Above The Creation of Adam, *in the Sistine Chapel, Rome, is one of the most famous paintings by the 16th-century artist Michelangelo.*

THE GOD OF THE JEWS

THE STORY OF THE JEWISH PEOPLE BEGAN IN MESOPOTAMIA. IT WAS HERE THAT SUCCESSIVE EMPIRES ROSE AND FELL BEFORE THE JEWS EMERGED AS A SEPARATE PEOPLE, BELIEVING IN ONE INVISIBLE GOD.

According to the Bible, Abraham was the father of the Jewish nation. Living in Ur of the Chaldeans, a Sumerian city near the head of the Persian Gulf, he was called by God to go to Canaan. As Genesis 12:1–2 records, God proclaimed: 'Go from your country and your kindred and your father's house to the land I will show you. And I will make of you a great nation.'

ANCIENT MESOPOTAMIAN RELIGION

The rise of ancient Mesopotamian civilization occurred at the end of the 4th century BCE in southern Mesopotamia, where the Sumerians created city states, each with its local

Right A vision of the prophet Jeremiah showing Greek fire, an incendiary weapon, being poured over Jerusalem. From the 12th-century Souvigny Bible.

gods. During the 3rd millennium BCE, waves of Semitic peoples settled amid the Sumerians, adopting their writing and culture. These Semites identified some of their gods with the Sumerian ones. In their view, life was under the control of the gods. To obtain happiness, it was essential to keep them in a good humour through worship and sacrifice – yet the gods were unpredictable. It was here in the 2nd century BCE that God called the Jewish nation to be his chosen people.

EARLY MONOTHEISM

According to some scholars, the origins of Israelite monotheism stemmed from Abraham's disillusionment with Mesopotamian religion. These scholars attribute this radical break to Abraham's discovery that the concept of universal justice must rest on the belief in one supreme God. Other scholars see Moses as the principal architect of Israelite monotheism. Such scholars point out that before Moses there was evidence of monotheistic belief in the religious reforms of the Egyptian Pharaoh Akhenaton in the 14th century BCE. In this light, Moses is seen as following the path of this Egyptian revolutionary figure.

MONOLATRY

There are other scholars, however, who contend that it is unlikely that monotheism can be attributed to Abraham or Moses. Such a view, they believe, conflicts with the biblical narratives of the tribal and monarchial periods that give evidence of a struggle on the part of some Israelites to remain faithful to God in the face of competing deities. For these writers, monotheism

Left Daily life in Mesopotamia, showing weaving and farming, from a wall painting in the Museum of the Jewish Diaspora in Tel Aviv, Israel.

Above The Hospitality of Abraham. *A Russian icon by Andrei Rublev, painted around 1410.*

THE PSALMIST

According to some scholars, Psalm 82 gives evidence of the transition from monolatry to monotheism: in it God rebukes the other gods for their injustice and deprives them of divine status and immortality:

God has taken his place in the
   divine council;
In the midst of the gods he holds
   judgement;
How long will you judge unjustly,
and show partiality to the wicked?
   Selah.
Give justice to the weak and the
   fatherless;

maintain the right of the afflicted
   and the destitute.
Rescue the weak and the needy;
deliver them from the hand of the
   wicked –
They have neither knowledge, nor
   understanding,
they walk about in darkness;
all the foundations of the earth are
   shaken –
I say, 'You are gods,
sons of the Most High, all of you;
nevertheless you shall die like men,
and fall like any prince.'
Arise, O God, judge the earth,
for to thee belong all the nations!

should be understood as the result of a clash of cults and religious concepts over the centuries.

According to this latter view, ancient Israelite religion was not monotheism but monolatry: the worship of one God despite the admitted existence of other gods. Arguably, this may have been the meaning of Deuteronomy 6:4: 'Hear, O Israel: the Lord our God is one

Below The Sacrifice of Isaac, *a 6th-century floor mosaic from the Bet Alpha synagogue, Israel.*

Lord.' With this view, the God of Israel was understood as the Divine Being who revealed his will to Israel, inspired its leaders, protected the Israelites in their wanderings, and led them to the Promised Land. The worship of any other deity was, according to Exodus 20:3, betrayal and blasphemy: 'You shall have no other gods before me.'

The God of Israel was not like any other gods of Mesopotamia, Egypt or Canaan, and it was forbidden to make an image of him. It was this God, not the Canaanite El, who was the creator of heaven and earth; he, not Baal, was the source of rain and agricultural fertility; it was through his action, rather than that of any of the gods of Mesopotamia, that the Assyrian and Babylonian conquest took place.

Monotheism is thus understood as a later development in the history of Israel; it took place when foreign gods were seen as simply the work of human hands. Possibly this was the view of Elijah in the 9th century BCE when, confronting the prophets of Baal, he declared: 'The Lord He is God; the Lord He is God' (1 Kings 18:39). But certainly by the time of Jeremiah (several decades before the

Babylonian exile in the 6th century BCE), monotheism appears to have taken a firm hold on the Israelite community. In the words of Jeremiah: 'Their idols are like scarecrows, in a cucumber field, and they cannot speak; they have to be carried for they cannot walk. Be not afraid of them, for they cannot do evil, neither is it in them to do good' (Jeremiah 10:5).

Below The Assyrian goddess of abundance, a stylised marble idol dating from around 1950–1700BCE.

UNITY OF GOD

THE MOST UNCOMPROMISING EXPRESSION OF GOD'S UNITY IS THE PRAYER IN DEUTERONOMY: 'HEAR, O ISRAEL, THE LORD OUR GOD IS ONE LORD.' THIS BELIEF HAS SERVED AS THE FOUNDATION OF THE FAITH.

THE REJECTION OF DUALISM

According to Scripture, the universe owes its existence to the one God, the creator of heaven and earth, and since all human beings are created in his image, all men and women are brothers and sisters. Thus the belief in one God implies that there is one humanity and one world.

At the heart of Jewish biblical teaching is an emphasis that God alone is to be worshipped. As the prophet Isaiah declared:

I am the Lord, and there is no other,
besides me there is no God; ...
I form light and create darkness,
I make weal and create woe,
I am the Lord,
  who do all these things.
  (Isaiah 45:5,7)

Within the Bible, the struggle against polytheism became a dominant motif, continuing into the rabbinic period. Combating the dualistic doctrine that there are two gods in heaven, the rabbis commented on Deuteronomy 32:39 ('See now that I, even I, am he, and there is no god beside me'): 'If anyone says that there are two powers in heaven, the retort is given to him: "There is no god with me".'

In a passage in the *Mekhilta* (midrash on Exodus), the dualistic doctrine is rejected since when God said, 'I am the Lord your God' (Exodus 20:2) no one protested. Again the Mishnah states that if a person says in his prayers, 'We acknowledge Thee, we acknowledge Thee', implying belief in two gods, he is to be silenced.

Above William Blake's vision of God writing on the Tablets of the Covenant, the laws given to Moses on Mt Sinai. For Jews, God is transcendent, yet directly involved in their history.

JUDAISM AND CHRISTIANITY

In the early rabbinic period Jewish sages were troubled by the Christian doctrine of the incarnation, which they viewed as dualistic in character. In 3rd-century CE Caesarea, for example, Abahu commented on the verse: 'God is not man, that he should lie, or a son of man, that he should repent. Has he said, and will he not do it? Or has he spoken, and will he not fulfil it?' (Numbers 23:19). According to Abahu, the last part of this verse refers to man rather than God. Thus he declared: 'If a man says to you, "I am a god", he is lying; "I am the Son of Man", he will not end by being sorry for it; "I am going up to heaven", he will not fulfil what he has said.'

In the Middle Ages the Christian doctrine of the Trinity was frequently attacked by Jewish scholars since it appeared to undermine pure monotheism. In contrast to Christian exegetes who interpreted the Shema with its three references to God as denoting the Trinity, Jewish scholars maintained that the Shema implies that there is only one God, rather

---

THE KABBALAH

In the Middle Ages. Kabbalistic belief in divine unity was also of major importance. The early Kabbalists of Provence and Spain referred to the Divine Infinite as En Sof – the absolute perfection in

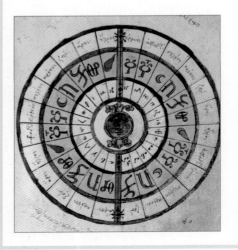

which there is no distinction or plurality. The En Sof does not reveal itself; it is beyond all thought. In Kabbalistic thought, creation is bound up with the manifestation of the hidden God and his outward movement. According to the Zohar, a mystical work of the time, the *sefirot*, or 'divine emanations', come successively from above to below, each one revealing a stage in the process. The ten sefirot together demonstrate how an infinite, undivided and unknowable God is the cause of all the modes of existence in the finite plane.

Left A 17th-century Greek codex showing the Moon surrounded by Kabbalistic symbols.

Above Torah scroll from the 16th-century Ha'ari synagogue in Safed, Israel, one of the homes of Kabbalah.

than Three Persons of the Godhead. For medieval Jewish theology, the belief in divine unity was a fundamental principle of Judaism. For a number of Jewish theologians the concept of God's unity implies that there can be no multiplicity in his being. Thus the 12th-century philosopher Moses Maimonides argued in *The Guide for the Perplexed* that no positive attributes can be predicated of God since the divine is an absolute unity. The only true attributes are negative ones; they lead to a knowledge of God because in negation no plurality is involved.

LURIANIC KABBALAH

The elaboration of early mystical ideas took place in the 16th century through the teachings of Isaac Luria. Of primary importance in the Lurianic system is the mystery of creation. In the literature of early Kabbalists, creation was understood as a positive act; the will to create

Right Prayer at the tomb in Meron, Israel, of Rabbi Simeon ben Yohai, traditionally the author of the Zohar, the most important medieval text of Kabbalistic Judaism.

was awakened within the Godhead and this resulted in a long process of emanation. For Luria, however, creation was a negative event: the En Sof had to bring into being an empty space in which creation could occur since divine light was everywhere, leaving no room for creation to take place. This was accomplished by the process of *zimzum* – the contraction of the Godhead into itself.

After this act of withdrawal a line of light flowed from the Godhead into empty space and took on the shape of the sefirot in the form of Adam Kadmon (primeval man). In this process divine lights created the vessels – the external shapes of the sefirot – which gave specific characteristics to each emanation. Yet these vessels were not strong enough to contain such pure light and they shattered. This breaking of the vessels brought disaster and upheaval to the emerging emanations: the lower vessels broke down and fell, the three highest emanations were damaged and the empty space was divided

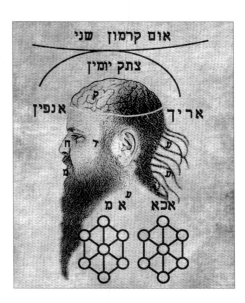

Above In Kabbalah, the term Adam Kadmon means Primeval Man. Copy of an illustration from Kabbala Denudata (1684) by Knorr von Rosenroth.

into two parts. Despite the complexity of this Kabbalistic theory of creation, Jewish mystics affirmed their belief in the unity of the Godhead. The sefirot were ten in number, yet God himself is one.

TRANSCENDENCE AND IMMANENCE

ACCORDING TO TRADITIONAL JUDAISM, GOD TRANSCENDS THE UNIVERSE YET IS MANIFEST IN HIS CREATION. THROUGHOUT SCRIPTURE GOD IS DEPICTED AS ACTIVE IN HUMAN HISTORY.

Transcendence is the concept of being entirely beyond the universe. For Jews, God is conceived as the transcendent creator of the universe. It is he who created the heavens and the earth; he reigns supreme over all creation. Yet, he does not remain remote from the cosmos. Repeatedly he is described as actively involved in the natural world and human affairs.

DIVINE TRANSCENDENCE

Throughout Scripture the theme of transcendence is repeatedly affirmed. Thus the prophet Isaiah proclaimed:

Have you not known?
Have you not heard?
Has it not been told you
　from the beginning?
Have you not understood from
　the foundations of the earth?
It is he who sits above the circle
　of the earth,

Left A 12th-century miniature of the prophet Job afflicted by boils. The book of Job considers the dual themes of God's justice and human suffering.

and its inhabitants are like
　grasshoppers;
who stretches out the heavens
　like a curtain
and spreads them like a tent
　to dwell in.
　(Isaiah 40:21–22)

Later in the same book, Isaiah declared that God is beyond human understanding:

For my thoughts are not
　your thoughts
neither are your ways my ways,
　says the Lord.
For as the heavens are higher than
　the earth,
so are my ways higher than
　your ways
and my thoughts than
　your thought.s
　(Isaiah 55:8–9)

In the Book of Job the same idea is repeated – God's purposes transcend human understanding:

Can you find out the deep things
　of God?
Can you find out the limit of the
　Almighty?
It is higher than heaven – what
　can you do?
Deeper than Sheol – what can
　you know?
Its measure is longer than the earth,
and broader than the sea.
　(Job 11:7–9)

Above North and South America from space. For Jews, God is seen as the transcendent creator of the universe.

IMMANENCE

Despite this view of God's remoteness from his creation, he is also viewed as actively involved in the created order. In the Bible his omnipresence is continually stressed.

Whither shall I go from thy Spirit?
Or whither shall I flee from thy
　presence?
If I ascend to heaven, thou art there!
If I take the wings of the morning
and dwell in the uttermost parts of
　the sea,
even there thy hand shall lead me.
　(Psalm 139:7–12)

In the rabbinic period, Jewish scholars formulated the doctrine of the *Shekhinah*, or 'divine presence', to denote God's presence in the world. The Shekhinah is compared to light. Thus the midrash paraphrases Numbers 6:25 ('The Lord make his face to shine upon you, and be gracious to you'): 'May He give thee of the light of the Shekhinah'. In another midrash, the 'shining' of the Shekhinah in the Tent of Meeting is compared to a cave by the sea. When the sea rushes in to fill the cave, it suffers no diminution of its waters. Likewise, the divine presence filled the Tent of Meeting, but simultaneously filled the world.

In the Middle Ages, the doctrine of the Shekhinah was further elaborated by Jewish scholars. According to the Jewish philosopher Saadia Gaon (9th to 10th century), the Shekhinah is identical with the glory of God, which serves as an intermediary between God and man during the prophetic encounter. For Saadia the 'Glory of God' is a biblical term whereas the Shekhinah is a rabbinic concept that refers to the created splendour of light that acts as an intermediary between God and human beings. At times this manifestation takes on human form. Thus when Moses asked to see God's glory, he was shown the Shekhinah. Similarly when the prophets in their vision saw God in human form, what they actually perceived was the Shekhinah.

In his *Guide for the Perplexed*, the 12th-century philosopher Moses Maimonides embraced Saadia's belief that the Shekhinah is a created light, identified with glory. In addition, he associated the Shekhinah with prophecy. According to Maimonides, prophecy is an overflow from God, which passes through the mediation of the active intellect and then to the faculty of imagination. It requires perfection in theoretical wisdom, morality and development of the imagination. On the basis of this conception, Maimonides asserted that human beings can be divided

Below The tide turns, and the sea floods into the cave. God is seen as actively present in his creation.

into three classes according to the development of their reasoning capabilities. First there are those whose rational faculties are highly developed and receive influences from the active intellect, but whose imagination is defective – these are wise men and philosophers. The second group consists of those where the imagination alone is in good condition, but the intellect is defective – these are statesmen, lawgivers and politicians. Thirdly there are prophets – those whose imagination is consistently perfect and whose active intellect is all developed.

In Kabbalistic teaching, the Shekhinah also played an important role. In early Kabbalistic thought it is identified as the feminine principle in the world of the *sefirot*, or 'divine emanations'. Later the Shekhinah was understood as the last in the hierarchy of the sefirot, representing

Above A vision of glory. Moses before the Burning Bush by Dieric Bouts the Elder, c.1465–70. According to Scripture, God was present in the Burning Bush.

the feminine principle. Like the moon, this sefirah has no light of her own, but instead receives the divine light from the other sefirot. As the divine power closest to the created world, she is the medium through which the divine light passes. Further, in Kabbalistic thought the Shekhinah is the divine principle of the Jewish people. Everything that happens to Israel is reflected upon the Shekhinah, which grows stronger or is weakened with every meritorious or sinful act of each Jew and of the people as a whole. Finally, the Shekhinah is viewed as the goal of the mystic who attempts to achieve communion with the divine powers.

ETERNITY

THROUGHOUT SCRIPTURE, GOD IS DESCRIBED AS HAVING NEITHER
BEGINNING NOR END. UNLIKE THE REST OF CREATION, WHICH MAY
SEE ETERNITY AS ENDLESS TIME, HE WAS, IS AND FOREVER WILL BE.

Many people have tried to define
the concept of God and eternity.
As the Psalmist declared:

Before the mountains were
    brought forth,
or ever thou hadst formed the
    earth and the world,
from everlasting to everlasting
    thou art God.
    (Psalm 90:2)

ETERNAL EXISTENCE
In the Bible the term *olam* is most
frequently used to denote the concept of God's eternity. In Genesis
21:33 he is described as the Eternal
God; he lives for ever (Deuteronomy
32:40), and reigns for ever (Exodus
15:18; Psalm 10:16). He is the living
God and everlasting King (Jeremiah

*Below Moses and Aaron show God's
power before Pharaoh by James Tissot.
For Jews, God is present in history,
having neither beginning nor end.*

10:10); his counsel endures for ever
(Psalm 33:11), as does his mercy
(Psalm 106:1). For the biblical writers, God's eternal existence is
different from the rest of creation –
he exists permanently without
beginning or end.

THE RABBIS
This biblical teaching was elaborated
by the rabbis. According to the
Talmud, there is an unbridgeable gap
between God and human beings. In
midrashic literature God's eternal
reign is similarly affirmed. Thus,
according to a midrash, when
Pharaoh was ordered by Moses and
Aaron in the name of God to let the
people go, Pharaoh declared that
God's name is not found in his list
of gods. In reply Moses and Aaron
declared: 'O fool! The dead can be
sought among the living but how
can the living be sought among the
dead. Our God lives, but those you
mention are dead. Our God is "the

*Above Some Jewish theologians think
that God is outside time altogether in
the way that sand dunes appear to
stretch on for ever.*

living God, and everlasting King"'
(Jeremiah 10:10). In response
Pharaoh asked whether this God is
young or old, how old he is, how
many cities he has conquered, how
many provinces he has subdued, and
how long he has been king. In reply
they proclaimed: 'The power and
might of our God fill the world. He
was before the world was created
and he will be when all the world
comes to an end and he has created
thee and gave thee the spirit of life.'

THEOLOGICAL SPECULATION
Although the rabbis were convinced
that God would endure for ever,
they discouraged speculation about
the nature of eternity. Such reluc-
tance is reflected in the Mishnah's
dictum: 'Whoever reflects on four
things, it were better for him that he
had not come into the world: What
is above? What is beneath? What is
before? What is after?'

In the Middle Ages, Jewish theologians debated this issue. In the
Guide for the Perplexed, the 12th-
century Jewish philosopher Moses
Maimonides argued that time itself
was part of creation. Therefore, when
God is described as existing before
the creation of the universe, the
notion of time should not be understood in its normal sense.

Above Maimonides argued that time was part of creation in his Guide for the Perplexed, *shown here in a 14th-century Italian illumination.*

This concept of time as part of creation was later developed by the 15th-century Jewish philosopher Joseph Albo. In his *Ikkarim* he maintained that the concepts of priority and perpetuity can only be applied to God in a negative sense. That is, when God is described as being 'before' or 'after' some period, this only means he was not non-existent before or after that time. However, these terms indicating a time span cannot be applied to God himself. Following Maimonides, Albo asserted that there are two types of time: measured time, which depends on motion, and time in the abstract. This second type of time has no origin – this is the infinite space of time before the universe was created.

ETERNAL NOW

According to other Jewish thinkers, God is outside time altogether – he is in the 'Eternal Now'. Thus the 13th-century theologian Bahya ibn Asher ibn Halawa, in his commentary on the Pentateuch, discussed the verse, 'The Lord will reign for ever and ever' (Exodus 15:18): 'All times, past and future, are in present so far as God is concerned, for he was before time and is not encompassed by it.' In the same way, the 16th-century scholar Moses Almosnino commented on the statement 'For now I know' (Genesis 22:12). According to Almosnino, God is in the 'Eternal Now', and he uses this notion to explain how God's foreknowledge is not incompatible with human free will.

According to these writers, God is outside time – he does not live in the present, have a past, or look forward to the future. On this view, God is experiencing every moment in the past and future history of the created world simultaneously and eternally. What for us are fleeting moments rushing by, bringing one experience after another, are for God a huge static tapestry, of which he sees every part continually. This conception of God's eternity – that he is outside time – and the alternative view that God exists in infinite duration before creation constitute the two central Jewish interpretations of the deity's relation to time. Yet for most Jews God's eternal existence is an impenetrable mystery.

None the less, the doctrine of God's eternity is a major feature of the Jewish faith. Through the centuries, Jews have been convinced that God was, is, and forever will be. Hence in Maimonides' formulation of the 13 central principles of the Jewish faith, the belief that God is eternal is the fourth tenet. In the Ani Maaimin prayer this principle is formulated as follows: 'I believe with perfect faith that the Creator, blessed be his name, is the first and the last.' And at the conclusion of synagogue services in all branches of Judaism, the faithful voice their commitment that God is eternal in time in the Adon Olam prayer:

He is the Lord of the universe,
Who reigned ere any creature yet
   was formed,
At the time when all things
   shall have had an end,
He alone, the dreaded one,
   shall reign:
Who was, who is, and who will
   be in glory.

Below Rain over the Golan Heights in Israel. Jewish thought suggests God sees every part of time continually – the time before, after and during the rain.

OMNIPOTENCE

AS LORD OF THE UNIVERSE, GOD IS CAPABLE OF ALL ACTIONS. IN
GUIDING HIS CHOSEN PEOPLE, HE BROUGHT ABOUT THEIR DELIVERANCE
AND REDEMPTION AND GUIDES THEM TO THEIR ULTIMATE DESTINY.

From biblical times, the belief in
God's omnipotence, that God is all
powerful, has been a central doctrine.

GOD IN SCRIPTURE

According to the Book of Genesis,
when Sarah expressed astonishment
at the suggestion that she should
have a child at the age of 90, she was
criticized: 'The Lord said to
Abraham, "Why did Sarah laugh,
and say 'Shall I indeed bear a child
now that I am old?' Is anything too
hard for the Lord?"' Again, in the
Book of Jeremiah, when the city was
threatened by invaders, God
declared: 'Behold I am the Lord the
God of all flesh: is anything too hard
for me?' (Jeremiah 32:27). Given
such a view, there is nothing God
cannot do. What appears impossible
is within his power.

IMPOSSIBLE ACTIONS

Despite the conviction that God can
do anything, in the Middle Ages
Jewish theologians wrestled with the
philosophical problems connected
with this belief. Pre-eminent among
their concerns was the question
whether God could do absolutely

everything. The 10th-century Jewish
philosopher Saadia Gaon, for example, in his *Book of Beliefs and Opinions*,
stated that the soul will not praise
God for causing five to be more
than ten without further addition,
nor for being able to put the world
through the hollow of a signet ring
without making the world narrower
and the ring wider, nor for bringing
back the day that has passed in its
original state. These, he argued, are
absurd acts.

Later, the 15th-century Jewish
philosopher Joseph Albo explored
the same issue. In his opinion, there
are two kinds of impossibility.

Some things are intrinsically
impossible so that even God cannot
make them possible. For example, we
cannot imagine that God can make
a part equal to the whole, a diagonal
of a square equal to one of its sides,
nor the angle of a triangle equal to
more than two right angles. Further,
it is impossible for God to make two
contradictory propositions true at
the same time, or the affirmative and
negative true simultaneously. Likewise,
it is impossible to believe that God
could create another being like himself. In all these cases, the human
intellect cannot conceive of such a
state of affairs.

The other kind of impossibility
is that which contradicts the law of
nature, such as the resurrection of
the dead. In such instances, it is possible to imagine such an occurrence.
Thus Albo argued, God can bring
about such events since they are not

inherently impossible. Hence logical
impossibilities are impossible for
God, but not physical impossibilities.

LOGICAL IMPOSSIBILITIES

The 12th-century Jewish philosopher Maimonides argued along
similar lines in his *Guide for the
Perplexed*. There he explored the
notion of God's omnipotence. In
Maimonides' view, although God is
all-powerful, there are certain actions
that he cannot perform because they
are logically impossible. That which
is impossible, he wrote, has a permanent and constant property which is

*Above The prophet Elijah wrote that
God's true spirit was not in the heart
of the storm but in the still small voice.
For Jews, God is the cause of all things.*

*Below Nothing is impossible with God.
Sarah, Abraham's ageing wife, hears
that she is to bear a son, and laughs.
Painting by French artist James Tissot.*

*Left The complex geometrical puzzles
of 20th-century artist M. C. Escher
reflect the complexity of the belief that
God can do anything.*

Above As the wave breaks on the shore and withdraws, so God allows humans space for the exercise of personal freedom.

not the result of some agent. It cannot in any way change, and thus it is a mistake to ascribe to God the power of doing what is impossible. It is impossible, he went on, for God to produce a square with a diagonal equal to one of its sides, or a solid angle that includes four right angles. Thus Maimonides concluded: 'We have thus shown that according to each one of the different theories there are things which are impossible, whose existence cannot be admitted, and whose creation is excluded from the power of God.'

THE HOLOCAUST

In addressing the religious perplexities connected with the Holocaust, a number of modern writers have advanced the concept of a limited God. In the view of these writers, God intentionally limited himself when he bestowed free will on human beings. Thus, the Orthodox rabbi and Jewish theologian Eliezer Berkovits (1908–92) argued in *Faith After the Holocaust* that if God did not respect human freedom, morality would be abolished and men and women would cease to be fully human. God, he

Right Jewish thought rules that God is all-powerful. The Creation of Adam by Michelangelo in the Sistine Chapel in Rome represents this idea.

insisted, did not intervene to save the Jewish nation because he had bestowed human free will on humanity at the time of creation.

In *God and Evil*, the Orthodox scholar David Birnbaum similarly argued that human beings must accept that God is 'Holy Potential', allowing through the process of divine contraction space for the exercise of personal freedom. In Birnbaum's view, men and women are able to attain spiritual maturity in the exercise of liberty, and thereby attain their fullest possible potential. This view serves as the basis for reconciling the tragedy of the Holocaust with the traditional understanding of God's nature.

RADICAL THEOLOGY

A more radical approach was adopted by the Reform rabbi Steven Jacobs in *Rethinking Jewish Faith*. Here he argued that the concept of God in the Bible and rabbinic Judaism must be reformulated in the post-Holocaust world. What is now needed, he wrote, is a notion of a deity compatible with the reality of radical evil at work and at play in our world. To continue to affirm the historically traditional notions of faith in God as omnipotent is a theological error. Similarly the feminist

Above Jewish quarter, Barcelona, Spain. Birthplace of Hasdai Crescas, author of Or Adonai, The Light of the Lord, *in which he wrestles with a range of theological issues.*

Jewish theologian Melissa Raphael argued in *When God Beheld God* that the patriarchal model of God should be set aside. Drawing on the records of women's experiences during the Nazi period, she offered a post-Holocaust theology of relation that affirms the redemptive presence of God at Auschwitz.

OMNISCIENCE

ACCORDING TO THE JEWISH TRADITION, GOD KNOWS ALL. YET THIS
CONCEPT GAVE RISE TO THEOLOGICAL SPECULATION ABOUT GOD'S
KNOWLEDGE OF THE FUTURE.

According to the Jewish tradition, God knows everything: past, present and future. Nothing is hidden from his sight. As an all-knowing deity, he looks down from heaven on all his creation. This does not imply that human beings lack free will since God knows in advance what their actions will be. Rather, Judaism asserts that God knows all, yet men and women possess freedom of the will.

FOREKNOWLEDGE AND FREE WILL

In line with this biblical view, rabbinic Judaism asserted that God's knowledge is not limited by space and time. Instead, nothing is hidden from him. Moreover, the rabbis stated that God's knowledge of events does not deprive human beings of free will. Thus in the Mishnah, the 2nd-century CE sage Akiva declared: 'All is foreseen but freedom of choice is given.'

In the *Guide for the Perplexed* Maimonides argued that God knows all things before they occur. None the less, human beings are unable to understand the nature of God's knowledge because it is of a different order from that of human beings. On this account, it is not possible to comprehend how divine foreknowledge is compatible with human freedom. Other medieval writers, however, were unconvinced by such an explanation. In *The Wars*

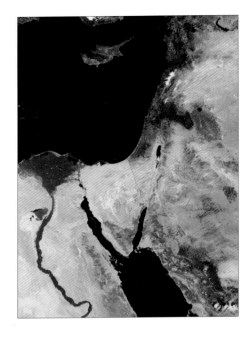

Above The Middle East and the Red Sea from the air. God's knowledge is not limited by time or space.

Below 15th-century painting of God as the divine architect. The act of creation is part of the tapestry of God's knowledge.

THE BIBLICAL VIEW
According to the Hebrew Bible, God is aware of all human action. As the psalmist proclaimed:

The Lord looks down from
  heaven,
He sees all the sons of men...
He who fashions the hearts of
  them all,
and observes their deeds.
  (Psalm 33:13,15)

Again, in Psalm 139:2–3, the psalmist declared:

Thou knowest when I sit down
  and when I rise up;
thou discernest my thoughts
  from afar.
Thou searchest out my path
  and my lying down,
and art acquainted
  with my ways.

of the Lord, the 14th-century theologian Gersonides argued that only God knows things in general. Hence the world is constituted so that a range of possibilities is open to human beings. Since men and women are able to exercise free will, these are possibilities rather than certainties, which they would be if God knew them in advance.

Thus, although God knows all it is possible to know, his knowledge is not exhaustive. He does not know how individuals will respond to the possibilities open to them since they are only possibilities. For Gersonides, such a view does not undermine God's providential plan. Although God does not know all future events, he is aware of the outcome of the whole process. In the same century, however, the Jewish theologian Hasdai Crescas (1340–1410) held a different view in *The Light of the Lord*. According to Crescas, human beings only appear to be free, but in reality all their deeds are determined by virtue of God's foreknowledge. Therefore, rather than attempting to reconcile free will and omniscience, he asserted that God's knowledge is absolute and free will is an illusion.

MODERN JUDAISM

In recent times the devout have been less concerned about such philosophical perplexities. Jewish scholar Michael Friedländer was best known for his English translation of Maimonides' *Guide for the Perplexed*. In 1890 he considered the subject of divine foreknowledge in *The Jewish Religion*: 'His knowledge is not limited, like the knowledge of mortal beings, by space and time. The entire past and future lies unrolled before his eyes, and nothing is hidden from

Above An omniscient eye on the Cao Dai temple in the Mekong Delta, Vietnam, portrays the idea of God's all-encompassing knowledge.

him. Although we may form a faint idea of the knowledge of God by considering that faculty of man that enables him within a limited space and time, to look backward and forward, and to unroll before him the past and the future, as if the events that have happened and those that will come to pass were going on in the present moment, yet the true nature of God's knowledge no man can conceive. ... It is the will of God that man should have free will and should be responsible for his actions; and his foresight does not necessarily include predetermination.'

In the modern period, there has been a universal reaffirmation of the traditional belief that God knows past, present and future and that men and women have freedom of choice.

Left The Creation from the Sarajevo Haggadah, c.1350, one of the oldest Sephardic Haggadahs. Images include the separation of light from darkness, and the spirit of God hovering over the waters of chaos. According to Judaism, God knows and does all things.

CREATION

THE DOCTRINE OF CREATION IS A CENTRAL ELEMENT OF THE JEWISH
FAITH. YET AMONG JEWISH THEOLOGIANS THIS BELIEF GAVE RISE TO
SPECULATION ABOUT THE CREATIVE PROCESS.

According to the Bible, God created
the cosmos. This belief became a
central feature of the synagogue
liturgy. Repeatedly, Jews praise God
for his creative works and extol
his providential concern for all that
he has formed. The doctrine of
divine creation also became a central doctrine of Jewish philosophy
and mysticism.

THE BIBLE
According to Genesis 1:1–4 God
created the universe:

In the beginning God created
   the heaven and the earth.
The earth was without form
   and void,
and darkness was upon the face
   of the deep;
and the Spirit of God was moving
   over the face of the waters.
And God said,

*Below This early 13th-century mosaic
for Monreale Cathedral, Sicily, shows
God creating Heaven and Earth.*

Right *According to the Bible God
created the cosmos and everything in it.
Animals in the* Rothschild Miscellany,
a 15th-century Italian illumination.

'Let there be light':
   and there was light.
And God saw that the light was good.
Based on the Psalms, synagogue liturgy
depicts God as the creator of all:

Blessed be He who spake, and the
   world existed:
Blessed be He;
Blessed be He who was the Master
   of the world in the beginning.

In the Ani Maamin prayer, the first
principle of the Jewish faith concerns creation:

I believe with perfect faith that
the creator, blessed be his name, is
the author and guide of everything
that has been created, and that He
   alone
has made, does make, and will
   make all things.

RABBINIC LITERATURE
In rabbinic sources, scholars speculated about the creative process. In
Genesis Rabbah (midrash on Genesis),
for example, the concept of the
world as a pattern in the mind of
God is expressed in relation to the
belief that God looked into the Torah
and then created the universe. Here
the Torah is conceived as a primordial blueprint. Regarding the order
of creation, the School of Shammai
stated that the heavens were created

EXTRATERRESTRIAL CREATION

Regarding the question whether in the process of creating the cosmos,
God also formed intelligent beings on other planets, the Bible provides no
information. Even though rabbinic sources attest to the creation of other
worlds, they similarly contain no reference to the existence of other sen-
tient creatures. However, in the 19th century Phineas Elijah ben Meir
Hurwitz of Vilna discussed this topic. On the basis of Isaiah 45:18 ('For
thus says the Lord who created the heavens, who formed the earth and
made it, he established it; he did not create it a chaos; he formed it to be
inhabited: "I am the Lord; and there is no other." '), he stressed that there
are creatures on other planets than the earth. He went on to say that creatures on other planets may have intelligence, yet he did not think that they
would have free will since only human beings have this ability. Consequently,
he wrote, there is only room for Torah and worship in this world, for neither Torah nor worship has any meaning where there is no free will.

Left Adam and Eve, the first created humans, in a scene from Genesis. From a 1438 manuscript of the Tur Even HaEzer, a compilation of Hebrew laws.

Kabbalah, the notion of God creating and destroying worlds before the creation of this world is viewed as referring to spiritual worlds. Thus *tohu*, or 'void', in Genesis denotes the stage of God's self-revelation known as world of the void that precedes the world of perfection. In later Kabbalistic thought, the 14th-century Kalonymus Kalman of Cracow in his *Maor Va-Shemsh* maintained that the void in Genesis is the primordial void remaining after God's withdrawal to make room for the universe. On this reading, God's decree 'Let there be light' (Genesis 1:3) means that God caused his light to be emanated into the void in order to provide sustaining power required for the worlds that were later to be formed.

Below Map showing the Earth, planets and zodiac circling the Sun, by Nicolaus Copernicus, c.1543.

first and then the earth. The School of Hillel, however, maintained that the heaven and the earth were created simultaneously. According to one rabbinic source, all things were formed at the same time on the first day of creation, but appeared on the other six days just as figs are gathered simultaneously in one basket but each selected individually.

Again, in the Genesis Rabbah midrash, scholars stressed that God created several worlds but destroyed them before creating this one. The goal of creation is summed up in the rabbinic claim that God created the world for his glory.

THE MEDIEVAL PERIOD

In the Middle Ages, a number of Jewish philosophers argued that God created the cosmos *ex nihilo*. The Kabbalists, however, interpreted the doctrine of *ex nihilo* in a special sense. In their view, God should be understood as the Divine Nothing because as he is in and of himself nothing can be predicated. This is because the divine is beyond human comprehension. Creation *ex nihilo* therefore refers to the creation of the universe out of God, the Divine Nothing. This took place, they stated, through a series of divine emanations.

For the Kabbalists the first verses of Genesis allude to the process within the Godhead prior to the creation of the universe. In Lurianic

GOODNESS

BIBLICAL AND RABBINIC SOURCES EXTOL GOD'S GOODNESS. TRADITION SAYS HE IS BENEVOLENT, MERCIFUL AND COMPASSIONATE. YET SUCH A BELIEF GAVE RISE TO SPECULATION ABOUT THE ORIGIN OF EVIL.

As the supreme ruler of the universe, God is depicted in biblical and rabbinic sources as all-good. He is the beneficent creator who watches over all he has formed and extends mercy to his chosen people. As the Psalmist declared, he is good and ready to forgive (Psalm 86:5).

THE RABBIS

According to rabbinic literature, God is the supremely beneficent deity who guides all things to their ultimate origin. In the unfolding of his plan, God has chosen Israel as his messenger to all peoples – as creator and redeemer, he is the father of all. Such affirmations about God's goodness have given rise to speculation about the existence of evil. In the Bible, the authors of Job and Ecclesiastes explore the

Below According to the Bible, Adam and Eve were expelled from the Garden of Eden because of their disobedience. 12th-century Spanish painting.

question why the righteous suffer, and this quest extended into the rabbinic period. However, it was not until the Middle Ages that Jewish theologians began to explore the philosophical perplexities connected with the origin of evil.

THE SOURCE OF EVIL

In the 12th century, the Jewish philosopher Abraham Ibn Daud argued that both human reason and the Jewish tradition teach that God cannot be the cause of evil. Reason demonstrates that this is the case because God is all-good; it would be self-contradictory for him to be the source of evil. Since God does not have a composite nature, it is logically impossible for him to bring about both good and evil. Why then does evil exist? Poverty, he argued, is in fact the absence of wealth; darkness the absence of light; folly the absence of understanding. It is an error to believe that God creates any of these

Above The Rabbi by Martin Archer-Shee, 1837, shows its subject as wise, knowing and benevolent.

things just as it would be an error to assume that God made no elephants in Spain. Such a lack of elephants is not divinely willed. Likewise, evil is not created by God. It occurs when goodness is not present. The absence of good is not an inherent evil. Rather, imperfections in the world exist so that God can benefit a multitude of creatures in different forms.

THE KABBALISTS

According to Jewish Kabbalists, the existence of evil constitutes a central problem for the Jewish faith. One tradition asserts that evil has no objective reality. Men and women are unable to receive all of the influx from the *sefirot*, or 'divine emanations'; it is this inability that is the origin of evil. Created beings are estranged from the source of emanation and this results in the illusion that evil exists. Another view depicts the sefirah of power as an attribute whose name is evil. On the basis of such teaching, Isaac the Blind (c. 1160–1235) concluded that there must be a positive root of evil and death. During the process of differentiation of forces below the sefirot, evil became

concretized. This interpretation led to the doctrine that the source of evil is the supra-abundant growth of judgement – this was due to the separation and substitution of the attribute of judgement from its union with compassion. Pure judgement produced from within itself the Sitra Ahra, or 'the other side'. The Sitra Ahra consists of the domain of emanations and demonic powers. Though it originated from one of God's attributes, it is not part of the divine realm.

THE ZOHAR

According to the Zohar, the major Kabbalistic source of the Middle Ages, evil is like the bark of a tree of emanation – it is a husk or shell in which lower dimensions of existing things are encased. Evil is perceived as a waste product of an organic process. It is compared to bad blood, foul water, dross after gold has been refined and the dregs of wine. Yet despite this depiction, the Zohar asserts that there is holiness even in the Sitra Ahra, whether it is understood as a result of

Below Evil can triumph when good men do nothing. The Holocaust Memorial at Mauthausen Concentration Camp is in the shape of a menorah.

the emanation of the last sefirah or a consequence of human sin. The domains of good and evil are intermingled, and it is a person's duty to separate them.

MODERN JEWISH THOUGHT

In modern times philosophical theories about the existence of evil have ceased to attract attention within Judaism, and most Jews have ignored the mystical theories in early and medieval Jewish literature. Instead, writers have wrestled with the question whether it is possible to believe in God's goodness after the Holocaust.

Above Peter Eisenman's Holocaust Memorial to the Murdered Jews of Europe, Berlin, 2005. For theologians, the Holocaust poses fundamental questions about human evil and God's omnipotence.

In *The Face of God after Auschwitz* (1965) Reform Jewish theologian Ignaz Maybaum contended Jews died in the concentration camps for the sins of humanity as God's suffering servant. For Maybaum, Jews suffer in order to bring about the rule of God over the world and its peoples – their God-appointed role is to serve the course of historical progress and bring human beings into a new era.

An alternative approach to the Holocaust is to see in the death camps a manifestation of God's will that his chosen people survive. Such a view was expressed by the Reform Jewish philosopher Emil Fackenheim (1916–2003), who asserted that God revealed himself to the Jewish people out of the furnaces and through the ashes of the victims of the death camps. Through the Holocaust, he argued, God issued an additional 614th commandment to the 613 commandments found in Scripture: 'Jews are forbidden to hand Hitler posthumous victories.' In this way, God commanded his people to survive as Jews, lest the Jewish people perish.

CHAPTER 6

GOD AND ISRAEL

According to traditional Judaism, God is understood as the providential Lord of all creation. In the Hebrew Bible, God is depicted as ever-present, directing the course of human affairs. In rabbinic sources, he is intimately involved with his people, continually leading them to their ultimate redemption. The revelation to Moses on Mount Sinai is the basis of the 613 commandments in the Torah, which were later interpreted by rabbinic scholars. According to tradition, God's eternal covenant with Israel means both the Written and the Oral Law are binding for all time.

As the all-good ruler of the universe, God chose the Jews as his special people. Israel was to be a messenger to all nations in the unfolding of God's divine plan for humanity. In acceptance of God's love, the Jewish people were to worship God and keep his commandments. In biblical times, worship and sacrifice were carried out in the Temple. Sacrifices were offered to God to obtain his favour and atone for sin. With the destruction of the Temple, the synagogue became the focus for divine worship. Prayers replaced sacrifices, which could no longer be offered. A new ritual, referred to as 'service of the heart', became a central focus of Jewish life.

Opposite This magnificent illustration from the Golden Haggadah of 1320 shows, anti clockwise from top right, Pharaoh letting the people of Israel go, the strangling of the firstborn, the Egyptians pursuing the people of Israel, and the drowning of the Egyptians in the Red Sea.

Above This 6th-century Byzantine mosaic from Madaba, Jordan, is the oldest extant map of Palestine.

PROVIDENCE

FOR THE JEWISH PEOPLE, GOD IS THE TRANSCENDENT CREATOR OF THE UNIVERSE AND ACTIVELY INVOLVED IN HISTORY. PROVIDENTIALLY, HE INTERVENES IN EVERYDAY LIFE, SUSTAINING AND GUIDING HIS CREATURES.

In Scripture, God is continually presented as controlling and guiding his creation. The Hebrew term for such divine intervention is *hashgahah*, derived from Psalm 33:14: 'From where he sits enthroned he looks forth [*hisgiah*] on all the inhabitants of the earth.' This view implies that the dispensation of a wise and benevolent providence is manifest everywhere.

THE BIBLE

According to the Hebrew Bible, there are two types of providence: general providence (God's provision for the world in general) and special providence (God's care for each person). In the Bible, God's general providence was manifest in his freeing the ancient Israelites from bondage; special providence relates to God's care for each individual. In the words

Below When God told Abraham to send Hagar and Ishmael into the desert, was this general or special providence? By Italian painter Veronese, 1580.

of Jeremiah: 'I know, O Lord, that the way of man is not in himself, that it is not in man who walks to direct his steps' (Jeremiah 10:23).

THE RABBINIC TRADITION

The doctrine of divine providence was developed in rabbinic sources. According to the Mishnah, 'everything is foreseen'. Developing this concept, the Talmud states: 'No man suffers so much as the injury of a finger when it has been decreed in heaven.' This belief became a major feature of the Rosh Hashanah, or New Year, liturgy where God, the judge of the world, provides for the destiny of individuals as well as nations on the basis of their actions.

THE MIDDLE AGES

Jewish medieval theologians were preoccupied with the problem of divine causality. In the *Guide for the Perplexed*, the 12th-century Jewish philosopher Moses Maimonides defended both general and special

Above 14th-century Spanish drawing of the ancient Hebrews as slaves in Egypt. For Jews, the Exodus from Egypt was an act of divine deliverance.

providence. Special providence, he argued, extends only to human beings and is in proportion to a person's intellect and moral character. This view implies God is concerned about non-human species, but not with every individual. Only men and women come under divine care as they rise in intellectual and moral stature.

However, in the 15th century, the Jewish theologian Hasdai Crescas (1340–1410) maintained that God created human beings out of his love for them. Therefore, his providential care is not related to their personal characteristics. Instead, all persons enjoy God's special providence.

THE KABBALISTS

Jewish Kabbalists were also concerned about providence. In his *Shomer Emunim*, the 18th-century scholar Joseph Ergas explained there are various types of providence. 'Nothing', he wrote, 'occurs by accident, without intention and divine providence, as it is written: "Then will I also walk with you in chance." (Leviticus 21:24). You see that even the state of chance is attributed to God, for all proceeds from him by reason of

HASIDIC TEACHERS

Such a restriction of special providence was rejected by a number of Hasidic thinkers. Divine providence, they insisted, is exercised over all things. In the 18th century, for example, Phineas of Koretz (1726–91) wrote in his *Peer La-Yesharim* that 'a man should believe that even a piece of straw that lies on the ground does so at the decree of God.' Hayim of Sanz (1793–1876), the founder of the Sanz Hasidic dynasty, stated: 'It is impossible for any creature to enjoy existence without the creator of all worlds sustaining it and keeping it in being, and it is all through divine providence.'

special providence.' None the less, Ergas limited special providence to human beings. 'The guardian angel', he continued, 'has no power to provide for the special providence of non-human species. For example, whether this ox will live or die, whether this ant will be trodden on or saved, whether this spider will catch this fly …There is no special providence for this kind of animals, to say nothing of plants and minerals.'

Below Cosmographical Diagram from the Catalan Atlas by Abraham Cresques, 1375. For Jews, God is both transcendent and immanent in human history.

Above The destruction of the Temple of Jerusalem can be seen as providentially willed or as the result of human action. Painting by Francesco Hayez, 1867.

MODERN JUDAISM

In the contemporary world, such theological issues have not been at the forefront of Jewish thought. Rather, the rise of science has challenged the traditional understanding of God's providential activity. In place of the religious interpretation of the universe as controlled by God, scientific investigation has revealed that nature is governed by complex natural laws. Thus it is no longer possible for most Jews to accept the biblical and rabbinic concept of divine providential activity. As a result, many Jews have simply abandoned the belief in providence.

Others envisage God as working through natural causes. As creator of all, he established the laws that regulate the natural order. Regarding special providence, many Jews would want to say that God is concerned with each individual, even though he does not miraculously intervene in the course of human affairs. Divine providential concern should thus be understood as a mode of interaction in which God affects the consciousness of individuals without curtailing their free will. Knowing the innermost secrets of the human heart, he introduces into the conscious awareness of individuals aims consonant with his will.

REVELATION

TRADITION IS THAT GOD REVEALED HIMSELF TO THE JEWISH NATION. THIS BELIEF SERVES AS THE FOUNDATION OF THE LEGAL SYSTEM AND THE AUTHORITATIVE BASIS OF JEWISH THEOLOGY.

Above Revelation at Sinai as Moses receives the Ten Commandments. From the mid 9th-century Moutier-Grandval Hebrew Bible.

According to the Jewish tradition, God revealed the Torah to Moses on Mount Sinai and, therefore, 613 commandments in the Five Books of Moses are binding for all time. In addition, God's revelation on Mount Sinai serves as basis for the conviction that the descriptions of God's nature and activity found in Scripture are authoritative and unchanging.

THE RABBIS

In rabbinic sources a distinction is drawn between the revelation of the Torah and the prophetic writings. This is frequently expressed by saying that the Torah was given directly by God, whereas the prophetic books were given by means of prophecy. The other books of the Bible, however, were conveyed by means of the holy spirit. Yet despite these distinctions, all the writings in the Hebrew Bible constitute the canon of Scripture. The Hebrew term referring to the Bible as a whole is Tanakh. This word is made of the first letters of the three divisions of Scripture: Torah, Neviim (Prophets), and Ketuvim (Writings).

THE ORAL TORAH

For the rabbis, the expositions and elaborations of the Written Law were revealed on Mount Sinai and passed down from generation to generation. This process is referred to as the Oral Torah. Hence, traditional Judaism affirms that God's revelation is two-fold and binding. Committed to this belief, Jews pray in the synagogue liturgy that God will guide them to do his will.

THE MEDIEVAL PERIOD

In the Middle Ages, the traditional belief in the Written and Oral Torah was repeatedly affirmed. The Jewish writer Nahmanides (1194–1270) stated in his *Commentary to the Pentateuch* that Moses wrote the Five Books of Moses at God's dictation. It is likely, he observed, that Moses wrote Genesis and part of Exodus when he came down from Mount Sinai. After 40 years in the wilderness, he completed the rest of the Torah.

Nahmanides stated that this view follows the rabbinic tradition that the Torah was given scroll by scroll. For Nahmanides, Moses was like a scribe who copied an older work. Underlying this conception is the mystical idea of a primordial Torah, which contains the words describing events long before they occurred. This entire record was in heaven before the creation of the world. Further, Nahmanides maintained that the secrets of the Torah were revealed to Moses and are referred to in the Torah by the use of special letters, and by the adornment of Hebrew characters.

KABBALAH

Parallelling Nahmanides' mystical interpretation of the Torah, the medieval mystical work the Zohar

Left The first Great Sanhedrin of French Jews in Paris, 1807. The Jewish legal system is based on God's revelation of Mount Sinai, as interpreted by rabbinic sages through the centuries.

asserts that the Torah contains mysteries beyond human comprehension. As Rabbi Simeon ben Yohai, traditionally thought to be the author of the Zohar, explained, 'Alas for the man who regards the Torah as a book of mere tales and everyday matters! If that were so, even we could compose a Torah dealing with everyday affairs, and of even greater excellence. Nay, even the princes of the world possess books of greater worth which we could use as a model for composing such Torah. The Torah, however, contains in all its words supernal truths and sublime mysteries.'

BIBLICAL SCHOLARSHIP

In the modern period it has become increasingly difficult to sustain the concept of divine revelation in the light of scholarly investigation and discovery. According to biblical scholars, the Torah is composed of various sources from different periods in the history of ancient Israel.

Below Tradition teaches that God revealed the Torah to Moses. This new Torah scroll is being completed before it is paraded in procession to an Ashkenazi synagogue in Stamford Hill, London.

Some scholars stress that these sources themselves contain early material; thus it is a mistake to think they originated in their entirety at particular periods. Other scholars reject the theory of separate written sources; instead, they argue that oral traditions were modified throughout the history of ancient Israel and only eventually were compiled into a single narrative. Yet, despite these rival claims, there is a general recognition that the Torah was not written by Moses; rather, it is seen as a collection of traditions originating at different times.

Above 1350 Passover Haggadah. In following such liturgy, Jews pray God will guide them to do his will.

MODERN JUDAISM

Orthodox Jews remain committed to the view that the Written and the Oral Torah were imparted by God to Moses on Mount Sinai. This is the basis of the legal system and doctrinal beliefs about God. Non-Orthodox Jews have a general acceptance of the findings of biblical scholarship. The Five Books of Moses are perceived as divinely inspired, but at the same time the product of human reflection.

THE TORAH

According to the Jewish tradition, the Torah was given by God to the Jewish nation. Moses Maimonides explained: 'The Torah was revealed from heaven. This implies our belief that the whole of the Torah found in our hands this day is the Torah that was handed down by Moses, and that it is all of divine origin. By this I mean that the whole of the Torah came unto him from before God in a manner which is metaphorically called "speaking". But the real nature of that communication is unknown to everybody except Moses.'

TORAH AND COMMANDMENTS

JEWISH OBSERVANCE IS BASED ON THE BELIEF THAT GOD REVEALED 613 COMMANDMENTS TO MOSES ON MOUNT SINAI – THESE ARE RECORDED IN THE TORAH AND SERVE AS THE BASIS OF JEWISH LAW.

Traditional Judaism affirms that Moses received the Oral Torah in addition to the Written Law. These commandments were passed down from generation to generation and were the subject of rabbinic discussion and debate.

THE RABBINIC TRADITION

The first authoritative compilation of the Oral Law was the Mishnah, composed by Yehuda Ha-Nasi in the 2nd century CE. This work is the most important book of law after the Bible – its aim was to supply teachers and judges with a guide to the Jewish legal tradition.

In later centuries, sages continued to discuss the nature of Jewish law. Their deliberations and conclusions are recorded in the Palestinian and Babylonian Talmuds. Both Talmuds incorporate the Mishnah and later rabbinic debate known as the Gemara. The Gemara text preserves the proceedings of scholarly academies in both Palestine and Babylonia. The central purpose of these works was to elucidate the Mishnah text.

CODES OF LAW

After the compilation of the Talmuds in the 6th century CE, outstanding scholars continued the development of halakha, or 'Jewish law', by issuing answers to specific questions. These responsa, or 'responses', touched on all aspects of the Jewish tradition and insured a standardization of practice. In time, various scholars felt the need to produce codes of Jewish law so that all members of the community would have access to the legal tradition. Isaac Alfasi (1013–1103) produced a work in the 11th century that became the standard code for Sephardic Jewry. Two centuries later, Asher ben Jehiel (c.1250–1327) wrote a code for Ashkenazi Jews. In the 12th century Moses Maimonides wrote the Mishneh Torah, which had a wide influence, as did the code by Jacob ben Asher in the 14th century. In the 16th century, Joseph Caro (1488–1575) published the *Shulkhan Arukh*, which together with the glosses by Moses Isserles (c.1525–72) has served as the standard code of Jewish law for Orthodox Jews.

THE KABBALAH

In Kabbalistic sources the observance of the *mitzvot*, or 'commandments', takes on cosmic significance. For the Jewish mystic, deeds of *tikkun*, or

Above Brass hanging lamp in the shape of a Jewish 'Sabbath lamp', lit on the eve of Sabbath and festivals. Jews are commanded to rest and worship on the Sabbath.

'cosmic repair', sustain the world, activate nature to praise God, and bring about the coupling of the 6th and 10th sefirot, or 'divine emanations'. Such repair is brought about

Below Dutch artist Rembrandt's painting of Moses with the Ten Commandments, 1659.

Below The rabbi in his pulpit reading a Torah scroll to his congregation, from the Barcelona Haggadah, c.1350.

LURIANIC KABBALAH

According to the 16th-century Kabbalist Isaac Luria (1534–72), when the vessels were shattered the cosmos was divided into two parts: the kingdom of evil in the lower part and the realm of divine light in the upper part. God, he believed, chose Israel to vanquish evil and raise up the captive sparks. The Torah was given to symbolize the Jews' acceptance of this task. Luria and his disciples believed they were living in the final stages of the last attempt to overcome evil, in which the coming of the Messiah would signify the end of the struggle. For Lurianic mystics, the concept of tikkun refers to the mending of what was broken during the shattering of the vessels. By keeping God's commandments it is possible for the righteous to redeem the world.

by keeping the commandments, which were conceived as vessels for establishing contact with the Godhead and for enduring divine mercy. Such a religious life provided the Jewish mystic with a means of integrating into the divine hierarchy of creation.

MYSTICAL CLEAVING

The highest rank attainable by the soul at the end of its sojourn on earth is mystical cleaving to God. Early Kabbalists of Provence defined such cleaving as the ultimate goal.

According to the 13th-century mystic Isaac the Blind, the principal task of the mystics and of those who contemplate the divine name is to cleave to God. This, he argued, is a central principle of the Torah and of prayer. The aim should be to harmonize one's thoughts above, to conjoin God in his letters and to link the ten sefirot to him. For the 13th-century writer Nahmanides, such cleaving is a state of mind in which one constantly remembers God and his love.

MODERN JUDAISM

In the modern world, such traditional mystical ideas have lost their force except among the Hasidim. Today the majority of those who profess allegiance to Orthodox Judaism do not live by the code of Jewish law. Instead, each individual Jew feels free to write his or her own *Shulkhan Arukh*. This is also the case within the other branches

Left Cover page of Leviticus, dated 1350, which covers laws about sacrifice, the sanctuary, impurity and holiness.

Above Jews kissing the Torah scrolls, Nevatim, Israel. Tradition states that God revealed the words of the Torah to Moses.

of Judaism. For most Jews the legal tradition has simply lost its hold on Jewish consciousness. This means that there is a vast gulf fixed between the requirements of legal observance and the actual lifestyle of the majority of Jews, both in Israel and the Diaspora.

Below Hasidic life is regulated by Jewish law. A Hasidic couple walk through the Mea Shearim, one of the oldest Jewish neighbourhoods in Jerusalem.

CHOSEN PEOPLE

ACCORDING TO TRADITION, GOD CHOSE THE JEWS FROM AMONG ALL
PEOPLES. THEY ARE TO BE HIS SERVANTS AND DO HIS WILL. THIS BELIEF
HAS ANIMATED JEWISH CONSCIOUSNESS THROUGH THE AGES.

According to Scripture, God chose the Jewish nation as his special people. As the Book of Deuteronomy proclaims: 'For you are a people holy to the Lord your God: The Lord your God has chosen you to be a people for his own possession out of all the peoples that are on the face of the earth' (Deuteronomy 7:6).

DIVINE LOVE
According to the Hebrew Bible, God's selection of Israel was motivated by divine love. The Book of Deuteronomy states: 'It was not because you were more in number than any other people that the Lord set his love but it is because the Lord loves you' (Deuteronomy 7:7–8). Such affection was later echoed in the synagogue liturgy, particularly in the prayer for holy days: 'Thou has chosen us from all peoples; thou has

Below The Book of Genesis from a 1472 Pentateuch, showing Adam, Eve and a unicorn, which in Jewish tradition stands for the final redemption of Israel.

loved us and found pleasure in us and hast exalted us above all tongues; thou hast sanctified us by thy commandments and brought us near unto thy service, O king, and hast called us by thy great and holy name.'

AN HISTORIC MISSION
By its election, Israel was given an historic mission to bear truth to all humanity. Hence, before God proclaimed the Ten Commandments on Mount Sinai, he admonished the people to carry out this role: 'You have seen what I did to the Egyptians, and how I bore you on eagles' wings, and brought you to myself. Now, therefore, if you will obey my voice, and keep my covenant, you shall be my own possession among all peoples; for all the earth is mine, and you shall be to me a kingdom of priests, and a holy nation' (Exodus 19:4–6).

OBLIGATION AND RESPONSIBILITIES
Such a choice of Israel carries with it numerous responsibilities: 'For I have chosen him, that he may charge his children and his household after him to keep the way of the Lord by doing righteousness and justice' (Genesis 18:19). Divine choice therefore brings about reciprocal response: Israel is obliged to keep God's law. In doing so, the nation will be able to persuade other nations that there is only one universal God. Israel is to be a prophet to the nations in that it will bring them to salvation. However, despite such an obligation, the Bible asserts that God will not abandon his chosen people even if they go astray. The wayward will be punished, but God

Above The Ark of the Law, 6th-century CE mosaic at Beth Alpha synagogue, Israel. Tradition says God chose the Jews from all nations to be his special people and observe his commandments.

will not reject them: 'Yet for all that, when they are in the land of their enemies, I will not spurn them, neither will I abhor them so as to destroy them utterly and break my covenant with them: for I am the Lord their God' (Leviticus 26:44).

THE RABBINIC VIEW
In rabbinic literature the concept of the chosen people is a constant theme. While maintaining that God chose the Jews from all peoples, the rabbis argued their election was due to an acceptance of the Torah. This belief was based on Scripture: 'If you will hearken to my voice, indeed, and keep my covenant, then you shall be my own treasure from among all the peoples' (Exodus 19:5). For the rabbis, the Torah was offered first to other nations of the world, but they all rejected it because its precepts conflicted with their way of life. Only Israel was willing to keep his covenant.

THE MEDIEVAL PERIOD
In the Middle Ages, the Jewish claim to be God's chosen people was disputed by Church authorities who

regarded the Church as the true Israel. In response, such Jewish philosophers as the 12th-century Spanish Jew Judah Halevi stressed that the entire Jewish people were endowed with a special religious sense. According to Halevi, this faculty was first bestowed on Adam, and then it was passed on through a line of Jewish representatives. As a result, the Jewish nation was able to enter into communion with God. Moreover, because of this divine influence, the election of Israel implies dependence on special providence, which sustains the people while the remainder of the human race is subject to the general workings of the laws of nature and general providence.

Below The Spanish philosopher Judah Halevi held that Jewish people had a special religious sense. Thus Moses could talk to God on Mount Sinai. A 14th-century Italian fresco by Bartolo di Fredi.

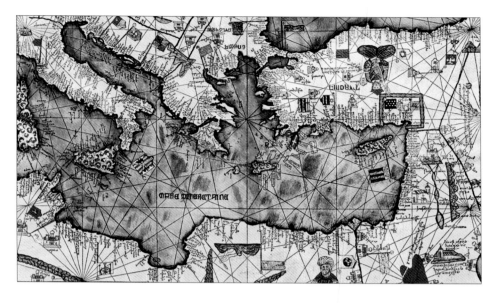

KABBALAH

The concept of Jewish chosenness is a central theme of medieval Kabbalistic thought. According to medieval Kabbalah, the Jewish people on earth has its counterpart in the Shekhinah, or 'divine presence', in the sefirotic realm – the sefirah, or 'divine emanation', *Malkhut* is known as 'the

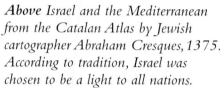

Above Israel and the Mediterranean from the Catalan Atlas by Jewish cartographer Abraham Cresques, 1375. According to tradition, Israel was chosen to be a light to all nations.

community of Israel' which serves as the archetype of the Israelite people on earth. For the Kabbalists, Israel's exile mirrors the cosmic disharmony in which the Shekhinah is cast into exile from the Godhead. The dynamic of Israel's exile and its restoration reflects the dynamic of the upper worlds.

MODERN JUDAISM

In the contemporary Jewish world, the notion of Israel's chosenness remains an important doctrine. Yet within Reform Judaism the concept of Jewish mission was developed, stressing the special message of God that is to be passed on to all peoples. Within the various non-Orthodox branches of the faith a number of writers have expressed unease about the claim that the Jews constitute a divinely chosen people. The rejection of this traditional doctrine derives from universalistic and humanistic tendencies. Although the Jewish community has a unique history, the people of Israel are not perceived as divinely chosen. Instead, the God of Israel is also the Lord of history who loves all peoples and guides their destiny.

LOVE OF GOD

OF CENTRAL IMPORTANCE IN JUDAISM IS THE LOVE OF GOD. THE OBLIGATION TO LOVE GOD INVOLVES BEING FAITHFUL, EVEN IF THIS REQUIRES THE LOSS OF ONE'S WEALTH OR ONE'S LIFE.

At the heart of Judaism lies the love of God. According to Scripture: 'You shall love the Lord your God with all your heart and with all your soul and with all your might' (Deuteronomy 6:5). The Mishnah teaches that this biblical verse implies that human beings must love God not only for the good that befalls them, but for their sufferings as well. This explanation is based on an interpretation of three expressions in this verse: 'with all your heart' means with both the good and evil inclinations; 'with all your soul' means even if God takes away your soul through martyrdom; 'with all your might' means with all your wealth.

MIDRASHIC TEACHING

Alongside the Mishnah, the midrash also comments on this biblical verse. Concerning the phrase 'You shall love the Lord your God', the *Sifra* (midrash on Exodus) declares: 'Do it out of love. Scripture distinguishes between one who does it out of love

and one who does it out of fear. Out of love, his reward is doubled and gain doubled. Scripture says: "You shall fear the Lord your God: you shall serve him and cleave to him" (Deuteronomy 10:20). A man who fears his neighbour will leave him when his demands become too troublesome, but you do it out of love. For love and fear are never found together except in relation to God.'

THE MIDDLE AGES

Among medieval Jewish writers, stress was placed on mystical love. Thus the Jewish philosopher Saadia Gaon (882–942 CE) in *Beliefs and Opinions* asked how it is possible to have knowledge of God, much less love him, since we have not perceived

Above I Will Worship toward Thy Temple. *A 19th-century painting of Jerusalem by the French artist James Tissot shows the obligation to love God.*

him with our senses. In response he asserted that certain statements are believed to be true even though they cannot be proved. For Saadia, it is possible to acquire knowledge of God through rational speculation and the miracle s afforded by Scripture. Hence, truth about God is able to mingle with the human spirit. For this reason the prophet Isaiah stated:

Below This carving of 1420 from Roskilde, Denmark, depicts Job, a righteous man who is put to the test with illness and the loss of his wealth and family, but remains faithful to God.

BAHYA IBN PAKUDAH

In the 11th century the Jewish philosopher Bahya Ibn Pakudah viewed the love of God as the final goal – this is the aim of all virtues. According to Bahya, the love of God is the soul's longing for the creator. When human beings contemplate God's power and greatness, they bow before his majesty until God stills whatever fear they might have. Individuals who love God in this fashion have no other interest than serving him. With complete faith they accept all their sufferings.

Above Paradise *by Lucas Cranach the Elder, 1530. Scripture says, Adam and Eve were driven out of Paradise for failing to observe God's commandments.*

'My soul yearns for thee in the night, my spirit within me earnestly seeks thee' (Isaiah 26:9). As a consequence, the soul is filled with love.

MOSES MAIMONIDES

In the Mishneh Torah, the 12th-century thinker Moses Maimonides discussed the love of God in relation to the nature of the universe. 'It is a religious obligation to love and fear this glorious and tremendous God,' he wrote. 'And it is said: "You shall love the Lord your God" (Deuteronomy 6:5). And it is said: "You shall fear the Lord your God" (Deuteronomy 6:13). How does a man come to love and fear God? No sooner does man reflect on his deeds and on his great and marvellous creatures, seeing in them his incomparable and limitless wisdom, than he is moved to love and to praise and to glorify and he has an intense desire to know the great Name.'

Right Jews praying before the Western Wall in Jerusalem. Such prayer should be based on love of God.

According to Maimonides, one who truly loves God serves him disinterestedly rather than out of an ulterior motive. When a person loves God, he automatically carries out the divine commandments. This state is like being lovesick, unable to get the person he loves out of his mind, pining constantly when he stands, sits, eats or drinks. Yet Maimonides maintained that not everyone is able to attain such a state of pure love. God, he maintained, can only be loved in proportion to the knowledge one has of him.

KABBALAH

In Kabbalistic literature the love of God is highly important. Concerning the verse, 'You shall love the Lord your God', the Zohar states that human beings are here commanded to cleave unto God with selfless devotion: 'It is necessary for man to be attached to God with a most elevated love, that all man's worship of the Holy One, blessed be he, should be with love; for no form of worship can be compared to the love of the Holy One, blessed be he.'

LATER KABBALISTS

In the writings of later Kabbalists the theme of the love of God was further elaborated. According to the 16th-century writer Elijah de Vidas in his *Reshite Hokhmah*, it is impossible for human beings to love a disembodied spirit. Here the love of God must refer to something that is embodied. Since God as En Sof has no body, human love of the divine must be understood as love of the Shekhinah (God's presence). For de Vidas, the Shekhinah is in no way apart from God; rather God manifests himself through the Shekhinah in order to provide human beings with something tangible they are able to grasp so as to rise above worldly desires.

FEAR OF GOD

THE FEAR OF GOD IS TO BE COUPLED WITH THE LOVE OF GOD.
ACCORDING TO MEDIEVAL JEWISH THINKERS, SUCH FEAR SHOULD BE
UNDERSTOOD AS AWE BEFORE GOD'S GREATNESS.

In the Jewish tradition, there are numerous references to the fear of God. In the Book of Job, for example, Job is described as 'blameless and upright, one who feared God and turned away from evil' (Job 1:1). In rabbinic sources the Hebrew terminology for such awesome reverence is *yirat shamayim*, or 'the fear of heaven'. In the medieval period a distinction was drawn between fear of punishment and fear in the presence of the exalted majesty of God.

MEDIEVAL THEOLOGIANS
In the 12th century, the Jewish philosopher Abraham Ibn Daud (1040–1105) discussed the concept of the fear of God in *Emunah Ramah*. Referring to Deuteronomy

Below The reading of the Torah in a synagogue is interrupted by a crowd led by a Christian priest, 1868. Out of love and fear of God, Jews have revered the Torah and God's commandments.

10:20 ('You shall fear the Lord your God'), he argued that the reference is to the fear produced by God's greatness, not to the fear of harm. There is a fundamental difference between these two types of fear, he stated. A person may be afraid of an honourable prophet who would certainly not harm him, or he might be afraid of a hyena or a snake. The first type is fear at the greatness of the one feared and shame in his presence. Fear of God, he asserted should be of this kind, not of the kind of fear we have for kings whom we are afraid will do harm to us.

In *Duties of the Heart*, the 11th-century theologian Bahya Ibn Pakudah drew a similar distinction. Only fear in the presence of the exalted majesty of God can lead to pure love. A person who attains this degree of reverence will neither fear nor love anything other than the creator. In this regard Bahya referred to a saint who found a God-fearing man sleep-

Above Breaking waves at Monteray Bay, California. Accepting the power of the natural world may be seen as a way of interpreting the fear of God.

ing in the desert. He asked if he were afraid of lions sleeping in such a place. In reply, the God-fearer said: 'I am ashamed that God should see that I am afraid of anything apart from him.'

LATER PHILOSOPHERS
In the 15th century, Jewish philosopher Joseph Albo defined fear as the receding of the soul and the gathering of all her powers into herself, when she imagines some fear-inspiring thing. Yet there is another type of fear in which the soul is awestruck not because of any fear of harm, but because of her unworthiness in the face of majesty. For Albo this higher fear is elevating. Fearing God in this way, a person will stand in awe before him and be ashamed to transgress his commandments.

In the following century, Elijah de Vidas maintained in *Reshite Hokhmah* that the fear of God is the gate through which every servant of the Lord must pass. It is a necessary condition for loving God and doing his will. Basing his views on Kabbalah, de Vidas stated that, since human beings are created after the pattern of the upper world, all acts have a cosmic effect. Good deeds cause the divine grace to flow through all worlds, whereas evil actions arrest this flow. The fear of sin thus has cosmic significance.

Right The fear of the Lord. Elijah curses the boys who have mocked his baldness, and they are eaten by bears. Painting by James Tissot (1836–1902).

HASIDIM

Among the Hasidim, the fear of God was also an important issue. In the 19th century, Zevi Elimelech Spira in *Bene Yisakhar* argued that effort is required to reach this state. He wrote: 'The disciples of the Ba'al Shem Tov wrote in the name of their master that human effort is only required in order to attain to the state of worship out of fear, whereas God himself sends man the love of him since the male pursues the female; and you know that fear is the category of the female and love that of the male.' In the 18th century Levi Isaac of Berdichev argued in *Kedushat Levi* that a distinction should be drawn between the lower fear of sin and the higher fear whereby one is over-awed by God's majesty. In this state a person has no self-awareness. Yet, this higher fear can only be attained as a product of the lower fear.

Right The fear of the Lord. Elijah curses the boys who have mocked his baldness, and they are eaten by bears. Painting by James Tissot (1836–1902).

THE ZOHAR

According to the medieval mystical work the Zohar, there are three types of fear. Two of these have no proper foundation, but the third is the main source of fear. A person may fear God in order that his sons may live and not die, or because he is afraid of some punishment. Because of this he is in constant fear. Or there is a person who fears God because he is terrified of punishment in the next world. Both these types of fear do not belong to the main foundation of fear. The fear that does have a proper foundation is when a person fears his master because he is the great and mighty ruler. This is the highest type of fear.

MUSAR

This was a movement for ethical education in the spirit of the halakha or Jewish law. It emerged in the 19th century in Lithuania, where fear of punishment was viewed as essential for those struggling to reach perfection. According to Isaac Blazer (1837–1907), the highest fear is the ultimate aim, but it is impossible to attain it without serious reflection on the fear of punishment. Only serious contemplation of severe punishment can penetrate the human heart so that this deeper understanding can be gained.

Below Living with fear. An anti-Semitic riot outside a synagogue in 1750, by Daniel Chodowiecki.

PROMISED LAND

TRADITIONAL JUDAISM MAINTAINS THAT THE HOLY LAND WAS PROMISED BY GOD TO ISRAEL. THROUGH THE CENTURIES, JEWS HAVE LONGED TO RETURN TO THEIR ANCESTRAL HOME.

According to Scripture, God told Abraham to travel to Canaan: 'Go from your country and your kindred and your father's house to the land that I will show you. And I will make of you a great nation' (Genesis 12:1–2). This divine promise became the basis of the Jewish claim to the Holy Land, a conviction that animated Jewish aspirations in the Diaspora to return to the land of their ancestors.

ANCIENT ISRAEL

God's promise to Abraham was repeated to his grandson Jacob who was renamed Israel (meaning 'he who struggles with God'). After Jacob's son Joseph became a vizier in Egypt, the Israelite clan settled in Egypt for several hundred years.

Below The fall of the Temple in 70CE marked the loss of the Jews' homeland for nearly 2,000 years. From the Hours of Neville of Hornby, c. 1340.

Eventually they were freed from Egyptian bondage by Moses, who led them into the desert. Under Joshua's leadership, the Jewish nation conquered the Canaanites and settled in the land, establishing a monarchy. A sacred Temple was built in Jerusalem by King Solomon which became the central cult for the nation. This was followed by a rebellion by the Northern tribes and the establishment of two kingdoms: Israel in the north and Judah in the south. In 722BCE the Northern Kingdom was devastated by Assyrian invaders, and two centuries later the Southern Kingdom was conquered by the Babylonians. Although Jews were allowed to return to Judah by Cyrus of Persia in 538BCE, the Romans destroyed the Temple in 70CE.

Below Palestine and the Promised Land; a map of 1603 after Flemish Abraham Ortelius, generally recognized as the creator of the first modern atlas.

Above The sack of Antioch, 1098. Some Jews saw Jewish deaths in this crusade as a sign that the Messiah was on his way.

MESSIANIC REDEMPTION

Following these events, the Jews were bereft of a homeland. In their despair the Jewish people longed for a messianic deliverer who would lead them back to Zion. Basing their beliefs on biblical prophecy, they foresaw a period of redemption in which earthly life would be transformed and all nations would bow down to the one true God. This vision animated rabbinic reflection about God's plan for his people.

According to rabbinic sources, the process of divine deliverance involved the coming of a messianic

Above View of Jerusalem Seen From the Mount of Olives *by the Russian artist N.G. Chernezov, 1863.*

figure, Messiah ben Joseph, who would serve as the forerunner of the second Messiah, Messiah ben David. This second messiah would bring back all the exiles to Zion and usher in the messianic age. At the end of this period all human beings would be judged: the righteous would enter into heaven whereas the wicked would be condemned to eternal punishment. This vision served as a means of overcoming the nation's trauma at suffering the loss of the Holy Land.

FALSE MESSIAHS
In the early rabbinic period some Jews believed that Jesus was the long-awaited redeemer of Israel. Although mainstream Judaism rejected such claims, the Jewish community continued to long for deliverance. In 132CE the Palestinian military leader Simeon bar Kochba was acclaimed by many Jews as the Davidic Messiah. When his rebellion against Rome resulted in failure, Jews put forward the year of redemption until the 5th century CE, when another messianic pretender, Moses from Crete, declared he would lead Jewish inhabitants from the island back to their homeland.

After this plan failed, Jews continued to hope for a future return and their aspirations are recorded in various midrashic sources.

This longing continued into the early Middle Ages. The traveller Eldad Ha-Dani brought news from Africa of the ten lost tribes, which stimulated messianic longing. Many Jews viewed the year of the First Crusade (1096) as a year of deliverance: when Jews were slaughtered, their suffering was viewed as the birth pangs of the Messiah. In later years the same yearning for a return to Zion was expressed by Jews who continued to be persecuted by the Christian population. The early modern period witnessed this same aspiration for redemption. In 1665 the arrival of Shabbetai Tzvi electrified the Jewish world. Claiming to be the Messiah, he attracted a large circle of followers; however, his conversion to Islam evoked widespread despair.

THE ZIONIST MOVEMENT
With the apostasy of Shabbetai Tzvi, the Jewish preoccupation with messianic deliverance diminished. Many Jews became disillusioned with messianic anticipation. Yet despite this shift in orientation, a number of Jews continued to pray for the coming of the Messiah, and linked this yearning to an advocacy of Zionism. Paralleling

these religious aspirations to establish a Jewish settlement in the Holy Land prior to the coming of the Messiah, modern secular Zionists encouraged such a development in order to solve the problem of anti-Semitism.

As time passed, the Zionist cause gained increasing acceptance in the Jewish world. The first steps towards creating a Jewish homeland were taken at the end of the 19th century with the first Zionist Congress. Subsequently, Zionists attempted to persuade the British government to permit the creation of a Jewish home in Palestine. Although Britain eventually approved of such a plan, the British government insisted that the rights of the Arab population be protected. After World War II, the creation of a Jewish state was approved by the United Nations. Yet despite such an official endorsement, this plan was rejected by the Arabs. In subsequent years, Arabs and Jews have engaged in a series of conflicts, and this antagonism has continued until the present day.

Below The Zionist dream. This Israeli poster shows a Hebrew soldier removing a yellow Star of David armband from an old man, c. 1950.

PRAYER

THROUGHOUT THE AGES, JEWS HAVE TURNED TO GOD IN PRAYER.
THROUGH PRAYERS OF PRAISE, THANKSGIVING AND PETITION, THEY
HAVE EXPRESSED THEIR LONGINGS AND ASPIRATIONS.

Within the Jewish faith, worship is of fundamental importance. From the biblical period to the present, Jews have turned to God in times of distress. In the synagogue, prayers are addressed to God during daily and Sabbath services and during festivals. In the belief that God listens to the voices of those who turn to him, Jews have expressed their deepest longings and hopes in words of prayer.

THE BIBLE
The Hebrew Scriptures list more than 80 examples of formalized and impromptu worship. Initially no special prayers were required for regular prayer. It was only later that worship services became institutionalized through sacrifices and offerings. Sacrifices to God were made to obtain his favour or atone for sinful acts. Unlike the Canaanites, who sacrificed human beings, the ancient

Below A French postcard for Jewish New Year showing worshippers in prayer shawls, c. 1920.

Israelites slaughtered only animals. In biblical times there were three types of sacrifice offered in the Temple: animal sacrifice, made as a burnt offering for sin; meal offerings; and libations. The rituals and practices governing these acts were set down in Leviticus 2, 23 and Numbers 28, 29.

FIXED WORSHIP
According to the Mishnah, priests serving in the Temple participated in a short liturgy comprising the Shema (Deuteronomy 6:4), the Ten Commandments (Exodus 20:3–17), and the priestly blessing (Numbers 6:24–6). During this period the entire congregation began to pray at fixed times; later, an order of service was established by the men of the Great Assembly. Regular services were held four times daily by the delegations of representatives from the 24 districts of the country. These services consisted of *shaharit*, or 'morning', *musaf*, or 'additional', and *neilat shearim*, or 'evening'.

Above A 5th-century Roman mosaic of Daniel in the lions' den, from Bordj El Loudi, Tunisia. According to Scripture, God protected Daniel from harm.

RABBINIC TIMES
Several orders of prayers coexisted until Gamaliel II produced a regularized standard after the Temple was destroyed in 70 CE. Prayers officially replaced the sacrificial system since they could no longer be offered in the Temple. This new ritual – the service of the heart – was conducted in the synagogue. The core of the liturgy included the prayer formula 'Blessed are You, O God', the Shema, and the Amidah (known also as the tefillah), consisting of 19 benedictions. On special occasions, an additional Amidah was included.

Prayers were recited by a *minyan*, or 'quorum of ten men': if such a number could not be found, certain prayers had to be omitted (including the Kaddish, Kedushah and the reading of the Law). The Alenu prayer, originating from the New Year liturgy, and the Kaddish were the two concluding prayers of all services.

HEBREW BIBLE READINGS
During the worship service, portions of the Torah (Five Books of Moses) and the Prophets were recited, and this became a normal practice by the time of the Mishnah in the 2nd

Above Prayer ceremony from an illustrated Hebrew prayer book, Germany, 1471.

century CE. By the end of the talmudic period (6th century CE), the prayer service was supplemented by piyyutim, or 'liturgical hymns'. These compositions were produced in Palestine as well as Babylonia from geonic times until the 12th century.

The Palestine rite was distinguished by a triennial cycle of reading from the Torah, a recension of the benedictions of the Amidah, and an introductory blessing before the recitation of the Shema.

The Babylonian rite was first recorded by Amram Gaon in the 9th century CE. This work served as the official ordering of prayers with their legal requirements. This act of setting down liturgical arrangements led to the dissolution of the ban against committing prayers to writing. In the 10th century CE the first authoritative prayer book (*siddur*) was edited by Saadiah Gaon (882–942CE).

JEWISH MYSTICISM

For Jewish mystics, *devekut*, or 'cleaving to God in prayer', was of fundamental importance. For the early Kabbalists of Provence devekut was the goal of the mystic way. According to the 13th-century Jewish philosopher Nahmanides,

devekut is a state of mind in which one constantly remembers God and his love to the point that when a person speaks with someone else, his heart is not with them at all but is still before God. In Nahmanides' view, the true Hasid, or 'pious individual', is able to attain such a spiritual state – devekut does not completely eliminate the distance between God and human beings. Rather, it denotes a state of beatitude and intimate union between the soul and its source.

MYSTIC PRAYER

In ascending to the higher worlds, the path of prayer paralleled the observance of the commandments. Yet, unlike the *mitzvot*, or 'commandments', prayer is independent of action and can become a process of mediation. Mystical prayer, which is accompanied by meditative *kavvanot*, or 'intention', focusing on each prayer's Kabbalistic content, became a feature of various stems of Kabbalah. For the Kabbalist, prayer was understood as the ascent of human beings into the higher realm where the soul can integrate with the higher spheres. By using the traditional liturgy in symbolic fashion, prayer repeats the hidden processes of the cosmos.

HASIDISM

In the 19th century, Hasidim incorporated Kabbalistic ideas into their understanding of prayer. According to Hasidic thought, the Kabbalistic type of kavvanot brings about an emotional involvement and attachment to God. In Hasidism, prayer is seen as a mystical encounter with the divine in which the human heart is elevated towards its ultimate source. Frequently the act of prayer was seen as the most important religious activity.

MODERN JUDAISM

In modern times the emergence of various Jewish movements led to the reinterpretation of the liturgical tradition. Reform Jews modified the worship service through eliminating various prayers, and introducing the organ and communal singing as well as addresses in the vernacular. The aim of Reform Judaism was to adapt Jewish worship to contemporary needs. Within the Conservative and Reconstructionist movements, prayer books adhered more closely to the traditional *siddur*, or 'prayer book'. Yet, despite such a diversity of approaches, prayer continues to serve as a focal point of the faith.

Below In the Synagogue, *c. 1900, the focus of divine worship and service.*

CHAPTER 7

THE SPIRITUAL PATH

The Bible serves as a guide to Jewish spirituality. Later Jewish sources – including the midrash and the Talmud – similarly provide a basis for the spiritual path. In this context, ethical values are of primary importance. Through their election, the Jewish people are to serve as God's servants, proclaiming God's truth and righteousness. Jews are called to action, to turn humanity away from wickedness and sin. In this quest, the Jewish nation is to become holy, just as God is holy. Through moral living, Jews are to reflect God's compassion, mercy and justice.

In the Jewish tradition, compassion is perceived as a cardinal virtue. Those who suffer are to be consoled. God's mission for his people is for them to act as comforters of the oppressed. This message is highlighted during the Passover *seder*, or 'religious meal'. The Jewish people are to remember that they were once enslaved; their responsibility is to free those who are in bondage. Yet such compassionate care is to be tempered by the quest for justice. By choosing such a moral life, the Jew is to complete God's work of creation.

Opposite Synagogue Service Imploring Divine Favour and Grace. *A devout Jew pictured by 19th-century Russian painter Nikolai Bogdanoff-Bjelski.*

Above Simchat Torah is the holy day on which the completion of the annual reading of the Torah is celebrated. This particular festival procession took place at Livorno synagogue, Italy, in 1850.

BIBLE

THE BIBLE SERVES AS THE BEDROCK OF THE JEWISH FAITH. IN THE
HEBREW SCRIPTURES, KNOWN AS THE TANAKH, THE ANCIENT
ISRAELITES RECORDED THEIR HISTORY AND RELIGIOUS BELIEFS.

For the Jewish people, the Hebrew
Scriptures serve as the basis of belief
and practice. Through the ages the
nation has looked to the Bible for
inspiration and sustenance. In times
of tribulation as well as joy, Jews have
turned to this sacred literature as a
source of comfort and hope.

THE HEBREW SCRIPTURES

The Jewish faith is a revealed religion. Its basis is the Bible. The
Hebrew name for the canon of
Scripture is *Tanakh*: the Hebrew
term is an abbreviation of the principal letters of the words standing
for its divisions: *Torah*, or 'teaching';
Neviim, or 'prophets'; *Ketuvim*,
or 'writings'. The Torah consists of
Genesis, Exodus, Leviticus, Numbers
and Deuteronomy. According to

*Below Samuel, prophet and judge in
the Bible, beheads Agad, king of the
Amalekites. From the North French
Hebrew Miscellany, compiled in 1278 at
a time of upheaval for European Jews.*

tradition, these five books were
revealed by God to Moses on
Mount Sinai. The second division of
the Hebrew Bible – the Prophets –
is divided into two parts. The first –
Former Prophets – contains the books
of Joshua, Judges, 1 and 2 Samuel and
1 and 2 Kings. The second part –
Latter Prophets – is composed of the
major prophets (Isaiah, Jeremiah and
Ezekiel) and the minor prophets
(Hosea, Joel, Amos, Obadiah, Jonah,
Micah, Nahum, Habakkuk, Zephaniah,
Haggai, Zechariah and Malachi). The
third division consists of a variety of
divinely inspired books: Psalms,
Proverbs, Job, Song of Songs, Ruth,
Lamentations, Ecclesiastes, Esther,
Daniel, Ezra, Nehemiah and 1 and
2 Chronicles.

NON-CANONICAL
LITERATURE

During the Second Temple period
and afterwards, a large number of
other books were written by Jews in
Hebrew, Aramaic and Greek that
were not included in the biblical
canon. None the less, these texts did
gain canonical status in the Roman
Catholic and Eastern Orthodox
churches. Known as the Apocrypha,
they had an important impact on
Christian thought. The most
substantial is the Wisdom of Jesus
Son of Sirah (also known as Ben
Sira or Ecclesiasticus). Other works
include: the Wisdom of Solomon,
1 and 2 Maccabees, Tobit and Judith.
Additional literary sources of
the Second Temple period are
known as the Pseudepigrapha –
these non-canonical books consist
of such works as the Testament of
the Twelve Patriarchs, 1 and 2 Enoch
and Jubilees.

*Above Samson, an Israelite judge and
man of great strength, defeats a lion in
a German illustration from 1360.*

RABBINIC JUDAISM

In rabbinic literature a distinction is
drawn between the revelation of the
Pentateuch (Torah in the narrow
sense) and the prophetic writings.
This is frequently expressed by saying that the Torah was given directly
by God, whereas the prophetic books
were given by means of prophecy.
The remaining books of the Bible
were conveyed by means of the holy
spirit rather than through prophecy.
Nevertheless, all these writings constitute the canon of Scripture.

According to the rabbis, the
expositions and elaborations of the
Torah She-Bi-Ketav, or 'Written Law',

*Below The Judgement of
Solomon, greatest of the judges, by
Valentin de Boulogne, 1625.*

Left The text of every Sefer Torah, kept in the synagogue, is identical because it is copied from an original by a sofer *(scribe).*

'Torah from Sinai', is a fundamental principle of the faith: 'The Torah was revealed from heaven. This implies our belief that the whole of the Torah found in our hands this day is the Torah that was handed down by Moses, and that it is all of divine origin. By this I mean that the whole of the Torah came unto him from before God in a manner which is metaphorically called "speaking"; but the real nature of that communication is unknown to everybody except to Moses to whom it came.'

Above The Book of Exodus recounts that the Israelites built cities for Pharaoh. From a Hebrew Haggadah, 1740.

were also revealed by God to Moses on Mount Sinai. Subsequently they were passed from generation to generation, and through this process additional legislation was incorporated. This process is referred to as the *Torah She-Be-Al-Peh*, or 'Oral Torah'. Thus traditional Judaism affirms that God's revelation is twofold and binding for all time. Committed to this belief, Orthodox Jews pray in the synagogue that God will guide them to do his will as recorded in their sacred literature.

THE MEDIEVAL PERIOD

In the Middle Ages this traditional belief was affirmed. Thus the 12th-century Jewish philosopher Moses Maimonides (1135–1204) declared that the belief in *Torah MiSinai*, or

Below The coming of the prophet Elijah, from the Washington Haggadah, created in Italy by Joel ben Simeon, 1478.

THE ZOHAR

The medieval mystical work the Zohar asserts that the Torah contains mysteries beyond human comprehension. According to Simeon ben Yohai, traditionally identified as the author of the Zohar: 'Alas for the man who regards the Torah as a book of mere tales and everyday matters! If that were so, even we could compose a Torah dealing with everyday affairs, and of even greater excellence. Nay, even the princes of the world possess books of greater worth which we could use as a model for composing such Torah. The Torah, however, contains in all its words supernal truths and sublime mysteries.'

MODERN JUDAISM

Orthodox Judaism remains committed to the view that the Written as well as the Oral Torah were imparted by God to Moses on Mount Sinai. This act of revelation serves as the basis for the entire legal system as well as doctrinal beliefs about God. Yet despite such an adherence to tradition, many modern Orthodox Jews pay only lip service to such a conviction. The gap between traditional belief and contemporary views of the Torah is even greater in

the non-Orthodox branches of Judaism. Here there is a general acceptance of biblical scholarship. Such a non-fundamentalist approach rules out the traditional belief in the infallibility of Scripture and thereby provides a rationale for changing the law and reinterpreting the theology of the Hebrew Scriptures.

THE PENTATEUCH

Like Maimonides, the 13th-century philosopher Nahmanides (1194–1270) in his *Commentary to the Pentateuch* argued that Moses wrote the Five Books of Moses at God's dictation. It is likely, he observed, that Moses wrote Genesis and part of Exodus when he descended from Mount Sinai. At the end of 40 years in the wilderness he completed the rest of the Pentateuch. Nahmanides observed that this view follows the rabbinic tradition that the Torah was given scroll by scroll. For Nahmanides, Moses was like a scribe who copied an older work.

MISHNAH, MIDRASH AND TALMUD

IN THE 2ND CENTURY CE, THE MISHNAH WAS COMPILED BY YEHUDA HA-NASI AS THE FIRST COLLECTION OF RABBINIC LAW. IN LATER CENTURIES, THE PALESTINIAN AND BABYLONIAN TALMUDS WERE PRODUCED.

With the rise of rabbinic Judaism, scholars engaged in the exposition of the biblical text and the interpretation of Jewish law. In academies in Erez Israel and Babylonia, sages devoted themselves to interpreting God's will and edifying the Jewish people. Initially their teachings were passed on orally, but in time they were written down in the Mishnah, Talmud and midrashic sources.

EARLY RABBINIC JUDAISM

During the early rabbinic period – between the 1st century BCE and the 6th century CE – rabbinic scholars referred to as Tannaim (70–200 CE) and Amoraim (200–500 CE) engaged in the interpretation of the biblical

Below The Talmud is a compilation of Jewish laws. This page, from a German Talmud of the early 1300s, shows when God created his world.

text. According to tradition, both the Written and the Oral Torah were given by God to Moses on Mount Sinai. This belief implies that God is the direct source of the *mitzvot*, or 'commandments', recorded in the Five Books of Moses and is also indirectly responsible for the legal judgements of the rabbis. Such a conviction serves as the justification for the rabbinic exposition of scriptural ordinances.

Alongside this halakha, or 'exegesis of Jewish law', Jewish sages also produced interpretations of Scripture in which aggadah, or 'new meanings of the text', were expounded in midrashim, or 'rabbinic commentaries', and in the Talmud. Within aggadic sources is found a wealth of theological speculation about topics such as the nature of God, divine justice, the coming of the Messiah and the afterlife. In addition, ethical considerations were of considerable importance in the discussions of these teachers of the faith.

MISHNAH

During the age of the Tannaim, Jewish scholars produced teachings dealing with Jewish law which were codified in the Mishnah by Yehuda Ha-Nasi (135–220CE) in about 200 CE. This work is a compilation of oral traditions (Oral Law); it is divided into six orders (which are subdivided into 63 tractates). The first order, Zeraim, or 'seeds', deals largely with agricultural law, although it begins with a section about prayer. The second order, Moed, or 'season', deals with the sacred calendar. In the third order,

Above Menorah, or seven-branched candlestick, and sarcophagus at Beit She'arim, where the great Mishnah scholar Yehuda Ha-Nasi lived.

Nashim, or 'women', matrimonial law is discussed in extensive detail. The fourth order, Nezikim, or 'damages', contains both civil and criminal law and also contains a tractate of Avot, or 'moral maxims'. The fifth order, Kodashim, or 'holy things', gives a detailed account of the rules for sacrifice. Finally, the sixth order, Tohorot, or 'purity', is concerned with ritual purity.

MIDRASH

Parallel with the legal tradition, Jewish sages also expounded the narrative parts of Scripture. In the Tannaitic period such midrashim dealt with the Five Books of Moses. Some of these traditions allegedly derive from the School of Akiva; others are attributed to the School of Ishmael. These midrashic sources are: the *Mekilta* on the book of Exodus; the *Sifra* on Leviticus; and the *Sifrei* on Numbers and Deuteronomy. Other midrashic sources deal with material from the Amoraic period.

Like the tannaitic midrashim, some are in the form of running commentaries known as exegetical midrashim. Others are collections of sermons arranged according to the

Above Studying the Scriptures with rabbinic commentary is an integral part of Jewish life. Photo taken in the Great Synagogue in Moscow, 1987.

sabbaths or festivals for which they were written. These are known as homiletical midrashim. The largest collection of midrashim is *Midrash Rabbah*, consisting of works that were separate commentaries on the Torah plus the Five Scrolls (the Song of Songs, Ruth, Lamentations, Ecclesiastes, Esther). Homiletical midrashim are exemplified by *Pesikta de-Rav Kahana*, *Pesikta Rabbati* and *Midrash Tanhuma* (known also as *Yelammedenu*).

TALMUD

In the centuries following the composition of the Mishnah and the early midrashim, Jewish sages in Palestine and Babylonia continued to expand Jewish law. By the 4th century CE scholars in Erez Israel had collected together the teachings of generations of sages in the academies of Tiberius, Caesarea and Sepphoris. The extended discussions of the Mishnah became the Palestinian Talmud. The text of this multi-volume work covers four sections of the Mishnah (seeds, set feasts, women and damages), but here and there various tractates are missing. No doubt the discussions in these academies included matters on these missing tractates, but it is

not known how far the recording, editing and transmission of these sections had progressed before they were lost.

The views of these sages had an important influence on scholars in Babylonia, though their work never attained the same prominence as that of the Babylonian Talmud. In Babylonia, sages completed the redaction of the Babylonian Talmud by the 6th century CE – an editorial task begun by Ashi in the 5th century CE. This massive work is largely a summary of the discussions that took place in the Babylonian academies. Although the Babylonian Talmud deals with slightly fewer

Mishnaic tractates, it is nearly four times larger than the Palestinian Talmud and came to be regarded as more authoritative.

The texts of these Talmuds consists largely of summaries of rabbinic discussion: a phrase of Mishnah is interpreted, discrepancies are resolved and redundancies are explained. In this compilation, conflicting opinions of the earlier sages are contrasted, unusual words are explained and anonymous opinions are identified. Frequently, individual teachers cite specific cases to support their views, and hypothetical eventualities are examined to reach a solution on the discussion. Debates between outstanding scholars in one generation are often cited, as are differences of opinion between members of an academy or a teacher and his students. The range of talmudic explorations is much broader than that of the Mishnah, and includes a wide range of teachings about such subjects as theology, philosophy and ethics.

Below A painting of a Jewish Wedding by Italian Pietro Longhi (1701/2–85). A section of the Mishnah concerns women, marriage, divorce and vows.

ETHICS

ETHICAL CONCERNS ARE OF PARAMOUNT IMPORTANCE IN THE JEWISH TRADITION. ALONGSIDE THE ETHICAL TEACHING IN SCRIPTURE, A WIDE RANGE OF MITZVOT DEAL WITH THE MORAL LIFE.

In the Jewish faith, ethical values are of primary importance. For Jews, moral action is fundamental – since it is through the rule of the moral law that God's kingdom on earth can be realized. This is the goal of the history of the world in which God's chosen people have a central role. It is their destiny to be a light to the nations.

THE MORAL LIFE

Through the centuries Judaism did not separate religion from life. Rather, the Jewish people were called to action. It was their duty to turn men and women away from violence, wickedness and falsehood. In this quest it was not the hope of bliss in a future life that was the

Right When God destroyed humanity with a flood because of its great wickedness, Noah's family were saved in an ark, shown here under a rainbow, in a mosaic from Kykko, Cyprus.

primary goal – rather, the aim was to establish a kingdom of justice and peace on earth. Ethical action is thus at the heart of the tradition. Each Jew was to be like the creator, mirroring the divine qualities revealed to Moses: 'The Lord, the Lord, a God merciful and gracious, slow to anger, and abounding in steadfast love and faithfulness, keeping steadfast love for thousands, forgiving iniquity and transgression and sin' (Exodus 34:6–7).

THE TORAH

In the Hebrew Scriptures, deeds and events involving ethical issues are found in abundance: the punishment of Cain for murdering his brother; the violence of the generation that brought about the flood; the early prohibition against murder; the hospitality of Abraham and his plea for the peoples of Sodom; the praise of Abraham for his ethical character; the condemnation of Joseph's brothers; Joseph's restraint in Egypt in the house of Potiphar; Moses' plea for the exploited.

Yet it is in the legal codes of the Torah that we encounter moral guidelines formulated in specific laws. The Ten Commandments in particular illustrate the centrality of Jewish ethics. The first commandments are theological in nature, but the last six deal with relationships between human beings. These *mitzvot*, or 'commandments', provide a means of expressing love of others. The Decalogue thus makes it clear that moral standards are fundamental to the Jewish faith.

Left Moses receives the Ten Commandments, a central part of Jewish ethics. From a 1305 Bible Historiale, the predominant medieval translation of the Bible into French.

THE PROPHETS

Ethical principles are at the core of prophetic teaching. The books of the prophets are rooted in the Torah of Moses. The prophets saw themselves as messengers of the divine word – their task was to denounce the nation for its transgressions and call it to repentance. In all this they pointed to concrete ethical action as the only means of sustaining their covenantal relationship with God. In their view, God demands righteousness and justice above all else.

Emphasis on the moral life was reflected in the prophetic condemnation of cultic practices that were devoid of ethical concern. These passages illustrate that ritual laws are of instrumental value – morality is intrinsic and absolute. The primacy of ethics was also reflected in the prophetic warning that righteous action is the determining factor in the destiny of the Jewish nation. Moral transgressions referred to in such contexts concern exploitation,

Below Jewish women in New York package excess donated produce from the Greenmarket. This was for delivery to programmes serving the hungry for the Rosh Hashanah holiday, 2010.

oppression and the perversion of justice. These transgressions have the potential to bring about the destruction of the nation.

PROVERBS

The Book of Proverbs reinforces the teaching of the Torah and the prophets. Here wisdom is conceived as a capacity to act morally. It is a skill that can be learned. Throughout the book of Proverbs dispositional traits are catalogued: positive moral types include the righteous person, the wise individual and the upright; negative ones include the evil person, the fool, the mocker and the simpleton. Thus, here as in the rest of Scripture, the moral life is seen as the basis of the faith. Theology is defined in relation to action – it is through the moral life that humanity encounters the divine.

RABBINIC LITERATURE

Rabbinic sages continued this emphasis on the moral life. Convinced that they were the authentic expositors of the Bible, the rabbis amplified scriptural law. In their expansion of the mitzvot, rabbinic exegetes differentiated between the laws governing human relationships to God and those that concern relationships to others. By choosing the moral life, the Jew is able to complete God's work of creation. To accomplish this task the sages formulated an elaborate system of traditions that

Above An old man blessing a child. Such ritual is a feature of Jewish ethical teaching on the relationship between children and adults.

were written down in the Mishnah, subsequently expanded in the Talmud and eventually codified in the Code of Jewish law. According to rabbinic Judaism, this expansion of biblical law is part of God's revelation. Both the Written and Oral Torah are binding on Jews for all time. Such a conviction implies that the entire corpus of moral law is an expression of the divine will and must be obeyed.

THE CODE OF JEWISH LAW

For Jews the moral law is absolute and binding. In all cases it was made precise and specific – it is God's word made concrete in the life of the nation. The commandment to love one's neighbour embraces all humanity. In the code of Jewish law the virtues of justice, honesty and humane concern are regarded as central to community life. Hatred, vengeance, deceit, cruelty and anger are condemned. The Jew is to exercise loving kindness to all: to clothe the naked, feed the hungry, care for the sick and comfort the mourner. By fulfilling these ethical demands, the Jewish nation can help bring about God's kingdom on earth in which exploitation, oppression and injustice are eliminated.

SIN AND REPENTANCE

IN THE JEWISH TRADITION, REPENTANCE IS REGARDED AS A VIRTUE.
SINNERS ARE TO RECOGNIZE THEIR WICKEDNESS, REPENT OF THEIR
ACTIONS, AND RESOLVE TO CHANGE THEIR EVIL WAYS.

According to the Jewish tradition, sin is understood in terms of the rejection of God's will. Human beings are thought of as being pulled in two directions: the *yetzer ha-tov*, or 'good inclination', draws individuals towards the good, whereas the *yetzer ha-ra*, or 'evil inclination', binds them in sin. Sin occurs when the evil inclination is overpowering in this struggle.

THE LEGAL SYSTEM
According to Jewish law, there are two types of sin: sins of commission and sins of omission. The former are more serious, but in some cases a positive commandment pushes aside

Below The serpent tempts Adam and Eve leading to their expulsion from the Garden of Eden. French manuscript of Ovid's Metamorphoses, *1494.*

a negative one if this is the only way that it can be carried out. Sins involving the transgression of negative precepts are of two types: offences against God and offences against one's neighbour. Yom Kippur, the Day of Atonement brings about forgiveness for those sins committed against God. But for offences against other human beings, the wrong done to the victim must be put right.

THE EVIL INCLINATION
The yetzer ha-ra is often identified with sexual lust, but the term also applies to physical appetites in general and aggressive desires. It is perceived as the force in human beings that drives them to gratify their instincts. Although it is referred to as 'evil' because it can lead to wrong-doing, it is essential to life. As the midrash remarks: 'Were it not for the yetzer

Above The shofar is blown at the end of Yom Kippur, to remind Jews of their sins during the previous year. From a 1400s German manuscript.

ha-ra, no man would build a house or marry or have children or engage in commerce.' This is the reason why Scripture states: 'And God saw everything that he had made and behold, it was very good' (Genesis 1:31). In a similar vein, there is a legend that the Men of the Great Synagogue wished to kill the yetzer ha-ra. But the yetzer ha-ra warned them that if they were successful, then the world would be destroyed.

REPENTANCE
Given the ever-present danger of sin, how are human beings to repent of their sinfulness? This is the constant theme of prophetic literature, and it continued into the rabbinic period. According to the 12th-century Jewish philosopher Moses Maimonides (1135–1204), if a person wittingly or unwittingly transgresses any commandment, he is required to repent and turn away from his wickedness and confess his sins to God. How should one confess one's sins? Maimonides wrote: 'He says, "O God! I have sinned, I have committed iniquity. I have transgressed before you by doing such and such. Behold now I am sorry for what I have done and am ashamed and

I shall never do it again."' True repentance takes place if the sinner has the opportunity of committing once again the sinful act, but he refrains from doing so. The sinner must strive to relinquish his sin, remove it from his thoughts and resolve never to repeat it.

LITERARY WORKS

In addition to the numerous references to repentance in rabbinic sources, there exist medieval works devoted to this theme. One of the most important, *Shaare Teshuvah* (Gates of Repentance) by Jonah ben Abraham Gerondi (1200–64), lists 20 essential features of sincere repentance: remorse; relinquishing the sin; pain for the sin; affliction of the body in fasting and weeping; fear of the consequences of the sin and of repeating it; shame for the sin; submission to God in humility and contrition; gentleness in future conduct; breaking the physical lusts by asceticism; the use by the sinner of that organ with which he sinned to do good; constant self-scrutiny; reflection by the sinner on the pun-

Right The Kapparot ceremony, in which a chicken is slaughtered and given to the poor, is performed before Yom Kippur, the annual Day of Atonement for sin.

ishment he deserves; the treatment of minor sins as major; confession; prayer; putting right the sin; almsgiving; the sinner should be conscious of his sin to refrain from repeating the sinful act when the opportunity presents itself; leading others away from sin.

PHYSICAL MORTIFICATION

For the rabbis, repentance is effected by such sincere resolve. There is no need for physical mortification in order to win pardon. The need for such mortification came into Jewish thought in the Middle Ages. The self-tortures required for true repentance are detailed in the ethical work *Rokeah* by Eleazer of Worms (1160–1238). No doubt Christian monasticism of the period influenced such practices. It is recorded that sages used to roll naked in the snow in the depths of winter, smear their bodies with honey and allow

themselves to be stung by bees and fast for days on end. However, such extreme practices were only carried out by a relatively few pietists, and in later centuries mortification of the flesh was condemned by the teachers of the Hasidic movement.

Below Penitence in a German synagogue, 1723. Flagellation was a practice influenced by Christian monks.

THE HUMAN STRUGGLE

According to rabbinic Judaism, human beings are engaged in a constant struggle against the evil that exists within themselves. The means whereby they can overcome this destructive force is provided by the Torah and its precepts. In the Talmud we read that when a person submits to the discipline provided by the Torah and studies it, then he will become free of morbid guilt. His life is then unclouded by the fear that the evil within will drag him down and bring his ruin. God has wounded human beings by creating the evil inclination – but the Torah serves as a plaster on the wound.

COMPASSION

JUST AS GOD IS COMPASSIONATE, JEWS ARE TO TREAT OTHERS WITH
COMPASSION. ALONGSIDE BENEVOLENCE AND MODESTY, IT IS REGARDED
AS AN IDENTIFYING CHARACTERISTIC OF THE JEWISH NATION.

Within the Jewish faith, compassion is regarded a central virtue. Empathy for the suffering of others and the desire to remove their pain are extolled as moral imperatives.

THE TRADITION OF COMPASSION

In Hebrew the word for compassion is *rahmanut*; this has the same root as the word *rehem*, or 'womb'. It denotes the tenderness and pity a mother should have for her child. According to the rabbis, compassion is one of the three distinguishing marks of Jews (the others being benevolence and modesty). This does not imply that non-Jews are less compassionate; rather compassion is understood as part of human nature. When compassion is ascribed to

Below Giving charity at the entrance to the grave of the Moroccan rabbi and Kabbalist Baba Saki in Netivot, Israel.

Right Compassion for the displaced. Fleeing anti-Semitism in the USSR in 1979, a Soviet Jewish child refugee and her mother arrive at Vienna.

Jews, this simply means that the Jewish people should be true to this basic element of human nature.

The Torah trains Jewry in the ways of compassion; the rabbis maintain that the ancestors of a person lacking in compassion did not stand at the foot of Mount Sinai. Just as God is described in the Bible as compassionate, so too should Jews strive to resemble the creator and be God-like in their sympathy for others.

THE CONCEPT

Rahmanut, or compassion, is understood as the tear which is shed for the sick and the poor; the hand that is outstretched in friendship; concern for the handicapped; commiseration with failure; and prayer for human-

ity overwhelmed with suffering. Even though rahmanut should result in action, it is in itself desirable. When a person is described as kind and sympathetic, this is compassion. Its opposite is indifference.

DIVINE COMPASSION

A common phrase used in the Talmud for 'God states' is 'The Compassionate says'. The second benediction of the Amidah prayer declares God's compassion for his creatures: 'Thou sustainest the living with loving kindness, revivest the dead with great compassion. Thou supportest the falling, healest the sick, loosest the bound, and keepest thy faith to them that sleep in the dust.'

One of God's names in the Jewish liturgy is *Av ha-Rahamin*, or 'Father of compassion'. The Grace after Meals speaks of God as feeding the world with goodness, with grace, with loving kindness, and with compassion. The end of the Amidah prayer refers twice to God's compassion.

UNIVERSAL RESPONSIBILITY

In Judaism, compassion is regarded as a virtue for all peoples. The prophets criticized non-Israelites for their lack of compassion to one another. Thus Jeremiah described people of the north country who 'lay hold on bow and spear, they are cruel and have no compassion' (Jeremiah 6:23). Amos pronounced God's verdict of doom on those nations who committed atrocities against one another, among them

Edom, who 'pursued his brother with the sword, and cast off all pity' (Amos 1:11).

COMPASSION FOR ANIMALS

According to the Jewish tradition, compassion must be extended to all of God's creatures. The principle of compassion toward animals is expressed by the Hebrew concept *tza'ar baalei hayyim*, or 'causing pain to living creatures'.

In the rabbinic tradition, this notion is developed in detail. Hence, according to the dietary laws, the purpose of *shehitah*, or 'ritual slaughter', is to adopt as painless a form of killing as possible. It is the principle of tza'ar baalei hayyim which underlies biblical prohibitions to avoid: muzzling the ox while ploughing (Deuteronomy 25:4), yoking an ox with an ass (22:10), taking the young before sending away the mother bird (22:76-7), and killing an animal and its young on the same day (Leviticus 22:28).

THOSE IN NEED OF COMPASSION

Judaism teaches that those whom fate has treated harshly should become objects of compassion. This applies particularly to the stranger, the widow and the orphan. According to rabbinic Judaism, it is wrong to suggest to those who mourn or suffer in other ways that this is the result of sin.

Although it is important to be self-critical, the temptation to be hard on others should be resisted. It is important in showing compassion that others should not be put to shame. Steps should always be taken not to cause distress. The Talmud, for example, asserts that in the presence

Right A 15th-century miniature showing sheitah, *the ritual slaughter of animals, which is carried out as painlessly as possible. According to Jewish law, animals are to be treated humanely.*

of a family of a criminal who has been hanged for murder, one should refrain from referring to anything that is hanging from the ceiling. Even when it is necessary to rebuke someone for his or her action, this should be done with tact.

THE LIMIT OF COMPASSION

Despite the importance of compassion, Judaism rules that there are limits. If a judge comes to the conclusion that a person is in the right and another in the wrong, it would be a perversion of justice if in feeling compassion for the guilty, there should be a miscarriage of justice. Thus the Talmud rules there must be no compassion in a law suit. The law must be decided objectively. What the judge must never do is to bend the law through a miscalculation based on sympathy for the accused.

Compassion is also misapplied when it is expressed to individuals who are deliberately cruel. There is a rabbinic dictum which states that whoever has compassion on the cruel will in the end be cruel to the compassionate.

BENEVOLENCE

LIKE THE ATTITUDE OF COMPASSION, THE PRACTICE OF BENEVOLENCE IS OF KEY IMPORTANCE IN THE JEWISH FAITH. COMPASSION SHOULD LEAD TO BENEVOLENCE – THE JEWISH IDEAL IS TO PRACTISE BOTH.

Above A man begs for alms in Israel. Giving to the needy is a means of exercising benevolence.

There are two related concepts of benevolence in Judaism. The first is *gemilut hasadim*, or 'bestowing loving kindness', and *tzedakah*, 'charity'. In the Bible, *tzedakah* means righteousness, and is synonymous with *mishpat*, or 'justice'. Yet, by rabbinic times, the word had assumed the meaning of charity. The Talmud states that there are three main differences between gemilut hasadim and tzedakah. Tzedakah is for the benefit of the poor, whereas gemilut hasadim is for everyone. It is not possible to contribute charity to the rich, but gemilut hasadim can be extended to all including the rich. Further, tzedakah refers to a contribution of money. The poor need financial assistance, but gemilut hasadim implies the giving of oneself. Finally, tzedakah is given to the living. One cannot give charity to the dead. But gemilut hasadim can be extended to those who have died by burying them and attending their funerals.

RABBINIC SOURCES

There are numerous examples of gemilut hasadim in rabbinic literature. Prominent among acts of benevolence is visiting the sick. An entire section of the Shulkhan Arukh, or 'Code of Jewish Law', is devoted to the rules for visiting the sick. The rabbis declared that the Shekhinah, or 'divine presence', is with the sick because God shares in that person's suffering. Comforting mourners is another example of gemilut hasadim. In talmudic times it was a custom to take gifts of food to those who had suffered loss. To attend a funeral is an act of benevolence. Other examples include lending money to help a person with a financial difficulty, speaking words of encouragement, greeting others warmly, helping the aged, and providing hospitality.

RELIEF FOR THE POOR

In giving charity, there should always be an element of benevolence. The poor should be spoken of kindly, and whatever is given should come from the heart without being patronizing. In ancient times there was a complex system of tzedakah: charity overseers made separate collections. One was for a weekly distribution; the other was for those who were passing through a town. Jewish communities provided a number of societies, each with its own charitable

Below Comforting mourners at a funeral is an example of gemilut hasadim. *Italian painting, 1750.*

DEGREES OF CHARITY

According to the medieval philosopher Moses Maimonides, there are eight degrees of charity:

1 A man gives, but is glum when he gives. This is the lowest degree of all.

2 A man gives with a cheerful countenance, but gives less than he should.

3 A man gives, but only when asked by the poor.

4 A man gives without having to be asked, but gives directly to the poor who know therefore to whom they are indebted, and he, too, knows whom he has benefited.

5 A man places his donation in a certain place and then turns his back so that he does not know which of the poor he has benefited, but the poor man knows to whom he is indebted.

6 A man throws his money into the house of a poor man. The poor man does not know to whom he is indebted but the donor knows whom he has benefited.

7 A man contributes anonymously to the charity fund, which is then distributed to the poor. Here the poor man does not know to whom he is indebted, neither does the donor know whom he has benefited.

8 Highest of all is when a man gives money to prevent another person from becoming poor, as by providing him with a job or by lending him money to tide him over during a difficult period. There is no charity greater than this because it prevents poverty in the first instance.

Above Charitable giving is a sign of benevolence. Donation box in Elijah's Cave synagogue, Haifa, Israel.

purposes. The education of poor children and other religious needs of the poor were also provided.

WHO ARE 'THE POOR'?

In determining who qualifies as a poor person, the Jewish tradition specifies that someone who has 200 zuz (an ancient silver coin) in ready cash or 50 zuz invested in business can no longer be considered poor and entitled to public assistance. A person who has a smaller amount does qualify since he meets the terms of the law. The official rabbinic view concerning the amount to be given is that a person should give a tenth of his income. However, the rabbis discourage giving more than a fifth of their income in case they might become poor themselves. Regarding the question who should come first in terms of preference, the rabbis state that when it is a question of food, a man should come before a woman because he has a family to support. If it is a question of clothing, a woman should take precedence because she suffers greater deprivation if she does not have proper clothes to wear. A person should help his poor relatives before he helps others; similarly, the poor of one's own town should be helped first.

Below Benevolence includes being with the sick. An Orthodox woman with a baby at the neonatal ICU in Shaarei Tzedek hospital, Jerusalem, Israel.

Below Russian Jewish refugees in the Poor Jews Temporary Shelter, Leman Street, east London, 1891.

JUSTICE

THE CONCEPT OF JUSTICE IS FUNDAMENTAL TO THE JEWISH TRADITION.
WITHIN RABBINIC SOURCES, JUSTICE IS UNDERSTOOD IN TERMS OF LAW.
THE PRACTICE OF GIVING A JUST RULING IS OF CENTRAL IMPORTANCE.

In legal cases, justice comes into operation when two parties are in conflict. For example, two individuals (A and B) might claim ownership of land: one (A) inherited the property from his father, while the other (B) claims he bought it from A and produces evidence to support this assertion. (A), however, denies ever having sold the land and rejects the evidence. In many instances, the available evidence does not provide a basis for reaching a just solution. Yet even here there is a possibility of solving the problem. Jewish law gives the benefit of the doubt to the person who is in possession of the disputed property. The general rule in such a dispute is that, in the absence of factual evidence, the court would not be justified in removing the property from where it is for this would be deciding, without sufficient cause, in favour of one of the parties. Where evidence is insufficient, the court has no right

Below The Bible records that after God had judged the world and sent the Great Flood, Noah emerged from the Ark. 13th-century mosaic, St Mark's, Venice.

to decide in favour of either party. The only fair procedure is to leave the property where it is until further evidence is available.

CRIME AND PUNISHMENT

In cases of crime, justice involves weighing the claims of society against the criminal. In a just society, the right of the criminal to prey on others should be rejected in favour of the right of society to protect itself. However, justice is involved when society has to determine how far to punish the offender. As far as the punishment affords such protection, it is just. But if it exceeds the degree of protection required, it is unjust to the criminal.

COURTS

Proper courts are necessary for the administration of justice. According to rabbinic sages, this is one of the demands of the Torah made even to non-Jews — it is one of the seven commandments of the sons of Noah to have a legal system. The Hebrew term for a court is *bet din*, or 'house of justice'. For civil cases, a bet din is composed of three Jewish scholars.

Above The bet din *shown here is the court of justice of the Sephardic Orthodox community in Israel.*

Here the decision of the majority is followed. Judges must be unbiased, and no one should serve as a judge if one of the parties is a friend or enemy. The laws regarding judges is contained in Deuteronomy 16:18–19: 'Judges and officers shalt thou make thee in all thy gates, which the Lord thy God giveth thee, tribe by tribe; and they shall judge the people with righteous judgement. Thou shalt not wrest judgement; thou shalt not show partiality; neither shalt thou take a bribe, for a bribe doth blind the eyes of the wise, and pervert the words of the righteous.' Scripture rules that judges must never take bribes, but the rabbis extend this ruling to include any form of gift even from the party he thinks is in the right.

COMPROMISE

According to rabbinic Judaism, if both parties to a dispute are willing to compromise, this is a form of justice. It is especially desirable in a complicated case, where it is unlikely right is solely on one side, for the parties to compromise with one another. In marital disputes, both parties may be right in some respects and wrong in others. In such cases, the path of compromise is often the best solution.

Above Arbitration at a bet din *(Jewish court that deals with religious questions) in a Czech Jewish community, 1925.*

Above The tombs of Zechariah and Jehoshaphat in the Kidron Valley, Israel. The prophet Zechariah stressed the importance of justice.

Witnesses in a law suit must be respectable individuals who can be relied on to tell the truth. Anyone who has a bad reputation in money matters is disqualified. No relative is permitted to serve as a witness.

THE VIRTUE OF JUSTICE

In the Mishnah, the first chapter of the Ethics of the Fathers concludes with a statement from Simeon ben Gamaliel: 'On three things the world rests: on justice, truth and peace.' Here the words of the prophet Zechariah are quoted: 'These are the things that ye shall do: Speak ye every man the truth with his neighbour; execute the judgment of truth and in your gates' (Zechariah 8:16). Commentators on this passage remark that where there is truth, there is justice; and where there is justice, there is peace. A peace based on injustice is no peace and will not endure.

JUSTICE IN PRACTICE

It is not only in courts that justice should be found – Judaism demands that Jews must be just in their dealings with one another. The relationship between employer and employee must

be based on fairness. Shopkeepers should charge fair prices and not take advantage of customers – they should have just weights and measures. A principle of everyday justice is the demand that no one should take advantage of another's helplessness. The Bible declares: 'Thou shalt not curse the deaf, nor put a stumbling block before the blind, but thou shalt fear thy God: I am the Lord' (Leviticus

19:14). This principle is extended in rabbinic sources to cover every instance of causing harm to another by allowing someone to err through weakness. Thus, the rabbis forbid giving advice one knows to be bad.

Right A horrifying vision of Hell by Renaissance painter Hieronymus Bosch. Belief in punishment in the Hereafter is a feature of rabbinic theology.

HOLINESS

WITHIN THE JEWISH FAITH, THE TERM HOLINESS REFERS TO WHAT IS
ELEVATED ABOVE THE MATERIAL PLANE. THE CONCEPT RELATES TO A
WIDE RANGE OF TOPICS INCLUDING GOD HIMSELF.

According to the Bible, holiness is a characteristic of God. He is apart from the universe and beyond its limitations. In the Book of Isaiah, the Serafim declare: 'Holy, holy, holy is the Lord of Hosts: the whole earth is full of his glory' (Isaiah 6:3). Here Scripture asserts that God is apart from the world he created, yet there are intimations of his holiness everywhere. Anything that is dedicated to God is called holy, such as the Temple or the synagogue. The implication is that to be near God it is necessary to be holy – such an idea is expressed in Leviticus 19:12: 'Speak unto all the congregation of the children of Israel, and say to them: Ye shall be holy; for I the Lord your God am holy.'

Below A 19th-century drawing of the Western Wall in Jerusalem by Alexandre Bida. Popularly known as the Wailing Wall, Jews regard it as a central holy site of pilgrimage.

THE JEWISH PEOPLE

According to the Jewish tradition, Jewish communities are referred to as holy: a community is called *kehillah kedoshah*, implying that where Jews are gathered together for sacred purposes, holiness is present. Holiness is not reserved for select individuals, but for persons living normal lives. Jews become holy through their involvement with spiritual affairs: this involves the willingness to give up worldly things as well as a separation from physical pleasures.

SELF-CONTROL

While it is true that Judaism does not encourage asceticism, self-denial is regarded as a virtue. Thus the rabbis stated: 'Sanctify yourself by denying yourself even something of that which is otherwise permitted.' This dictum implies that self-control must be exhibited even when doing what the Torah permits. Whatever the Torah forbids is

Above Seraphim with wings (Isaiah 6) decorated with an all-seeing eye motif, from a 1537 Romanian fresco.

forbidden; but this does not mean that one should indulge oneself. Each person must exercise restraint. It is ultimately left to each individual to determine how much self-control should be exercised so that worldly pleasure does not become a barrier to spiritual growth.

THE QUEST FOR HOLINESS

For ordinary people, Judaism prescribes various aids to holiness. Prominent among these are the 'holy days', which include the Sabbath and festivals when secular concerns are set aside and there is time for spiritual refreshment. Yom Kippur (the Day of Atonement) in particular is referred to as Yom ha-Kodesh (the Holy Day); this is a time when the needs of normal physical life are transcended and Jews are called to be near to God. Classical Jewish sources are called 'holy' – by studying these it is possible for the individual to achieve a degree of spirituality. Further, there are various symbols of the Jewish religion including *tefillin*, or 'phylacteries', the *Sefer Torah*, or 'Torah scroll', and the

mezuzah, or 'rolled parchments with scriptural references', which are connected with holiness. Conversely, there is the need to avoid the opposite of what is holy.

SELF-DENIAL

According to the Talmud, there are two views of self-denial. One is that those who deny themselves are sinners, presumably because they reject legitimate gifts of food and drink which God has given to them. The second is that on the contrary those who pursue self-denial are holy. A number of thinkers hold that it all depends on one's motives. If a person is sincere in the quest for God and appreciates how necessary it is to forego many of life's pleasures to attain a spiritual state, then he is holy.

Below Blowing the shofar to signal the end of the Yom Kippur fast, London, 1929. The High Holy Days begin with Rosh Hashanah and end with Yom Kippur.

But if his reasons are a hatred of life or a wish to demonstrate religious superiority, he is a sinner.

PRAISE OF HOLINESS

Rabbinic sources extol the state of holiness. Hence, the rabbis ruled that before carrying out a *mitzvah*, or 'commandment', it is essential to recite the benediction: 'Blessed art thou, O Lord our God, King of the universe, who has sanctified us with his commandments.' Through observing God's laws we become holy. In rabbinic sources the usual name for God is *Ha-Kadosh Barukh Hu*, or 'The Holy One, blessed be he'. There are degrees of holiness and one should make an attempt to ascend to a higher level. The Zohar states nothing is more holy than the Torah, and both students of the Torah and those who help them to study are to be called holy.

THE GIFT OF HOLINESS

According to the tradition, the attainment of holiness is not possible through one's own efforts. Rather, it is a gift from God. According to the Talmud, a person who makes a little effort to be holy is given much holiness from on high. In this quest, there are stages of development. As the 2nd-century CE teacher Phinehas ben Yair explained: 'The knowledge of the Torah leads to watchfulness, watchfulness to zeal, zeal to cleanliness, cleanliness to abstinence, abstinence to purity, purity to saintliness, saintliness to humility, humility to the fear of sin, and the fear of sin to holiness. Holiness leads to the holy spirit and the holy spirit leads to the resurrection of the dead.'

CHAPTER 8

MESSIAH AND THE HEREAFTER

For thousands of years the Jewish people have longed for messianic deliverance; sustained by this belief the community has endured persecution and suffering, confident that they will ultimately be rescued from earthly travail. In the Hebrew Bible, God declared to Abraham, Isaac and Jacob that their descendants will inherit a land of their own. In biblical times, such deliverance was understood as pertaining to human history. Yet, with the emergence of rabbinic Judaism, the concept of the Messiah was transformed. In rabbinic sources, sages maintained that prior to the coming of the Messiah, the world would be subject to a series of tribulations defined as the 'birth pangs of the Messiah'. The Messiah would then usher in a period of deliverance, and all Jewish exiles would be returned to Zion. This messianic age would usher in the concept of perfect peace in the end of days. At the end of this messianic period, all human beings would undergo judgement and either be rewarded with heavenly bliss or punished everlastingly.

Opposite The Resurrection of the Dead, *an important expectation of the messianic tradition. From the* Très belles heures of Notre Dame, *1410, commissioned by the Duc de Berry.*

Above Section of The Last Judgment *showing the deceased in Paradise. A painting c. 1465 by Giovanni di Paolo, one of the most important painters of the Sienese School.*

BIBLICAL MESSIAH

IN SCRIPTURE THE MESSIAH IS CONCEIVED OF AS THE REDEEMER OF ISRAEL. AS GOD'S ANOINTED, HE WILL USHER IN A PERIOD OF PEACE IN WHICH ALL PROPHECIES WILL BE FULFILLED.

Biblical history foretells of a future redemption, which will be brought about through an appointed agent of the Lord. According to the early prophets, such a kingly figure will be a descendant of David. Eventually there arose the view that the house of David would rule over Israel as well as neighbouring peoples. Later prophets predicted the destruction of the nation because of its iniquity, yet they were convinced that God would eventually deliver the Israelites and usher in a new redemption of the nation.

THE CONCEPT OF THE MESSIAH

The term 'Messiah' is an adaptation of the Hebrew *Ha-Mashiah*, or 'the anointed'. In time it came to refer to the redeemer at the End of Days.

Below Ethiopian icon from the 18th–19th century, showing the Messiah celebrating Passover with his disciples.

Although there are no explicit references to such a figure in the Torah, the notion of the redemption of the Jewish nation is alluded to in the promises made to the patriarchs. Such references form the background to the development of the doctrine of deliverance.

It was in the Book of Samuel that the notion of redemption through a divinely appointed agent was explicitly expressed; here Scripture asserts that the Lord had chosen David and his descendants to rule over Israel to the end of time.

This early biblical doctrine assumed that David's position would endure throughout his lifetime and would be inherited by a series of successors who would carry out God's providential plan. With the fall of the Davidic empire after the death of King Solomon in the 10th century BCE, there arose the view that the house of David would eventually rule over the two divided

Above The Prophet Amos, *who foretold the coming of the Day of the Lord, by Juan de Borgoña, 1535.*

kingdoms as well as neighbouring peoples. Yet despite such a hopeful vision of Israel's future, the pre-exilic prophets were convinced that the nation would be punished for its iniquity. Warning the people of this impending disaster, the Northern 8th-century BCE prophet Amos spoke of the Day of the Lord when God would unleash his fury against those who had rebelled against him. None the less, the prophets predicted that those who had been led away into captivity would eventually return to their own land.

Below Prophet Jonah rests under a *gourd vine in Nineveh; a 4th-century* CE *mosaic pavement from the basilica in Aquileia, northern Italy.*

Above The Earthly Paradise, 1607, Jan Brueghel the Elder. According to tradition, the Messiah will bring about God's kingdom on earth.

REDEMPTION AND REBIRTH

In the Southern Kingdom the 8th-century BCE prophet Isaiah predicted that the inhabitants of Judah would be destroyed because of their iniquity. None the less, he predicted the eventual triumph of God's kingdom on earth. In his view, only a faithful remnant will remain, from which a redeemer will issue forth to bring about a new epoch in the nation's history. A contemporary of Isaiah, the prophet Micah, also predicted that the nation would not be cut off. God, he stated, had a purpose for them in the future. Confident of the restoration of the people, he looked forward to an age of fulfilment and prosperity. Like Isaiah, he predicted a time of messianic redemption. All nations will go to the mountain of the Lord and dwell together in peace. In those days swords will be turned into ploughshares and each man will sit under his vine and fig tree.

POST-EXILIC PROPHECY

Dwelling in Babylon in the 6th-century BCE, the prophet Ezekiel castigated Israel for their iniquity – because they had turned away from

God further punishment would be inflicted on them. Yet, despite the departure of God's glory from the Temple, the prophet reassured the nation that it will not be abandoned. In his view, God takes no delight in the death of sinners; what he requires instead is a contrite heart. Using the image of a shepherd and his flock, Ezekiel reassuringly declared that God will gather his people from exile and return them to the Promised Land. In a vision of dry bones, Ezekiel predicts that, although the nation had been devastated, it will be renewed in a future

deliverance: a future king will rule over his people and under his dominion Jerusalem will be restored. In a similar vein Second Isaiah offers words of consolation to those who had experienced the destruction of Judah. In place of oracles of denunciation, the prophet offered the promise of hope and restoration.

The Bible thus presents a picture of destruction that is followed by redemption. According to the prophets, the Lord will have compassion upon his chosen people and return them to their former glory. Reassured by these words of comfort, the ancient Israelites were secure in the knowledge that they had not been forsaken. The Messiah will usher in an era of peace and tranquillity. God will be reunited with his people and Zion will undergo future glory. These words of comfort provided the framework for the evolution of the concept of messianic deliverance, which was expanded by Jewish writers during the Second Temple period.

Below The prophet Samuel anoints David. From a wall painting in the Dura-Europos synagogue, Syria, c. 2nd century CE.

POST-BIBLICAL MESSIAH

DRAWING ON BIBLICAL THEMES, POST-BIBLICAL JEWISH LITERATURE DEVELOPED THE CONCEPT OF THE MESSIAH. IN THESE WRITINGS THE STAGES OF MESSIANIC DELIVERANCE ARE DESCRIBED IN DETAIL.

In post-biblical Jewish literature, which is known as the Apocrypha and Pseudepigrapha, the concept of a future redemption was not forgotten, and there are frequent references to the ingathering of the exiles. Although the messianic predictions in these writings vary considerably, they bear witness to the deep longing for divine deliverance and redemption.

MESSIANIC ANTICIPATION

Throughout the book of Ben Sira composed in the 2nd century BCE, the love of Israel is manifest. In this work the author outlines the various stages of messianic anticipation – the destruction of Israel's enemies, the sanctification of God's name by elevating the Jewish nation, the performance of miracles, the ingathering of the exiles, the glorification of Jerusalem and the Temple, reward for the righteous and punishment for the wicked, and the fulfilment of prophetic expectations. Although Ben Sira does not specify that redemption will come through Davidic rule or an individual Messiah, the author does specify that the house of David will be preserved.

RETURN OF THE EXILES

In the Apocryphal Baruch, which was also written in the 2nd century BCE, there is a reference to the idea that God will bring about the return of the exiles to the land of their fathers once they have turned from their evil ways. Later in the book the author describes Jerusalem,

Above Head of the Messiah, *1648, by Rembrandt, who lived in the Jodenbreestraat in Amsterdam, in what was then becoming the Jewish quarter.*

which is to be renewed. The book continues with a description of the return of the exiles: 'Arise, O Jerusalem, and stand upon the height; And look about thee toward the east; And behold thy children gathered from the going down of the sun unto the rising thereof.' Alluding to Second Isaiah's vision of the ingathering of the exiles, the author depicts the re-establishment of Zion in glowing terms.

THE MESSIANIC AGE

Composed after the destruction of the Temple, the author of the Apocryphal Baruch presented a variety of reflections about the messianic age beginning with the Day of Judgement. During this period the Day of the Lord was identified with the 'birth pangs of the Messiah' – this did not refer to any suffering of the Messiah himself, but to the tribulations of the messianic age. In his view the Holy Lord will come from his dwelling, appear from the highest

---

THE WORLD TO COME

Unlike other post-biblical work, the Wisdom of Solomon is preoccupied with the world to come, eternal life, and divine retribution. In chapter 3

the author describes the reward for the righteous: 'But the souls of the righteous are in the hand of God; and no torment shall touch them. In the eyes of fools they seemed to die; and their departure was accounted to be their hurt; and their going from us to be their ruin: but they are in peace.' Turning to the destruction of the wicked, he described the future Day of the Lord: 'He shall sharpen stern wrath for a sword: and the world shall go forth with him to fight against his insensate foes; shafts of lightning shall fly with true aim; and from the clouds, as from a drawn bow, shall they leap to the mark.'

Left The Last Judgement *by Hieronymus Bosch, 1500.*

---

their spirits will grow strong when they see the Messiah, and heaven and earth will be transformed. The elect will then dwell in a new and blessed earth upon which sinners and evildoers will not set foot. The Messiah will be a staff to the righteous and holy and a light to the gentiles. All who dwell on earth will worship and bless him and praise the God of Spirits.

REDEMPTION

Another work of this period, *The Testaments of the Twelve Patriarchs*, consists of stories about the tribal patriarchs. In the Testament of Judah, there are vivid descriptions of messianic redemption. The star of peace

will arise and walk in meekness among men. The heavens will be opened and pour out their blessings. The spirit of truth will come upon the children of Judah. A shoot will come forth from the stock of Judah and the rod of righteousness will be in his hand to judge and save all those who call upon him. All the tribes will become one people and have one language. Those who died in grief will arise and awake to everlasting life.

Above Satan Arousing the Rebel Angels, *1808. An illustration by English visionary William Blake for John Milton's poem* Paradise Lost.

of heavens and tread on Mount Sinai. Not only will the wicked be chastised, so too will Satan and the angels who have corrupted the earth be brought to judgement. At the end of days the righteous will be delivered, beget a thousand children, and complete all their days in peace. The whole earth will be filled with righteousness and the fields prosper. The Lord will open the storehouses of heavenly blessing, which he will pour out upon the faithful.

THE MESSIAH

The Ethiopic Book of Enoch, another apocryphal work, continues with a description of the Messiah himself. According to the author, the Messiah existed before the creation of the world, and his dwelling place is under the wings of the God of Spirits where the elect shall pass before him. On that day the Elect One will sit on the throne of glory and choose the occupations of men and their dwelling places;

Below German engraving of the Tribes of Israel around the Ark of the Covenant, c.1630. Tradition says the Messiah will transport the scattered people of Israel back to Zion.

RABBINIC MESSIAH

DURING THE RABBINIC PERIOD, JEWISH SAGES DEVELOPED THE CONCEPT OF THE MESSIAH: MESSIANIC REDEMPTION WOULD BE DIVIDED INTO A SERIES OF STAGES LEADING TO THE WORLD TO COME.

Once the Temple had been destroyed and the Jewish people driven out of their homeland, the nation was bereft. In their despair the rabbis longed for a kingly figure who would deliver them from exile and rebuild their holy city. Drawing on messianic ideas that are found in Scripture, the Apocrypha and Pseudepigrapha, they foresaw the coming of a future deliverance when all peoples would be converted to the worship of the one true God.

THE COMING OF THE MESSIAH

In rabbinic sources, sages elaborated the themes found in Scripture as well as in Jewish literature of the Second Temple period. In midrashic collections and the Talmud they formulated a complex eschatological scheme divided into a series of stages. In their view, this chain of

Right This 1400s Russian icon shows the Messiah's entry into Jerusalem.

events will begin with devastation. As in the Pseudepigrapha, such sufferings are referred to as the 'birth pangs of the Messiah'. As the Talmud states: 'With the footprints of the Messiah, insolence will increase and death reach its height; the vine will yield its fruit but the wine will be costly. There will be none to offer reproof, and the whole empire will be converted to heresy.'

Not only will natural disasters come upon the land, the word of the Lord will also be forgotten during the time of messianic travail. As the Talmud states: 'When our teachers entered the vineyard (school) at Yabneh, they said: "The Torah is destined to be forgotten in Israel, as it is written (Amos 8:11): 'Behold the days come, saith the Lord God, that

I will send a famine in the land, not a famine of bread, nor a thirst for water, but of hearing the words of the Lord.'"'

THE PROPHET ELIJAH

Despite these dire predictions, the rabbis maintained that the prophet Elijah will return prior to the coming of the Messiah to solve all earthly problems. In addition, his role in the messianic era will be to certify the ritual uncleanliness of families that suffered from mixed marriages or forbidden unions, and also to grant permission to hitherto excluded peoples from marrying Jews. Moreover, Elijah's task will be to bring back to the Jewish people those who had been wrongfully excluded from the community. All this is to be done in anticipation of the coming of the Messiah. As a forerunner of messianic redemption, Elijah will announce from the top of Mount Carmel that the Messiah is coming who will initiate the end of history and the advent of God's kingdom on earth.

Left Gog and Magog. A woodcut for the Martin Luther Bible of 1534, from the workshop of Lucas Cranach the Elder. According to tradition, the Messiah will engage in battle with Gog and Magog.

MESSIAH BEN JOSEPH

Drawing on earlier conceptions, the rabbis formulated the doctrine of a second Messiah – the son of Joseph – who will precede the King-Messiah, the Messiah ben David. According to legend, this Messiah will engage in battle with God and Magog, the traditional enemies of Israel, and be slain. Only after his defeat will the Messiah ben David arrive in glory. As a hero, the Messiah ben Joseph will be mourned by the Jewish people. As the Talmud states, quoting Scripture: 'And the land shall mourn, every family apart; the family of the house of David apart, and their wives apart' (Zechariah 12:12).

In this final struggle against the nation's enemies, God will act on behalf of Israel. Thus in the midrash, the rabbis maintain that: 'There are four shinings forth: the first was in Egypt, as it is written (Psalm 80:1), "Give ear, O Shepherd of Israel, thou that leadest Joseph like a flock, thou that art enthroned upon the cherubim shine forth"; the second was at the time of the giving of the Law, as it is written (Deuteronomy 33:2), "He shone forth from Mount Paran"; the third will take place in the days of Gog and Magog, as it is

Above The beloved city. View of Jerusalem, *Russian painting, 1821, by Maxim N. Vorobyev.*

written (Psalm 94:1), "Thou God to whom vengeance belongeth shine forth"; the fourth will be in the days of the Messiah (ben David) as it is written (Psalm 50:2), "Out of Zion, the perfection of beauty, shall God shine forth."'

Regarding this struggle, the rabbis speculated that God had already revealed the defeat of Gog and Magog to Moses. Hence Rabbi Nehemiah stated that in Numbers 11:26 Eldad and Medad prophesied concerning this battle: 'As it is written (Ezekiel 38:17), "Thus saith the Lord God: Art thou he of whom I spoke in old time by my servants the prophets of Israel, that prophesied in those days [from many] years that I would bring thee against them?"' and so on. According to Simeon ben Yohai (2nd century CE), the war with Gog and Magog was one of the most terrible evils to befall humanity. Yet after Israel is delivered from this struggle, the King-Messiah will come to bring about the messianic age.

MESSIAH BEN DAVID

During the early rabbinic period, numerous legends emerged about the names and personality of this glorious figure. His moral character and spiritual integrity were frequently exalted and with his coming

the dispersion would cease. Thus Simeon ben Yohai proclaimed: 'Come and see how beloved is Israel before the Holy One, blessed is he; for wherever they went into exile the Shekinah [God's presence] was with them, as it is written (I Samuel 2:27), "Did I indeed reveal myself unto the house of thy father when they were in Egypt." They went into exile in Babylonia, and the Shekinah was with them, as it is written (Isaiah 43:14), "For your sake I was sent to Babylonia." Likewise, when they shall be redeemed in the future, the Shekinah will be with them, as it is written (Deuteronomy 30:3), "Then the Lord thy God will return with thy captivity." It does not say "will bring back thy captivity" but "will return with thy captivity" – teaching that the Holy one, blessed is he, returns with them from the places of exile.'

Here God is described as accompanying his chosen people in exile, sharing their sufferings. Yet with messianic redemption, the exiles will return to Zion in triumph with God at their head. Clouds of glory shall be spread over them, and they will come singing with joy on their lips.

Below The Return to Jerusalem, after Raphael. Tradition is that the Messiah will bring about the return of all Jews to the Holy Land.

THE MESSIANIC AGE AND HEAVEN

AT THE CULMINATION OF THE MESSIANIC AGE, ALL WILL BE JUDGED. THE RIGHTEOUS WILL ENTER HEAVEN. THIS IS DIVIDED INTO A SERIES OF CHAMBERS FOR VARIOUS CLASSES OF INDIVIDUALS.

Rabbinic literature contains frequent speculation about the Days of the Messiah (also referred to as 'The World to Come'). At the end of this messianic period, all human beings will undergo judgement and either be rewarded with heavenly bliss or punished everlastingly. This vision of a future hope was animated by the Jewish conviction that God will not abandon his people.

THE MESSIANIC AGE

In their depictions of the messianic age, Jewish sages stressed that the Days of the Messiah will be totally different from the present world. Concerning the fruitfulness of the harvest, for example, they stressed his

Below Adam and Eve driven from the Garden of Eden by James Tissot. In the tradition, Heaven is referred to as Gan Eden *(Garden of Eden).*

Right Detail of a Turkish Jewish rug showing Adam and Eve, late 19th century. The Garden of Eden symbolizes heavenly bliss.

era 'is not of this world. In this world, there is the trouble of harvesting and treading [grapes]; but in the world to come a man will bring one grape on a wagon or in a ship, put it in the corner of his house, and use its contents as if it had been a large wine cask...There will be no grape that will not contain 30 kegs of wine.'

Speculating on the length of this period, the early rabbinic sages differed as to its duration. Eliezer, for instance, stated: 'The Days of the Messiah will be 40 years; for it is written in one place (Deuteronomy 8:3), "And he afflicted thee, and suffered thee to hunger and fed thee with manna", and in another place it is written (Psalm 90:15), "Make us

HEAVEN

The principal qualification for divine reward is obedience to God's law; those who are judged righteous will enter into Heaven (Gan Eden). One of the earliest descriptions is in a compilation called Midrash Konen:

There are five chambers for various classes of the righteous. The first is built of cedar with a ceiling of transparent crystal. This is the habitation of non-Jews who become true and devoted converts to Judaism. The second is built of cedar, with a ceiling of fine silver. This is the habitation of the penitents, headed by Manasseh, king of Israel, who teaches them the Law. The third chamber is built of silver and gold, ornamented with pearls ... [here] rest Abraham, Isaac, and Jacob, the tribes, those of the Egyptian exodus, and those who died in the wilderness, headed by Moses and Aaron ...The fourth chamber is made of olive-wood and is inhabited by those who have suffered for the sake of their religion... The fifth chamber is built of precious stones, gold and silver, surrounded by myrrh and aloes. ... This chamber is inhabited by the Messiah ben David, Elijah and the Messiah ben Joseph.

Above Vine of the Promised Land. 12th-century Romanesque enamel from the Rhenish School.

glad according to the days wherein thou hast afflicted us according to the years wherein we have seen evil."' Dosa said: 'Four hundred years; for it is written in one place (Genesis 15:13), "And they shall serve them, and they shall afflict them 400 years"; and in another place it is written (Psalm 90:15), "Make us glad according to the days wherein thou has afflicted us."' Jose the Galilean said: 'Three hundred and sixty-five years, according to the number of days in the solar year, as it is written (Isaiah 63:4), "For the day of vengeance was in my heart, and my year of redemption has come."'

According to another Baraitha: 'It was taught in the school of Elijah: The world will endure 6,000 years;

Right The Valley and Lower Pool of Gihon, Jerusalem, c.1870, by W. Dickens. According to tradition, the exiles will return to Jerusalem at the time of Messianic redemption.

2,000 in chaos, 2,000 under the Law and 2,000 during the messianic age; but because of our many iniquities time has been lost from the last period (that is, 4,000 years have already passed, yet the Messiah has not yet arrived).' Other traditions, however, stress that such reckoning is fruitless. Hence the Talmud records: 'Seven things are hidden from men. These are the day of death, the day of consolation, the depth of judgement, no man knows what is in the minds of his friend; no man knows which of his business ventures will be profitable, or when the kingdom of the house of David will be restored or when the sinful kingdom will fall.'

WORLD TRANSFORMATION

Despite such disagreement about the length of this period, there was a general acceptance among the sages that at the end of the Days of the Messiah all will be changed. At the close of this era, a final judgement will come upon all humankind. Yet for such judging to take place, all those who have died will need to be resurrected. Given that there is no explicit belief in eternal salvation in the Bible, the rabbis of the post-biblical period were faced with the difficulty of proving that the doctrine of resurrection of the dead is contained in Scripture that they regarded as authoritative. To do this, they employed a number of principles of exegesis based on the assumption that each word of the Torah was transmitted by God to Moses.

HELL

ACCORDING TO JEWISH SAGES, THOSE WHO SIN WILL BE CONDEMNED TO ETERNAL TORMENT. RABBINIC LITERATURE DEPICTS THEIR SUFFERING IN GRAPHIC DETAIL.

As with heaven, we find extensive and detailed descriptions of hell in Jewish literature. In the Babylonian Talmud, Joshua ben Levi deduces the division of hell from biblical quotations. This talmudic concept of the sevenfold structure of hell was greatly elaborated in rabbinic sources.

DIVISIONS OF HELL

According to one midrashic source, it requires 300 years to traverse the height or width or the depth of each division, and it would take 6,300 years to go over a tract of land equal in extent to the seven divisions. Each of these seven divisions of hell is in turn divided into seven subdivisions, and in each compartment there are seven rivers of fire, and seven of hail. The width of each is 100 ells (measurement equivalent to about 45 ins/114cm), its depth 1,000, and its length 300. They flow from each other and are supervised by the Angels of Destruction. Besides, in each compartment there are 700 caves, and in each cave there are 7,000 crevices. In each crevice there are 7,000 scorpions. Every scorpion has 300 rings, and in every ring 7,000 pouches of venom from which flow seven rivers of deadly poison. If a man handles it, he immediately bursts, every limb is torn from his body, his bowels are cleft, and he falls upon his face.

PUNISHMENT

Confinement to hell is the result of disobeying God's Torah as is illustrated by a midrash concerning the evening visit of the soul to hell before it is implanted in an individual. There it sees the Angels of Destruction smiting with fiery scourges; the sinners all the while crying out, but no mercy is shown to them. The angel guides the soul and then asks: 'Do you know who these are?' Unable to respond the soul listens as the angel continues:

Above The Ungodly Shall Not Stand *by the 19th-century French artist James Tissot.*

'Those who are consumed with fire were created like you. When they were put into the world, they did not observe God's Torah and his commandments. Therefore they have come to this disgrace, which you see them suffer. Know, your destiny is also to depart from the world. Be just, therefore, and not wicked, that you may gain the future world.'

VISIT TO HELL

According to this midrash, the soul was not alone in being able to see hell; a number of biblical personages entered into its midst. Moses, for example, was guided through hell by an angel, and his journey there gives us the most complete picture of its torments: 'When Moses and the Angel of Hell entered hell together, they saw men being tortured by the Angels of Destruction. Some sinners were suspended by their eyelids, some by their ears, some by their hands, and some by their tongues. In addition, women were suspended by their hair and their breasts by chains of fire. Such punishments were inflicted on the basis of sins

Left Dante's Divine Comedy, *1465, by Domenico di Michelino. Hell on the left, Purgatory in the background, with Adam and Eve at the summit; on the right Dante's home city of Florence and Brunelleschi's dome.*

Right Fire, the devil and separation in a 19th-century Japanese painting of Hell.

that were committed: those who hung by their eyes had looked lust-fully upon their neighbours' wives and possessions; those who hung by their ears had listened to empty and vain speech and did not listen to the Torah; those who hung by their tongues had spoken slanderously; those who hung by their hands had robbed and murdered their neigh-bours. The women who hung by their hair and breasts had uncovered them in the presence of young men in order to seduce them.

In another place, called Alukah, Moses saw sinners suspended by their feet with their heads down-wards and their bodies covered with long black worms. These sinners were punished in this way because they swore falsely, profaned the Sabbath and the Holy Days, despised the sages, called their neighbours by unseemly nicknames, wronged the orphan and the widow, and bore false witness. In another section,

Below The Angel of Death and Destruction visits Rome during a plague. Painting by Jules-Elie Delaunay, 1869.

Moses saw sinners prone on their faces with 2,000 scorpions lashing, stinging and tormenting them. Each of these scorpions had 70,000 heads, each had 70,000 mouths, each mouth 70,000 stings, and each sting 70,000 pouches of poison and venom. So great was the pain they inflicted that the eyes of the sinners melted in their sockets. These sin-ners were punished in this way because they had robbed other Jews, were arrogant in the community, put their neighbours to shame in pub-lic, delivered their fellow Jews into the hands of the gentiles, denied the Torah, and maintained that God is not the creator of the world.

THE NATURE OF HELL

This eschatological scheme, which was formulated over the centuries by innumerable Jewish scholars, should not be seen as a flight of fancy. It was a serious attempt to explain God's ways. Israel was God's chosen peo-ple and had received his promise of reward for keeping his law. Since this did not happen on earth in this life, the rabbis believed it must occur in the World to Come. Never did the rab-bis relinquish the belief that God would justify Israel by destroying the power of the oppressing nations. This would come about in the messianic age. The individual who had died without seeing the justification of God would be resurrected to see the ultimate victory of the Jewish peo-ple. And just as the nations would be judged in the period of messianic redemption, so would each individ-ual. Those deemed wicked would be punished everlastingly. In this way, the vindication of the righteous was assured in the hereafter.

JEWISH MESSIAHS

OVER THE YEARS VARIOUS PSEUDO-MESSIAHS APPEARED, EACH CLAIMING
THEY HAD COME TO USHER IN THE MESSIANIC AGE. THEY ALL FAILED
TO FULFIL THE EXPECTATIONS OF DELIVERANCE AND REDEMPTION.

JESUS THE MESSIAH

From the Gospels it appears that a
Jewish sect of Christians emerged in
the 1st century BCE. In consonance
with messianic expectations of this
period, these believers expected their
Messiah to bring about the fulfilment of human history. According
to the New Testament, Jesus of
Nazareth spent most of his life in
Galilee where he preached the coming of the Kingdom of God. After a
brief association with John the
Baptist, he attracted disciples from
among the most marginalized sec-
tors of society to whom he
proclaimed his message.

Despite his popularity among the
masses, he soon aroused suspicion
and hostility from both Jewish and
Roman officials and was put to
death during the reign of Pontius
Pilate in about 30CE. Afterwards his
followers believed he had risen from
the dead, appeared to them and
promised to return to usher in the
period of messianic rule. The Jewish
community, however, rejected these
claims; in their view, Jesus did not
fulfil the messianic role as outlined
in Scripture and portrayed in rabbinic sources. Despite the growth of
the Christian community in the
years after Jesus' death, Jews continued to wait for the advent of a
Messiah-King who would return the
exiles to Zion, resurrect the dead
and usher in a period of messianic
redemption.

EARLY MESSIAHS

The destruction of Jerusalem and
the Temple in 70CE profoundly
affected Jewish life and led to intensified longing for messianic
deliverance. With the loss of both the

*Above Jesus talking to Moses and
Elijah with his disciples Peter, John
and James below, c. 1278, by Duccio
di Buoninsegna.*

Northern and Southern Kingdoms,
Jews looked to the advent of the
messianic age when the nation
would be restored to its ancient
homeland. Although mainstream
Jewry rejected Jesus as the long-
awaited Messiah, the Jewish
community continued to long for
divine deliverance.

In 132CE a messianic revolt
against Rome was led by the war-
rior Simeon bar Kochba. This
rebellion was inspired by the conviction that God sought to
overthrow Roman oppression.
When this uprising was crushed,
Jews put forward the year of messianic deliverance until the 5th
century CE. In fulfilment of this pre-
diction, a figure named Moses
appeared in Crete, declaring that he
would be able to lead Jews across the
seas to Judaea. However, after this
plan failed, Jews continued to engage
in messianic speculation, believing
that they could determine the date
of their deliverance on the basis of
scriptural texts.

*Left Herodium, the ancient palace-
fortress built by Herod the Great on a
Judean hilltop, who lived at the time of
Jesus, the Christian Messiah.*

MEDIEVAL MESSIAHS

During the early medieval period a series of messianic pretenders appeared such as Abu Isa al-Isphani, Serene and Yugdhan, and the traveller Eldad Ha-Dani brought reports of the ten lost tribes, an event which stimulated the Jewish desire to return to Zion. At the end of the 11th and throughout the 12th century a number of pseudo-Messiahs appeared in the Jewish world. In 1096 the arrival of the Crusaders gave rise to widespread excitement among Jews living in the Byzantine empire. As a consequence, the French Jewish community sent a representative to Constantinople to obtain information about the advent of the Messiah. In Khazaria 17 communities marched to the desert to meet the ten lost tribes. In Salonika the arrival of the prophet Elijah was announced. During this period a proselyte, Obadiah, journeyed to northern Palestine, where he

Below Shabbetai Tzvi, a Jewish rabbi and Kabbalist who claimed to be the long-awaited Jewish Messiah, 1670s.

Above Bishop John of Speyer (r. 1090–1104) protecting Jews from Crusaders, from A Popular History of Germany, 1878. *Messianic expectations increased during the Crusades.*

encountered the Karaite Solomon ha-Kohen who declared he was the Messiah and would soon redeem the Jewish nation. In Mesopotamia another messianic figure, ben Chadd, appeared but was subsequently arrested by the caliph of Baghdad.

In the next century a messianic forerunner in Yemen was described by the 12th-century Jewish philosopher Moses Maimonides. But the most important pseudo-Messiah of this period was David Alroy who appeared in 1147 at the time of the Second Crusade. Born in Amadiya, his real name was Menahem ben Solomon, but he called himself David owing to his claim to be king of the Jews. The movement to recognize his messiahship probably began among mountain Jews of the north-east Caucasus before 1121 and gathered momentum in the ferment accompanying the struggles between Christianity and Islam following the First Crusade and during the wars preceding the Second Crusade.

EARLY MODERN MESSIAHS

In the following centuries other messianic pretenders appeared, including Solomon Molko, a 16th-century Kabbalist and mystic. When Rome was sacked in 1527 he believed he saw the signs of impending redemption. In 1529 he preached about the coming of the Messiah. To fulfil the talmudic legend about the suffering

of the Messiah, he dressed as a beggar and sat for 30 days, fasting among the sick on a bridge over the Tiber. Eventually he was burned at the stake for refusing to embrace Christianity. After his death, many of his disciples refused to accept that he had died and remained loyal to the belief that he was the long-awaited Messiah.

THE MYSTICAL MESSIAH

At the beginning of the 17th century, Lurianic mysticism had made a major impact on Sephardi Jewry, and messianic expectations had become a central feature of Jewish life. In this milieu, the arrival of Shabbetai Tzvi brought about a transformation of Jewish life and thought. In 1665 his messiahship was proclaimed by Nathan of Gaza. Eventually Shabbetai was brought to court and given the choice between conversion and death. In the face of this alternative, he converted to Islam. Despite this act of apostasy, a number of his followers remained loyal, justifying his action on the basis of Kabbalistic ideas. In subsequent years such belief was continued by various branches of the Shabbatean movement.

ANTI-MESSIANISM

DESPITE THE CENTRALITY OF BELIEF IN THE MESSIAH IN THE JEWISH TRADITION, IN RECENT TIMES THE WORLD HAS WITNESSED THE EROSION OF SUCH CONVICTION.

With the conversion of Shabbetai Tzvi in the 17th century, the Jewish preoccupation with messianic calculation diminished. As time passed, many Jews found it increasingly difficult to believe in a miraculous divine intervention that will change the course of human history.

DISILLUSIONMENT

Not surprisingly the failure of the Messiah to appear through thousands of years of history coupled with the repeated appearance of false messiahs throughout the centuries led to widespread disillusionment with the Jewish eschatological hope. As a consequence,

Below A Rabbinical Disputation *by Jacob Toorenvliet (1640–1719). As messianic expectations faded, Jews debated whether a Jewish homeland should be established in Palestine.*

the longing for the Messiah who will bring about the end of history appeared to many Jews as a misguided aspiration. Instead, 18th- and early 19th-century Jewry hailed the breaking down of the ghetto walls and the elimination of social barriers between Jews and Christians. In this milieu the belief in the Kingdom of God inaugurated by the Messiah-King receded in importance; in its place the clarion call for liberty, equality and fraternity signified the dawning of a golden age for the Jewish people.

REFORM JUDAISM

Within Reform Judaism in particular, the doctrine of messianic redemption was radically modified in the light of these developments. In the 19th century, Reform Jews interpreted the new liberation in the Western world as the first step

Above Moses Hess (1812–75), German socialist who argued for the creation of a Jewish homeland.

towards the realization of the messianic dream. For these reformers messianic redemption was understood in this-worldly terms. No longer, according to this view, is it necessary for Jews to pray for a restoration in Erez Israel. Rather, Jews should view their own countries as Zion, and their political leaders as bringing about the messianic age.

Such a conviction was enshrined in the Pittsburgh Platform of the Reform movement, which was formulated in 1885. As a central principle of the Platform, the belief in a personal Messiah was replaced by the concept of a messianic age, which will come about through social causes: 'We recognize in the modern era of universal culture of heart and intellect the approach of the realization of Israel's great messianic hope for the establishment of the kingdom of truth, justice and peace among all men. We consider ourselves no longer a nation but a religious community, and therefore expect neither a return to Palestine, nor a sacrificial worship under the administration of the sons of Aaron, nor a restoration of any of the laws concerning the Jewish state.'

Right *Jewish ghetto in Rovigo, Italy, 1867, by Giovanni Biasin. At the end of the 19th century, Zionists pressed for the creation of a Jewish state to solve the problem of discrimination against Jews in Europe and elsewhere.*

ZIONISM

These sentiments were shared by secular Zionists who similarly rejected the traditional belief in the coming of the Messiah and the in-gathering of the exiles. The early Zionists were determined to create a Jewish homeland, even though the Messiah had not yet arrived.

Rejecting the religious categories of the Jewish past, such figures as Moses Hess (1812–75), Leo Pinsker (1821–91) and Theodor Herzl (1860–1904) pressed for a political solution to the problem of anti-Semitism. In their view there is no point in waiting for a supernatural intervention to remedy Jewish existence.

As Pinsker explained: 'Nowadays, when in a small part of the earth our brethren have caught their breath and can feel more deeply for the sufferings of their brothers; nowadays, when a number of other dependent and oppressed nationalities have been allowed to regain their independence, we, too, must not sit even one moment longer with folded hands; we must not admit that we are doomed to play on in the future the hopeless role of the "wandering Jew" ... it is our bounded duty to devote all our remaining moral force to re-establish ourselves as a living nation, so that we may finally assume a more fitting and dignified role.'

BEYOND MESSIANISM

Such attitudes are representative of a major transformation in Jewish thought. In the past, Jews longed for the advent of a personal Messiah who would bring about the messianic age, deliver the Jewish people to their homeland, and inaugurate the fulfilment of human history.

Although this doctrine continues to be upheld by a large number of devout Orthodox Jews, it has been largely eclipsed by a more secular outlook. Most contemporary Jews prefer to interpret the messianic hope in naturalistic terms, abandoning the belief in the coming of the Messiah, the restoration of the sacrificial system, and the idea of direct divine intervention. On this view, it is argued that Jews should free themselves from the absolutes of the past. Jewish views about the Messiah should be seen as growing out of the life of the people. In the modern world, these ancient doctrines can be superseded by a new vision of Jewish life, which

Right *This Israeli poster of Theodor Herzl celebrates the 50th anniversary of the meeting of the first Zionist Congress in Basle, Switzerland, in 1897, which later became the World Zionist Organization.*

is human-centred in orientation. Rather than await the coming of a divinely appointed deliverer who will bring about peace and harmony on earth, Jews should themselves strive to create a better world for all peoples.

DEATH OF THE AFTERLIFE

IN THE PAST JEWS BELIEVED EARTHLY LIFE WAS NOT THE END. AFTER DEATH THE RIGHTEOUS WOULD BE REWARDED AND THE WICKED PUNISHED. SUCH A CONVICTION HAS LOST ITS HOLD ON MODERN JEWISH CONSCIOUSNESS.

On the basis of the scheme of salvation and damnation – which is at the heart of rabbinic theology throughout the centuries – it might be expected that modern Jewish theologians of all shades of religious observance and opinion would attempt to explain contemporary Jewish history in the context of traditional eschatology. This, however, has not happened: instead many Jewish thinkers have set aside doctrines concerning messianic redemption, resurrection, final judgement and reward for the righteous and punishment for the wicked.

JEWISH THEOLOGY

This shift in emphasis is in part due to the fact that the views expressed in the narrative sections of the midrashim and Talmud are not binding. All Jews are obliged to accept the divine origin of the law, but this is not so with regard to theological concepts and theories expounded by the rabbis. Thus it is possible for a Jew to be religiously pious without accepting all the central beliefs of mainstream Judaism. Indeed,

Above Joseph Hertz (1872–1946) was born in Hungary, became chief rabbi of Great Britain, and wrote on the theme of resurrection.

throughout Jewish history there has been widespread confusion as to what these beliefs are. In the 1st century BCE, for example, the sage Hillel stated that the quintessence of Judaism could be formulated in a single principle: 'That which is hateful to you, do not do to your neighbour. This is the whole of the Law; all the rest is commentary.' Similarly, in the 2nd century CE, the Council of Lydda ruled that under certain circumstances the laws of the Torah may be transgressed in order to save one's life, with the exception of idolatry, murder and unchastity.

PRINCIPLES OF JEWISH FAITH

In both the above cases, the centre of gravity was in the ethical rather than the religious sphere. However, in the medieval period Moses Maimonides (1135–1204) formulated what he considered to be the 13 principles of the Jewish faith. Other thinkers, though, challenged this formulation. Hasdai Crescas (1340–1410), Simon ben Zemah

Below A 19th-century photograph of the city of Lydda, where the Council of Lydda ruled c. 135 CE that in certain circumstances the laws of the Torah could be transgressed in order to save life.

Above Sigmund Freud (1865–1939), Austrian Jewish psychologist, was critical of traditional Jewish theology.

Duran (1361–1444), Joseph Albo (c.1380–c.1444) and Isaac Arami elaborated different creeds, and some thinkers argued that it is impossible to isolate from the whole Torah essential principles of the Jewish faith. As David ben Solomon Ibn Abi Zimra (c.1479–1573) stated: 'I do not agree that it is right to make any of the perfect Torah into a "principle" since the whole Torah is a "principle" from the mouth of the Almighty.' Thus when formulations of the central theological tenets of Judaism were propounded, they were not universally accepted since they were simply the opinions of individual teachers. Without a central authority whose opinion in theological matters was binding on all Jews, it has been impossible to determine the correct theological beliefs in Judaism.

REINTERPRETING MESSIANIC REDEMPTION

Given that there is no authoritative bedrock of Jewish theology, many modern Jewish thinkers have felt fully justified in abandoning the various elements of traditional rabbinic eschatology, which they regard as untenable. The doctrine of messianic redemption, for example, has been radically modified. In the 20th century, Reform Jews interpreted the new liberation in the Western world as the first step towards the realization of the messianic dream. But messianic redemption was understood in this-worldly terms. No longer, according to this view, was it necessary for Jews to pray for a restoration in Erez Israel; rather they should view their own countries as Zion and their political leaders as bringing about the messianic age. Secular Zionists, on the other hand, saw the return to Israel as the legitimate conclusion to be drawn from the realities of Jewish life in Western countries, thereby viewing the State of Israel as a substitute for the Messiah himself.

THE JEWISH HOPE

Traditional rabbinic eschatology has thus lost its force for a large number of Jews in the modern world, and in consequence there has been a gradual this-worldly emphasis in Jewish thought. Significantly this has been accompanied by a powerful

RESURRECTION

The earlier doctrine of the resurrection of the dead has in more recent times been largely replaced by the belief in the immortality of the soul.

The original belief in resurrection was an eschatological hope bound up with the rebirth of the nation in the Days of the Messiah, but as this messianic concept faded into the background, so did this doctrine. For most Jews, physical resurrection is simply inconceivable in the light of a scientific understanding of the world. As the former Chief Rabbi of Great Britain, Joseph Herman Hertz (1872–1946) wrote: 'Many and various are the folk beliefs and poetical fancies in the rabbinical writings concerning Heaven, Gan Eden, and Hell, Gehinnom. Our most authoritative religious guides, however, proclaim that no eye hath seen, nor can mortal fathom, what awaiteth us in the Hereafter; but that even the tarnished soul will not forever be denied spiritual bliss.'

attachment to the Jewish state. For many Jews, the founding of Israel is the central focus of their religious and cultural identity. Jews throughout the world have deep admiration for the astonishing achievements of Israelis in reclaiming the desert and building a viable society. As a result, it is not uncommon for Jews to equate Jewishness with Zionism, and to see Judaism as fundamentally nationalistic in character – this is a far cry from the rabbinic view of history that placed the doctrine of the hereafter at the centre of Jewish life and thought.

Left Partying in a Tel Aviv nightclub. For many young Jews, enjoying this life is more important than the afterlife.

PART III

JEWISH PRACTICE

According to the Jewish heritage, God revealed the Five Books of Moses to Moses on Mount Sinai. Traditional Judaism maintains that in addition Moses received the Oral Tradition. This was passed down from generation to generation and was the subject of rabbinic debate. This first authoritative compilation of the Oral Law was the Mishnah, composed by Yehuda Ha-Nasi in the 2nd century CE. In subsequent centuries sages continued to discuss the content of Jewish law; their deliberations are recorded in the Palestinian and Babylonian Talmuds.

In time, Jewish scholars felt the need to produce codes of Jewish law so that all members of the community would have access to the legal tradition. The most important code, the *Shulkhan Arukh*, was composed in the 16th century by Joseph Caro, together with glosses by Moses Isserles. This has served as the standard Code of Jewish Law for Orthodox Jewry until the present day. Alongside the Orthodox community, the various non-Orthodox branches of Judaism draw on this sacred tradition in their reinterpretation of Jewish observance for the modern world.

Opposite Members of a Hasidic community dancing on Simchat Torah as the scrolls of the Torah are carried round a synagogue at Bnei Brak, Israel.

Above A 17th-century illustration from the Barcelona Haggadah of the Passover Seder meal, celebrated in Jewish homes each year.

CHAPTER 9

WORSHIP

Throughout the history of the nation, Jews have turned to God for comfort and support. In ancient times the Tabernacle and the Temple served as the focus of religious life; subsequently the synagogue became the place for public worship.

The Jewish year consists of 12 months based on the lunar cycle, and is 354 days long. Throughout the year, believers gathered together to recite the traditional liturgy. According to Scripture, God rested on the Sabbath day; as a consequence, the Jewish people are to rest from all forms of labour on *Shabbat*, or 'the Sabbath'. During the rabbinic era, Jewish sages formulated 39 categories of work that were later interpreted by scholars as forbidding a wide range of activities. For Orthodox Jews these regulations are authoritative and binding. Alongside the Sabbath, the pilgrim festivals (Passover, Sukkot and Shavuot) occupy a central place in the Jewish calendar. In ancient times pilgrims went to offer sacrifices in the Temple in Jerusalem. Later special prayers were recited in the synagogue, and each festival has its own special liturgical characteristics, ceremonies and customs.

Opposite Morning service in a synagogue in Teaneck, New Jersey, USA. Young boys gather round the Scrolls of the Law.

Above Jews praying in the Portuguese Sephardic Synagogue in Amsterdam, the Netherlands, built in 1671 by Jews who escaped from the Inquisition in Iberia.

JEWISH CALENDAR

RUNNING FROM NISAN TO ADAR, A VARIETY OF FESTIVALS ARE CELEBRATED THROUGHOUT THE JEWISH YEAR, MANY OF WHICH COMMEMORATE HISTORICAL EVENTS IN THE LIFE OF THE NATION.

According to tradition, the first work of chronology is the *Seder Olam* attributed to Yose ben Halafta (2nd century CE). In this work, calculation is based on biblical genealogical tables, the length of lives recorded in the Hebrew Bible, and the creation of the world in six days. On this basis the year of creation was 3761BCE. The Jewish calendar is lunar, not solar, consisting of a lunar year of 12 months of 29 or 30 days. The year is thus 354 days. The shortage of 11 days between lunar and solar years is made up by adding a 13th month (Adar 2) in certain years. In 356CE the sage Hillel II introduced a permanent calendar based on mathematical and astrological calculations.

CALENDAR REFORM

In modern times there have been several attempts at calendar reform so as to arrange a calendar with the same number of days in each month.

This would result in a uniform pattern so that the same date would fall on the same day of the week each year. The year would be divisible into two equal halves and four quarters. The main objection to such an alteration is that it would disturb the regularity of a fixed Sabbath after every six working days. If the reform were carried out, it would fall on a different day each year.

THE MONTHS

There are 12 months in the Jewish calendar. New Year (Rosh Hashanah) takes place in the seventh month in autumn and begins the spiritual year.

1 NISAN

Shabbat ha-Gadol This Sabbath takes place before Passover.
14 The Fast of the First-Born A fast is observed by every male first-born in gratitude for God's deliverance during the Exodus.
15–22 Passover Passover lasts for eight days and commemorates God's deliverance of the Israelites from Egypt. It is also referred to as the festival of unleavened bread. This term refers to the unleavened bread which the Israelites baked when they fled from the Egyptians.
16 The Counting of the Omer The Israelites were commanded to count 49 days from the second day of Passover when the omer was brought to the Temple. The 50th day was celebrated as a wheat harvest.
17–20 Hol Hamoed Intermediate days of Passover and Sukkot which are observed as semi-holy days.

Left Rabbis drinking with pilgrims at Lag B'Omer at the El Ghriba synagogue, Djerba, Tunisia.

Above Passover lamb being taken into a synagogue. Copper plate from the Verdun Altar, Klosterneuburg, of 1181 made by Nicholas of Verdun.

23 Isru Hag Day after the festival of Passover.
28 Yom Yerushalaim Jerusalem Reunification Day.

2 IYYAR

5 Yom ha-Atsmaut Celebration of the day of the State of Israel's independence.
Second, fifth and seventh days of the week During the month of Iyyar and Marheshvan these days are kept as fast days to atone for any sins committed during the preceding Passover or Sukkot.
14 Second Passover The Paschal lamb was to be sacrificed only on 14 Nisan. Those who were unable to make this sacrifice because they were in a state of ritual impurity or a long way from home could make this offering on 14 Iyyar.
18 Lag B'Omer The period between Passover and Shavuot was a time of tragedy. During the days of Akiva a plague occurred among his disciples and only stopped on 18 Iyyar. This day became known as the Scholars' Feast. The day itself is a time of joy when pilgrims go to Meron where Simeon ben Yohai (2nd century CE) is buried.

3 SIVAN

3–5 Three Days of Bordering This day commemorates the time when the Israelites prepared themselves for the revelation on Mount Sinai.

6–7 Shavuot This festival is celebrated seven weeks after the bringing of the omer on the second day of Passover. It commemorates the giving of the law on Mount Sinai.

8 Isru Hag Day after Shavuot.

4 TAMMUZ

17 The Fast of the 17 of Tammuz This fast commemorates the day when the walls of Jerusalem were breached by the Romans as well as other disasters.

5 AV

Sabbath of the 'Vision' The Sabbath before Tishah B'Av.

9 Tishah B'Av This fast commemorates the day when the Temple was destroyed by Nebuchadnezzar (604–561BCE), and the Second Temple by Titus (ruled 79–81CE).

Sabbath of 'Comfort Ye' The Sabbath after Tishah B'Av.

15 The 15 of Av A joyous day in ancient times when the people participated in a wood offering.

6 ELLUL

7 TISHRI

1–10 Ten Days of Penitence The period begins with Rosh Hashanah and concludes with Yom Kippur. It is a time for spiritual cleansing.

1–2 Rosh Hashanah The New Year festival.

3 Fast of Gedaliah This fast commemorates the assassination of Gedaliah, the Governor of the Jews appointed by Nebuchadnezzar.

10 Yom Kippur Day of Atonement.

15–21 Sukkot This festival commemorates God's protection of the Israelites in the wilderness. Sukkot, or 'booths', are built during this festival to symbolize the temporary shelter used by the Israelites.

17–21 Hoi Hamoed Atzeret Intermediate days of the festival, observed as semi-holy days.

21 Hoshanah Rabbah Name given to the seventh day of Sukkot since seven circuits are made around the Torah while Hoshanah prayers are recited.

22–3 Shemini Atzeret This two-day festival is observed at the end of Sukkot. A special prayer for rain is recited during the Musaf or additional service.

23 Simchat Torah On this festival the annual cycle of Torah readings is completed and begun again.

24 Isru Hag The day after the Sukkot festival.

8 MARHESHVAN

Second, fifth and seventh During Iyyar and Marheshvan these days are kept by some as fast days to atone for sins committed during Sukkot.

9 KISLEV

25–2/3 of Tevet Hanukkah This festival is celebrated for eight days. It commemorates the re-dedication of the Temple by the Maccabees after the Seleucids were defeated in 165BCE.

10 TEVET

10 The Fast of 10 Tevet This day commemorates the siege of Jerusalem by Nebuchadnezzar.

11 SHEVAT

15 New Year for Trees Joyous festival celebrated in Israel by the planting of trees.

Sabbath relating to the shekels Sabbath that takes place before or on 1 Adar.

12 ADAR

Sabbath of 'Remember' Sabbath before Purim.

13 Fast of Esther This fast commemorates Queen Esther's fast before she asked Ahasuerus (486–465BCE) to revoke his decree against the Jews.

14 Purim This festival commemorates the defeat of Haman's plot against the Jews.

15 Shushan Purim This festival commemorates the victory of the Jews of Shushan.

Sabbath of the Red Heifer Sabbath that occurs on the first or second Sabbath after Purim.

Sabbath of the Month Sabbath that occurs before or on 1 Nisan.

NAMES OF THE MONTHS

The names of the months in the Jewish year are of Babylonian origin. In the pre-exilic books they are identified by their numerical order. Concerning the days themselves, they begin at sunset and end at nightfall on the next day. As a result, the Sabbath begins at sunset on Friday and ends the next night when three stars appear. This same pattern apples to all holy days. The Hebrew date is normally given by indicating the name of the month first; this is followed by the date and then the year. When the year is written in Hebrew, it is usual to omit the thousands.

Above Calendar page from a Spanish Bible manuscript of 1301.

PLACES OF WORSHIP

AT FIRST, JEWISH WORSHIP TOOK PLACE IN THE SANCTUARY. LATER THE TEMPLE BECAME THE CENTRAL PLACE OF PRAYER. AFTER ITS DESTRUCTION IN 70CE, IT WAS REPLACED BY THE SYNAGOGUE.

Throughout their history Jews have gathered together for worship. In the desert the ancient Israelites transported a portable shrine; this was subsequently superseded by the Temple built in Jerusalem by King Solomon (10th century BCE). In later centuries the synagogue served as a meeting place for prayer and study.

SANCTUARY

Scripture relates that Moses made a portable shrine (sanctuary) following God's instructions in the Book of Exodus. This structure travelled with the Israelites in the desert and was placed in the centre of the camp in an open courtyard. The fence surrounding it consisted of wooden pillars from which a cloth curtain was suspended. Located in the eastern half of the courtyard, the Sanctuary measured 50 cubits by 10

Below A modern synagogue in Teaneck, New Jersey, USA, with a beautiful stained-glass window.

cubits (about 75 x 15 ft/23 x 4.5m; at its end stood the Holy of Holies, which was separated by a veil hanging on five wooden pillars on which were woven images of the cherubim. Inside the Holy of Holies was the Ark of the Covenant, the table on which the shewbread was placed, the incense altar, and the *menorah*, or 'candelabrum'. In the courtyard there was also an outer altar on which sacrifices were offered, as well as a brass laver for priests.

TEMPLE

In time this structure was superseded by the Temple, which was built by King Solomon in Jerusalem in the 10th century BCE. From the time of Solomon's reign, the Temple served as the site for prayer and the offering or sacrifices to God. In addition to the communal sacrifices made daily, there were additional communal sacrifices offered on the Sabbath, festivals, and the New Moon. The Temple was also the site to which the *omer*, or the first barley measure harvested on the second day of Passover, and the first fruits were brought on Shavuot. On Passover all families were required to come to Jerusalem to offer the paschal sacrifice.

ORIGINS OF THE SYNAGOGUE

In the 6th century BCE the Temple was destroyed by the Assyrians when they invaded the country. After the exile during the same century, Jews in Babylonia established a new institution for public worship: the synagogue (meaning 'assembly' in Greek). There they came together to study and pray. On their return to Jerusalem in the latter part of the 6th century BCE, the Jewish populace

Above Am imaginary view of the Temple of Solomon. Copper engraving by Pierre Mariette, 1670.

continued to gather in synagogues as well as offer sacrifice in the Temple. Thus the synagogue developed alongside the Second Temple.

THE SYNAGOGUE

In the synagogue itself, there are a number of elements, which parallel the Sanctuary and the Temple. Firstly, there is the Holy Ark – this is symbolic of the Holy of Holies, the most important part of the Sanctuary and the Temple. The Ark itself is located on the eastern wall so that Jews are able to pray in the direction of the Temple in Jerusalem. Secondly, the eternal light hangs before the Ark. This represents the lamp that burned continually in the Sanctuary.

The third major element in the synagogue is the Torah scroll, which is placed in the Ark. The Torah is written in Hebrew by a scribe who uses a special ink on parchment. A breastplate covers the Torah, and over it hangs a pointer, which is used for the chanting or recitation of the Torah. There are two rollers on which the Torah scroll is wrapped; in addition, various ornaments, usually in silver, adorn the Scroll. These are symbolic of the ornaments of the High Priest in Temple times.

A fourth feature of the synagogue is the *bimah*, or 'platform', which was in previous times used only for the

Above Siege of Jerusalem by Assyrians under Nebuchadnezzar, 587BCE. From Merian's Illustrated Bible, c.1627.

reading of the Law and the Prophets, as well as for rabbinical sermons. Finally, men and women sit separately; the women are usually seated in a balcony during the service.

SYNAGOGUE HISTORY

According to tradition, there were about 400 synagogues in Jerusalem when the Second Temple fell. Although this figure may be exaggerated, there is considerable evidence of synagogue building in the Jewish world during the Second Temple period. By the 5th century BCE it was widely attested that wherever Jews lived they built structures which became the focus of Jewish life and thought. Unlike the Temple, where ritual was carried out exclusively by priests, the only requirement for synagogue worship was the presence of a *minyan*, or 'quorum of ten men'. Any service could be led by a lay person. This shift away from Temple hierarchy marked a fundamental democratization of Jewish life.

THE MIDDLE AGES

The medieval synagogue dominated Jewish life; in most communities it

Right Moses receives the Tablets of the Law, builds the Ark of the Covenant and makes offerings. From the medieval Bible by Guiars de Moulins.

was at the heart of the Jewish quarter. Men attended services three times a day, and the local rabbinic court frequently convened there. Classes took place in the sanctuary or in an annexe, and oaths as well as banns of excommunication were pronounced in its environs. In addition, communal offices, the ritual bath, a library, a hospice for travellers and a social hall were located in synagogue rooms or adjacent buildings.

THE MODERN PERIOD

In the early modern period, synagogues were constructed in Western European ghettos; Poland's wooden synagogues influenced synagogue architecture all over Eastern Europe. From the 19th century, reformers influenced major innovations. Reform synagogues (temples) were large, imposing buildings with organs. The section for women was abolished, and decorum during the service was

Above Eternal light or Ner Tamid burns before the Ark in a synagogue in Westchester County, New York.

emphasized. Head coverings for men were abandoned, and the reader's platform was shifted from the centre to the area in front of the Ark.

Yet, despite such changes, Reform temples, together with Orthodox synagogues have reassumed a major role in Jewish life.

WORSHIP

ACTS OF WORSHIP MAY BE PERFORMED INDIVIDUALLY OR IN A GROUP
WITH OR WITHOUT A LEADER. THROUGH IT JEWS EXPRESS THEIR JOYS,
SORROWS AND HOPES, ESPECIALLY IN TIMES OF CRISIS AND CALAMITY.

In the Hebrew Bible, the patriarchs often addressed God through personal prayer. Abraham, for example, begged God to spare Sodom since by destroying the whole population the righteous as well as the wicked would be destroyed. At Beth-El Jacob vowed: 'If God will be with me, and will keep me in this way that I go,

Below A watercolour by Richard Moser of the elaborately decorated interior of a synagogue in Vienna, 1920.

and will give me bread to eat, and raiment to put on ... then shall the Lord be my God (Genesis 28:20–1). After Israel made a golden calf to worship, Moses begged God to forgive them for this sin (Exodus 32:31–2).

THE TEMPLE

In ancient times the Temple in Jerusalem served as the central focus for worship. Twice daily – in the morning and afternoon – the priests offered sacrifices while the Levites

Above An engraving by Bernard Picart showing the Simchat Torah ceremony at an Amsterdam synagogue, Holland.

chanted psalms. Additional services were added on Sabbaths and festivals. As time passed it became customary to include other prayers with the recitation of the Ten Commandments and the Shema (Deuteronomy 6:4–9, 11, 13–21; Numbers 15:37–41). When the Temple was destroyed in 70CE, sacrificial offers were replaced by the prayer service in the synagogue. To enhance uniformity, the sages introduced fixed periods for daily prayer, which corresponded with the times sacrifices had been offered in the Temple. By the completion of the Talmud in the 6th century CE, the major elements of the synagogue service were established. In the 8th century CE the first prayer book was composed by Rav Amram, Gaon of Sura.

THE ORDER OF SERVICE

Jews are commanded to recite the Shema during the morning and evening services in accordance with the commandment, 'You shall take of them when you lie down and when you rise' (Deuteronomy 6:7), The first section (6:4–9) opens with 'Shema Yisrael' ('Hear, O Israel: the Lord our God is one Lord'). This teaches the unity of God, and emphasizes the duty to love God, meditate on his commandments and impress them on one's children. In addition, it contains laws about the tefillin and the mezuzah.

Above Amsterdam Jews at Yom Kippur, 1723, in the Second Synagogue built when the Great Synagogue proved too small.

Tefillin consists of two black leather boxes containing scriptural verses, which are bound by black leather straps on the arm and forehead in accordance with the commandment 'you shall bind them as a sign upon your hand, and they shall be frontlets between your eyes' (Deuteronomy 6:8). They are worn by men during morning prayer except on the Sabbath and festivals. The mezuzah consists of a piece of parchment containing two paragraphs of the Shema, which is placed into a case and fixed to the right-hand side of an entrance. Male Jews wear an undergarment with

Below Stained-glass window featuring the menorah at the Great Synagogue in Jerusalem, Israel.

fringes (the smaller tallit) and a larger tallit, or 'prayer shawl', for morning services. The silk or wool shawl has black or blue stripes with tzizit, or 'fringes', at each of the four corners.

A central feature of the synagogue service is the *Shemoneh Esreh*, or '18 Benedictions' or the Amidah. Composed over a long period of time, the prayers received their full form in the 2nd century CE. They consist of 18 separate prayers plus an additional benediction dealing with heretics. The first and last three benedictions are recited at every service; the 13 other prayers are recited only on weekdays. On Sabbaths and festivals they are replaced by one prayer dealing with the Holy Day. Other prayers are added on special occasions.

THE SYNAGOGUE SERVICE

From earliest times, the Torah was read in public gatherings; later regular readings of the Torah on Sabbaths and festivals were instituted. The entire Torah is divided into 54 sections, each of which is known as a *sidrah*. Each of these sections is subdivided into parashot, or 'portions'. Before the reading of the Torah in the synagogue, the Ark is opened and the Torah Scroll is removed.

The number of men called up to the reading on the Sabbath is seven; on other occasions the number varies. In former times those who were called up to the Torah read a section of the weekly sidrah; later an expert in Torah reading was appointed to recite the entire sidrah, and those called up recited blessings instead. After the reading of the Torah, a section from the *Haftarah*, or 'prophetic books', is recited. Once the Torah scroll is replaced in the Ark, a sermon is usually delivered based on the sidrah of the week. Another central feature of the synagogue service is the kaddish prayer. Written in Aramaic, it takes several forms in the prayer book and expresses the hope for universal

peace under the kingdom of God – this prayer is recited by mourners at the end of the service.

THE MODERN PERIOD

The traditional liturgy was essentially the same until the Enlightenment. Reformers in Central Europe then altered the worship service and introduced new prayers into the liturgy. They decreed that the service should be shortened and conducted in the vernacular as well as in Hebrew. In addition, they introduced melodies accompanied by a choir and organ and replaced the chanting of the Torah with the recitation of the sidrah. Prayers viewed as anachronistic were abandoned, and prayers of a particularistic character were amended so they became more universalistic in scope.

In recent years, all groups across the Jewish spectrum have produced new liturgies. Moreover, a wide range of occasional liturgies exist for camps, youth groups and *havurot*, or 'informal prayer groups'. Among non-Orthodox denominations there is a growing emphasis on more egalitarian liturgies with gender-free language and an increasing democratic sense of responsibility.

Below Rabbi carries the Torah scrolls during a Yom Kippur service in the Great Synagogue, Budapest, Hungary.

SABBATH

WITHIN THE JEWISH FAITH, SABBATH DAY OBSERVANCE IS OF PARA-
MOUNT IMPORTANCE. JEWS GATHERED TOGETHER TO COMMEMORATE
THE CREATION OF THE UNIVERSE AND GOD'S SPECIAL DAY OF REST.

According to Genesis, God finished the work he had made on the seventh day. He blessed the seventh day and hallowed it and ceased his labour. Genesis 2:1–3 is the basis of the decree no work is to be done on the Sabbath.

During their time in the wilderness, the Israelites were commanded to observe the Sabbath. They were told to work on five days and collect a single portion of manna. On the sixth day they were told to collect a double portion for the following day, was to be 'a day of solemn rest, a holy sabbath of the Lord' (Exodus 16:23). On the seventh day when several people looked for manna, the Lord said: 'How long do you refuse to keep my commandments and my laws? See! The Lord has given you the sabbath, therefore on the sixth day He gives you bread for two days; ... let no man go out of his place on the seventh day' (Exodus 16:23–9).

Below Table set for the Sabbath meal with candles, wine and a challah loaf.

Several weeks later God revealed the Ten Commandments, including regulations concerning the Sabbath day: 'Remember the sabbath day, to keep it holy. Six days you shall labour, and do all your work, but the seventh day is a sabbath to the Lord your God; in it you shall not do any work, you, or your son, or your daughter, your manservant, or your maidservant, or your cattle, or the sojourner who is within your gates; for in six days the Lord made heaven and earth, the sea, and all that is in them, and rested the seventh day; therefore the Lord blessed the sabbath day and hallowed it' (Exodus 20.8–11).

RABBINIC JUDAISM

By the time of the Sanhedrin, Sabbath observance was regulated by Jewish law. Following Exodus 20:10, the primary aim was to refrain from work. In the Torah only a few provisions are delineated. Such regulations were expanded by the rabbis who listed 39 categories of work.

According to the Mishnah, the 39 categories of work are: sowing; ploughing; reaping; binding sheaves; threshing; winnowing; sorting; grinding; sifting; kneading; baking; shearing sheep; washing wool; beating wool; dyeing wool; spinning; sieving; making two loops; weaving two threads; separating two threads; tying; loosening; sewing two stitches; tearing in order to sew two stitches; hunting a deer; slaughtering; flaying; salting; curing a skin; scraping the hide; cutting; writing two letters; erasing in order to write two letters; building; pulling down a structure; extinguishing a fire; lighting a fire; striking with a hammer; and, finally, moving something.

Above A Jewish woman lighting Sabbath candles. A 17th-century Dutch woodcut.

In the Talmud these 39 categories were discussed and expanded to include within each category a range of activities. In order to ensure that individuals did not transgress these prescriptions, the rabbis enacted further legislation, which serves as a fence around the law.

SABBATH OBSERVANCE

The Sabbath begins on Friday at sunset. Candles are lit by the woman of the house about 20 minutes before sunset, as she recites the blessing: 'Blessed are you, O Lord our God, King of the universe, who has hallowed us by your commandments and commanded us to kindle the Sabbath light.' In the synagogue service preceding Friday *maariv*, or 'who brings on twilight', takes place at twilight. Known as Kabbalat Shabbat, it is a late addition dating to the 16th century when Kabbalists in Safed went to the fields on Friday afternoon to greet the Sabbath queen.

Traditionally, when the father returns home from the synagogue he blesses his children. With both hands placed on the head of a boy, he says: 'May God make you like Ephraim and Manasseh'; for a girl: 'May God make you like Sarah, Rebekah, Rachel and Leah.' In addition, he recites the priestly blessing.

Those assembled then sing Shalom Aleikhem, which welcomes the Sabbath angels. At the Sabbath table the father recites the Kiddush prayer over a cup of wine. This is followed by the washing of the hands and the blessing of the bread. The meal ends with the singing of *zemirot*, or 'table hymns', and concludes with the *Birkhat ha-Mazon*, or 'grace after meals'.

SYNAGOGUE SERVICE

On Sabbath morning the liturgy consists of a morning service, a reading of the Torah and the *Haftarah*, or 'selective readings from the prophets', and the additional service. In the service itself, introductory prayers prior to the Shema differ from those of weekdays, and the Amidah is also different. Seven individuals are called to the reading of the law, and an eighth for the reading from the prophets. In the Reform movement the worship is abridged and has no additional service. On returning home, the morning Kiddush and the blessing over bread are recited, followed by the Sabbath meal and then the grace after meals. In the afternoon service, the Torah is read prior

Below A woman praying before the Shabbat candles.

to the Amidah; three persons are called to the Torah, and the first portion of the reading of the law for the following week is recited. Customarily three meals are to be eaten on the Sabbath day; the third meal is known as the Seudah Shelishit. It should take place just in time for the evening service. At the end of the Sabbath, the evening service takes place and is followed by the Havdalah service.

HAVDALAH

The Havdalah ceremony marks the conclusion of the Sabbath period; it is divided and consists of four blessings. Three are recited over wine, spices and lights, and the service concludes with the Havdalah blessing. The final blessing opens with the phrase, 'Blessed are you, O Lord our God, King of the universe, who distinguishes'; it is followed by a series of comparisons: between the holy and the profane, light and darkness, Israel and the nations, between the seventh day and the six days of the week. The hymn Ha-Mavdil follows the Havdalah ceremony and asks for forgiveness of sins and for the granting of a large number of children. A number of customs, including filling

Above Abraham sees Sodom in Flames by James Tissot, shows the importance of keeping God's law.

a cup and extinguishing the Havdalah candle in wine poured from it, are associated with the Havdalah ceremony. Within Reform Judaism an alternative Havdalah service incorporates additional readings with traditional blessings.

Below An Orthodox Jew at daily prayer at the Western Wall in Jerusalem.

SPECIAL SABBATHS

IN THE JEWISH CALENDAR, A NUMBER OF SABBATHS ARE OF SPECIAL IMPORTANCE AND CELEBRATED IN TRADITIONAL SYNAGOGUES. ON THESE OCCASIONS, THE WORSHIP SERVICE ALTERS IN VARIOUS WAYS.

Throughout the Jewish year, special sabbaths are held to mark the coming or ending of a festival.

THE SABBATH OF BLESSING
On this Sabbath before a New Moon, worshippers using the Ashkenazi liturgy recite a formula based on sage Rav's prayer that 'it will be God's will to renew the coming month for good service' and with four expressions of hope it will be God's intention to re-establish the Temple, rescue his people from all afflictions, maintain Israel's sages and grant a month of good tidings. The service continues with the prayer 'He who performs miracles', an announcement of the date of the New Moon, and a benediction.

SHABBAT MAHAR HODESH
This Sabbath, which falls on the eve of the New Moon, has a biblical origin (1 Samuel 20:18). The Torah reading

Left Silver goblet used for kiddush, a prayer recited before the meal on the eve of Shabbat and Jewish holidays.

is that for the week. The Haftarah (1 Samuel 20:18–42) depicts the covenant between Jonathan and David on the eve of the New Moon.

SABBATH OF THE NEW MOON
In the Sabbath service which falls on the New Moon the Hallel is recited after the morning service. The Torah reading is that for the week and the additional reading is Numbers 28:9–15. The Haftarah is Isaiah 66:1–24.

SABBATH OF RETURN
The origin of the name of this Sabbath is derived from the opening words of the Haftarah: 'Return [*shuvah*], O Israel, to the Lord your God.' Since this Sabbath occurs during the Days of Penitence, it is also known as the Sabbath of Repentance.

SABBATH DURING SUKKOT
In the service for this Sabbath, which occurs during the intermediate days of Sukkot, the Hallel and the Book of Ecclesiastes are read after morning service. In some traditional congregations, religious poems are recited.

SABBATH OF GENESIS
The origin of the name of this Sabbath is derived from the opening words of the Book of Genesis which are included in the reading of the law for this Sabbath (which follows the Simchat Torah festival): 'In the beginning God created ...' On this Sabbath the annual reading cycle of the Torah commences with Genesis 1:1–6,8, and the Haftarah is that for the week. Included among

Above David's Farewell from Jonathan by Rembrandt, commemorated on Shabbat Mahar Hodesh.

those who are called to the Torah is the person chosen as 'bridegroom of Genesis' on Simchat Torah. He normally provides a festival meal to which all are invited after the Sabbath morning service.

SABBATH OF HANUKKAH
This Sabbath takes place during the Hanukkah festival. After the morning service, the Hallel is recited. The Torah reading is that for the week. The additional reading is Numbers 7:1–7. If the Sabbath also falls on the eighth day of Hanukkah the weekly portion is Genesis 41:1–44.17 and the additional reading is Numbers 7:54–8.4. If this Sabbath coincides with the New Moon, Numbers 28:9–15 is recited from a second scroll before the additional reading.

SABBATH OF THE SONG
The origin of the name of this Sabbath is the song Moses and the Israelites sang at the Red Sea (Exodus 15:1–18), which is included in the Torah reading. In some congregations special religious poems are also recited. The Torah reading is the weekly portion (Exodus 13:17–17:16).

Above The Parting of the Red Sea, *an 18th-century lithograph by Becquet for a French catechism, forms a part of the Exodus story. The Hallel and Song of Songs are recited on the Sabbath during Passover.*

SABBATH OF THE SHEKEL TAX

The origin of the name of this Sabbath, which precedes or coincides with the New Moon, Rosh Hodesh Adar, is derived from the Mishnah that states that 'on the first day of Adar they gave warning of the shekel dues.' The additional reading concerns the half-shekel levy, which was used to support the Sanctuary. In some congregations the rabbi urges that contributions be made to religious institutions in Israel.

SABBATH OF REMEMBRANCE

On the Sabbath before Purim, the additional reading emphasizes the obligation to 'remember what Amalek did to you' (since traditionally Haman was regarded as a descendant of Amalek).

SABBATH OF THE RED HEIFER

This Sabbath precedes the Sabbath of the New Moon. The additional reading deals with the red heifer whose ashes were used for ritual purification by the ancient Israelites.

SABBATH OF THE MONTH

The origin of the name for this Sabbath is derived from the opening words of the additional reading: 'This month [ha-Hodesh] shall mark for you the beginning of the months.'

THE GREAT SABBATH

The origin of the name of this Sabbath is uncertain but it may derive from the last verse of the Haftarah: 'Lo, I will send the prophet Elijah to you before the coming of the awesome [gadol], fearful day of the Lord '(Malachi 4:5).

SABBATH DURING PASSOVER

This Sabbath takes place during the intermediate days of Passover. In the service the Hallel and Song of Songs are recited after the morning service.

SABBATH OF PROPHECY

The Sabbath precedes the ninth day of Av. Its name is derived from the Haftarah, which refers to Isaiah's vision [hazon] about the punishments that will be inflicted on Israel.

SABBATH OF COMFORT

The origin of this name is derived from the opening words of the Haftarah: 'Comfort [nahamu], O comfort my people.' The Torah reading is Deuteronomy 3:23–7:11 which includes the Ten Commandments and the first paragraph of the Shema.

Below Jewish high priests, a 14th-century fresco from Ohrid, Macedonia. The high priesthood ended with the fall of the Temple, and synagogue services took the place of Temple worship.

PASSOVER

THE FESTIVAL OF PASSOVER COMMEMORATES THE EXODUS FROM EGYPT. THE SEDER MEAL TAKES PLACE ON THE FIRST NIGHT. DURING THE PASSOVER CELEBRATIONS, JEWS ARE COMMANDED TO EAT MATZAH.

Through the centuries the Jewish people celebrated the festival of Passover, which commemorates the exodus from Egypt. The term 'passover' is derived from the account of the tenth plague in Egypt when first-born Egyptians were killed, whereas God passed over the houses of the Israelites (whose door-posts and lintels were sprinkled with the blood of the paschal lamb).

THE FESTIVAL OF UNLEAVENED BREAD

Passover is also known as the festival of unleavened bread. Once the Egyptian Pharaoh gave permission for the Israelites to go, they were in such a hurry to leave that they did not wait for their bread to rise. Subsequently God commanded that no leaven was to be eaten at future Passover celebrations, nor should any leaven be found in the house. As a consequence, it became the custom just before the festival to conduct a thorough spring-clean. All leavened foods were removed, and special Passover cutlery and crockery were brought out. This was accompanied by a final ritual search for leaven.

FESTIVAL CELEBRATIONS

Passover is also described as the festival of spring – this refers back to its traditional agricultural connections. Primarily the festival is perceived as a celebration of liberation. Traditionally it is kept for eight days and its main focus is the Passover Seder (meal), which takes place on the first night. Even the most secular Jews often attend a Passover Seder: it is an opportunity for the extended family to meet one another in an atmosphere of fellowship and joy.

PREPARATION

In preparation for Passover, Jewish law stipulates that all leaven must be removed from the house. On the

Above Three matzahs. The unleavened breads play an important part in the Seder meal.

14th of Nisan a formal search is made for any remains of leaven. This is then put aside and burned on the following morning. The first night of Passover is celebrated in the home; the ceremony is referred to as the Seder. This is done to fulfil the biblical commandment to relate the story of the Exodus to one's son: 'And you shall tell thy son on the day, saying: "It is because of what the

---

ORDER OF THE SEDER

At the Seder, the Haggadah, or 'Passover prayer book', details the order of service. It is as follows:

The kiddush is recited.
The celebrant washes his hands.
Parsley is dipped in salt water.
Celebrant divides the middle matzah and sets the afikoman aside.
Celebrant recites the Haggadah narration.
Participants wash their hands.
Blessing over bread is recited.
Blessing over matzah is recited.
Bitter herbs are eaten.
The matzah and *maror*, or 'bitter herbs', are combined.
The meal is eaten.
The afikoman is eaten
Grace after meals is recited.
The Hallel is recited.
The service is concluded.
Hymns and songs are sung.

Below Passover Seder, from a 15th-century missal; manuscript attributed to the school of Van Eyck.

Below Father distributing loaves of unleavened bread and haroset, from the Spanish Golden Haggadah, c.1320.

Lord did for me when I came out of Egypt'" (Exodus 13:8). The order of the service dates back to Temple times. During the ceremony celebrants traditionally lean on their left sides – this was the custom of freemen in ancient times.

MATZAH

Three *matzot*, or 'unleavened bread', are placed on top of one another, usually in a special cover. The upper and lower matzot symbolize the double portion of manna that provided for the Israelites in the wilderness. The middle matzah (which is broken in two at the beginning of the Seder) represents the 'bread of affliction'.

The smaller part of the matzah is eaten to comply with the ancient commandment to eat matzah. The larger part is set aside for the *afikoman*, which recalls Temple times when the meal was completed with the eating of the paschal lamb. These

Below Clockwise from top: Plague of the first born, the Israelites leave Egypt, the passage of the Red Sea and the pursuit by the Egyptians. From the Golden Haggadah, c. 1320.

three matzot also symbolize the three divisions of the Jewish people: Cohen, Levi and Yisrael.

FOUR CUPS OF WINE

According to tradition, each Jew must drink four cups of wine at the Seder. The first is linked to the recital of Kiddush; the second with the account of the Exodus and the Blessing for Redemption; the third with the grace after meals; and the fourth with the *Hallel*, or 'psalms', and prayers for thanksgiving. These

cups also symbolize four expressions of redemption in Exodus 6:6–7. Today the cups are usually small.

CUP OF ELIJAH

This cup symbolizes the hospitality awaiting the passer-by and wayfarer. According to tradition, the Messiah will reveal himself at the Passover, and Malachi declared that he will be preceded by Elijah. The cup of Elijah was also introduced because of the doubt as to whether five cups of wine should be drunk rather than four.

THE SEDER PLATE

The Seder plate displays a number of other symbols for Passover in addition to the matzah. Bitter herbs symbolize the bitterness of Egyptian slavery. Parsley is dipped in salt water and eaten after the Kiddush, or 'prayer over wine'. It is associated with spring. Haroset is a mixture of apples, nuts, cinnamon and wine. It is a reminder of the bricks and mortars that Jews were forced to use in Egypt. A roasted shankbone symbolizes the paschal offering. A roasted egg commemorates the festival sacrifice in the Temple. Salt water recalls the salt that was offered

Above Table set for Seder meal with foods associated with Passover.

with all sacrifices. It also symbolizes the salt water of the tears of all ancient Israelites.

SHAVUOT

THE FESTIVAL OF SHAVUOT COMMEMORATES THE GIVING OF THE LAW ON MOUNT SINAI. IT CULMINATES THE PROCESS OF LIBERATION OF THE JEWISH NATION WHICH BEGAN WITH THE EXODUS AT PASSOVER.

The festival of Shavuot, or 'Festival of Weeks', is based on Leviticus 23:15: 'and from the day you bring the *omer*, or 'sheaf offering', of 'wave offering', you shall count off seven weeks [Shavuot].' Through the centuries, this festival has been observed as a celebration of the giving of the law.

ORIGINS

On the second day of Passover a meal offering was brought to the Temple, consisting of a sheaf of barley that was waved by the priest. This accounts for the fact that it is referred to as a 'wave offering'. Strictly speaking, the word *omer* is the name of a 'measure'. A sheaf that had this measure was brought as an offering in thanks for the barley harvest. Seven weeks were counted from the second day of Passover. At the end of seven weeks (on the 50th day), Shavuot was celebrated.

Below A mid-19th-century image of a festival procession at a synagogue at Livorno, Italy.

Initially, Shavuot was a harvest festival. However, the revelation on Mount Sinai took place during the month of Sivan according to Exodus 19: the date of Shavuot (on the sixth of Sivan) and Sinaitic revelation thus occurs at the same time. For this reason Shavuot came to be seen as a celebration of revelation, rather than a harvest festival. During the prayers for the day, Shavuot is referred to as 'the season of the giving of the Torah'.

SHAVUOT RITUALS

There are no special rituals for Shavuot as there are for Passover and Sukkot. Originally, Shavuot appears to have been an adjunct of Passover. But an adjunct festival does not require its own rituals. Further, even when Shavuot became the festival celebrating the giving of the law, new rituals expressing this theme were not created. Yet, during the Middle Ages, Shavuot customs began to develop. It is the practice, for example, to decorate the synagogue

Above Children celebrate Shavuot in a kindergarten in Jerusalem.

with flowers and plants. This symbolizes what occurred on Mount Sinai when the Torah was given. When God gave the law, it was covered with luxuriant plants and fragrant flowers.

Another custom is to eat dairy dishes. One of the reasons given is that the Torah is like milk, which soon turns sour if it is left in vessels of gold or silver. Students of the Torah who have golden opinions of themselves and lack humility are not true representations of Jewish scholarship. They turn sour the nourishing milk of the Torah.

Below Ruth harvesting, from the 1520s Latin Bible of St Amand Abbey, France. The Book of Ruth is read on Shavuot.

Above A boy learning how to fire an arrow from a bow. Archery plays a part in the celebration of Lag B'Omer.

CELEBRATION

Shavuot is celebrated for two days on the 6th and 7th of Sivan. Seven weeks are counted from the bringing of the omer on the second day of Passover. The festival is also referred to as Pentecost, a Greek word meaning 50, since it was celebrated on the 50th day. Symbolically, the day commemorates the culmination of the process of emancipation, which began with the Exodus at Passover. It is concluded with the proclamation of the Law on Mount Sinai.

During the Temple period, farmers set out for Jerusalem to offer a selection of the first ripe fruits as a thanks-offering. In post-Temple times, the festival focuses on the giving of the law on Mount Sinai. In some communities it is a practice to remain awake during Shavuot night. In the 16th century, Solomon Alkabets and other Kabbalists began the custom of *tikkun*, in which an anthology of biblical and rabbinic material was recited. Today in the communities where this custom is observed, this lectionary has been replaced by a passage of the Talmud or other rabbinic literature.

Right Poem for the first day of Shavuot from Laudian Mahzor, a German book of Jewish liturgy for festivals, c.1275.

Some congregations in the Diaspora read a book of psalms on the second night. Synagogues are decorated with flowers or plants. Jews should count the days until the Law was given on Sinai. This is like a slave counting the days to his freedom, or lovers counting the days until reunion. In the Middle Ages, the omer period was one of mourning. One reason given for this is that the disciples of Akiva died during this period. It is the custom not to have a haircut during this time, except on certain days. In addition, weddings are not to be celebrated except at specific times.

LAG B'OMER

The word 'lag' has the numerical equivalent of 33. This day, which is the 33rd day of the omer, is a minor festival because Simeon ben Yohai, traditionally viewed as the author of the Zohar, died on this day. The ascent of his soul to Heaven is described as his wedding, the reunion of the soul with God. Weddings are permitted on this day, even though it takes place during the omer. Lag B'Omer became a scholars' festival, celebrated as a day of joy. In some communities, teachers and students go out into the woods to shoot bows and arrows.

SUKKOT

THE FESTIVAL OF SUKKOT COMMEMORATES THE WANDERING OF THE ISRAELITES IN THE DESERT. DURING THIS FESTIVAL JEWS ARE COMMANDED TO CONSTRUCT SUKKOT (BOOTHS) AND DWELL IN THEM.

Sukkot is a pilgrim festival prescribed in the Bible: 'On the 15th of the month and for seven days is the feast of tabernacles to the Lord' (Leviticus 23:34). Beginning on the 15th of Tishri, it commemorates God's protection of the Israelites during their sojourn in the desert. Leviticus demands that Jews are to construct booths during this period as a reminder that the people of Israel dwelt in booths when they fled from Egypt (Leviticus 23:42–3).

BIBLICAL LAW
The Book of Leviticus goes on to explain how the festival of Sukkot is to be celebrated: 'You shall take on the first day the fruit of goodly trees, branches of palm trees and boughs of leafy trees and willows of the brook; and you shall rejoice before

Below An Orthodox Jew and a secular youth blessing the four species during the Feast of Tabernacles in Jerusalem.

the Lord your God for seven days ... You shall dwell in booths for seven days ... that your generation may know that I made the people of Israel dwell in booths when I brought them up out of the land of Egypt' (Leviticus 23:40, 42–3).

THE SUKKAH
The feast of tabernacles was thus ordained to remind Jews of their wandering in the wilderness before they reached the Promised Land. This was a time when they were particularly close to God. Today Jews are expected to build their own *sukkah*, or 'tabernacle', and the sages of the Talmud explained how this is to be done. The sukkah has to be at least four square cubits in size (a cubit is about 18ins/45 cm). It must have at least three walls and it should have a covering of things that were once growing. However, this does not imply that it should have a complete roof. When pious Jews stand in

Above Serving food at a Sukkot celebration in the Grand Choral Synagogue, St Petersburg, Russia.

the sukkah, they should be able to see the stars through the branches of the covering. Meals should be eaten in the sukkah for the duration of the festival, although in cold climates there is no obligation to sleep in it or even to remain in it if it rains.

LULAV
In addition to constructing a sukkah, Jews are to perform a ceremony involving the fruit and the branches. This is done by holding an *etrog*, a citron, which is a large citrus fruit, in one hand and branches of palm, willow and myrtle (which are collectively known as the *lulav*) in the other. During the synagogue service, the lulav is waved in six directions: north, south, east, west, up and down. In all likelihood this symbolizes God's control of all the points of the compass and space.

Various explanations have been given regarding the composition of the lulav: possibly the most attractive is that it symbolizes the different types of Jews that make up the community, that all are necessary and should work in harmony while keeping their individuality. In any case, the lulav is waved while the Hallel (Psalms 113–118) is recited, and it is taken in a circuit around the synagogue while a prayer is recited for a good harvest.

Above *Hollow eggs with sacred texts were used to decorate European sukkahs for the holiday of Sukkot. This 19th-century Polish egg is decorated with text from the Song of Solomon.*

THE GREAT HOSHANAH

On the seventh day of the festival known as the Great Hoshanah (God saves), seven circuits are made in the synagogue. This is often viewed as the culmination of the whole season of repentance (the New Year, the Ten Days of Penitence and the Day of Atonement). Since Sukkot is celebrated during the course of the Tabernacles

Below *Jews eating in a public sukkah during Sukkot. Some congregations build community sukkahs.*

festival, it is a mixture of joy and solemnity. The next day, the day of the holy convocation, is Shemini Atzerert (the eighth day of the solemn assembly) and Simchat Torah (the rejoicing of the law). Shemini Atzeret and Simchat Torah are traditionally commemorated on the same day, but it has become customary for Shemini Atzeret to be observed on the eighth day and Simchat Torah on the ninth.

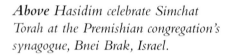

Above *Hasidim celebrate Simchat Torah at the Premishian congregation's synagogue, Bnei Brak, Israel.*

SIMCHAT TORAH

Simchat Torah is a time of joy. It is a holy day on which the annual reading of the Torah is finished and the whole cycle begins again with the first portion from the Book of Genesis. It is considered to be an honour to be called up to read the last section of the Book of Deuteronomy, and the person chosen is called 'Bridegroom of the Torah'. The next person who is called up to read the first section of the Book of Genesis is known as the 'Bridegroom of Genesis'.

During the service, the Torah scrolls are taken from the Ark and carried in procession around the synagogue. In Hasidic communities, the enthusiasm is overwhelming and the procession spills out into the street amid singing and dancing. Children are called up and given sweets and fruits. In some communities it is the custom for the two 'bridegrooms' to give a party for the whole community.

CHAPTER 10

FESTIVALS

Celebrating Jewish high days and holidays is a vital part of being a Jew. Communities come together to mark not just the happiest festivals but also those that commemorate sad and serious times such as Holocaust Remembrance Day and Yom Kippur. The Jewish New Year begins in the autumn of the first day of Tishri and marks the start of the Ten Days of Penitence, which end on the Day of Atonement. In the Bible, Rosh Hashanah is referred to as falling on the first day of the seventh month (Leviticus 23:24). During the rabbinic period, it came to be regarded as a day of judgement for the entire world, on which each person's fate is inscribed in the Book of Life. Today the High Holy Days can continue to serve as the focus for reflection and introspection. Throughout the Jewish year, the community also celebrates a numbers of days of joy, including Hanukkah, Purim, Rosh Hodesh, the New Year for Trees, the Fifteenth of Av and Israel Independence Day. During these celebrations, Jews remember joyous historical events and times of tragedy in the history of their nation as well as seasons of the year when thanks are due to God for his blessings.

Opposite Blowing the shofar, a ceremonial wind instrument originally made from a ram's horn, on Rosh Hashanah to mark the beginning of the Jewish New Year.

Above A late 18th-century engraving showing Jews in a synagogue in Amsterdam, Holland, celebrating Purim. At Purim, Esther delivered the Jews from Haman's plot to destroy them.

ROSH HASHANAH

ROSH HASHANAH (NEW YEAR) MARKS THE COMMENCEMENT OF THE
SPIRITUAL YEAR. AT THIS TIME JEWS ARE COMMANDED TO REPENT OF
THEIR SINS AND RESOLVE TO IMPROVE DURING THE NEXT 12 MONTHS.

The New Year is commemorated for two days on the 1st and 2nd of Tishri. It marks the beginning of the Ten Days of Penitence, which ends on Yom Kippur, or 'the Day of Atonement'. From ancient times to now, Rosh Hashanah has been seen as the start of the spiritual year. It is a time for reflection and self-examination.

BIBLICAL JUDAISM
In ancient times, the Jewish New Year took place on one day; in subsequent centuries it became a two-day festival. The term Rosh Hashanah occurs only once in Scripture – in Ezekiel 40:1. Nevertheless, this festival had three other biblical designations: (1) Shabbaton – a day of solemn rest to be observed on the first day of the seventh month; (2) Zikhron Teruah – a memorial proclaimed with the blast of the horn (Leviticus 23:24); and (3) Yom Teruah – a day of blowing the horn (Numbers 29:1). Later it

Below Sounding the shofar on Rosh Hashanah. 1723 engraving by Bernard Picart from his series on Judaism.

was referred to by the sages as Yom ha-Din (the Day of Judgement) and Yom ha-Zikkaron (the Day of Remembrance).

DIVINE JUDGEMENT
The Mishnah declares that all human beings will appear before God on the New Year. The Talmud expands this idea by stressing the need for self-examination. In rabbinic sources each individual stands before the throne of God, and judgement on each person is entered on the New Year and sealed on the Day of Atonement.

According to the Talmud, there are three ledgers opened in heaven: one is for the completely righteous, who are immediately inscribed and sealed in the Book of Life. Another is for the thoroughly wicked, who are recorded in the Book of Death. A third is for the intermediate, ordinary type of individual, whose fate hangs in the balance and is suspended until the Day of Atonement. In this light, Rosh Hashanah and Yom Kippur are called *Yamim Noraim*, or 'Days of Awe'.

Above At Rosh Hashanah it is customary to eat apples dipped in honey for 'a good and sweet year'.

SYNAGOGUE OBSERVANCE
On New Year Day, the Ark curtain, reading desk and Torah scroll mantles are decked in white, and the rabbi, cantor and person who blows the *shofar*, or 'ram's horn', all wear a white *kittel*, or 'robe'. In the synagogue service the Amidah or the Musaf service contains three sections relating to God's sovereignty, providence and revelation: Malkhuyyot deals with God's rule; Zikhronot portrays God's remembrance of the ancestors of the Jewish people when he judges each generation; Shofarot contains verses relating to the shofar, and deals with the revelation on Mount Sinai and the messianic age. Each introductory section is followed by three verses from the Torah, three from the Writings; three from the Prophets, and a final verse from the Torah.

Below A poem for Rosh Hashanah, has a drawing of the sacrifice of Isaac by Abraham. From a 14th-century German Jewish book of prayers for festivals.

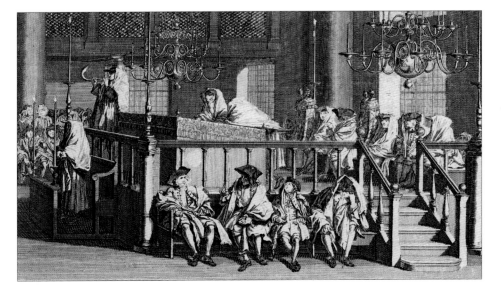

Above A Central European postcard from 1900 showing the blowing of the shofar, or horn, for Rosh Hashanah.

AVINU MALKENU

Avinu Malkenu is said from Rosh Hashanah to Yom Kippur. The phrase means 'Our father, our king'.

Avinu Malkenu, we have no king but you.

Avinu Malkenu, help us for your own sake.

Avinu Malkenu, grant us a blessed New Year.

Avinu Malkenu, annul all evil decrees against us.

Avinu Malkenu, annul the plots of our enemies.

Avinu Malkenu, frustrate the designs of our foes.

Avinu Malkenu, rid us of tyrants.

Avinu Malkenu, rid us of pestilence, sword, famine, captivity, sin and destruction.

Avinu Malkenu, forgive and pardon all our sins.

Avinu Malkenu, ignore the record of our transgressions.

Avinu Malkenu, help us return to you fully repentant.

Avinu Malkenu, send complete healing to the sick.

Avinu Malkenu, remember us with favour.

Avinu Malkenu, inscribe us in the book of happiness.

Avinu Malkenu, inscribe us in the book of deliverance.

Avinu Malkenu, inscribe us in the book of prosperity.

Avinu Malkenu, inscribe us in the book of merit.

Avinu Malkenu, inscribe us in the book of forgiveness.

The Torah readings at Rosh Hashanah concern the birth (Genesis 12:1–34) and the binding of Isaac (Genesis 22:1–24). On both days the shofar is blown at three points during the service: 30 times after the reading of the Law; 30 times during Musaf; and 10 before Alenu. In the liturgy there are three variants of the blowing of the shofar: *tekiah*, or 'a long note'; *shevarim*, or 'three tremulous notes'; and *teruah*, 'nine short notes'. According to the 12th-century Jewish philosopher Moses Maimonides, the shofar is blown to call sinners to repent.

TASHLICH

Traditionally, it was the custom to go to the seaside or the banks of a river on the afternoon of the first day. The ceremony of Tashlich symbolizes the casting of one's sins into a body of water. The prayers for Tashlich and the three verses from the Book of Micah (Micah 7:18–20) express confidence

Right A Rosh Hashanah service at the Moscow Choral Synagogue, Russia.

in divine forgiveness. In the home, a piece of bread is dipped in honey followed by a piece of apple, and a prayer is recited that the year ahead may be good and sweet.

A SOLEMN DAY

The Ten Days of Penitence begin with the New Year and last until the Day of Atonement. This is regarded as the most solemn time of the year when all are judged and their fate determined for the coming year. During the Ten Days various additions are made to the liturgy, especially in the morning service. Selihot Penitential prayers are recited during the morning service, and various additions are made to the Amidah and the reader's repetition of the Amidah. The reader's repetition is followed by the Avinu Malkenu prayer.

YOM KIPPUR

YOM KIPPUR CONCLUDES THE TEN DAYS OF PENITENCE, WHICH BEGINS WITH ROSH HASHANAH. DURING YOM KIPPUR, JEWS ARE COMMANDED TO REPENT OF THEIR SINS AND SEEK FORGIVENESS.

Yom Kippur is the holiest day of the Jewish year. Observed on the 10th of Tishri, it is prescribed in Scripture: 'On the tenth day of the seventh month is the Day of Atonement; and you shall afflict yourselves. It shall be to you a sabbath of solemn rest, and you shall afflict yourselves; on the ninth day of the month, beginning at evening, from evening to evening' (Leviticus 23: 27, 32).

The rabbis stress that the Day of Atonement enables human beings to atone for sins committed against God. However, regarding transgressions committed against others, pardon cannot be obtained unless forgiveness has been sought from the persons injured. As a result, it is customary for Jews to seek reconciliation with anyone they might have offended during the year.

Below *The Day of Atonement as observed by Ashkenazi Jews in the 18th century, by Bernard Picart.*

KAPPAROT

The kapparot ritual takes place before Yom Kippur among Sephardi and Eastern communities as well as among some Ashkenazim. During this ceremony a fowl is slaughtered and either eaten before the fast or sold for money, which is given to charity. Its death symbolizes the transfer of guilt from the person to the bird that has been killed. In some congregations, Jews substitute coins for the fowl, and charity boxes are available at the morning and afternoon services before Yom Kippur.

Previously *malkot*, or 'lashes', were administered in the synagogue to impart a feeling of repentance, but this custom has largely disappeared.

YOM KIPPUR RITUAL

Customarily, Jews were able to absolve vows on the eve of Yom Kippur. In addition, afternoon prayers are recited earlier than normal, and the Amidah is extended by two formulae

Above *Emperor Hadrian expelled the Jews from Jerusalem. His persecution is referred to in the Yom Kippur liturgy.*

A DAY OF FASTING

According to the sages, afflicting one's soul involves abstaining from food and drink. Thus every male over the age of 13 and every female over 12 is obliged to fast from sunset until nightfall the next day. Sick people may take medicine, and small amounts of food and drink. Those with chronic illnesses like insulin-dependent diabetes may be forbidden to fast. During the day normal Sabbath prohibitions apply, but worshippers are to abstain from food and drink, marital relations, wearing leather shoes, using cosmetics and lotions and washing the body, except for fingers and eyes.

Below *Leather shoes are not worn on the day of Yom Kippur.*

Right The Kol Nidre, the first of the Yom Kippur services, in the Great Synagogue, Budapest, Hungary.

of confession. Some pious Jews immerse themselves in a *mikveh*, or 'ritual bath', in order to undergo purification before the fast. In the home, a final meal is eaten, and, before lighting the festival candles, a memorial candle is lit to burn throughout the day. Leather shoes are replaced by non-leather shoes. The *tallit*, or 'prayer shawl', is worn throughout all the services, and a white curtain adorns the Ark and Torah scrolls. The reader's desk and other furnishings are covered in white. Among Ashkenazim, rabbis, cantors and other officials also wear a white kittel (gown).

CONFESSION

On Yom Kippur five services take place. The first, Kol Nidre, takes place on Yom Kippur eve. Among the Orthodox, it was a custom to spend the night in the synagogue reciting the entire Book of Psalms as well as other readings. Among Sephardim and Reform Jews the memorial prayer is recited on Kol Nidre. In addition to selihot and other hymns, the morning service includes a Torah reading describing the Day of Atonement ritual in the Sanctuary. Before the Musaf service, a special prayer – Hineni He-Ani Mi-Maas – is recited. A number of liturgical hymns are included in the reader's repetition of the Amidah, including the 11th-century U-Netanneh Tokef passage, which states that prayer and charity avert judgement.

MARTYROLOGY

Interpolated among the selihot and confessions towards the end of Musaf is the Elleh Ezkerah martyrology. Based on a medieval midrash, this describes the plight of the Ten Martyrs persecuted for defying Hadrian's ban on studying of the Torah. In some rites this part of the service is expanded to

include Holocaust readings. In the afternoon service, Leviticus 18 is read, dealing with prohibited marriages and sexual offences. The second reading is the Book of Jonah.

CONCLUDING SERVICE

Before the neilah, or 'concluding service', the hymn El Nora Alilah is chanted among the Sephardim. This part of the liturgy is recited as twilight approaches. In some congregations, the Ark remains open and worshippers stand throughout the service. They ask God to inscribe each person for a good life and to seal them for a favourable fate. At the end of the service, the shofar is blown, and the congregations recite *La-Shanah ha-Baah Bi-Yerushalayim*, or 'next year in Jerusalem'. After the service concludes, it is customary to begin the construction of the sukkah, or 'booth'.

Below Jews in preparation for Yom Kipper perform the kapparot ritual, in which a chicken is sacrificed.

FASTS

THROUGHOUT THE JEWISH YEAR, THE COMMUNITY COMMEMORATES
A VARIETY OF EVENTS WITH FASTING. ALONGSIDE YOM KIPPUR, THERE
IS A RANGE OF FAST DAYS WHICH HIGHLIGHT TRAGIC PAST EVENTS.

Fasting or abstinence from food plays its part in Jewish religion. Individuals may fast as a sign of repentance or mourning, or to make atonement.

THE FIRST TEMPLE

In the ritual of the First Temple, fasting was a permanent feature: the death of a national leader such as King Saul could initiate a day-long fast or even a weekly fast. The purpose of such fasting was manifold: its most important function was to avert or terminate calamities. In addition, fasting served as a means of obtaining divine forgiveness.

THE BIBLE

In Scripture, there is no record of specific fast days in the annual calendar except for the Day of Atonement. Fixed fast days were first mentioned in the post-exilic period by the prophet

Below On the 9th of Av, Jews wearing jute bags gather to pray at the Western Wall in Jerusalem, to mark the fall of the First and Second Temples.

Zechariah. According to tradition, these fasts commemorate events which resulted in the destruction of the Temple: the 10th of Tevet – the beginning of the siege of Jerusalem; the 17th of Tammuz – the breaching of the walls; the 9th of Av – the destruction of the Temple; the 3rd of Tishri – the assassination of Gedaliah, the Babylonian-appointed governor of Judah. As a result, the practice of fasting, which was initially spontaneous, later entered the calendar as a recurring event in the commemoration of historical tragedies.

OBSERVANCE

Jewish texts lay down a series of prescriptions to regularize the process of fasting. During the First Temple period, the devout offered sacrifice, confessed sins and uttered prayers. From the Second Temple period onwards, public fasts were accompanied by a reading from Scripture. On solemn fasts, four prayers were recited as well as Maariv. The Amidah of the fast day consisted of 24 benedictions (the normal 18 and six others), and the liturgy was elaborated with passages of *selihot*, or 'supplication', and prayers for mercy. During the service the shofar, or 'ram's horn', was sounded, accompanied by other horns.

In the Temple, the blowing of shofarot and trumpets was performed differently from other localities. Prayers were normally uttered in the open, and all the people tore their clothes, wore sackcloth and put ashes or earth on their heads. Holy objects were also humiliated. It was common for the altar to be covered with sackcloth and the Ark, containing the Torah scrolls, was

Above The Suicide of Saul, 1562, *by Pieter Brueghel the Elder. Saul's death initiated fasting and mourning.*

frequently taken into the street and covered with ashes. During the mass assembly, one of the elders rebuked the people for their failings, and the affairs of the community were scrutinized. It was normal for young children and animals to fast as well. The sages, however, exempted young children and animals, the sick, those obliged to preserve their strength and pregnant and nursing women.

ORDINARY AND
IMPORTANT FAST DAYS

Ordinary fast days lasted during the daylight hours; important fasts were 24 hours in length. Fasts were held either for one day, or, on some occasions, for a series of three or seven days. In some cases they took place daily for a continued period.

In unusual cases, fasts were held on Sabbaths and festivals, but it was normally forbidden to fast on these days. So as not to mar the celebration of joyful events in Jewish history, Hananiah ben Hezekiah ben Garon (1st century CE) formulated a Scroll of Fasting which lists 35 dates on which a public fast should not be proclaimed. Eventually, however, this list was abrogated. It was customary to hold fast days on Mondays and Thursdays. After the destruction of the Second Temple, individuals took upon themselves to

Left This 13th-century fresco from Anagni, Italy describes the events in 1 Samuel 6 when the Philistines returned the Ark of the Covenant. During fasts, the Ark was taken into the streets covered with ashes.

5 7th of Adar is a traditional date of the death of Moses.

6 Yom Kippur Katan is a fast day which takes place on the last day of each month.

7 The Fast of the First-Born takes place on 14th Nisan to commemorate the sanctification of the first-born who were saved during the time of the last plague of Egypt.

8 Days commemorating various calamitous events in the history of the Jewish nation.

fast every Monday and Thursday. Jewish law specifies that in such cases these persons should fast during the afternoon of the preceding day. It was also possible to fast for a certain number of hours. On some occasions, the fast was only partial, with those fasting refraining only from meat and wine.

BIBLICAL FASTS

1 The Day of Atonement (Yom Kippur) is to be a fast day.

2 The Ninth of Av (Tishah B'Av) was the day when Nebuchadnezzar (fl. 7th–6th centuries BCE) destroyed the Temple in 586BCE and Titus later devastated the Second Temple in 70CE.

3 The Seventeenth of Tammuz commemorates the breaching of the walls of Jerusalem, which occurred on 9th of Tammuz in the First Temple period.

4 The Tenth of Tevet is a fast that commemorates the commencement of the siege of Jerusalem by Nebuchadnezzar.

5 The Fast of Gedaliah takes place on 3rd of Tishri to commemorate the fate of Gedaliah, the governor of Judah who was assassinated on this day.

6 The Fast of Esther takes place on the 13th of Adar, the day before Purim.

RABBINIC FASTS

1 The especially pious are encouraged to fast during the Ten Days of Penitence and for as many days as possible during the month of Elul.

2 The first Monday and Thursday and the following Monday after Passover and Sukkot are observed as fast days.

3 Shoavim Tat is observed during the Three Weeks of Mourning.

4 A fast is observed during the Three Weeks of Mourning between 17th of Tammuz and 9th of Av.

PRIVATE FASTS

1 The anniversary of the death of a parent.

2 Grooms and brides fast on the day before their wedding.

3 Fasting occurs to prevent the consequences of nightmares taking place.

4 Fasting takes place if a Torah scroll is dropped.

Below German Jews from Nuremberg, 1734, commemorate Tishah B'Av in memory of the destruction of the Temple in Jerusalem.

HANUKKAH

HANUKKAH IS A JOYOUS FESTIVAL COMMEMORATING THE TRIUMPH OF THE JEWS OVER THEIR ENEMIES IN ANCIENT TIMES. FOR EIGHT DAYS A HANUKKAH MENORAH IS LIT AND TRADITIONAL PRAYERS RECITED.

The festival of Hanukkah, or 'dedication', is celebrated for eight days beginning on the 25th of Kislev – it commemorates the victory of the Maccabees over the Seleucids in the 2nd century BCE. Originally a Jewish rebel army the Maccabees took control of Judea, which had been a client state of the Seleucid empire, and founded the Hasmonean dynasty, which ruled from 164BCE to 63BCE, reasserting the Jewish religion and expanding Israel's borders.

At this time the Maccabees were engaged in military conflict with the Seleucids who had desecrated the Temple. After a three-year struggle (165–163BCE), the Maccabees under Judah Maccabee (*d.* 160/161 BCE) conquered Jerusalem and rebuilt the altar. According to the Talmud, one day's worth of oil miraculously kept the menorah burning in the Temple for eight days.

I MACCABEES

The First Book of Maccabees 4:36–59 states that Judah Maccabee, after defeating Lysias, entered Jerusalem and purified the Temple. The altar, which had been defiled, was destroyed and a new one was constructed.

Judah then made new holy vessels including a candelabrum, an altar for incense and a table, and established the 25th of Kislev as the date for the rededication of the Temple. This day coincided with the third anniversary of the proclamation of the edicts of Antiochus Epiphanes (*c.*215–164BCE) in which he decreed idolatrous sacrifices should be offered in the Temple. The altar was to be consecrated with the renewal of the daily sacrificial service; this was to be accompanied by song, the playing of musical instruments, the chanting of the Hallel, and the offering of sacrifice.

Above In this scene from 1 Maccabees, Mattathias kills a Jew who comes to make a sacrifice at an altar. By Gabriel Bodenehr the Elder (1673–1765).

These festivities lasted for eight days, and Judah decreed they should be designated as a time for rejoicing.

II MACCABEES

The Second Book of Maccabees 1:8; 10:1–5 parallels 1 Maccabees. It adds that the eight-day celebration was performed on an analogy with Solomon's consecration of the Temple. The eight days were celebrated with gladness like the Feast of Tabernacles, which recalled how the ancient Israelites had been wandering like wild beasts in the mountains and caves. Thus, bearing wands wreathed with leaves, boughs and palms, they offered hymns of praise.

Hanukkah is therefore called Tabernacles or Tabernacles and Fire. Fire had descended from heaven at the dedication of the altar during the time of Moses and at the sanctification of the Temple of Solomon. At the consecration of the altar in the time of the prophet Nehemiah there was also a miracle of fire, and similarly in the days of Judah Maccabee.

Left A menorah dominates this fresco of preparations for a Jewish festival by Luigi Ademollo. In the 2nd century BCE, the Maccabees under Judah Maccabee drove out the Seleucid oppressors, rebuilt the Temple and rekindled the menorah.

Right Children playing with dreidels at Hanukkah. This traditional Jewish toy bears the initial letters of the Hebrew words 'A great miracle happened there.'

THE KINDLING OF LIGHTS

None of these early sources mention the kindling of lights on Hanukkah. This is referred to first in a *baraita*, or 'religious law outside teaching': 'The precept of light on Hanukkah requires that one light be kindled in each house; the zealous require one light for each person; the extremely zealous add a light for each person each night. According to Bet Shammai: "On the first day, eight lights should be kindled, thereafter they should be progressively reduced" while Bet Hillel held that: "On the first night one light should be kindled, thereafter they should be progressively increased."'

HANUKKAH OBSERVANCE

The main observance of this festival is the kindling of the festive lamp on each of the eight nights. This practice gave this holiday the additional

Below Hanukkah recalls when a day's oil kept the Temple menorah burning for eight days. In this 1299 Hebrew Bible from Spain, oil is poured into a menorah.

name of *Hag ha-Urim*, or 'festival of lights'. In ancient times this lamp was placed in the doorway or in the street outside; subsequently the lamp was placed inside the house. The lighting occurs after dark (except on Friday night, when it must be done before the kindling of the Sabbath lights). The procedure for lighting the Hanukkah candles is to light one candle (or an oil lamp) on the first night, and an additional candle each night until the last night when all eight candles are lit. The kindling should go from left to right. An alternative tradition prescribes that the eight candles are lit on the first night, seven on the second night and so forth. These candles are lit by an additional candle called the *shammash*, or 'serving light'. In addition to this home ceremony, candles are lit in the synagogue.

THE SYNAGOGUE LITURGY

In the synagogue this festival is commemorated by the recitation of the Al ha-Nissim prayer in the Amidah, and Grace after Meals. In the morning service the Hallel is recited, and a special reading from the law takes place on each day. In both the home and the synagogue the hymn Maoz Tsur is sung in Ashkenazi communities; the Sephardim read Psalm 30 instead. During Hanukkah it is customary to hold parties, which include games and singing. The most

well-known game involves a *dreidel*, or 'spinning top'. The dreidel is inscribed with four Hebrew letters (*nun, gimmel, he, shin*) on its side – this is an acrostic for the phrase *nes gadol hayah sham*', or 'a great miracle happened there'. During Hanukkah, *latkes*, or potato pancakes, and *sufganiyyot*, or doughnuts, are eaten. In modern Israel the festival is associated with national heroism and a torch is carried from the traditional burial site of the Maccabees at Modiin to various parts of the country.

Below Children lighting a menorah for the eight-day holiday of Hanukkah, commemorating the rededication of the Holy Temple in Jerusalem.

PURIM

THE FESTIVAL OF PURIM CELEBRATES THE DELIVERANCE OF THE JEWISH PEOPLE FROM THEIR OPPRESSORS. THE BOOK OF ESTHER IS READ DURING THE FESTIVAL.

According to Scripture, this feast was instituted by Mordecai to celebrate the deliverance of the Jews from the plot by Haman, chief minister of King Ahasuerus (486–465BCE), to kill them. The term 'purim' refers to the lots cast by Haman in order to determine the month when this massacre was to take place. Purim is celebrated on the 14th of Adar, and is a time of joy and thanksgiving.

OBSERVANCE

The central feature of this festival is the reading of the Book of Esther, from the *megillah*, or 'scroll', with special cantillation (ritual chanting or intoning). Megillot scrolls are often decorated, sometimes with scenes from the narrative. It is customary to fold the megillah over and spread it out before the reading. The

Below Mordecai and Haman. A 2nd-century fresco from Dura-Europos Synagogue, Syria.

four verses of redemption (Esther 2:5; 8:15–16 and 10:3) are read in a louder voice than other verses. It is the custom of children to make a loud noise with rattles whenever the name of Haman is read. It is the practice for the reader to recite the names of the ten sons of Haman (Esther 9:7–9) in one breath to demonstrate that they were executed simultaneously. According to one interpretation, this is done so that a person will not gloat over the downfall of one's enemies.

GIFTS

The Book of Esther (9:22) describes the practice of sending portions to friends on Purim and giving gifts to the poor. The rule is to send at least two portions of eatables, confectionery and so forth to a friend and to give a present of money to at least two poor men. A special festival meal is often consumed on Purim afternoon: among Purim foods are boiled

Above Children in Old Jerusalem dress in colourful costumes as angels, clowns and police officers for Purim.

beans and peas, which are viewed as a reminder of the cereals Daniel ate in the king's palace in order to avoid infringing dietary laws. Three-cornered pies, known as *hamantashen*, or 'Haman's hats', are also eaten. According to the Babylonian sage Rava (270–350CE), a person is obliged to drink so much wine on Purim that he becomes incapable of knowing whether he is cursing

SACRED LITERATURE

Parodies of sacred literature produced for Purim include *Massekeht Purim*, a parody of the Talmud with its theme of the obligation to drink wine and abstain from water. The institution of the Purim rabbi as a merry fool became a norm in many communities. This can be seen as an annual attempt to find psychological relief from an overwhelming burden of loyalty to the Torah. Under influence from the Italian carnival, people dressed up on Purim in fancy dress. Men were even allowed to dress as women, and vice versa.

Above *Jews celebrating Purim in a synagogue in Amsterdam, Holland. A late 18th-century engraving.*

Haman or blessing Mordecai. The laws concerning this festival are found in the Code of Jewish Law.

KABBALAH

In Kabbalistic and Hasidic literature much is made of Purim as a day of joy and friendship. Unlike Passover, which celebrates God's intervention in human life, God is not mentioned in the Book of Esther. The lots of Purim are compelled with the 'lots' cast on the Day of Atonement when human beings call fate and luck into being. Kabbalists esteemed Purim so highly that they reported in the name of Isaac Luria that the Day of Atonement is like Purim. Although a few Reform congregations abolished Purim, the majority continue to regard the day as one of encouragement and hope.

PURIM KATAN

Following the talmudic injunction that one must recite a special thanksgiving benediction on returning to the place where one was once miraculously saved from danger, the custom arose of celebrating the anniversary of the Jews escape from destruction by reciting special prayers with a ritual similar to that of Purim. These communal Purims are referred to as 'Purim Katan' or 'Moed Katan' or 'Purim', followed with the name of the community. In some cases special Purims were preceded by a fast comparable to the Fast of Esther.

In addition, on the Purim Katan itself the story of personal or communal salvation is recited from a scroll in the course of the synagogue service in which special prayers are recited. Sometimes the Al ha-Nissim prayer and the Hallel are inserted into the ritual. The traditional Purim observance of enjoying a festival meal and giving charity to the poor were also added to these Purims.

PURIM-SHPIL

The term *Purim-shpil*, or 'Purim play', refers to the group performances or monologues given at the traditional family meal held on the festival of Purim. There is evidence that the use of the term 'Purim-shpil' was widespread among Ashkenazi communities as early as the mid-16th century. At the beginning of the 18th century, the biblical Purim-shpil reflected various trends of the contemporary European theatre in its literary style, choice of subject and design.

As time passed, the Purim-shpil became a complex drama with a large cast, comprising thousands of rhymed lines performed to musical accompaniment. The play invariably maintained a strong connection with Purim.

Below *Kurdish Jews celebrating the festival of Purim wearing traditional dress and reading from a scroll of the Book of Esther.*

FESTIVALS OF JOY

DURING THE YEAR JEWS CELEBRATE A NUMBER OF JOYOUS FESTIVALS. IN MODERN TIMES, ISRAEL INDEPENDENCE DAY HAS GAINED CONSIDERABLE SIGNIFICANCE IN THE JEWISH CALENDAR.

In addition to the festivals of Hanukkah and Purim, Jews celebrate several other festivals of joy. The first, Rosh Hodesh, celebrates the New Moon; the second, Tu b'Shevat, is related to tree planting; the third, 15th of Av, is a folk festival; and the fourth, Israel Independence Day, commemorates the creation of the State of Israel.

NEW MOON

Originally Rosh Hodesh, or 'new moon', was not fixed by astronomical calculations; instead it was proclaimed after witnesses had observed the reappearance of the crescent of the moon. On the 30th of every month, members of the High Court assembled in a courtyard in Jerusalem; there they waited

Above A young boy pats down the soil around a sapling he has planted for Tu b'Shevat in Herzlia, Israel.

to receive information from reliable witnesses. They then sanctioned the New Moon. If the moon's crescent was not seen on the 30th day, the New Moon was celebrated on the next day. To inform the population of the beginning of the month, beacons were lit on the Mount of Olives and from there throughout the country as well as in the Diaspora.

Later the Samaritans began to light beacons, and the High Court sent out messengers to far-removed communities. Those Jews who lived far from Jerusalem always celebrated the 30th day of the month as Rosh Hodesh. On these occasions, when they were informed of its postponement to the next day, they also observed a second day as Rosh Hodesh. By the middle of the 4th century CE, however, the sages established a permanent calendar and the public proclamation of the New Moon ceased. A relic of this original practice is retained in the synagogue custom of announcing the New Moon on the Sabbath preceding its celebration.

Although the biblical commandment of joy is not prescribed in relation to Rosh Hodesh, the rabbis

Left A lighted beacon in a window at the Great Synagogue, Jerusalem, for the New Moon or Rosh Hodesh.

ISRAEL INDEPENDENCE DAY

Israel's national day is Israel Independence Day, which commemorates the proclamation of its independence on the 5th of Iyyar 1948. The Chief Rabbinate of Israel declared it a religious holiday and established a special order of service for the evening and morning worship. This service includes the Hallel, and a reading from the Book of Isaiah. The rabbinate also suspended any fast that takes place on the day and various other restrictions. In Israel, the preceding day is set aside as a day of remembrance for soldiers who died in battle. Memorial prayers are recited, and next-of-kin visit the military cemeteries. At home, memorial candles are lit, and Psalm 9 is recited in many synagogues.

Right *Celebrating Independence Day at the Western Wall, Jerusalem.*

inferred its relevance from the fact that the Bible equated the New Moon with the festivals as well as from the duty to recite the following on Rosh Hodesh: 'This is the day which the Lord hath made. We will rejoice and be glad in it' (Psalm 118:24). Hence it is forbidden to fast on the New Moon, and any funeral service is abbreviated. On the New Moon it is customary to partake of a festive meal.

During the period of the First Temple, Rosh Hodesh was observed with the offering of special sacrifices, the blowing of shofars, feasting and a rest from work. By the end of the 6th century BCE, Rosh Hodesh became a semi-holiday. Eventually this status disappeared, and Rosh Hodesh became a normal working day except for various liturgical changes. In the morning service the Hallel psalms of praise are recited. The Bible reading is from Numbers

and describes the Temple service for the New Moon. An additional service is also included, corresponding to the additional sacrifice which was offered on the New Moon.

NEW YEAR FOR TREES

A further joyous festival is Tu b'Shevat (New Year for Trees), which occurs on the 15th of Shevat. Even though this festival is not referred to in the Bible, it appeared in the Second Temple period as a fixed cut-off date for determining the tithe levied on the produce of fruit trees. Once the Temple was destroyed, the laws of tithing were no longer applicable. As a consequence, this festival took on a new character. Wherever Jews resided, it reminded them of their connection with the Holy Land.

During the 15th century, a number of new ceremonies and rituals were instituted by the mystics of

Safed. Owing to the influence of Isaac Luria (1534–72), it became customary to celebrate the festival with gatherings where special fruits were eaten and hymns and readings from the Bible were included. Among the fruits eaten on Tu b'Shevat were those of the Holy Land. In modern Israel new trees are planted during this festival.

15TH OF AV

Another joyous occasion is the 15th of Av, which was a folk festival during the Second Temple period. At this time bachelors selected their wives from unmarried maidens. According to the Mishnah, on both this day and the Day of Atonement, young girls in Jerusalem dressed in white garments and danced in the vineyards where young men selected their brides. In modern times this festival is marked only by a ban on eulogies or fasting.

HOLOCAUST REMEMBRANCE DAY

THE HOLOCAUST HAS CAST A SHADOW OVER THE MODERN JEWISH COMMUNITY. HOLOCAUST MEMORIAL DAY COMMEMORATES THOSE WHO LOST THEIR LIVES AT THE HANDS OF THE NAZIS.

It is now well over half a century since the Holocaust took place. For survivors, the Holocaust is an ever-present memory, but for others it is an event of the past. To ensure that this tragedy is not forgotten, *Yom ha-Shoah*, or 'Holocaust Remembrance Day', is now commemorated throughout the Jewish world. Inaugurated in 1959, Holocaust Remembrance Day was signed into law by the Prime Minister of Israel, David Ben-Gurion (1886–1973), and the President of Israel, Yitzhak Ben-Zvi (1884–1963).

The original proposal was to hold Holocaust Remembrance Day on the anniversary of the Warsaw ghetto

Below The women's compound at Bergen-Belsen concentration camp, where Margot and Anne Frank died in March 1945. Painting by Leslie Cole.

uprising on 19 April 1943, but this was problematic since the 14th of Nisan is the day before Passover. The date was therefore moved to the 27th of Nisan, eight days before Israel Independence Day. Most Jewish communities hold a ceremony on this day but there is no institutional ritual. Generally Jews light a memorial candle and recite the Kaddish prayer for the dead.

ORTHODOX JUDAISM
After the war, the Chief Rabbinate of Israel decided that the 10th of Tevet should be a national remembrance day for victims of the Holocaust. It recommended traditional forms of remembering the dead, such as the study of the Mishnah section about ritual baths, saying psalms, lighting a yahrzeit candle and saying Kaddish. On other occasions, the Chief

Above Holocaust memorial in Miami Beach, Florida, USA, designed by Kenneth Treister.

Rabbinate recommended Tisha b'Av as the appropriate day for remembrance. In April 1951, the Knesset decreed that 27th Nisan should become Yom ha-Shoah, ignoring the Rabbinate's decision. In turn, the Chief Rabbinate decided to

Above Dr Laszlo Tauber, Holocaust survivor, lights a menorah in memory of victims and survivors of the Holocaust at a service in Washington DC, 1985.

ignore the Knesset's chosen date. Although there are Orthodox Jews who commemorate the Holocaust on Yom ha-Shoah, others in the Orthodox world – especially the Hasidim – remember the victims of the Holocaust on traditional days of mourning which were in place before World War II, such as Tishah B'Av. In Israel most Orthodox Zionists stand still for two minutes during the siren. Others, especially in Haredi areas, do not pay attention to this event: most stores remain open, schools continue, and most people carry on with their activities when the siren sounds. The non-participation of the Haredim has caused friction with the rest of the Israeli population.

NORTH AMERICA
Jews in North America observe Yom ha-Shoah within the synagogue as well as in the broader American community. Commemorations range widely from synagogue services to communal vigils and educational programmes. Some congregations find it more practical to have a commemorative ceremony on the closest Sunday to Yom ha-Shoah. It is usual to have a talk by a Holocaust survivor, recitation of songs and reading, and viewing of a film dealing with the Holocaust. Some communities stress the loss that Jews experienced during the Holocaust by reading out the names of Holocaust victims.

HOLOCAUST RITUALS
Rituals associated with Yom ha-Shoah are continually being created and vary widely. Attempts have also been made to observe this day of mourning and remembrance in the home. A common practice is to light a yahrzeit candle.

There have also been attempts to compose a Holocaust liturgy such as the 'Six Days of Destruction' produced by the Reform movement. It was intended to serve as a modern addition to the five scrolls that are read on special holidays.

It has also been suggested that a programme of observance for Yom ha-Shoah should include fasting, and a Holocaust Haggadah has been written in which the story of the Holocaust is told.

Despite the variations in practice, the overriding theme of Yom ha-Shoah or Holocaust Remembrance Day is the importance of remembering this tragedy and ensuring that it never occurs again.

Below Memorial in Berlin for the murdered Jews of Europe, designed by Peter Eisenman; comprising a field of thousands of concrete steles.

TISHAH B'AV

THE FESTIVAL OF TISHAH B'AV RECALLS THE DESTRUCTION OF THE
TEMPLE BY THE BABYLONIANS IN THE 6TH CENTURY BCE, AND LATER
THE ROMAN CONQUEST OF JERUSALEM IN THE 1ST CENTURY CE.

This day of mourning commemorates the destruction of the Temple in Jerusalem by the Babylonians and later by the Romans. In synagogues throughout the Jewish world Jews gather together to mourn this tragic event as well as other calamities in Jewish history which occurred at about the same time. Tishah B'Av serves to remind Jewry of its vulnerability throughout the ages.

HISTORICAL BACKGROUND

In 586BCE the Temple (First Temple) was destroyed by King Nebuchadnezzar of Babylonia (7th–6th century BCE) on the 10th of Av. The

Below A dramatic reconstruction of The Destruction of Jerusalem *by David Roberts (1796–1864).*

rebuilt Temple (Second Temple) was destroyed by the Romans in 70CE on the same day. In time the 9th of Av became the anniversary of both destructions. The Talmud justifies this date because a series of calamities occurred on this day throughout Jewish history in addition to the destruction on the Temples on the 10th of Av.

MOURNING RITES

It is uncertain whether the 9th of Av was observed as a day of mourning before 70CE, in memory of the destruction of the First Temple. The Talmud recounts that Eliezer ben Zadok, who lived before and after the destruction of the Second Temple, did not fast on the 9th of Av, which was deferred because of

Above Romans carrying the Menorah and Jewish holy vessels in triumph, following the destruction of the Second Temple in 70CE. From the Triumphal Arch of Titus, Rome, 81CE.

the Sabbath to the following day since it was his family's traditional holiday of wood offerings for the altar. This indicates that fasting on the 9th of Av was observed during the period of the Second Temple. In any event, fasting on the 9th of Av was observed during the mishnaic period. Some rabbis advocated

Above Rebuilding the Temple in Jerusalem, *manuscript illumination from a 13th-century Bible.*

permanent abstention from wine and meat in memory of the destruction of the Temple, but this was regarded as excessive.

The general rule in the Talmud for the mourning rites of Tishah B'Av is that a person is obliged to observe on it all mourning rites that apply in the case of the death of a next of kin. These rites have to be followed from sunset to sunset. Some mourning rites are already observed during the weeks prior to Tishah B'Av from the fast of the 17th of Tammuz. On the 1st of Av, the mourning rites are intensified. On the eve of Tishah B'Av, at the final meal before the fast, one should not partake of two cooked dishes nor eat meat nor drink wine. It is customary to eat a boiled egg at this meal, and to sprinkle ashes on it. Grace after this meal is said silently by each individual.

RULES FOR TISHAH B'AV

These rules are observed on the fast of Tishah B'Av:

1 There should be complete abstention from food and drink.

2 Bathing is forbidden. Washing of the hands and the face, however, are permissible for cleansing.

3 The use of oils for anointing or the application of perfumes is forbidden.

4 Sexual intercourse is forbidden.

5 Footwear made of leather is not to be worn.

6 One should sit on the ground or on a low stool.

7 It is customary to abstain from work.

8 The study of Torah is forbidden, except for the reading of the Book of Lamentations and its midrash, the Book of Job, the curses in the Book of Leviticus (Leviticus 26:14–42), several chapters in the Book of Jeremiah, and aggadic tales in the Talmud describing the destruction of Jerusalem.

NIGHT OF TISHAH B'AV

On the night of Tishah B'Av pious individuals used to sleep on the floor with a stone as a pillow. It was customary to fast until noon of the 10th of Av. Meat and wine should not be consumed until the afternoon of the 10th, although some of the mourning rites are lessened from Tishah B'Av afternoon onwards based on the belief that Tishah B'Av will again be a holiday since the Messiah will be born then. At the end of the 17th century, strict observance of Tishah B'Av also became a mark of adherence to traditional Judaism after Shabbetai Tzvi abolished the fast of Tishah B'Av and turned the day into a time of joyous celebration.

SYNAGOGUE OBSERVANCE

In the synagogue the following practices are observed:

1 The lights are dimmed and only a few candles lit. This is a symbol of the darkness which befell Israel.

2 The curtain of the Ark is removed in memory of the curtain in the Holy of Holies in the Temple. According to talmudic legend, it was stabbed and desecrated by Roman emperor Titus (39–81 BCE).

3 Congregants sit on low benches or on the floor.

4 The cantor recites the prayers in a monotonous and melancholy fashion.

5 Some people change their customary seats.

6 In some congregations the Torah Scroll is placed on the floor and ashes are sprinkled on it.

7 The prayer service is the regular weekday service with a number of changes.

8 In some congregations it is customary not to wear prayer shawls and *tefillin*, or 'phylacteries', during the morning service. Instead they are worn during the afternoon service.

9 It is customary to sprinkle ashes on the head as a symbol of mourning. In Jerusalem, it is customary to visit the Western Wall where the Book of Lamentations is recited.

Below Prayer with Torah scroll at the Western Wall, Jerusalem, on the 9th of Av, the anniversary of the destruction of both the First and Second Temples.

CHAPTER 11

HOME CEREMONIES

In Judaism religious observance in the home is of central importance. According to the sages, the home is a *mikdash me-at*, or 'minor sanctuary'. Like the synagogue, home continues various traditions of the ancient Temple. The Sabbath candles, for example, recall the Temple menorah and the dining table symbolizes the altar. *Kashrut* or dietary laws and the discipline of keeping a kosher kitchen, together with ritual immersion, are seen as a part of a person's freewill choices about aligning one's life with God. In this context, honouring and respecting parents is regarded as an ideal. Most significantly, in the home family life is sanctified.

This chapter also considers personal piety and duties of the heart in Jewish religious practice. A good person shows humility, compassion, mercy and justice. Alongside the home, communal life is of fundamental importance. Within the context of community and synagogue, Jews express their loyalty to the traditions of their ancestors and their dedication to God.

Opposite A father putting the Passover basket on his son's head in the ritual meal held annually to mark the Exodus from Egypt. From the Barcelona Haggadah c.1340.

Above A family in Seattle, Washington DC, USA, holding a Passover seder, to commemorate the Jews' escape from slavery in Egypt.

HOME

ACCORDING TO THE TRADITION, THE HOME IS REGARDED AS A MINOR SANCTUARY. THROUGHOUT THE YEAR VARIOUS RELIGIOUS CEREMONIES TAKE PLACE IN A FAMILY SETTING.

The Jewish home is a *mikdash me'at* or minor sanctuary. Religious observance is of fundamental importance.

THE HOME AND THE TEMPLE

Like the synagogue, the home continues various traditions of the ancient Temple. The dining table symbolizes the altar and the Sabbath candles recall the Temple menorah.

Most significantly, within the home, family life is sanctified. As head of the family, the father is to exercise authority over his wife and children. He is obligated to circumcise his son, redeem him from Temple service in a special ceremony if he is the first-born, teach him the Torah, marry him off and teach him a craft. Moreover, the father of the family is required to serve as a role model for the transmission of Jewish ideals to his offspring.

Below A Jewish woman hiding leavened bread for her husband to find, 1723. At the beginning of Passover, leavened bread must be removed from the house.

WIFE AND MOTHER

The prevailing sentiment is that the wife's role is to bear children and exercise responsibility for family life.

According to Jewish law, womanhood is a separate status with its own sets of rules. In terms of religious observance, women were classed as slaves and children, disqualified as witnesses, excluded from the study of the Torah and segregated from men. Moreover, they were viewed as ritually impure for extended periods of time. In general, they were exempted from time-bound commandments. As a consequence, they were not obliged to fulfil those commandments that must be observed at a particular time. The purpose of these restrictions was to ensure that their attention and energy be directed towards completing their domestic duties.

In the modern world, however, a growing number of women have agitated for equal treatment and the role of women has undergone a major transformation.

Above An Orthodox Jewish father from Tiberias, Israel, holding his son. Family life is central to Judaism.

CHILDREN

Young people are to carry out the commandment to honour and respect their parents. For the rabbis, the concept means providing parents with food, drink, clothing and transportation. Respect requires children do not sit in a parent's seat, interrupt them, or express an opinion in a dispute involving a parent. The Talmud extols this: 'There are three partners in man, the Holy One, blessed be He, the father and the mother. When a man honours his [parents], the Holy One, blessed be He, says, "I will ascribe [merit] to them as though I had dwelt among them and they had honoured me."'

DOMESTIC HARMONY

The ideal of home life is domestic harmony. The Talmud specifies the guidelines for attaining this goal: 'A man should spend less than his means on food, up to his means on clothes, and more than his means in honouring wife and children because they are dependent on him.' Such harmony is attained through give and take, as well as the observance of Jewish ritual. When the family follows God's commandments, the home is permeated with sanctity.

SYMBOLS AND OBSERVANCE

Mezuzah on each doorpost characterize the Jewish home. In Scripture it is written that 'these words' shall be written on the mezuzot, or 'doorposts', of the house (Deuteronomy 6:4–9; 11:13–21). This is understood literally; these two passages are copied by hand on to parchment, put into a case and fixed to the doorpost of every room in the house.

Sabbath candles are important home ritual objects. At least two candles should be used in honour of the dual commandment to remember and observe the Sabbath day. This ceremony is performed before sunset on Sabbath eve as well as at festivals symbolizing light and joy. Lighting the candles is normally the wife's task.

The cycle of the year provides various opportunities for home observances. On Passover normal dishes are replaced. Traditional law excludes the use of all domestic utensils, crockery and cutlery. As a result sets are kept especially for this holiday. The seder, or 'religious meal', itself is observed on the first night of Passover. On Sukkot it is customary to dwell in a *sukkah*, or 'booth', built for the festival in a yard, garden or balcony. It is covered by foliage through which the stars can be seen at night. During Hanukkah a festival lamp is kindled at home on each day of the festival in memory of the victory of the Maccabees over the Seleucids. Life-cycle events also provide an occasion for special observances in the home.

MODERN JUDAISM

In contemporary society Orthodox Judaism continues to carry out these home activities. However, within the various branches of non-Orthodox Judaism modifications have been made to those traditions and a number of home festivities have been eliminated because they are no longer viewed as spiritually significant. None the less, there is a universal recognition among Jewry that the home is central to Jewish existence and survival.

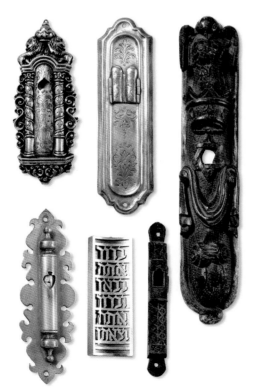

Left Mezuzah cases. Such cases contained Bible scrolls and were fixed to doorposts to protect the household.

Below Taking part in home ceremonies. A mother and father help their daughter light the Friday night candles.

COMMUNITY LIFE

IN THE JEWISH WORLD, COMMUNAL LIFE IS OF FUNDAMENTAL SIGNIF-
ICANCE. IT IS WITHIN THE COMMUNITY THAT JEWS ARE ABLE TO CARRY
OUT THEIR RITUAL AND MORAL RESPONSIBILITIES.

Through the centuries, community life had been of central importance in the Jewish faith. Alongside the home, Jews have encouraged active participation within the community. Community centres, synagogues and other venues help unite the Jewish people into a collective whole.

THE ANCIENT WORLD
In ancient Israel, Jews constituted a Hebrew clan. Later, as they changed from a nomadic to an agricultural existence, they lived in towns. As a result, their leadership became urbanized. Leaders were responsible for administering justice and towns were organized into territorial units. During the Babylonian exile, Jewish institutions established a pattern for later communal development. As early as the 2nd century BCE, Jews in Alexandria formed their own cor-

Below Conversation in the street. Polish Jews in the ghetto at Vienna, Austro-Hungary, c.1873.

poration with a council that regulated its affairs in accordance with Jewish law. It also constructed synagogues and sent taxes which were collected for the Temple in Jerusalem. In the Roman Empire, Jews were judged by their own courts: this system established the basis for legal autonomy which became a standard for Jewish life throughout the world.

THE DIASPORA
When the Temple was destroyed in 70CE, Jewish life underwent a transformation. In Israel the patriarchate together with the Sanhedrin served as the central authority. In Babylonia, on the other hand, the exilarch was the leader of the community along with the heads of the rabbinical academies. Jews were bound together by the law, and synagogues, law courts, schools, philanthropic institutions and ritual baths constituted the framework of communal life. In North Africa and Spain, the *nagid* ('prince') was the

Above A kosher butcher weighing beef in his shop at the Orthodox Jewish community headquarters in Budapest. Kosher (Kashrut) meat is required as part of Jewish dietary law.

head of the community. Later in the medieval period in the Franco-German region, rabbinical authorities exercised communal leadership. As in Babylonia, a wide range of institutions regulated daily life, and taxes were raised to provide for the needy. In this milieu the synagogue served as the centre for Jewish worship and study.

COMMUNAL STATUTES
In order to regulate communal affairs, *takkanot ha-kahal*, or 'statutes', were established; these were amplified by special ordinances and enactments. To ensure their enforcement, a *bet din*, or 'court', was presided over by a panel of *dayyanim*, or 'judges'. These courts excommunicated offenders. The parnas, or 'community's head', was recognized by the secular or church authorities. He and the local rabbi were often designated as Master of the Jews or Bishop of the Jews. From the 14th century, Polish Jewry gained dominance in Eastern Europe and communal autonomy was often invested in the Jewish community of a central town which had responsibilities for smaller communities

in the region. In Poland – Lithuania, the Council of the Four Lands functioned as a Jewish parliament. By contrast, in the Ottoman empire a chief rabbi was recognized as the Jewish community's representative. Each province of the empire had its own chief rabbi.

THE ENLIGHTENMENT

With the advent of the Enlightenment in the 18th century, the traditional pattern of Jewish life was fundamentally altered. Previously, Jews were unable to opt out of the community. However, with full citizenship rights, Jews assimilated into the wider community. In modern times, Jews have adjusted communal life to contemporary demands. In contrast with previous centres where Jewish life was uniform in character, the Jewish community has fragmented into a number of different religious groupings.

MODERN JUDAISM

On the far right of the Jewish spectrum, Orthodoxy has sought to preserve the beliefs and practices

Below A bet din *(Jewish court dealing especially with religious questions) in London's East End, 1930s.*

Above The circular city of Nahalal, Israel. An aerial view of the first moshav, a co-operative settlement consisting of small separate farms, founded in the Jezreel Valley.

of the past. From the late 18th century, Orthodox Jews opposed changes to Jewish existence brought about by the Enlightenment. Moving to the centre of the religious spectrum, Conservative Judaism advocates a moderate stance in which traditional law is observed, but modified according to contemporary needs. As an offshoot of the Conservative movement, Reconstructionist Judaism rejects supernaturalism while adopting a moderately traditional approach to Jewish life. Reform Judaism has adopted a more liberal stance, intent on modernizing Judaism for the contemporary world. Humanistic Judaism espouses a more radical position; like Reconstructionist Judaism it rejects any form of supernaturalism and focuses on humanistic values. Alongside these movements, there are a variety of alternative approaches to Jewish existence that espouse a range of differing ideologies.

THE COMMUNAL IDEAL

Throughout Jewish history, communal life has undergone enormous change. Yet despite the variations in form, the Jewish people have been united in their determination to preserve and transmit their religious traditions. Despite their varied forms of organization, Jews remain loyal to the concept of *K'lal Yisrael*, or 'the community of Israel', and are intent on ensuring the survival of Judaism and the Jewish people. It is within the context of community that Jewry continues to gain spiritual sustenance and strength.

PRAYERS AND BLESSINGS

PRAYER IS AT THE HEART OF THE JEWISH TRADITION. THE TALMUD DESCRIBES IT AS BELONGING TO THE HIGHEST THINGS OF THE WORLD. IT LETS JEWS ESTABLISH A DIRECT CONTACT WITH THE CREATOR.

Jewish prayer is usually recited in Hebrew; this is the language of the Bible, the prophets and the sages of Israel. It is customary for prayers to be chanted, since this endows the words with a more profound meaning. The Ashkenazim and the Sephardim use different traditions of chant, and there are also different chants in the traditions of German, French, Italian, Lithuanian and Polish Jews. These forms of chanting vary depending on the context: the weekday mode of chanting differs from that of the festivals. On Rosh Hashanah and Yom Kippur the chanting is more solemn.

Below An illuminated heading from a German prayer book, c.1320, for the Day of Atonement, which is observed by praying and fasting.

Right An Ashkenazi Rabbi of Jerusalem by George S. Hunter, (1846–1919) wearing the prayer shawl.

GESTURES

Traditionally a number of movements and gestures are made during various parts of the liturgy. Bowing and prostrating the body are frequently described in the Bible. The Talmud limits bowing to four stages in the Amidah prayer, which is recited while standing. These four bows take place at the beginning and end of the first benediction and at the beginning and end of the thanksgiving benediction near the end of the Amidah. The correct procedure for bowing is to bend the head and the body from the waist while reciting *Barukh Atah*, or 'Blessed art Thou'. Then one should straighten

the head and after it the body so that head and body are upright when saying *Adonai*, or 'O Lord'.

During the biblical period it was customary for total prostration of the body to take place with the face to the ground and arms and legs outstretched. Today this only takes place during the Alenu prayer on Rosh Hashanah and Yom Kippur and while reciting the account of the Temple service on Yom Kippur. Some Jews also cover the eyes with the right hand while reciting the first verse of

SWAYING

It is customary for traditional Jews to sway while reciting prayer. In Yiddish this is known as *shocklen*. In the past some sages were opposed to swaying since they believed it lacked decorum. Other scholars permitted a gentle form of swaying of the head as an aid to concentration. Others, such as the Hasidim, however, advocated the use of violent movements and gestures. Advocates of such a practice cite Psalm 35: 10 to emphasize the necessity of swaying: 'All my bones shall say, Lord who is like unto Thee' – in their view, this verse suggests that the entire body should move in praise of God.

Above Tashlich prayer by the Yarkon River, Israel. On the first day of Rosh Hashanah, prayers are recited near water.

the Shema: 'Hear, O Israel, the Lord our God, the Lord is One.' This is done so that one is not distracted during the recitation of this prayer.

TEMPLE AND SYNAGOGUE

Since the destruction of the Temple in Jerusalem in the 1st century CE, the synagogue has become the central place of prayer. No longer are sacrifices offered as they were in ancient times, and the use of incense, which was associated with the Temple cult, has been abandoned. It is also incorrect to have a seven-branched menorah in the synagogue like the one used in the Temple. However, since the 19th century, Reform Jews have referred to their place of worship as a 'temple', but such a designation is regarded by traditional Jews as a misnomer.

COVERING THE HEAD

During the talmudic period, it was a mark of piety to cover the head. This is because heaven is described as above in both spatial and spiritual terms. For this reason it has become customary for Jewish men to cover their head; by doing so they create a barrier between themselves and the heavenly domain. Both Orthodox and non-Orthodox men cover their head during worship services, and recently this practice has been adopted by some women in non-

Above Rabbi's Blessing, 1871, by Moritz Daniel Oppenheim, one of the leading German Jewish artists.

Orthodox synagogues. It is also common for Orthodox men (as well as some traditionalists) to wear head coverings at all times.

SYNAGOGUE DECORUM

According to tradition, the synagogue should be a place where Jews worship in a spirit of holiness. One should not eat or drink in the synagogue; conversation during prayers should be avoided unless necessary for the conduct of the service; and a synagogue should not be used as a short-cut from one place to another. Yet, despite such a spirit of decorum, traditionally the synagogue should be regarded as a familiar place where Jews gather together for religious purposes.

BLESSINGS

There are four types of blessings in Judaism. The first are blessings to be recited when enjoying God's bounty. For each type of enjoyment (such as eating bread or fruit) a specific blessing was introduced. Another group of blessings is recited before the performance of a *mitzvah* or commandment: 'Blessed art thou ... Who has sanctified us with his commandments and has commanded us to ...'. A third

type of blessing consists of those said on beholding the wonders of nature. Finally, there are blessings of general praise such as the blessing of the kiddush on the Sabbath and festivals, or the blessings at a wedding.

PRAYERS OF THE DAY

There are three daily prayers: *shaharit* or morning prayer, *minhah* (afternoon) and *ma'ariv* (evening). Morning prayer should be recited just after sunrise; afternoon prayer can be recited from 20 minutes after midday until nightfall; evening prayer can be recited at any time during the night until dawn, but it is customary for minhah and ma'ariv to be recited one after the other. The central feature of all three prayers is the Amidah, which is arranged in three sets of blessings. First there are three in praise of God; these are followed by 11 blessings of petition; finally there are three blessings of further praise. Before the Amidah in the morning and evening service, the Shema is recited together with a number of blessings.

PARENTS AND CHILDREN

ACCORDING TO SCRIPTURE, IT IS THE DUTY OF CHILDREN TO HONOUR AND REVERE PARENTS. IN RABBINIC LITERATURE, SUCH DUTIES ARE ELABORATED IN DETAIL.

In the Jewish faith respect for parents is a cardinal virtue. Scripture uses two different expressions to describe such an attitude. In Exodus 20:12 Jews are instructed to 'honour thy father and thy mother'; Leviticus 19:3 states: 'Each one of you shall revere his mother and his father'.

RABBINIC JUDAISM
On the basis of these two passages, rabbinic sages taught that there is a double obligation to honour parents and revere them. They point out that in the verse from Exodus the father is mentioned first, whereas in the verse from Leviticus the mother is referred to first. The reason given is that children are more ready to honour their mother than their father, but are more ready to revere their father than their mother. As a result, the parent who might be neglected is mentioned first. This is as if to say, you may not need reminders to honour your father and to revere your mother. But do not forget to honour both and to revere both.

Above Father, son and great grandfather at a circumcision ceremony in Israel.

PARENTAL DUTIES
According to rabbinic Judaism, the duty to honour parents is defined as the obligation to provide them with food and drink, clothe them and escort them. The duty to revere parents is defined as the obligation not to stand or sit in their place, contradict them or take sides in a dispute involving them. The duty to honour parents is conceived as positive – to do what they require. But the duty to revere them is a negative requirement: not to do that which causes them distress.

OBLIGATIONS OF CHILDREN
These requirements require clarification. For example, to give parents food and drink and clothe them can mean either it is the responsibility of children to support their parents financially or, alternatively, it could mean simply that children should be courteous to their mother and father, serving them with their meals, and helping them on with their clothes – in such cases food and clothing would have been purchased by the parents themselves. This issue was debated by later scholars. The final ruling is that children have no obligation to support their parents financially. Yet, if their parents are too

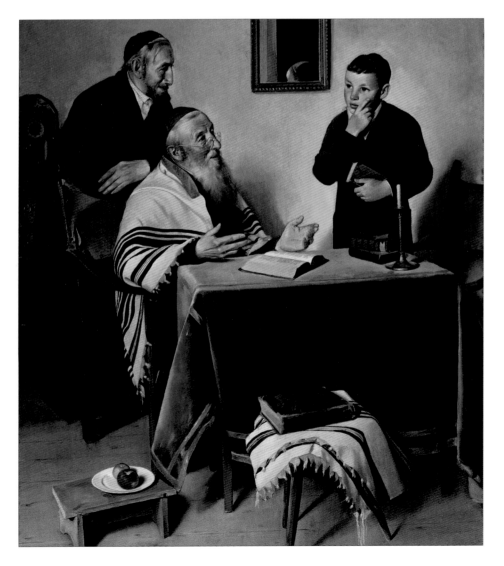

Left The Lesson. A boy studies the Talmud in this Austrian painting of 1930 by F.X. Wolf.

Left *Across the generations.*
Grandparents and grandchildren
lighting candles for Hanukkah.

When parents divorce, children can be tempted to take sides, but this should be resisted. Children should avoid playing one parent against another. When there are contradictory demands to the father and mother, the children must do their best to be impartial.

HONOUR

The obligation to honour and revere parents is extended by rabbinic sages in various ways. Honour is to be paid to parents who are no longer alive. The institutions of *kaddish*, or 'reciting a prayer for the dead', and *yahrzeit*, or 'lighting a memorial candle', were introduced for this purpose. There are also other categories of individuals to whom respect is due – this is a further extension of this commandment. These include grandparents, parents-in-law, step-parents, older siblings, and teachers. Yet, duties to parents must always come first.

poor to provide for their own needs, then their children must support them financially. Regarding the obligation not to contradict parents or patronize them, this does not imply that children are not permitted to disagree with their mother and father. It means instead that children should not give the impression of judging their parents' opinions in a patronizing fashion. Children do not have to forfeit their own opinions; on the contrary, they have a right to their own views. The obligation not to stand or sit in a parent's place is understood both literally and figuratively. If a father has a special place at home, a child should not occupy it unless a parent has no objection. Further, the injunction means that if a parent has a special position in the community, children should not take the same role. However, it is permitted for parents to forgo their rights in these matters.

LIMITATIONS

Despite such obligations to parents, there are limits to what a mother and father can demand. The commandment to honour parents does not give parents the right to act in a dictato-

rial fashion. Children have rights, and the wishes of parents should be set aside if children are expected to commit a crime or disobey the *mitzvot*, or 'commandments'. According to a number of authorities, there is not an obligation for children to obey their parents other than in the cases specified by Jewish law. Thus, if a parent objects to the person their son or daughter chooses to marry, the parents' wishes do not have to be respected.

Below *Grandfather, father, son. Three*
generations of Jews reading from the
Torah for the son's bar mitzvah.

DIETARY LAWS

SCRIPTURE DIFFERENTIATES BETWEEN FOOD WHICH IS KOSHER AND FOOD WHICH IS FORBIDDEN. THESE REGULATIONS WERE EXPANDED IN RABBINIC SOURCES.

According to Scripture, food must be *kosher*, or 'ritually fit', if it is to be consumed. Through the centuries, Jews have observed these biblical regulations as well as rabbinic pre-scriptions. The laws of *kashrut* are of seminal importance in the tradition.

BIBLICAL LAW
The Bible declares that laws of kashrut were given by God to Moses on Mount Sinai. As a result, Jews are obligated to follow this legislation due to its divine origin. Nevertheless, various reasons have been adduced for such observance. Allegedly, forbidden foods are unhealthy; that is why they are forbidden. Another explanation is that those who refrain from eating particular kinds of food serve God even while eating. Thereby they are able to attain an elevated spiritual state. Some of these laws, such as refraining from eating pork,

Below A Jewish bakery in the le Marais district of Paris.

have gained such significance that Jews were prepared to sacrifice their lives rather than violate God's law.

ANIMALS, BIRDS AND FISH
The laws concerning which animals, birds and fish may be eaten are contained in Leviticus 11 and Deuteronomy 14:3–21. The Bible states that only those animals that chew the cud and have split hooves may be eaten. Such animals include cows and sheep. However, no similar formula is stated concerning which birds may be consumed; instead a list is given of forbidden birds. Although no reasons are given to explain these choices, it has been suggested that forbidden birds are in fact birds of prey. By not eating them, human beings are able to express their abhorrence of cruelty as well as the exploitation of the weak over the strong. Regarding fish, the law states that only fish that have both fins and scales are allowed. Again, no reason is given to support

Above A rabbi wearing a prayer shawl supervises production of kosher wines at a winery in Tuscany, Italy.

this explanation. Yet various explanations have been proposed, such as the argument that fish that do not have fins and scales frequently live in the depths of the sea, which was regarded as the abode of the gods of chaos.

SLAUGHTER
A further category of kashrut deals with *shehitah*, or 'the method of killing animals for food'. Even though the Torah does not specify the details of this procedure, the Talmud states this method has divine authority since it was explained by God to Moses on Mount Sinai. According to tradition, the act of slaughter must be done with a sharpened knife without a single notch, because that might tear the animal's food pipe or windpipe.

Numerous other laws govern this procedure. A person must be trained in the law if he is to act as a *shohet*, or 'slaughterer'. According to rabbinic scholars, the central idea underlying the laws of ritual slaughter is to give the animal as painless a death as is possible. Judaism does not require that the devout become vegetarians, but when animals are

killed for food this must be done so as to cause the least amount of suffering possible.

Another aspect of ritual slaughter is the concern that no animal is eaten if it has a defect. In such cases it is referred to as *terefah*, or 'torn'. The prohibition against terefah is based on Exodus 22:31. This law is elaborated in the Mishnah where the sages decree that terefah refers not only to the meat of an animal torn by wild beasts but to any serious defect in an animal's or a bird's organs. On the basis of this law, the shohet is obliged to examine the lungs of an animal after it has been slaughtered to ensure that no defect is found. If any irregularity is found in an animal that has been slaughtered it should be taken to a rabbi to determine if it is kosher. In the preparation of meat, it is imperative that adequate salting takes place. This prescription is based on the biblical prohibition against consuming blood.

MILK AND MEAT

Another restriction concerning ritual food is the prohibition against eating milk and meat together. This stipulation is based on Exodus 23:19: 'Thou shalt not boil a kid in its mother's milk'. According to

Below A German Jewish slaughtering yard in the 1700s. Animals are killed according to Jewish dietary laws by cutting the animal's throat and allowing the blood to drain out.

rabbinic Judaism, this rule does not refer only to the act of boiling a kid in its mother's milk. Tradition stipulates that it is forbidden to cook meat and milk together. Later, this law was expanded to eating milk and meat products at the same time. Eventually the law was introduced that dairy dishes should not be eaten after a meal until a stipulated period of time had passed. Meat, on the other hand, may be eaten after dairy produce; none the less, it is usual to wash the mouth out beforehand. Not only should milk and meat products not be consumed at the same time, dairy food should not be cooked in meat utensils, and vice versa.

MODERN JUDAISM

Although the Bible does not attempt to explain the origin of these various dietary laws, it does associate them with holiness. The rabbis of the Talmud and midrash explored the rationale of the system of kashrut. Generally they believed that observance of such laws aids the development of self-discipline and moral conduct.

Today, kosher food is obtainable in kosher food stores and some supermarkets. Observant Jews eat in kosher restaurants, which have been inspected by supervisors.

Above Purifying dishes for Passover, an important part of the preparations, in Mea Shearim neighbourhood, Jerusalem.

Up until modern times the rules of kashrut were universally practised by Jewry. Yet, in the 19th century, the Reform movement broke with tradition. For this reason, most Reform Jews have largely ignored the prescriptions of the dietary system. Conservative Judaism, however, adheres to the laws of kashrut, although allowance is made for personal selectivity. Orthodox Judaism, on the other hand, strictly follows the tradition.

Below Seal of approval. Packaged kosher food is sealed with a label, often called a hechsher.

CONVERSION

ACCORDING TO TRADITION, A PERSON IS JEWISH IF HIS OR HER MOTHER IS JEWISH. HOWEVER, CONVERSION HAS ALWAYS BEEN A ROUTE OF ENTRY INTO THE JEWISH COMMUNITY.

Although there is no formal term for the process of conversion in the Hebrew Bible, there are several biblical terms that are suggestive of such an act. Such terms illustrate that conversion was practised during the biblical period in order to assimilate conquered peoples as well as those who came to live within the Israelite community. During the tannaitic and amoraic periods (100BCE–600CE), conversion was frequently extolled by various authorities. According to the early rabbinic sage Elazar, for example, conversion was viewed as part of God's salvationist scheme. According to Hoshiah, another early rabbinic authority, God acted righteously towards Israel when he

Below Passover Haggadah showing Savants at the Table of Maimonides. *From left: Joseph Caro, Isaac Alfasi, Maimonides, Jacob ben Asher and Rashi. Laws regulating conversion are contained in compendiums of Jewish law compiled by such rabbinic scholars.*

scattered them among the nations. In another passage in the Talmud it is asserted that the proselyte is dearer to God than the Israelite since he has come of his own accord.

As a result of such openness to converts, a number of gentiles converted to Judaism during the early rabbinic period. However, the rise of Christianity led to the cessation of Jewish missionizing. None the less, during the talmudic and post-talmudic period occasional conversions did take place in accordance with rabbinic law. Eventually the regulations governing conversion were drawn together and edited by Joseph Caro (1488–1575), the compiler of the *Shulkhan Arukh*, which since its publication in 1565 has served as the authoritative Code of Jewish Law.

CANDIDATE CONVERSION

In the *Shulkhan Arukh* the requirements for conversion as laid down in the Talmud and other codes are detailed. When a man or woman

Above Ethiopian immigrants to Israel *demonstrate against a ruling by the rabbinate that they must undergo conversion to be considered Jews, 1996.*

appears as a candidate, the person is asked: 'What motivates you? Do you know that, in these days, Jews are subject to persecution and discrimination, that they are hounded and troubled?' If the individual replies: 'I know this and yet I regard myself as unworthy of being joined to them,' the convert is accepted immediately. The root principles of the faith, namely the unity of God and the prohibition of idol worship, are expounded to the candidate at considerable length. The proselyte is taught, too, some of the simpler and some of the more difficult commandments, and is informed of the punishment involved in violating the commandments.

Similarly, the convert is told of the rewards of observing them, particularly that by virtue of keeping the commandments he or she will merit the life of the world to come. He or she is told that no one is considered wholly righteous except those who understand and fulfil the commandments. Further, the convert is told that the world to come is intended only for the righteous. If the male convert finds these doctrines acceptable, he is circumcised immediately. After his circumcision has completely healed, he undergoes ritual immersion. Three learned Jews

Above Jews washing in a small spring mikveh *(ritual bath) outside the Tomb of the Prophet Samuel, north of Jerusalem. Traditionally, converts undergo ritual immersion in a mikveh.*

stand by while he is in the water and instruct him in some of the easy and some of the difficult commandments.

In the case of the female proselyte, Jewish women accompany her and supervise her immersion. The three learned male Jews remain outside the *mikveh*, or 'pool', and give the convert instruction while she is in the water.

THE CANDIDATE'S MOTIVES

The *Shulkhan Arukh* states: 'When the would-be proselyte presents himself, the convert should be examined lest the person be motivated to enter the congregation of Israel by hope of financial gain or social advantage or by fear. A man is examined lest his motive be to marry a Jewish woman, and a woman is questioned lest she have similar desires towards some Jewish man.' If no unacceptable motive is found, the candidate is told of the heaviness of the yoke of the Torah and how difficult it is for the average person to live up to the commandments of the Torah. This is done to give the candidate a chance to withdraw if he so desires. Once a man

Right Harvest scene from the Book of Ruth, 1320. According to Scripture, Ruth was a Moabite woman who joined the Jewish people.

is circumcised and a man or woman is ritually immersed, the convert is no longer a non-Jew. The central feature of these regulations governing the traditional conversion procedure is the emphasis on joining the Jewish community and accepting the law.

MODERN JUDAISM

Up until the present day, the procedure outlined in the *Shulkhan Arukh* has been rigorously followed. Within modern Orthodox Judaism, the emphasis is on living a Jewish way of life within the community. For this reason, converts are given extensive religious instruction. Conservative Judaism generally follows these legal requirements, but Reform Judaism has departed from the traditional practice in a variety of ways.

Above American entertainers Frank Sinatra and Sammy Davis Jr were members of the Rat Pack. Both championed Jewish civil rights and causes in the USA, and Davis became a Jew.

Emphasizing the universalistic mission of Judaism, Reform Jews very early in their history abrogated the necessity of ritual immersion for converts. On the question of circumcision, opinion was at first divided. Eventually, however, it was generally accepted that the only requirements were that the person freely seek membership, that the candidate be of good character and be sufficiently acquainted with the faith and practices of Judaism. Unlike Orthodoxy, Reform Judaism accepts conversion for the sake of marriage.

DUTIES OF THE HEART

NOT ONLY ARE JEWS OBLIGATED TO FULFIL RITUAL AND MORAL DUTIES, THEY ARE ALSO COMMANDED TO DIRECT THEIR SPIRITUAL LIFE IN ACCORDANCE WITH GOD'S WILL.

In the Middle Ages the 11th-century Jewish philosopher Bahya Ibn Pakudah wrote an important treatise *Duties of the Heart*. In this he described Jewish obligations as comprising duties which he calls practices of the limbs: these are acts a Jew is obliged to perform. In addition, he listed a second category – duties of the heart – which relate to the inner life.

SPIRITUALITY

In the past, Jewish writers promoted inwardness. What is clear is that the norm for these sages was different from the attitude of modern Jews. For example, Bahya discussed the concept of equanimity. In his view, it is essential for a person to adopt such an attitude if God is to be truly worshipped. In other words, a spiritual person must be indifferent to the praise and blame of others. Such an individual should so love God

Above Prayer at Home, c.1470. A facsimile of a Hebrew book of sacred texts painted by the Italian Renaissance master Leonardo Bellini.

that he does not care what others think. His mind and heart should be directly focused on the Divine. Yet, for most Jews today such an attitude of disinterestedness is not based on the love of God, but on a disdain of the opinions of others. Moreover, such an attitude can result in indolence. If a person does good only to satisfy others, his motivation is not adequate. On the other hand, one who aspires to do good only for the sake of heaven is leaving it up to himself to decide if and when God is satisfied. Indeed, he may in fact trying to deflect criticism by believing that his motives are for God alone. This can result in complacency and self-satisfaction.

CHARACTER

According to Judaism, one who has a good character should possess the traits of humility, compassion, love of mercy and a sense of justice. Conversely, he or she should avoid such attitudes as pride, vanity, cruelty, falsehood and bad temper. To be humble does not mean that a person should be unaware of his talents. Rather, such an individual should regard all his positive qualities as a

Left When Joseph's brothers sold him into slavery they betrayed their brotherly duty. From a painting by Raphael.

THE ASCETIC LIFE

Bahya and others' views on the ascetic life should be viewed with caution by those with no saintly pretensions. Judaism demands correct action. But there is no requirement to be a saint. Ascetics in previous centuries have denied themselves food and drink and rarely slept in a comfortable bed. At times they flogged themselves and performed other acts of self-torture. Such actions are not required; indeed, such can even lead to morbid self-hatred.

*Right A cantor reads the Haggadah to
illiterate members of a Spanish
synagogue so that all can take part.
14th-century Sephardi manuscript.*

gift from God for which he can
claim no credit. In this regard, there
is a religious dimension of a good
character. The pursuit of truth, for
example, is connected with the God
of truth. Falsehood is a distortion of
reality, an affront to God.

PEACE

Rabbinic sages stated that it is
permitted to tell harmless lies for
the sake of peace. An example of
this is Joseph's statement to his
brothers that their father, Jacob, had
ordered him to forgive them for
their wrongdoing. This was not true,
but Joseph was telling a lie to
preserve family peace. The rabbis
also say that a lie is in order if a person is asked indelicate questions
about his married life. In such a
case, he has no obligation to tell the
truth. Again, it is permissible to lie
about how much Torah learning
one has in order to avoid appearing
as a braggart.

*Right A cantor reads the Haggadah to
illiterate members of a Spanish
synagogue so that all can take part.
14th-century Sephardi manuscript.*

*Below A woman prays at the Tomb of
the Righteous Rabbi Ovadia in the
Upper Galilee, Israel.*

BAD TEMPER

Within the Jewish tradition, a bad
temper is severely criticized. A person who breaks things in a fit of
temper is compared to an idolator
because the loss of self-control is due
to an inadequate awareness of God's
presence. Even when a parent or
teacher is obliged to show disap-
proval, they should retain control,
making only the outward signs of
displeasure. As the Ethics of the
Fathers states in the Mishnah: 'The
man who is quick to become angry
but is easily appeased, his virtue outweighs his fault. The person who
rarely flies into a rage but when he
does so is hard to appease – his fault
outweighs his virtue. The man who
is quick to be angry and hard to
appease is wicked. The man who

rarely loses his temper and on the
occasions when he does so is easily
appeased – that person is a saint.'

THE LOVE AND FEAR OF GOD

Love and fear of God are duties of
the heart that have received a range
of interpretations. In the Bible, they
are usually synonymous with righteous action. It is not only that justice
and righteousness lead to love and
fear of God, but in a sense they are
the love and fear of God. In rabbinic
literature the love of God generally
means love of God's law; the fear of
God refers to the avoidance of sin.
Among medieval mystics, the love
and fear of God is viewed as a yearning of the human soul for the
nearness of the Creator and its dread
and awe at his majesty.

RITUAL IMMERSION

A MIKVEH, OR 'COLLECTION OF WATER', REFERS TO ANY POOL OR
BATH OF CLEAR WATER WHICH IS USED FOR RITUAL IMMERSION. SUCH
IMMERSION RENDERS A PERSON RITUALLY CLEAN.

From ancient times to the present, the mikveh has played a central role in Jewish life. By immersing in a mikveh a person who has become ritually unclean through contact with the dead or any other defiling object, or through an unclean flux from the body, can become ritually clean. The mikveh is also used for vessels that have become unclean.

In the modern world, the chief use of the mikveh is for a woman who has just menstruated. According to Jewish law, the contracting of marital relations with a wife who is in an unclean state is a serious offence.

The mikveh is also commonly used for the immersion of proselytes, or converts to Judaism, as part of the ceremony of conversion.

In addition, immersion in the mikveh is practised by various groups as an aid to spirituality, particularly on the Sabbath and festivals, especially the Day of Atonement.

SPIRITUALITY

The purpose of immersion is not physical, but spiritual. According to the 12th-century philosopher Moses Maimonides, the laws about immersion as a means of freeing oneself from uncleanness are decrees laid down by Scripture. They are not matters that human beings can rationally comprehend. Uncleanliness thus should not be viewed as mud or filth which water can remove, but rather of a spiritual nature and depending on the intention of the heart. For this reason the sages stated: 'If a man immerses himself, but without special intention, it is as though he has not immersed himself at all.'

THE MORAL RATIONALE

There is a moral basis for immersion. Just as one who sets his heart on becoming clean becomes clean as soon as he has immersed himself (although nothing new has occurred to his body), so, too, one who sets his heart on turning away from evil becomes clean as soon as he resolves to change his ways. For this reason, Scripture states: 'And I will sprinkle clean water upon you and you shall be clean, from all your uncleanliness and from all your idols will I cleanse you' (Ezekiel 36:25).

THE WATER

All natural spring water, provided it is clean and has not been discoloured by any admixtures, is valid for a mikveh. With regard to rainwater, melted snow or ice, care must be taken to ensure the water flows freely. The water must

Above Mikveh (ritual bath) at Masada, Israel. The water in a mikveh should come from a natural spring or river.

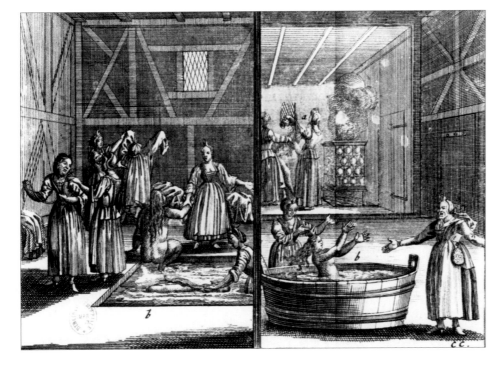

Left Jewish women in the mikveh or ritual bath. An engraving from 1726 by Johann Georg Puschner.

Below A non-traditional Jewish group in Pennsylvania, USA, have a mikveh (ritual bath) in a swimming pool.

the correct amount of valid water, it does not become invalid even though someone adds drawn water to it.

TYPES OF MIKVEH

When there is a plentiful supply of valid water which can replenish the mikveh, the only condition to be fulfilled is to ensure the water does not become invalidated by the construction of the mikveh, which renders it a vessel, or by going through metal pipes, which are not sunk into the ground. Since most mikvaot are constructed in urban areas where such supplies are not freely available, the technological and halakhic solution of a valid mikveh depends essentially upon constructing a mikveh with valid water and replenishing it with invalid water, taking advantage of the fact the addition of this water to an originally valid one does not invalidate it.

Below A Hungarian Orthodox Jew prays in the yard of the mikveh (ritual bath) after making his dishes kosher.

BIBLICAL LAW

According to biblical law, any collection of water, drawn or otherwise, is suitable for a mikveh as long as it contains enough for a person to immerse himself. The rabbis, however, enacted that only water which has not been drawn in a vessel or receptacle may be used. The rabbis further established that the minimum quantity for immersion is 250–1,000 litres/55–220 gallons. A mikveh containing less than this amount becomes invalid should a specified amount of drawn water be added to it. If the mikveh contains more than this amount, it can never become invalid no matter how much water is added. A mikveh may be be hewn out of rock or built in or put on the ground, and any material is suitable. It must be watertight, otherwise it becomes invalid. Finally, the height must be 47 inches (119.3 cm) to enable a person standing in it to be completely immersed even though he has to bend the knees.

not reach the mikveh through vessels made of metal or other materials. This is avoided by attaching the pipes and other accessories to the ground, which means they cease to have the status of vessels. The mikveh should be emptied from above by hand, by vacuum or by electric or automatic pumps. There is one regulation that eases the problems of constructing a valid mikveh. Once the mikveh has

CHAPTER 12

LIFE CYCLE EVENTS

The Jewish life cycle is marked by a series of religious events which celebrate various stages of development. Beginning at birth, a number of ceremonies mark the acceptance of the child into the Jewish community. For male infants, the act of circumcision symbolizes the child's identification as a Jew. The Redemption of the First-Born recalls the ancient practice of redeeming the child from Temple service. Bar and bat mitzvah constitute steps towards Jewish adulthood. Finally, the Jewish marriage service binds the bride and groom in the presence of God.

At the end of life, the utmost regard and consideration is shown to the dying. Jewish law stipulates that the body must be buried as soon as possible after death. The general pattern for funerals involves the ritual rending of garments, the funeral procession, the eulogy, either in a funeral chapel or beside the grave, and memorial prayers. Once the funeral is over, it is customary for the family to return home to begin a period of mourning.

Opposite A Jewish marriage contract from the Netherlands, 1648. The purpose of Jewish marriage is to create a Jewish home and a family and thus continue the Jewish community.

Above The Jewish Bride, 1667, by the leading artist of the Dutch Golden Age, Rembrandt van Rijn, is a portrait that explores marital tenderness.

BIRTH

IN THE BIBLE THE FIRST COMMANDMENT IS TO BE FRUITFUL AND
MULTIPLY. IT IS THEREFORE AN OBLIGATION FOR JEWISH PARENTS TO
HAVE CHILDREN WHO WILL CONTINUE THE TRADITION.

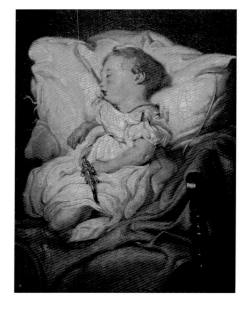

*Above Painting by English Jewish
painter Abraham Solomon of his
brother Simeon as a baby, 1841.*

From ancient times there have
been various ceremonies connected
with childbirth.

THE BIBLE

In biblical times childbirth took
place in a kneeling position or sit-
ting on a special birthstool. Scriptural
law imposes various laws on ritual
purity and impurity of the mother.
If she gives birth to a boy, she is considered ritually impure for seven
days. For the next 33 days she is not
allowed to enter the Temple
precincts or handle sacred objects.
For the mother of a girl, the number of days are respectively 14 and
66. According to Jewish law, if a
woman in childbirth is in mortal
danger, her life takes precedence over
that of an unborn child. Only when

more than half of the child's body
has emerged from the womb is it
considered to be fully human so that
both lives are of equal worth.

THE BIRTH OF A CHILD

In ancient times the birth of a child
was accompanied by numerous
superstitious practices, including the
use of amulets to ward off the evil
eye. After the birth, family and
friends gathered nightly to recite
prayers to ward off evil spirits such
as Lilith, the female demon who
allegedly attempts to kill off all
newly born children. Among
German Jews it was frequently the
practice for parents of a son to cut
off a strip of swaddling in which the
child was wrapped during his circumcision; this is known as the
wimple, and it is kept until his bar
mitzvah, when it is used for tying
the scroll of the law. From the
medieval period Ashkenazi mothers
visited the synagogue after the birth

of a child to recite a blessing that
expresses gratitude to God as well as
other prayers. It was also customary
for the congregation to recite a
prayer for the welfare of the mother
and the child.

BABY NAMING

The naming of a child takes place
either when a baby boy is named at
the circumcision ceremony or when
a baby girl is named in the synagogue on the first time the Torah is
read after her birth. The Hebrew
form of a person's name consists of
the individual's name followed by
ben, or 'son', or *bat*, or 'daughter', of
the father. This form is used in all
Hebrew documents as well as for the
call to the reading of the Torah. In
contemporary society it is still the
practice to give a child a Jewish
name in addition to their ordinary
name. Ashkenazi Jews frequently
name a child after a deceased relative; Sephardi Jews after a person
who is still alive. Alternatively, a
Hebrew name is selected that is
related to the ordinary name either
in meaning or sound, or the secular
name may be transliterated in

*Below In this 1900 lithograph, people
are giving offerings for sacrifice to the
priests at the Temple in Jerusalem.
First-born boys were dedicated to God.*

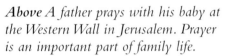

Above A father prays with his baby at the Western Wall in Jerusalem. Prayer is an important part of family life.

Above The redemption of the first-born son ritual requires payment of gold to a Cohen, a member of a priestly clan that traces its paternal lineage back to Aaron, the first priest in the Jewish religion.

redeem first-born sons from this service is referred to in Numbers 3:44–51. Here redemption is to take place by a payment of five shekels to the priest. Detailed laws are outlined in the Mishnah tractate Bekhorot and further expanded in the talmudic commentary on this passage.

Hebrew characters. Traditionally it was customary to change the name of a person at the time of a serious illness. According to rabbinic Judaism, changing the name is a way of misdirecting the angel of death. On this basis, it became a custom to add a further name to the ill person's. From that point the individual was known by their original name, together with the new one.

REDEEMING THE FIRST-BORN
The custom of redeeming first-born male children (*Pidyon ha-Ben*) is based on the scriptural prescription that first-born sons should be consecrated to the Temple. Just as first fruits and first-born animals had to be handed over to the priests, so first-born boys were dedicated to God. The obligation to

According to Jewish law, the sons of priests and Levites are exempt from redemption. Similarly, first-born sons whose mother is the daughter of either a priest or Levite are exempt. During the geonic period, a ceremony was instituted in which the father of the child declares to the priest on the 31st day after its birth that the child is the first-born son of his mother and the father, and that as a father, he is obliged to redeem him. The priest then asks the father if he prefers to give his son to the priest or redeem his son, and the father hands the priest the required amount. The father then recites a blessing concerning the fulfilment of the precept of redeeming the child, and another expressing gratitude to God. This procedure has served as the basis for the ceremony since the Middle Ages.

Left A mother reading to her young daughter in Shirat Hayam, a Gaza settlement, in 2005.

RITES OF PASSAGE

ACCORDING TO SCRIPTURE, ABRAHAM WAS COMMANDED BY GOD
TO CIRCUMCISE HIS SON ISAAC. THE PRACTICE OF CIRCUMCISION HAS
CONTINUED THROUGH THE AGES.

From ancient times, Jewish male children were circumcised; this practice was based on biblical law and was perceived as a sign of the covenant. At the age of 13, Jewish boys reach the age of adulthood, which is celebrated by a bar mitzvah ceremony. In modern times, a bat mitzvah ceremony has been introduced for Jewish girls.

CIRCUMCISION

According to Jewish law, all male children are to undergo circumcision in accordance with God's command to Abraham in the Book of Genesis. Jewish ritual involves the removal of the entire foreskin of the

Below Circumcision, from The Rothschild Miscellany, *the most lavish Hebrew manuscript of the 15th century, which details almost every custom of religious and secular Jewish life.*

penis. This act is to be performed on the eighth day after the birth of the child by a person who is qualified (*mohel*). The Jewish law specifies that this ceremony can be performed even on the Sabbath, festivals and the Day of Atonement. However, postponement is permitted if there is a danger to the child's health.

Laws concerning the ceremony are derived from both biblical and rabbinic sources. Traditionally circumcision is to take place in the presence of a *minyan*, or 'quorum of ten adult Jewish men'. On the morning of the eighth day, the child is taken from the mother by the godmother who hands him to the *sandak*, or 'godfather'. The sandak then carries the child in to the room where circumcision is to take place. He then hands him to the individual who places the child on a chair called the Chair of Elijah. Another person then takes him and passes him

Above A 17th-century circumcision set from Prague, elaborately ornamented and engraved, in gold and steel.

to the child's father who puts him on the lap of the godfather who holds the boy during the ceremony. The circumcision is performed by a mohel or specially trained person who performs circumcision. Formerly, blood was drawn orally but today an instrument is used. The infant is then handed to the person who will hold him during the ceremony of naming, and circumcision ends with a special blessing over a cup of wine, followed by the naming of the child.

BAR MITZVAH

At the age of 13, a boy attains the age of Jewish adulthood. From this point he is considered as part of a minyan. According to Jewish law, the 13th year is when a boy should observe the commandments. The essentials of the bar mitzvah ceremony involve prayer with *tefillin*, or 'phylacteries', for the first time, and reading from the Torah. It is now a universally accepted practice that the bar mitzvah boy is called to the reading at Sabbath morning services where he recites the Torah blessings, chants a maftir, or 'portion of the Law', and reads from the Prophets.

Above A bar mitzvah is held at the Western Wall in Jerusalem, a remnant of the ancient Temple.

In both Ashkenazi and Sephardi communities the bar mitzvah ceremony included a discourse by the bar mitzvah boy, which demonstrates his knowledge of rabbinic sources. In time other practices became associated with the ceremony. Some boys chanted the entire weekly reading; others were trained as prayer leaders; some conducted the Sabbath eve service on Friday night as well as the Sabbath morning. In some communities the bar mitzvah boy reads a special prayer standing before the Ark. In modern times it is usual for the rabbi to address the bar mitzvah boy after the reading of the law.

BAT MITZVAH

Unlike the bar mitzvah, there is no legal requirement for a girl to take part in a religious ceremony to mark her religious majority. None the less, a ceremonial equivalent of bar mitzvah has been designed for girls. In Orthodoxy this was an innovation in the 19th century and subsequently became widespread. In the early 20th century the Conservative scholar Mordecai Kaplan (1881–1983) pioneered the bat mitzvah

ceremony in the USA as part of the synagogue service, and since then this has become widely accepted by many American communities. In non-Orthodox congregations, a 12-year-old girl celebrates her coming of age on a Friday night or during the Sabbath morning service where she conducts the prayers, chants the Haftarah or reading from the Prophets, and in some cases also reads from the Torah and delivers an address. In Orthodox

synagogues, however, the bat mitzvah's participation in services is more limited. At a woman's minyan or quorum for prayer, she is called to the reading of the Torah and may even chant one of the portions, together with the Haftarah.

Outside the USA the bat mitzvah ceremony takes various forms. In Reform congregations the ceremony is in line with the American pattern. Orthodox girls, however, do not participate in the synagogue service. Rather, a bat mitzvah's father is called to the Torah on the appropriate Sabbath morning. His daughter then recites a prayer, and the rabbi addresses her in the synagogue or at a Kiddush reception afterwards. Alternatively, the ceremony takes place at home or in the synagogue hall on a weekday.

In Britain and South Africa the procedure is different; bat mitzvah girls must pass a special examination enabling them to participate in a collective ceremony.

Below Surrounded by friends, a Jewish girl lights candles at her bat mitzvah celebration in Manhattan, New York.

EDUCATION

IN JUDAISM EDUCATION IS OF CENTRAL IMPORTANCE. IT IS A PARENTAL DUTY TO ENSURE THEIR CHILDREN RECEIVE EDUCATION AND ARE FAMILIAR WITH THE VARIOUS ASPECTS OF THEIR RELIGIOUS HERITAGE.

Judaism stipulates that it is the responsibility of parents to educate children. The Book of Deuteronomy declares: 'And you shall teach them diligently to your children, and shall talk of them when you sit in your house, and when you walk by the way, and when you lie down and when you rise' (6:7). For this reason, Jewish education has been of paramount importance through the ages.

PARENTAL DUTY

The Hebrew Bible repeatedly refers to a father's obligation to teach his children about their religious past. The Book of Exodus states: 'You may tell in the hearing of your son and of your son's son how I have made sport of the Egyptians and what signs I have done among them' (Exodus 10:2). Exodus 13:8 says: 'And you shall tell your son on that day, "It is because of what the Lord did for me when I came out of Egypt."' The Book of Deuteronomy stipulates

Below Morning prayer in this Jewish girls' school in Jerusalem takes place in the classroom.

that 'When your son asks you in the time to come, "What is the meaning of the statutes and the ordinances which the Lord our God has commanded you?" then you shall say to your son, "We were Pharaoh's slaves in Egypt; and the Lord brought us out of Egypt with a mighty hand"' (Deuteronomy 6:20–21). In addition to such parental duties, it was the responsibility of the Levites to teach the people: 'They shall teach Jacob thy ordinances, and Israel the law' (Deuteronomy 33:10).

THE BIBLE

From the earliest times the study of the tradition was of central importance in the life of the nation. For this reason, the Hebrew Bible contains numerous references to the process of learning. The Book of Joshua, for example, states: 'This book of the law shall not depart out of your mouth, but you shall meditate on it day and night, that you may be careful to do according to all that is written in it' (Joshua 1:8). Again, the Book of Proverbs contains a number of references to the process of education:

Above Orthodox Jewish boys studying the Torah at the Yeshiva Kol Yaakov in Monsey, New York, USA.

'He who spares the rod hates his son' (Proverbs 13:24); 'Train up a child in the way he should go, and when he is old he will not depart from it' (Proverbs 22:6).

When the Israelites returned from Babylonian exile, Scripture records that Ezra gathered the people and taught them the law. When they heard his words, they vowed to observe the religious practices and festivals of their ancestors. According to the rabbis, it was Ezra who instituted the Torah reading on Monday and Thursday when people attended local markets.

Below A rabbi teaching boys Hebrew in a synagogue after school hours, 1891, from the London Illustrated News.

RABBINIC JUDAISM

According to the tradition, parents are obliged to begin a child's education as soon as possible. When the child begins to speak, he should be taught the verse: 'Moses commanded us a law, as a possession for the assembly of Jacob' (Deuteronomy 33:4). During this period the 1st century BCE sage Simeon ben Shetah (120–40BCE) established schools. However, it was his contemporary Joshua ben Gamla who is credited with the establishment of a formal system of education. He decreed that teachers had to be engaged in each locality at the community's expense and all children were to be given an education. Later the Talmud stipulated the size of classes. One teacher was permitted to handle up to 25 students. If students exceeded this number, an assistant was to be hired. More than 40 students required two teachers.

THE PALESTINIAN ACADEMY

Instruction in the law was to be carried out in the Palestinian academy. The first such institution was founded in Javneh after the destruction of the Temple in 70CE. According to tradition, Johanan ben Zakkai (fl. 1st century CE) arranged

Below A male teacher gives a lesson at a religious school for primary-level children in Jerusalem, Israel.

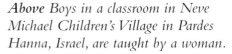

to have himself smuggled out of the city in a coffin. He was then brought before the Roman commander, Vespasian (9–79CE) and requested permission to found a centre of learning. This institution took over from the great Sanhedrin. Later other academies flourished under Johanan ben Zakkai's disciples.

BABYLONIAN ACADEMIES

In Babylon, schools of higher learning were also established in the 1st century CE. In the next century, under the leadership of Rav Shila and Abba bar Abba, the academy of Nehardea became the Babylonian spiritual centre, maintaining contact with the Palestinian Jewish community. When Rav returned to Babylonia from Palestine, he founded another academy at Sura in 200CE. In 259CE the Nehardea acad-

Above Boys in a classroom in Neve Michael Children's Village in Pardes Hanna, Israel, are taught by a woman.

emy was destroyed; under Judah ben Ezekiel it was transferred to Pumbedita where it remained for the next 500 years. From then it functioned in Baghdad until the 13th century.

THE POST-TALMUDIC AND MODERN PERIOD

During the period between the completion of the Talmud in the 6th century CE and the Enlightenment the majority of male Jews received some sort of education. This was generally limited to the study of sacred texts. However, in some periods secular subjects were also included. Prior to Jewish emancipation, the typical pattern of Jewish study involved a teacher with several students who studied religious texts. In the 19th century, organized *yeshivot*, or 'rabbinical seminaries', emerged in eastern Europe. In these institutions students progressed from one level to another – throughout the subject matter was Talmud and halakha, or 'Jewish law'. With the emancipation of Jewry, Jews began to study in secular schools and this has been the pattern up until the present. Jewish religion schools operating alongside secular schooling as well as Jewish day schools now serve as the primary means of Jewish education.

HIGHER EDUCATION AND COURTSHIP

AMONG THE ORTHODOX, JEWISH LEARNING CONTINUES AT A HIGH LEVEL. TRADITIONALLY, YOUNG MEN CONTINUED THEIR EDUCATION IN YESHIVOT OR ACADEMIES DEDICATED TO STUDYING SACRED TEXTS.

For the strictly Orthodox, in the modern world religious education does not end with bar or bat mitzvah. Four years of Jewish high school follow which combine secular and Jewish studies. Then young men go off to a *yeshiva* for several years.

ANCIENT ACADEMIES
A yeshiva (pl. yeshivot) is an academy dedicated to the study of the Talmud and other sacred texts. Academies of higher learning were created in Palestine and Babylonia in the 1st century CE. These institutions kept in contact with one another and attracted students from other lands. In Palestine the most famous was the academy founded by Johanan ben Zakkai (fl. 1st century CE) in Javneh after the destruction of Jerusalem in 70CE. In Babylonia the academies of

Below Male students in a yeshiva in Efrat, an Israeli settlement established in 1983.

Sura and Pumbedita, founded in the 3rd century CE, exerted an enormous influence on Jewish learning.

NON-ORTHODOX YOUTH
Most young people in the Diaspora do not pursue such a rigorous course of study. They go to secular schools and attend Jewish religious schools at the weekend. In non-Orthodox congregations, boys and girls attend confirmation classes, culminating in a confirmation ceremony. Alongside such study, summer camp offers opportunities for Jewish youth to learn about the tradition. Many Jewish children go on a trip to the Holy Land, where they are given a chance to experience Jewish life in Israel.

ORTHODOX COURTSHIP
According to the tradition, marriage is a sacred institution. Jews are expected to marry. Early marriage is the norm for the strictly Orthodox. Boys and girls are taught separately,

Above An engaged couple at a meal, facsimile of Schecken Bible of 1470, painted by Leonardo Bellini of Venice.

THE YESHIVA WORLD
In the 19th century, yeshivot were organized throughout Eastern Europe, however they were destroyed in the Holocaust. After World War II, new yeshivot were set up in the United States, Israel and Europe. Today most yeshivot are organized along the traditional Lithuanian lines. Students generally study in pairs in a large hall; together they argue the meaning of ancient sources. The debate is often conducted in Yiddish as they pore over the Aramaic text. Twice a week, the head of the yeshiva will give a lecture on the portion of the Talmud that is being studied. There is also a moral tutor who gives regular talks on *musar*, or 'ethics'. Such study does not necessarily lead to a career in the practical rabbinate. The majority of graduates earn their living in secular occupations. However, almost every yeshiva has a kolel, an advanced section in which married men and their families are supported as they continue their studies.

Above A couple under a huppah (bridal canopy), 1438, from Jacob ben Asher's Even ha'Ezer, *on marriage and divorce.*

and they are largely kept apart during adolescence. During a young man's final years at a yeshiva, he is expected to get married and families, friends and teachers are co-opted to find a suitable bride. In the past, in Eastern Europe villages, an official matchmaker organized the brokering between families. Today, this process is more informal. Marriages are not exactly arranged, but parents keep a close eye on the proceedings.

THE NON-ORTHODOX

Most Jewish children go to secular, co-educational schools. They then attend secular universities, often far from home. As a result, parents are able to exert far less control. According to Jewish law, certain marriages have no validity – in particular those that are incestuous, those that are adulterous, and those between a Jew and a gentile. In contemporary society intermarriage poses a major threat to Jewish life. In the past, when Jews were isolated in their own communities or when there was rampant anti-Semitism, the danger of intermarriage was small. Today in the State of Israel, Jews are likely to marry Jews. But in the Diaspora, the rate of intermarriage is very high.

INTERMARRIAGE

The religious establishment is anxious to combat this trend. Part of the drive behind the creation of non-Orthodox Jewish day schools is to help children grow up in a more Jewish milieu. Children are sent to Jewish summer camps where they meet other Jews. There are university Jewish societies, and Jewish single events take place in major cities around the globe.

Parents also exert considerable pressure. In the past, if a child married a gentile, then he or she was cut off from the Jewish community. Today this state of affairs is usually inconceivable, and most families are touched by intermarriage.

SINGLE JEWS

Despite the importance of marriage in the Jewish tradition, a significant number of Jewish men and women remain unmarried. In some cases this is because they are homosexual. Others are happier to live by themselves. Some have had a bad early experience, or simply leave it too long. Non-marriage combined with intermarriage poses a danger to the survival of the Jewish way of life. It has been calculated that if present trends continue, the Jewish community will significantly diminish in size.

Below A group of young Jews in the 1980s at a Jewish summer camp in Saratoga, California.

OUTWARD SIGNS

IN LIVING A JEWISH LIFE, JEWISH ADULTS ARE OBLIGED TO FOLLOW A RANGE OF LAWS RELATING TO OUTWARD SIGNS. SOME OF THESE REGULATIONS MUST BE OBSERVED BY MEN, OTHERS BY WOMEN.

All outward signs express determination to fulfil God's will as revealed to Moses on Mount Sinai and interpreted by rabbinic sages.

PHYLACTERIES

Once a Jewish boy has reached the age of maturity, he is required to wear *tefillin*, or 'phylacteries', for prayer. These consist of special boxes containing biblical verses written by hand on parchment. The verses are: (1) Exodus 13:1–10, concerning the laws relating to the dedication of the first born to God's service; (2) Exodus 13:11–16, repeating the laws of the first-born and the commandment to teach children about the miraculous deliverance from slavery in Egypt; (3) Deuteronomy 6:4–9, the first paragraph of the Shema prayer stressing the oneness of God; and (4) Deuteronomy 11:13–21, containing the second paragraph of the Shema prayer on reward and punishment. These boxes are attached to straps. One is placed over the head so that the box sits squarely upon the forehead and between the eyes. The other is wound round the left arm so that the box faces the heart. The strap is placed in a special

Above A prayer book and tefillin, worn to fulfil the law to bind the commandments on hands and before the eyes.

way so that it forms the Hebrew letter *shin*, the first letter of God's name Shaddai – God Almighty.

LAYING TEFILLIN

The action of putting on the boxes is known as laying tefillin. It is an ancient practice and should be observed by all male Jews of bar mitzvah age and above. It is performed every weekday at home or in the synagogue. Phylacteries are not worn on the Sabbath or festivals. The tradition among Ashkenazim is to wind the straps round the arm anti-clockwise whereas the Sephardim wind them clockwise. The Talmud emphasizes the importance of fulfilling this commandment, and it states that even God lays tefillin. Among the Hasidim it is said that if only every male Jew were to perform this duty then the Messiah would come.

THE BEARD

According to Leviticus, it is forbidden to cut the corners of the beard. In the medieval period, it was customary for Jewish men to have beards, and the Talmud describes the beard as the 'ornament of the face'. Later, this biblical verse was interpreted to mean Jews should not shave, but it was permissible to clip facial hair. Today many

Left Jew in Black and White, 1923, by Marc Chagall, showing the characteristic prayer shawl and tefillin.

Jewish men are clean-shaven – they use an electric razor or a chemical depilatory. Among the Hasidim and the strictly Orthodox, the passage from Leviticus is also understood to mean that men should let their *peot*, or side-locks grow.

FRINGES

An element of Orthodox appearance is *tziztzit*, or 'fringes'. According to the Book of Numbers, God told the Israelites to make tassels on the corners of their garments. Orthodox men wear an undergarment with

Below The Rabbi, *1892, by Jan Styka. The leather box and straps are the tefillin and contains four Torah texts.*

fringes on the four corners; these are tied in a particular way to symbolize the numerical value of the name of God. Known as a *tallit katan*, it is largely hidden, though the fringes are brought out above the trouser waistband and are discreetly tucked into a pocket. Similar fringes are put on the four corners of the *tallit gadol*, or 'prayer shawl', which is worn in the synagogue during the morning service. A special blessing is said when both the prayer shawl and the undergarment are put on each day.

MODESTY

Women's dress is characterized by modesty. Traditionally, married women cover their heads, and the Orthodox continue this practice by wearing a wig or by swathing the head in a scarf. Skirts cover the knee and sleeves the elbow. The Book of Deuteronomy teaches that a woman shall not wear anything that pertains to a man, nor shall a man put on a woman's garment. Thus among the strictly Orthodox any unisex garment is perceived as an abomination. However, non-Orthodox women ignore these customs.

Right A customer tries on a wig at a shop in Israel. Many ultra-Orthodox Jewish women cover their heads once they marry to obey religious modesty edicts.*

Above A Jewish father wraps his son's arm in phylacteries at his bar mitzvah at the Western Wall, Jerusalem.*

FORBIDDEN CLOTH

The Book of Deuteronomy states it is forbidden to wear a *shatnes*, or mingled stuff, such as wool or linen mixed together. This regulation is one of many laws against mixing. Today modern technology can be employed to determine the precise composition of fabrics, and certify the legality of a particular material. The commandment is understood as forbidding the mingling of linen and wool. Any other combination is permissible. Again, this law is ignored by the non-Orthodox.

MARRIAGE

ACCORDING TO TRADITION, MARRIAGE IS GOD'S PLAN FOR HUMANITY. IN THE JEWISH FAITH IT IS VIEWED AS A SACRED BOND AS WELL AS A MEANS TO PERSONAL FULFILMENT.

In Judaism the purpose of marriage is to create a Jewish home, have a Jewish family and thereby perpetuate the Jewish community. Marriage is an institution with cosmic significance, legitimized through divine authority. Initially Jews were permitted to have more than one wife, but this practice was banned in Ashkenazi countries by Rabbenu Gershom (c.960–1028CE) in 1000. In modern society all Jewish communities follow this ruling.

ANCIENT JUDAISM

In the Bible, marriages were arranged by fathers. Abraham, for example, sent his servant to find a wife for Isaac, and Judah arranged the marriage of his first-born son. When the proposal of marriage was accepted by the girl's father, the nature and amount of the *mohar*, or

Below A classic image of the relationship of husband and wife in this Dutch painting of The Jewish Bride *by Rembrandt, 1667.*

'payment by the groom', was agreed. By Second Temple times, there was a degree of choice in the selection of a bride: on 15th of Av and the Day of Atonement, young men could select their brides from among the girls dancing in the vineyards.

According to tradition, a period of engagement preceded marriage itself. The ceremony was a seven-day occasion for celebration during which love songs were sung in praise of the bride.

In the talmudic period, a major development occurred concerning the mohar. Since it could be used by the father of the bride, a wife could become penniless if her husband divorced or predeceased her. As a consequence, the mohar evolved into the *ketubah*, or 'marriage document', which gave protection to the bride. In addition, the act of marriage changed from being a personal civil procedure to a public religious ceremony, which required the presence of a *minyan*, or 'quorum', and the recitation of prayers.

Above A Jewish couple share in a Passover Seder meal. From a 15th-century illuminated manuscript.

MARRIAGE PROCEDURES

In biblical and rabbinic times marriage was divided into two stages – betrothal and marriage.

Betrothal involved the commitment of a couple to marry and the terms of financial obligations, and also a ceremony establishing a nuptial relationship independent of the wedding ceremony. In the Bible, the betrothal or nuptial ceremony takes place prior to the wedding and is referred to as *erusin*; in the rabbinic period the sages called it *kiddushin* to indicate the bride was forbidden to all men except her husband. According to the Mishnah, the bride could be acquired in marriage in three ways: by money, deed or intercourse. Traditionally, the method involved placing a ring on the bride's finger. At this stage the groom declared: 'Behold, you are consecrated unto me with this ring according to the law of Moses and Israel.' Then the blessing over wine was recited.

After this ceremony the bride remained in her father's house until the *nissuin*, or 'marriage ceremony'. During the second stage of this procedure the *sheva berakhot*, or 'seven blessings', are recited.

THE WEDDING

From the Middle Ages it became customary for Jewish communities to postpone the betrothal ceremony until just before the nissuin wedding ceremony. Prior to the wedding itself, the bride immerses herself in a mikveh, or 'ritual bath', usually on the evening before the ceremony. To facilitate this the wedding date is determined so that it does not occur during her time of menstruation, or the following week. In some Ashkenazi circles the bride when reaching the *huppah*, or 'marriage canopy', is led around the groom seven times. The wedding ceremony can be held anywhere, but from the Middle Ages, the synagogue or synagogue courtyard was commonly used. In modern times, the Orthodox wedding ceremony normally follows a uniform pattern based on traditional law.

Normally the groom signs the ketubah. He is then led to the bride and covers her face with her veil; the couple are next led to the marriage canopy with their parents walking with the groom and the bride. According to custom, those leading the couple carry lighted candles.

Below Marc Chagall painted The Wedding *in 1918, three years after his marriage. The fiddler and house symbolize their wedded state and a baby is drawn on the cheek of the bride.*

When the participants are under the canopy, the rabbi recites the blessing over wine. Then the bride and groom drink from the cup. The groom then recites the traditional formula: 'Behold you are consecrated unto me according to the law of Moses and of Israel.' He then puts the ring on the bride's right index finger. To demonstrate that the act of marriage consists of two ceremonies, the ketubah is read prior to the nissuin ceremony. The seven blessings are

Above Indian–Jewish wedding in Mumbai. Tradition says the Bene Israel were shipwrecked while fleeing persecution in Galilee and reached India some 2,100 years ago.

then recited over a second cup of wine. The ceremony concludes with the groom stepping on a glass and breaking it. Within Conservative and Reform Judaism the wedding service follows the traditional pattern with varying alterations.

THE *SHEVA BERAKHOT* OR SEVEN BLESSINGS

Blessed are you, O Lord Our God, King of the Universe, who creates the fruit of the vine,
• Who has created all things to your glory.
• Creator of man.
• Who has made man in your image, after your likeness ...
• Made she who was barren (Zion) be glad and exult when her children are gathered within her in joy. Blessed are you, O Lord, who makes Zion joyful through her children.
• O make these loved companions greatly to rejoice, even as of old you did gladden your creatures in the Garden of Eden. Blessed are you, O Lord, who makes bridegroom and bride to rejoice.
• Who has created joy and gladness, bridegroom and bride, mirth and exultation, pleasure and delight, love, brotherhood, peace and fellowship. Soon may there be heard in the cities of Judah and in the streets of Jerusalem, the voice of joy and gladness, the voice of the bridegroom and the voice of the bride, the happy sound of bridegrooms from their canopies, and of youths from their feasts of song.
• Blessed are you, O Lord, who makes the bridegroom to rejoice with the bride.

DIVORCE

MARRIAGE IS REGARDED AS AN IDEAL IN JUDAISM, BUT RELATION-
SHIPS BETWEEN MEN AND WOMEN DO BREAK DOWN. JEWS RECOGNIZE
THIS, AND THE BIBLE SPECIFIES A PROCEDURE FOR DIVORCE.

'When a man takes a wife and marries her, if then she finds no favour in his eyes because he has found some indecency in her, he writes her a bill of divorce and puts it in her hand and sends her out of his house' (Deuteronomy 24:1).

BIBLICAL AND RABBINIC LAW

This verse in Deuteronomy stipulates that the power of divorce rests with the husband, and the act of divorce must be in the form of a legal document. Among early rabbinic sages there was disagreement as to the meaning of the term 'indecency'. The School of Shammai interpreted it as referring to unchastity, whereas the School of Hillel understood the term more widely. It was not permitted for divorce to take place in two instances: if a man claimed that his

Below The Bet Din grants a divorce. *From* Jüdisches Ceremoniell *(1717) published by Paul Christian Kirchner, following his conversion to Judaism.*

wife was not a virgin and his charge was disproved; or if he raped a virgin whom he later married. Conversely, a person was not allowed to remarry his divorced wife if she had married someone else and had not been divorced or widowed. Nor could a priest marry a divorced woman.

THE TALMUDIC PERIOD

During the talmudic period, the law of divorce underwent considerable change, including the elaboration of various situations under which a court could compel a husband to divorce his wife. This applied if she remained barren over a period of ten years, if the husband contracted a loathsome disease, if he refused to support her or was not in a position to do so, if he denied his wife her conjugal rights, or if he beat her despite the court's warnings. In these cases the Talmud states that the husband is coerced by the court only to the extent that he would in fact want to divorce his wife.

Above A 1906 edition of the Gittin tractate of the Talmud, which deals with the concepts of divorce.

DIVORCE PROCEDURE

The procedure for a divorce is based on the Code of Jewish Law. The officiating rabbi asks the husband if he gives the get or bill of divorce of his own free will. After receiving the writing materials from a scribe, he

---

THE BILL OF DIVORCE

A get, or 'bill of divorce', is to be drawn up by a scribe following a formula based on mishnaic law. This document is to be written almost entirely in Aramaic on parchment. Once it has been given to the wife, it is retained by the rabbi, who cuts it in a criss-cross fashion so that it cannot be used a second time. The husband then gives the wife a document that affirms that he has been divorced, and may remarry. The wife is permitted to remarry only after 90 days, so as to determine whether she was pregnant at the stage of divorce. This document must be witnessed by two males over the age of 13 who are not related to each other or to the divorcing husband and wife.

Above Marriage breakdown. An estranged couple sit at opposite ends of a sofa, deliberately avoiding each other.

Left A bet din *(rabbinical court) in Jerusalem granting a divorce for a woman whose husband has left her.*

instructs the scribe to write a get. The get is written, and the witnesses should be present during this process. They then make a distinguishing mark on the get. When it is completed, the witnesses read the get. Eventually the rabbi asks the husband if the get was freely given. The wife is then asked if she freely accepts the get.

The rabbi then tells the wife to remove all jewellery from her hands and holds her hands together with open palms upward to receive the bill of divorce. The scribe holds the get and gives it to the rabbi. The rabbi then gives the get to her husband; he holds it in both hands and drops it into the palms of the wife. When the wife receives the bill of divorce, she walks with it a short distance and returns. She gives the get to the rabbi who reads it again. The four corners of the get are cut, and it is placed in the rabbi's files. The husband and wife then receive written statements certifying that their marriage has been dissolved in accordance with Jewish law.

DIVORCE PROCEEDINGS

It is customary for the husband and wife to be present during the divorce proceedings. If this is not possible, Jewish law stipulates an agent can take the place of either party. The husband may appoint an agent to deliver the

get to his wife. If this agent is unable to complete this task, he has the right to appoint another one, and the second agent yet another. The wife can also appoint an agent to receive the get. Thus it is possible for the entire procedure to take place without the husband or wife seeing one another.

NON-ORTHODOX JUDAISM

Since it is the husband who must give the bill of divorce to his wife, if he cannot be located, this presents an insurmountable obstacle. Similarly, in the Diaspora rabbinic scholars have the status of a woman who is an *agunah*, or 'chained person', who is not

able to remarry according to traditional Jewish law. To vitiate this the Conservative movement has called for the insertion of a clause in the marriage contract whereby both groom and bride in grave circumstances agree to abide by the decision of the *bet din*, or 'religious court'. Within Reform Judaism the traditional practice of granting a bill of divorce has been largely abandoned. Instead civil divorce is regarded as valid.

Below At these divorce proceedings in Amsterdam, Netherlands, the Ashkenazi Jew passes a writ of divorce into the hands of a surrogate for his wife.

DEATH AND MOURNING

THE JEWISH RELIGION SPECIFIES A DETAILED PROCEDURE FOR DEALING
WITH THE DEAD. BURIAL SHOULD TAKE PLACE AS SOON AS POSSIBLE AFTER
THE MEMBERS OF THE BURIAL SOCIETY HAVE TAKEN CARE OF THE BODY.

Above At a Jewish cemetery in Budapest, Hungary. The rabbi chants prayers as family members use a shovel to put dirt on the casket in the open grave.

According to Scripture, human beings will return to the dust of the earth (Genesis 3:19). The Bible teaches that burial – especially in the family tomb – was the normal procedure for dealing with the deceased. Such a practice has been superseded by burial in the earth, preceded by a number of procedures. This is followed by a period of mourning for the dead.

THE ONSET OF DEATH

The rabbis of the Talmud decreed that death takes place when respiration has ceased. However, with the development of modern medical technology, this concept has been changed. It is now possible to resuscitate those who previously would have been viewed as dead. For this reason the Orthodox scholar Moshe Sofer (1762–1839) stated that death is considered to have occurred when there has been respiratory and cardiac arrest. Mosheh Feinstein (1895–1986) ruled that a person is considered to have died with the death of his brain stem. Despite such disagreements, it is generally accepted that a critically ill person who hovers between life and death is alive. It is forbidden to hasten the death of such a person by any positive action. However, it is permitted to remove an external obstacle, which may be preventing death.

DEALING WITH THE DEAD

Once death has been determined, the eyes and mouth of the person are to be closed, and if necessary the mouth is tied shut. The body is then put on the floor, covered with a sheet, and a lighted candle is placed close to the head. Mirrors are covered in the home of the deceased, and any standing water is poured out. A dead body is not to be left unattended, and it is considered a good deed to sit with the person who has died and recite psalms.

BURIAL

The burial of the body should occur as soon as possible. No burial is allowed to take place on the Sabbath or on Yom Kippur, the Day of Atonement, and in contemporary practice it is considered unacceptable for it to take place on the first and last days of a pilgrim festival.

After the members of the burial society have taken care of the body, they prepare it for burial. It is washed and dressed in a white linen shroud. The corpse is then placed in a coffin. Traditional Jews only permit the use of plain wooden coffins. The deceased is then borne to the grave face upwards. Adult males are buried wearing their prayer shawl. A marker should be placed on a newly filled grave, and a tombstone should be erected and unveiled as soon as possible.

Among Reform Jews, burial practice differs from that of the Orthodox. Embalming and cremation are usually permitted and Reform rabbis often officiate at crematoria. Burial may be delayed for several days, and the person who has died is usually buried in normal clothing. No special places are reserved for priests, nor is any separate arrangement made for someone who has committed suicide or married out of the faith.

Below The Acafoth, or seven turns around the coffin. A 1723 French engraving by Bernard Picart.

Right An Orthodox Jew gestures while praying as he stands in a Jewish cemetery on the Mount of Olives in Jerusalem.

BURIAL SERVICE

Despite the differences between Ashkenazi and Sephardi Jews, there are a number of common features of the burial service. In both rites, mourners rend their garments and liturgical verses are chanted by the rabbi as he leads the funeral procession to the cemetery. Often a eulogy is given either in the funeral chapel or as the mourners help to fill the earth. Memorial prayers and a special mourners' kaddish are recited. Mourners present words of comfort to the bereaved, and all wash their hands before leaving the cemetery.

SHIVAH

The mourning period is known as *shivah*, 'seven', and lasts for seven days beginning with the day of burial. During this time mourners sit on the floor or on low cushions or benches and are forbidden to shave, bathe, go to work, study the Torah, engage in sexual relations, wear leather shoes,

Below A mother mourns at the grave of her son in the military section of Mount Herzl cemetery, Jerusalem.

greet others, cut their hair or wear laundered clothing. Through these seven days, it is customary to visit mourners. Those comforting mourners are not to greet them but rather offer words of consolation.

SHELOSHIM

Shivah concludes on the morning of the seventh day and is followed by mourning of a lesser intensity for 30 days known as *sheloshim*, or 'thirty'. At this time mourners are not permitted to cut their hair, shave,

wear new clothes or attend festivities. Those who mourn are not permitted to attend public celebrations or parties. Mourners are to recite kaddish daily throughout the period of mourning. In the case of those whose mourning continues for a year, it is at times customary to recite kaddish till one month or a week before the first anniversary of death.

Below Four sons saying Kaddish over the coffin of their father in the Gaza Strip settlement of Ganei Tal, Israel.

GLOSSARY

ADAM KADMON primordial man, in Kabbalah the spiritual prototype of man created by God

ADAR twelfth month of the Jewish year. In leap years, Adar is followed by a month called Adar 2

ADON OLAM poem that begins, 'Lord of eternity'

AFIKOMAN part of the middle matzah

AKEDAH the binding of Isaac

ALENU prayer at the end of a service

AMIDAH major prayer originally consisting of 18 benedictions

AMORAIM Palestine sages (200-500CE)

ANTI-SEMITISM hostility towards Jews

ARK OF THE COVENANT chest in which the two ancient Tablets of the Law were placed

ASHKENAZIM one of the two main divisions of Jews. Initially applied to a biblical people, but now Jews originating in Eastern Europe

ASIYAH Kabbalistic realm ('making')

ATZILUT Kabbalistic term ('emanation')

AV fifth month of the Jewish year

BARAITA teachings not included in the Mishnah

BAR MITZVAH male adolescent ceremony ('son of the commandment') when a Jewish youth comes under the obligation to fulfill the commandments

Below A dreidel used at Hanukkah.

BAT MITZVAH female adolescent ceremony ('daughter of the commandment')

BERIYAH Kabbalistic realm ('creation')

BET DIN rabbinic court

BIBLE the Hebrew Bible is divided into three sections: the Torah (Pentateuch), Nevim (Prophets) and Ketuvim (writings)

BIMAH platform

BINAH God's wisdom

CANTOR chanter

CHALLAH braided bread eaten on the Sabbath and holidays

CHOSEN PEOPLE the belief that God chose the Jews based on the covenant between Abraham and God

COHEN priest

COMMANDMENTS *see* Halakha, Mitzvah and Ten Commandments

CONSERVATIVE JUDAISM religious movement, which emerged in the mid-19th century as a mid-way between Orthodoxy and Reform

COVENANT binding agreement between person's nations or parties

DEVEKUT mystical cleaving to God

DIASPORA outside Israel

DREIDEL a spinning top used in a game at Hanukkah

ELUL sixth month of the Jewish year

ELOHIM one of the names of God.

EN SOF Infinite

EREZ ISRAEL land of Israel

ESSENES monastic Jewish sect, one of three main Jewish sects before the destruction of the Temple in 70CE

EXILE exclusion from the Promised Land, especially to Babylonia in the 6th century BCE

FRANKISTS Heretical movement founded by Jacob Frank

GAN EDEN Garden of Eden (or heaven)

GAON head of a Babylonian academy

GEHINNOM Hell

GEMARA rabbinic discussions on the Mishnah

GET bill of divorce

HABAD Hasidic movement whose name is based on the initials of the words *hokhmah* (wisdom), *binah* (understanding), and *daat* (knowledge)

HAFTARAH prophetic reading

HAGGADAH Passover prayer book

HALAKHA Jewish law

HALLEL Psalms 113-118

HANUKKAH festival of lights (dedication), lasting eight days

HAREDIM Strictly Orthodox Jews

HAROSET paste of fruit, spices, wine and matzah eaten at the Passover seder

HASID pious person

HASIDISM mystical Jewish movement founded in the 18th century

HASKALAH Jewish enlightenment

HAVDALAH service at the end of the Sabbath and festivals

HEDER school for children

HESHVAN eighth month of the Jewish year

HOKHMAH God's wisdom

HOLOCAUST destruction of the European Jewish community during the Second World War. Six million Jews are estimated to have died during the Holocaust.

HUMANISTIC JUDAISM non-supernaturalistic and humanistically oriented movement

HUPPAH marriage canopy

IYAR second month of the Jewish year

JEWISH RENEWAL Judaism inspired by counter-culture

JUBUS Jewish Buddhists

KABBALAH mystical teachings

KADDISH Aramaic prayer praising God

KARAITES Jewish sect, which rejected the rabbinic tradition

KASHRUT dietary laws

KETUVIM Writings (third section of the Hebrew Scriptures)

Above Matzot, eaten at Passover.

KIBBUTZ collective village in Israel
KIDDUSH prayer recited over wine to consecrate the Sabbath or a festival
KIPPAH skullcap
KISLEV ninth month of the Jewish year
KITTEL robe
KNESSET Parliament of Israel
KOLLEL advanced institute for Talmud study
KOL NIDRE evening service, which starts the Day of Atonement ('all vows')
KOSHER ritually fit food

LADINO Judeo-Spanish dialect
LAG BA-OMER scholars' feast
LEKHAH DODI Sabbath hymn ('come, my beloved')
LEVITE priest
LULAV palm branch (used on Sukkot)
LURIANIC KABBALAH mysticism based on the teachings of Isaac ben Luria

MAARIV evening service
MAFTIR reader of the *Haftarah*
MAMZER offspring of any sexual relationship forbidden in Jewish law (that is, incest, or sexual intercourse between a married woman and a man who is not her husband)
MAROR bitter herbs
MARRANOS Jews who converted to Christianity (in Spain and Portugal)
MASKILIM followers of the Jewish Enlightenment
MATRIARCHS the wives of the three Patriarchs: Sarah, Rebecca, Leah and Rachel
MATZAH unleavened bread for Passover
MEGILLAH scroll
MENORAH a seven-branched candlestick. A menorah with eight branches is used at Hanukkah.

MERKAVAH divine chariot
MESSIAH the anointed one
MESSIANIC JUDAISM a movement with a belief in Jesus (Yeshua)
MEZUZAH scroll in a box fixed to the doorpost of a Jewish home
MIDRASH rabbinic commentary on Scripture
MIKDASH ME-AT minor sanctuary
MIKVEH ritual bath. Used for immersion and ritual cleansing of both individuals and vessels
MINHAH meal offering (or afternoon service)
MINYAN quorum of ten men
MISHNAH compendium of the Oral Torah
MITNAGGEDIM rabbinic opponents of the Hasidim
MITZVAH commandment
MOHEL person who performs a circumcision
MOURNERS' KADDISH prayer said at the end of service
MUSAF additional service
MUSAR movement of return to traditional ethics founded in the modern period

NAGID head of a Spanish or North African community
NEILAH concluding service, originally recited daily one hour before sunset and the closing of the Temple
NEVIIM Prophets (second section of the Hebrew Scriptures)

Below A Hanukkah menorah.

Above A ritual Seder plate.

NISAN first month of the Jewish year
NISSUIN second stage of the marriage procedure

OLAM HA-BA the hereafter. Olam ha-Ba will begin with the resurrection of the dead and a final judgement. The righteous will be rewarded and the wicked punished.
OMER barley offering
ORTHODOXY Torah-observant Judaism

PARASHAH Torah portion
PARNAS head of the community
PASSOVER festival commemorating the Exodus from Egypt
PATRIARCHS the biblical ancestors of the Jewish people: Abraham, Isaac and Jacob
PENTATEUCH the Five Books of Moses (Genesis, Exodus, Leviticus, Numbers and Deuteronomy)
PESACH Passover festival
PHARISEES one of three main Jewish sects before the destruction of the Temple in 70CE
PIYYUTIM hymns
PURIM feast of Esther, marking the deliverance of the Jews from Haman

RABBI teacher
REBBE Hasidic leader
RECONSTRUCTIONIST JUDAISM modernizing movement founded by Mordecai Kaplan
REFORM JUDAISM progressive modernizing movement
RESPONSA answers to specific legal questions
ROSH HASHANAH New Year. The Jewish New Year begins on the 1st day of Tishri, the 7th month of the Jewish year

ROSH HODESH 1st of the month, celebrating the appearance of the new moon

SABBATH day of rest. Observed every week from before sunset on Friday until nightfall on Saturday
SADDUCEES priestly class, one of three main Jewish sects before the destruction of the Temple in 70CE
SAMARITANS people descended from the tribes of Ephraim and Manasseh
SANDAK godfather
SANHEDRIN central rabbinic court in ancient times
SEDER Passover ceremony at home
SEFER YETZIRAH Early Babylonian or Palestinian mystical tract
SEFIROT divine emanations
SELIHOT penitential prayers
SEPHARDIM Jews originating in Spain or North Africa
SEUDAH SELISHIT third meal
SHABBAT first tractate of the Mishnah and Talmud. It discusses Sabbath law and outlines the thirty-nine categories of work, forbidden on the Sabbath
SHABBATEANS followers of Shabbetai Tzvi
SHAHARIT morning service
SHAVUOT Festival of Weeks, commemorating the giving of the law on Mount Sinai
SHEHITAH ritual slaughter
SHEKHINAH divine presence

Below Sabbath challah and wine.

SHELOSHIM 30 days of mourning
SHEMA prayer ('Hear, O Israel')
SHEMINI ATZERET final day of the festival of Sukkot
SHEMONEH ESREH Amidah
SHEVAT eleventh month of the Jewish year
SHEWBREAD bread laid out in the Temple on the golden table
SHIVAH seven days of mourning
SHOFAR ram's horn
SHOHET slaughterer
SHTETL small town in eastern Europe with Jewish population
SHULKHAN ARUKH Jewish law code
SIDDUR traditional prayer book
SIDRAH section of the Torah reading
SIMHAT TORAH Festival of the Rejoicing of the Law
SITRA AHRA demonic realm
SIVAN third month of the Jewish year
SUKKAH booth built at Sukkot
SUKKOT Feast of Tabernacles, marking the end of the agricultural year
SYNAGOGUE place of worship

TABLETS OF THE LAW the Ten Commandments given by God to Moses on Mount Sinai
TALLIT (larger) prayer shawl
TALLIT (smaller) fringed undergarment
TALMUD compilation of the legal discussions based on the Mishnah
TAMUZ fourth month of the Jewish year
TANAKH Hebrew Bible
TANNAIM Jewish sages (70–200CE)
TASHLIKH casting away sin
TEFILLAH prayer (also the Amidah)
TEMPLE principal place of worship of the Jews in Jerusalem until 70CE
TEN COMMANDMENTS laws given by God to Moses on Mount Sinai
TENAIM betrothal document
TEVET tenth month of the Jewish year
TIK the wooden or metal case in which the Scroll of the Law is stored
TIKKUN cosmic repair
TISHA B'AV ninth of Av, commemorating the destruction of the Temples and other Jewish tragedies
TISHRI seventh month of the Jewish year
TORAH Law (or Pentateuch)
TOSEFTA additions to the Mishnah

Above Masks are worn at Purim.

TWELVE TRIBES according to the Bible Israel is divided into 12 tribes descended from the sons of Jacob: Reuben, Simeon (Levi), Judah, Issachar, Zebulun, Benjamin, Dan, Naphtali, Gad, Asher, Ephraim and Manasseh
TU b'SHEVAT New Year for Trees
TZIZTZIT fringes

YAD pointer used in the synagogue when reading the Torah
YAHRZEIT lighting a memorial candle
YAHWEH God's sacred name, which is never pronounced
YARMULKE skullcap
YARTZEIT anniversary of a death
YESHIVAH (pl. yeshivot) Jewish rabbinical college
YETSIRAH Kabbalistic realm
YETZER HA-RA evil inclination
YETZER HA-TOV good inclination
YHWH it is forbidden to pronounce the Hebrew name of God (YHWH), so substitutions were used
YIDDISH language of Ashkenazi Jews
YIZKOR memorial prayers
YOM ATZMAUT Israel Independence Day
YOM KIPPUR Day of Atonement

ZADDIK righteous person
ZEMIROT hymns
ZIMZUM contraction of the Godhead into itself
ZIONISM movement for a Jewish homeland
ZOHAR medieval mystical work

FURTHER READING

GENERAL INTRODUCTIONS

Baron, S.W., *A Social and Religious History of the Jews* (Columbia University Press, 1952–76)

Beck, L., *The Essence of Judaism* (Schocken, 1948)

Cohn-Sherbok, D., *Introduction to Zionism and Israel* (Continuum, 2012)

—, *Judaism Today* (Continuum, 2011)

—, *Judaism: History, Belief and Practice* (Taylor & Francis, 2003)

De Lange, N., *Judaism* (Oxford University Press, 1986)

Epstein, I., *Judaism* (Penguin, 1975)

Jacobs, L., *The Book of Jewish Practice* (Behrman House, 1987)

—, *The Book of Jewish Belief* (Behrman House, 1984)

—, *A Jewish Theology* (Darton, Longman and Todd, 1973)

—, *Principles of the Jewish Faith* (Jason Aaronson, 1988)

Joffe, L., *An Illustrated History of the Jewish People* (Lorenz Books, 2012)

Katz, S.T., *Jewish Ideas and Concepts* (Schocken Books, 1972)

Margolis, M. L. and Marx, A., *A History of the Jewish People* (Harper and Row, 1965)

Neusner, J., *The Way of Torah: An Introduction to Judaism* (Dickenson, 1974)

Pilkington, C.M., *Judaism* (Hodder and Stoughton, 1991)

Rosten, L., *The Joys of Yiddish* (W.H. Allen, 1968)

Roth, C., *A History of the Jews* (Schocken, 1973)

Scheindlin, R.P., *A Short History of the Jewish People* (Oxford University Press, 2000)

Trepp, L., *A History of the Jewish Experience* (Behrman House, 1973)

Waskow, A.I., *Seasons of Our Joy: Modern Guide to the Jewish Holidays* (Bantam, 1982)

Werbolowsky, R.J. and Wigoder, G. (eds), *Encyclopedia of the Jewish Religion* (Holt, Reinhardt and Winston, 1966)

Above A Passover haggadah.

DICTIONARIES AND ENCYCLOPEDIAS

Abrahamson, G. (ed.), *The Blackwell Companion to Jewish Culture* (Blackwell, 1989)

Brisman, S. (ed.), *A History and Guide to Judaic Bibliography* (Hebrew Union College Press and Ktav, 1977)

Cohn-Sherbok, D., *A Concise Encyclopedia of Judaism* (Oneworld, 1992)

—, *Dictionary of Kabbalah and Kabbalists* (Impress Books, 2009)

—, *Dictionary of Jewish Biography* (Oxford University Press, 2005)

De Lange, N., *Penguin Dictionary of Judaism* (Penguin, 2008)

Encyclopedia Judaica (Keter, 1972), second edition (Macmillan, 2007)

The Jewish Encyclopedia (Funk and Wagnalls 1901–6)

Kantor, M., *The Jewish Time Line Encyclopedia* (Jason Aaronson, 1989)

Shamir, I. and Shavit, S., *Encyclopedia of Jewish History* (Massada, 1986)

Shunami, S., *Bibliography of Jewish Bibliographies* (Magness Press, 1965; supplement, 1975)

Solomon, N., *Historical Dictionary of Judaism* (Scarecrow Press, 2006)

Waxman, M., *A History of Jewish Literature* (Thomas Yoseloff, 1960)

Wigoder, G., *Dictionary of Jewish Bibliography* (Jerusalem Publishing House, 1991)

Wigoder, G., *The Encyclopedia of Judaism* (Macmillan, 1989)

ATLASES

Barnavi, Eli (ed.), *A Historical Atlas of the Jewish People* (Hutchinson, 1992)

Cohn-Sherbok, D. *Atlas of Jewish History* (Routledge, 1994)

De Lange, N., *Atlas of the Jewish World* (Phaidon, 1984)

Friesel, E., *Atlas of Modern Jewish History* (Oxford University Press, 1994)

Gilbert, M., *Jewish History Atlas* (Weidenfeld & Nicolson, 1988)

ELECTRONIC TEXTS

Bar-Ilan's Judaic Library (Torah Education Software, 1990)

Dead Sea Scrolls Database (Brill, 1999)

Encyclopedia Judaica (TES, 1997)

Judaic Classic Library (Davka Corporation, 1991–5)

INTERNET

Useful web addresses at the time of publication include (please note that addresses may change):

www.jewishencyclopedia.com (the 1901–6 edition)

http://www.jewfaq.org

http://www.torah.org/

Below The Torah is at the heart of Judaism.

INDEX

Below Fall of the Second Temple, 70CE.

Above Caves in the Judean desert.

Below Jewish quarter, Barcelona, Spain.

Above The Shrine of the Book, Jerusalem.

Below Modern-day Tel Aviv, Israel.

FOR LAVINIA, and thanks to my editor Joy Wotton for all her splendid work and support.

This edition is published by
Lorenz Books
an imprint of Anness Publishing Ltd, Blaby Road, Wigston, Leicestershire LE18 4SE; info@anness.com
www.lorenzbooks.com; www.annesspublishing.com

Anness Publishing has a new picture agency outlet for images for publishing, promotions or advertising. Please visit our website www.practicalpictures.com for more information.

© Anness Publishing Ltd 2013

Publisher: Joanna Lorenz
Editor: Joy Wotton
Maps: Anthony Duke
Designer: Nigel Partridge
Production Controller: Wendy Lawson

PUBLISHER'S NOTE

p. 1 14th-century Spanish Jews celebrating Passover.
p. 2 Rabbi's Blessing, 1871, by Moritz Daniel Oppenheim.
p. 3 Menorah window, Great Synagogue, Jerusalem, Israel.
Above Seder plate used at Passover.

PICTURE ACKNOWLEDGEMENTS

AKG-Images: 2, 6br, 14b, 17b, 18t, 19bl, 20b, 26br, 27b, 33b, 36b, 50b, 56t, 57t, 58b, 76b, 82t, 83b, 87b, 109t, 114b, 123t, 133t, 138t, 142b, 154, 158t, 160t, 161t, 177, 178t, 196bl, 217tl, 226bl, 230t&b; British Library 1; © Sotheby's 116t, 218b; Bible Land Pictures, 35bl&br, 51tr, 191bl, 203b; Bildarchiv Pisarek 80t, 96t, 151tl, 215b; British Library 8, 120t, 125bl, 132bl, 138bl, 139tr, 144b, 160b; Cameraphoto 121t; Electa 31b; Erich Lessing 15bl, 26bl, 32bl, 40bk, 54t, 57b, 82b, 100, 103bl, 120b, 126t, 135b, 138br, 148b, 157t, 176t, 185b; Horizons 94b, 220b; IAM 239bl; Israel Images 3, 19br, 34b, 35t, 40t, 41, 48t, 52b, 62t, 63bl, 99, 125br, 143t, 146b, 150t, 153t, 169b, 181bl, 190b, 192, 209b, 218t, 219t, 221t&br, 225b, 231bl, 235t&b, 236b, 238t, 241t, 245bl, 251; János Kalmár 43; Joseph Martin 156t; Jürgen Raible 12, 207b; Laurent Lecat 152b; North Wind Picture Archives 18b; Rabatti – Domingie 155; RIA Nowosti 195b; Suzanne Held 52t, 81t, 81b, 105tl; ullstein – Archiv Gerstenberg 131t; ullstein bild, 117t, 170b, 181t, 199b; World History Archive/IAM 130b.

Alamy: © john norman 55b; © 19th era 2, 59t, 221bl; © Arcaid 61; © Art Directors & TRIP 68b; © ASAP

182b; © david sanger photography 93tl; © Eddie Gerald 75t, 149br; © Eden Akavia 242t; © Eitan Simanor 77b, 198b; © Frances Roberts 143b; © Hanan Isachar 55t; © INTERFOTO 88t; © Israel images 145t, 204b; © J. Wolanczyk 59b; © Jean Dominique Dallet 48b; © Jeff Morgan 06, 73b; © Jim West 73t; © Lebrecht Music and Arts Photo Library 27t, 45tr, 54b, 167b, 242b; © moris kushelevitch 105b; © Nathan Benn 97b, 175t, 181br, 197t, 243b; © ohad reinhartz 140t; © PhotoStock-Israel 90t; © Richard Levine 77tl; © Ruby 243tl; © Stefano Paterna 111tr, 253; © The Art Gallery Collection 32t; © The Print Collector 163b; © www.BibleLandPictures.com 4l, 19t, 29b, 30t, 32br, 47b, 63t.

The Art Archive: 167t, 179tl, 208t, 250; American Colony Photographers / NGS Image Collection, 34t; Anagni Cathedral Italy / Collection Dagli Orti 199t; Basilica Aquileia Italy / Collection Dagli Orti 156br; Biblioteca Nacional Lisbon / Gianni Dagli Orti 201bl; Biblioteca Nazionale Marciana Venice / Gianni Dagli Orti 104b; Bibliothèque de l'Arsenal Paris 186bl; Bibliothèque Mazarine Paris / CCI, 28bl, 112b; Bibliothèque Municipale Amiens / Kharbine-Tapabor / Coll. J.Vigne 209t; Bibliothèque Municipale Moulins / Gianni Dagli Orti 102t; Bibliothèque Municipale Valenciennes / Gianni Dagli Orti 28br, 188br; Bibliothèque Nationale Paris 132t; Bibliothèque Universitaire de Mèdecine, Montpellier / Gianni Dagli Orti 46t, 179b; Bodleian Library Oxford, 42, 115t, /Arch Selden A 5 folio2v, 140b, / Canon Or 62 folio 1r, 126b, / Canon or 79 folio 2v, 237t, /Laud Or 321 folio127v, 189b, / Mich 619 folio 130r, 216b, / MS. Reggio 1 fol. 159v, 194br, / Opp 776 folio 20v, 135t; British Library, 4r, 44t, 45tl, 115b, 118, 124br, 173, 186bm, 187bl, 210, 223b, 225t; Castello della Manta Piemonte / Collection Dagli Orti 39t; CCI 134b, 195t, 213t; Collection Antonovich / Gianni Dagli Orti 156bl; Collection Dagli Orti 128b; Culver Pictures 56b; DeA Picture Library / G. Nimatallah 158b; Eileen Tweedy 49br; Fondation Thiers Paris / Gianni Dagli Orti 122b, 145b, 180t, 194bl, 212b, 244b; Gemaldegalerie Dresden 129t; Gianni Dagli Orti 119, 129b, 252; Art Archive, Hermitage Museum Saint Petersburg / Superstock, 184t; Horniman Museum / Eileen Tweedy 165t; Hunt Add E (R)/ Bodleian Library Oxford 49bl; Imperial War Museum 206b; Israel Museum Jerusalem / Gianni Dagli Orti 141b; Jewish Museum, New York / Superstock 108b, 110br, 128t, 131t, 162b, 164t, 183t; Kunsthistorisches Museum Vienna / Superstock 198t; Laud. Or.234 fol. 83V/ Bodleian Library Oxford 51tl; Library of Congress 139b; Minneapolis Institute of Fine Art / Superstock 165b; Moldovita Monastery Romania / Collection Dagli Orti 152b; Museo del Bargello Florence / Gianni Dagli Orti 163t; Museo del Prado Madrid 227t; Museum der Stadt Wien / Collection Dagli Orti 180b; Museum of Anatolian Civilisations Ankara / Gianni Dagli Orti 103br; Museum of London 124t, 149bl, 234br; Art Archive, National Gallery London / Eileen Tweedy 166t; National Museum of Bosnia Herzegovina, Sarajevo 14t; Palatine Library Parma / Gianni Dagli Orti 28t; Palazzo Comunale Rovigo Italy / Collection Dagli Orti 169t; Palazzo Leoni-Montanari Vicenza / Gianni Dagli Orti 47t; Palazzo Pitti Florence / Collection Dagli Orti 200b; Private Collection / Gianni Dagli Orti 184b, 185t, 193, 203t; Private Collection Istanbul / Gianni Dagli Orti 224t; Rijksmuseum Amsterdam / Superstock 229, 240b; San Apollinare Nuovo Ravenna / Collection Dagli Orti 38b; Sistine Chapel Vatican / Superstock 101; St. Peter's Basilica, The Vatican / Superstock 224b; Steve Raymer / NGS Image Collection 125t; Superstock, 7t, 136; University Library Istanbul / Gianni Dagli Ort 29t, 46b, 122t, 137, 188bl, 236t;Victoria and Albert Museum London /V&A Images 159t.

The Bridgeman Art Library: 4m, 9, 37b, 37b, 40t, 49t, 58t, 96b, 102b, 124bl, 127t, 132br, 134t, 151bl, 162t, 164b, 168t, 191tl, 213bl, 228; Gift of James A. de Rothschild, London 114t; Photo © Bonhams, London, UK 5l, 80b; © British Library Board. All Rights

Reserved 33t; © National Gallery of Scotland, Edinburgh, Scotland 104t; Alinari 127b; Archives Charmet 144t, 159b, 161b, 222b; Bibliotheque Nationale, Paris, France 17t; DaTo Images 78, 95, 133b; Gift of James A. de Rothschild, London 10, 44b, 232b; Giraudon 15t, 37tl; Museo Diocesano de Solsona, Lleida, Spain 116b; Photo © AISA 98–9; Photo © Bonhams, London, UK 80b; Photo © Christie's Images 216t; Photo © Zev Radovan 5m, 24, 26t, 38t, 39br, 113b, 139tl, 157b, 201br, 202b; The Stieglitz Collection and donated with contribution from Erica & Ludwig Jesselson 232t.

Corbis: 25, 65tl, 72b; © Mark Weiss 196br RF; © ABIR SULTAN/epa 223tl; © Alfredo Dagli Orti/The Art Archive 150b, 240t; © Andrew Aitchison/In Pictures, 123b; © Andrew Aitchison/In Pictures/, 64t; © Aristide Economopoulos/ Star Ledger, 71t; © Austrian Archives 153b; © Bettmann 21tl, 62b, 66b, 67, 87tr, 88bl, 171t, 182t, 207t, 214b; © Bojan Brecelj 45b; © Catherine Karnow 91b; © Catherine Ledner 84t; © Chris Hellier 196t; © Christie's Images 6bl, 168b; © Courtesy of Museum of Maritimo (Barcelona), Ramon Manent 121b; © DANIELE LA MONACA/X01660/Reuters 220t; © Dave Bartruff 202t; © David H. Wells 226br, 237b; © David Rubinger 222t; © Ed Kashi 90b; © Eldad Rafaeli 148t; © ELIANA APONTE/Reuters 239br; © Envision 186t; © Eyal Ofer 231b; © Frans Lanting 130t; © Gene & Karen Rhoden/Visuals Unlimited 110t; © Gianni Dagli Orti 30bl; © Gideon Mendel 187b; © Godong/Robert Harding World Imagery 149t; © Hanan Isachar 204t, 215t, 217tr, 226t; © Hanan Isachar/JAI 65b; © Herbert Spichtinger 107b; © Heritage Images 36t; © Historical Picture Archive 200t, 208b; © Hulton-Deutsch Collection 21tr, 170t; © Jacques Loew/Kipa 88br; © Jason Horowitz 63br; © Jim Hollander/epa 79; © Jim Zuckerman 111b; © John Bryson/Sygma 223tr; © John Stanmeyer/VII 97t; © Jonathan Ernst/Reuters 74t; © Karen Kasmauski 231tr; © Lalage Snow 171b; © Lebrecht Music & Arts 86b; © Leland Bobbé 66t, 183bl, 201t, 219b, 256; © Les Stone/Sygma 85t&b; © Luca Tettoni 113t; © Lucy Nicholson/Reuters 91t; © Mark Peterson 5r, 65tr, 233b; © Michael Nicholson 31t; © Michael St. Maur Sheil 117b; © Nathan Benn 7b; © Nathan Benn/Ottochrome 64b, 146t, 214t, 239t, 244t; © Neal Preston 93b; © Nik Wheeler 176b; © Nir Alon / Demotix/Demotix/Demotix 197b; © NIR ELIAS/Reuters 245br; © Oscar White 87tl; © P Deliss/Godong 234bl; © Pauline St. Denis 189t RF; © Peter Turnley 141t; © Philadelphia Museum of Art 107t; © Philippe Lissac/Godong 212t; © Richard T. Nowitz 13, 53b, 84b, 166b, 174, 178b, 183br, 188t, © 205; © Robert Mulder/Godong 233t; © Roger Hutchings/In Pictures 109b; © Ron Dahlquist 111tl; © Roy Morsch 213br; © Scott Speakes 194t; © Shai Ginott 22–3, 39bl, 151tr; © Silvia Morara 23; © Sonntag/beyond 243tr RF; © Steve Raymer 190t; © STR/Reuters 53t; © Sung-Il Kim 108t; © Ted Spiegel 60, 69b, 179tr, 211; © Tetra Images/Tetra Images 187br; © The Gallery Collection 103t; © Tony Savino/Sygma 206t; © William Whitehurst 110bl; © YANNIS BEHRAKIS/Reuters 94t; Image © Bettmann 68t; 69t, 83tl, 83tr; IMAGE © Hanan Isachar 172–3, 191tr.

Photo12: 20t, 37tr, 106b, 147; Ann Ronan Picture Library 15br, 16t; Eye Ubiquitous 142t; Oronoz 6t, 50t.

Rex Features: Alinari 77tr, 238b, 241b; Europress Photo Agency 227b; Everett Collection 86t; Sipa Press 245t.

Rodger Kamenetz: © Rodger Kamenetz 74b, 75b, 92b; John Bigelow Taylor/ courtesy of the International Campaign for Tibet 93tr.

Eisenstein Reconstructionist Archives, Reconstructionist Rabbinical College, Wyncote, PA: 70t, bl&r, 71b.

Society for Humanistic Judaism (www.shj.org; www.hujews.org): 72t.